CICERO, *PHILIPPIC* 2, 44–50, 78–92, 100–119

Cicero, *Philippic* 2, 44–50, 78–92, 100–119

Latin text, study aids with vocabulary, and commentary

Ingo Gildenhard

OpenBook Publishers

Digital material and resources associated with this volume are available at https://www.openbookpublishers.com/product/845#resources

Classics Textbooks, vol. 6 | ISSN: 2054-2437 (Print) | 2054-2445 (Online)

ISBN Paperback: 978-1-78374-589-0
ISBN Hardback: 978-1-78374-590-6
ISBN Digital (PDF): 978-1-78374-591-3
ISBN Digital ebook (epub): 978-1-78374-592-0
ISBN Digital ebook (mobi): 978-1-78374-593-7
DOI: 10.11647/OBP.0156

Cover image: Portrait of a political personality, probably Mark Antony, from the oration area of the Roman Forum, Centrale Montemartini, Rome. Wikimedia, https://bit.ly/2OQRxNy

Cover design: Anna Gatti.

All paper used by Open Book Publishers is SFI (Sustainable Forestry Initiative), PEFC (Programme for the Endorsement of Forest Certification Schemes) and Forest Stewardship Council(r)(FSC(r) certified.

Printed in the United Kingdom, United States, and Australia by Lightning Source for Open Book Publishers (Cambridge, UK)

To Vivi and in memory of Lucio (3.6.1932–23.8.2016)

Contents

Preface and Acknowledgements

The sections from *Philippic* 2 included in the present textbook will serve as one of the set texts for the OCR Latin AS and A Level specifications from 2019–2021. It is a challenging pick, not least since Cicero serves up a smorgasbord of topics in his invective assault on Antony: he finds occasion to weigh in on modes of fornication, electoral procedures, Rome's civic religion, political incidents and developments before and after the assassination of Caesar, and many other matters, all the while deploying a wide range of generic and discursive registers. Luckily, the availability of excellent resources facilitates engagement with the speech, including the commentaries by Mayor (1861), Denniston (1926), Ramsey (2003), and Manuwald (2007) (on *Philippics* 3–11, but of relevance to the entire corpus), the bilingual edition with commentary by Lacey (1986), and the translation by Shackleton Bailey (1986).

As in earlier commentaries, I have tended to summarize and cite (also at length), rather than refer to, primary sources and pieces of secondary literature: for my primary audience (students, but also teachers, in secondary education), a 'see e.g.' or a 'cf.' followed by a reference is at best tantalizing, but most likely just annoying or pointless. Gestures to further readings are not entirely absent, however, since I have tried to render this commentary useful also for audiences who have more time at their hand and can get access to scholarly literature, such as students wishing to do an EPQ. The commentary tries to cater for various backgrounds: it contains detailed explication of grammar and syntax, bearing in mind students who study the text on their own; and it tries to convey a flavour of Latin studies at undergraduate level for those who are thinking of pursuing classical studies at university.

© Ingo Gildenhard, CC BY 4.0   https://doi.org/10.11647/OBP.0156.01

Unless otherwise indicated, texts and translations of Greek and Latin texts are (based on) those in the Loeb Classical Library.

Along with my other volumes in this series, this one would not have been possible without the gallant support of John Henderson, who kindly explained to me what *Philippic* 2 is all about while turning around an unusually unwieldy draft with his customary speed and bountiful comments, now all incorporated in the commentary, and Alessandra Tosi, who has shepherded this project from first idea to final product with much-appreciated patience and enthusiasm. I am also grateful to Liam Etheridge for his nifty copy-editing, Bianca Gualandi for her magically swift generation of the proofs, and King's, my College at the University of Cambridge, which has generously contributed a grant to help cover the cost of publication.

Dedico questo libro ai miei suoceri, Vivi e Lucio.

INTRODUCTION

 https://doi.org/10.11647/OBP.0156.02

When one day the head of Cicero was brought to them [sc. Antony and his wife Fulvia] — he had been overtaken and slain in flight —, Antony uttered many bitter reproaches against it and then ordered it to be exposed on the speakers-platform more prominently than the rest, in order that it might be seen in the very place where Cicero had so often been heard declaiming against him, together with his right hand, just as it had been cut off. And Fulvia took the head into her hands before it was removed, and after abusing it spitefully and spitting upon it, set it on her knees, opened the mouth, and pulled out the tongue, which she pierced with the pins that she used for her hair, at the same time uttering many brutal jests.

Cassius Dio 47.8.3–4[1]

Like few other periods in (ancient) history, late-republican and early-imperial Rome pullulated with memorable personalities. The years that saw the fitful transformation of a senatorial tradition of republican government into an autocratic regime produced a gallery of iconic figures that have resonated down the ages: Julius Caesar ('Cowards die many times before their deaths | the valiant never taste of death but once'), Marcus Tullius Cicero ('But for my own part [what he said] was Greek to me'), Marcus Brutus ('This was the noblest Roman of them all'), Gaius Cassius ('Men at some time are masters of their fates'), Marcus Antonius, a.k.a. Mark Antony ('Friends, Romans, countrymen, lend me your ears'), and Octavian, the future *princeps* Augustus ('The time of universal peace is near'), have all remained household names,

---

1   Cassius Dio (c. 155–c. 235 CE) was a Roman statesman and historiographer, writing in Greek.

partly because they have continued to inspire creative individuals also in post-classical times — not least Shakespeare.[2] They are certainly good to think with, evoking Big Issues and Ideas, such as Civil War and Dictatorship (Caesar), Republican Liberty (Cicero), Tyrannicide (Brutus and Cassius), Power and Love (Antony and Cleopatra), and Empire (Augustus).

Consisting of selections from *Philippic* 2, the text set by OCR offers an excellent introduction to, intervention in, and commentary on this period of turmoil and transition. Composed in the autumn of 44 BCE, the year of Caesar's assassination, it includes a sustained attack by Cicero on Mark Antony, who was consul at the time — but whom Cicero suspected of aiming at autocratic power, another tyrant-in-waiting. *Philippic* 2 is conceived as Cicero's (imaginary) response to the verbal abuse Antony had hurled at him in a meeting of the senate on 19 September, but was in all likelihood never orally delivered: Cicero unleashed his sh•tstorm as a literary pamphlet sometime towards the end of the year (late November or December). Further efforts followed, all aimed at pushing a reluctant senate and the people of Rome into a violent confrontation with Antony, whom Cicero deemed (and managed to transform into) Public Enemy No 1. But when political fortune swung, Cicero found himself on the killing list of a triumvirate comprising Antony, Caesar Octavianus (the future Augustus), and M. Aemilius Lepidus ('a slight unmeritable man | meet to be sent on errands').[3] And thus the maestro of the needling tongue was heading for decapitation — and Fulvia, Antony's wife at the time, made sure (or so Dio Cassius' story goes) that the reprisal stuck also postmortem, pricking republican *libertas* and *eloquentia* to death. Against the orator who knew how to use his word as sword, the sword got the final word. (Or has it? Ask yourself: why am I reading Cicero on Antony, not Antony on Cicero…? And you also might want to challenge the all-too-easy binary between word / sword in other ways as well: arguably the warmonger here was Cicero, while Antony, too, had considerable talent as orator.)

Much, then, is at stake with this text, and it is not easy to do it critical justice. The 'double whammy' of *Philippic* 2 — 'as on the one

---

2   The quotations are, respectively, from *Julius Caesar* 2.2, 1.2, 5.5, 1.2, 3.2, and *Antony and Cleopatra* 4.6.

3   So says Antony to Octavian in Shakespeare, *Julius Caesar* 4.1.

hand lengthiest and most hysterically warped, and on the other hand undelivered fake up' — invites analysis from a range of perspectives.[4] To begin with, the text is a historical document: the speeches are crammed full with facts and figures about the political culture of republican Rome and, more specifically, the changes that happened in the wake of Caesar's victory in the civil wars and his rise to the dictatorship. This calls for some basic orientation about author, title, date, circumstances of composition, and whatnot (1). Secondly, the abusive pyrotechnics Cicero fires off in *Philippic* 2 should not blind us to the fact that the speech is carefully scripted rhetoric and repays close study as a literary artifact designed to intervene in a specific historical situation: it is meant to change (our perception of) reality, even though it would be a mistake to think that (m)any of the salacious secrets Cicero shares with us about (say) Antony's supposedly sordid sex life have a factual basis (2). Finally, Cicero *also* conceived of *Philippic* 2 as a monument of eloquence and political activism designed to *outlive* its context of production — and invites us to consider his speech as enacting a mode of politics and as a personal manifesto of political eloquence that possesses trans-historical relevance and universalizing import (3).

---

4   Henderson (2010).

1. Contexts and Paratexts

1.1 (Character) Assassination as a Means of Politics in Late-Republican Rome

The convulsive showdown between Cicero (berating) and Antony (beheading) is just one episode in a long series of violent confrontations between members of Rome's ruling elite that eventually resulted in the collapse of the republican commonwealth. But the 'extremist' politics of Cicero and Antony (and their generation) that aimed at the complete verbal and/or physical annihilation of a peer-turned-enemy, was a fairly recent phenomenon in Roman history. While we should not imagine early and mid-republican Rome as a conflict-free zone where sober ancestors beholden to a set of peasant values practised consensual politics in happy harmony, the murderous savagery of civil warfare, so familiar from the last generation of the Roman republic, did not really take off until the second half of the second century BCE. True, narratives that bemoan a decline in personal and political morality began to circulate from c. 200 BCE onwards. This was (not coincidentally) the time when Rome's imperial success and exploitation started to take off in earnest and resulted in increasing inequalities in wealth within Rome's ruling elite, which opened up novel possibilities for specific individuals to accumulate degrees of wealth and political power difficult to accommodate within an oligarchic system. But one could do worse than single out 133 BCE as the moment in time when the fabric of Rome's political culture first started to unravel violently: in that year, the *pontifex maximus* and ordinary senator Scipio Nasica, unaided by the consuls, took charge of the murder of one of the tribunes of the plebs,

Tiberius Gracchus, and around three hundred of his supporters, on the suspicion that he aimed for tyranny.

In a commonwealth fundamentally grounded in power sharing, consensus politics, and default friendship among members of the ruling elite — but also with a pronounced ethics of revenge — the phenomenon of political murder proved deeply divisive.[5] It was the moment when Romans first started to become deadly serious about turning 'adversaries' into 'enemies' — to use a distinction recently made by Michael Ignatieff.[6] From then on, political measures designed to validate 'extremist' politics (such as the so-called '*hostis* declaration', the decision to regard a Roman citizen as an external enemy), which amounted to the 'othering' of part of the self, coincided with repeated episodes of outright civil war. The series of violent clashes (Marius with Sulla, Caesar with Pompey, Cicero and the senate with Mark Antony, to name only the most obvious) only ended in 31 BCE at the battle of Actium between Caesar Octavianus and Antony and Cleopatra. This led to the establishment of the principate, an autocratic form of government prefigured, not least, by the dictatorships of Sulla and Caesar. *Philippic* 2 is an explosive exhibit of 'the Roman culture of civil conflict'[7] — composed in the brief period of republican revival that began with the murder of Caesar in March 44 and ended with the battle of Philippi in Northern Greece in October 42, where Antony and Caesar Octavianus triumphed over Caesar's foremost assassins, Brutus and Cassius. Philippi sounded the ultimate death knell of politics in

---

5   On default friendship: you might get a thought-provoking kick out of reading the exchange of letters between Cicero and Antony attached to Cicero's *Letter to Atticus* 14.13 = 367 SB, dating to 26 April 44 BCE.

6   See Michael Ignatieff, 'Enemies vs. Adversaries', http://www.nytimes.com/2013/10/17/opinion/enemies-vs-adversaries.html, an op-ed piece for *The New York Times* à propos the emergence of new forms of radical or even extremist politics across the globe, including Western democracies: 'For democracies [and, one might add, the Roman republic] to work, politicians need to respect the difference between an enemy and an adversary. An adversary is someone you want to defeat. An enemy is someone you have to destroy. With adversaries, compromise is honorable: Today's adversary could be tomorrow's ally. With enemies, on the other hand, compromise is appeasement'.

7   For the phrase (and a gloss), see the conference announcement by Wolfgang Havener, 'A Culture of Civil War? — *bellum civile* in the Late Republic and the Early Principate', https://www.hsozkult.de/event/id/termine-34304

a republican key. Previously, Cicero's *Philippics*, not least *Philippic 2*, arguably hastened along the final demise of the *libera res publica* by advocating a second act of (prospective) tyrannicide and pushing the senate into an armed confrontation with Antony that turned out to be ill-advised. (Savour the paradox!)

1.2 The Antagonists: Cicero and Antony

Born in 106 BCE, Cicero reached political maturity during the reign of Sulla (82–79 BCE), who first introduced proscriptions (the drafting of 'kill lists') into Rome's political repertory, and lost his life in 43 BCE when the triumvirs resorted once more to the same measure (or, in the words of Seneca the Elder, *Suasoria* 6.3, when 'Sulla's thirst for citizen blood returned to the state' (*civilis sanguinis Sullana sitis in civitatem redit*). The autobiography that emerges from Cicero's oratorical self-fashioning throughout his career as a public speaker reflects the tumultuous historical context in which he was operating. The following six stages can be distinguished:

(i)   c. 81–66 BCE: in his early defence speeches Cicero adopts the stance of the inexperienced novice, who, in the name of justice, dares to speak truth to power and gradually rises to the top. This early period culminates in the speeches against Verres, who stood accused of imperial exploitation, through which he dethroned Hortensius (a part of Verres' defence team) as 'king of the courts'.

(ii) In his first political speech the *De Imperio Gnaei Pompei* or *Pro Lege Manilia* delivered in 66 BCE, the year he held the praetorship (the second highest political office after the consulship), Cicero promotes himself as the 'new man made good', who puts himself at the service of the commonwealth.

(iii) He follows up on this with the consular ethos (optimate or *popularis*, as the occasion demanded) he projects in the orations he gave during and shortly after his consulship (63–59 BCE) — the apex of his political ambitions, which tragically also resulted in his first devastating career break: in 58 BCE, Cicero was driven into exile for his illegal execution of the Catilinarians without trial.

(iv) Upon his return in 57 BCE, he tries to regain lost political prestige by adopting a 'L'État, c'est moi' ['The state am I'] posture, starting with his two speeches of thanks-giving to the senate and the people for his recall and culminating in the *pro Milone* (52 BCE).

(v) Soon after the *pro Milone*, Cicero left Rome on a pro-consular appointment in the Near East and returned just shortly before the outbreak of civil war. With a dictator in charge, Cicero turns himself into a principled republican, who struggles to find, but manages to assert, a meaningful voice in the presence of autocratic omnipotence: all three speeches he delivered before Caesar — the *pro Marcello* and *pro Ligario* in 46; and the *pro Rege Deiotaro* in 45 — testify to his republican convictions (but also his willingness to enter into dialogue with the dictator), though the mood of the orations progressively darkens.

(vi) After Caesar's assassination, Cicero, in his *Philippics* (1–14, dating to 44–43 BCE), casts himself in the role of an ardent patriot, who tries to rally the senate and the people under the slogan 'give me liberty or give me death'. *Philippic* 2 thus belongs to the last phase of Cicero's career, leading up to — indeed helping to bring about — his murder.[8]

Born in 83 or 82 BCE, Antony, unlike Cicero, was not a *homo novus*:[9] the *gens Antonia* belonged to the nobility (though was not of patrician origins). The most illustrious representative of the family clan was Antony's grandfather, the eponymous Marcus Antonius (I), one of the consuls of 99 BCE and immortalized by Cicero as one of the two principal interlocutors in his dialogue *On the Ideal Orator* (*de Oratore*).

---

8   Writing in the early imperial period, Seneca the Elder (54 BCE–39 CE) put together collections of materials for declamatory exercises. Two of his *Suasoriae* deal with the circumstances of Cicero's death: *Suasoria* 6 debates whether Cicero should have begged Antony's pardon if the opportunity had presented itself (and concludes with a collection of accounts of his actual death, including Livy's); *Suasoria* 7 explores the (again fictional) scenario: 'Antony Promises To Spare Cicero's Life If He Burns His Writings: Cicero Deliberates Whether To Do So'. Debate Away!

9   For his date of birth (disputed), see Denniston (1926: 100).

The next generation failed to live up to his lofty standards: Marcus Antonius (II), son of Marcus Antonius (I) and father of our Mark Antony did reach the praetorship in 74, but soon after suffered a fatal career break because of military failure followed by bankruptcy. His brother Gaius Antonius Hybrida got chucked out of the senate in 70, though managed a comeback as Cicero's colleague in the consulship in 63. Cicero quite literally bought his support against Catiline, not least by agreeing to swap pro-consular provincial assignments. But upon his return from Macedonia in 59, Hybrida was dragged into court for his approach to provincial government and went into exile. If Hybrida harboured significant sympathies for Catiline, Antony's stepfather P. Cornelius Lentulus Sura, one of the consuls of 71, but (just like Antonius Hybrida) stricken off the senatorial register the following year, was one of Catiline's ringleaders and among those whom Cicero had executed without trial.

Antony therefore had to overcome the failings of the previous generation of Antonii, but he could rely on the distinction of his grandfather and some family resources, which 'included the large Antonian *clientela* and access to wealth, arising both from the family's business interests in the East and from a possibly lucrative first marriage to Fadia, the daughter of a freedman'.[10] His talents in the military sphere served as catalyst for a remarkable career. Antony first distinguished himself in service under Gabinius in the Near East (57–55), before joining Caesar in Gaul and becoming one of his most trusted lieutenants.[11] With the help of Caesar's patronage, he started on his *cursus honorum* in Rome, holding the quaestorship in 52 and the tribuneship in 49. The outbreak of civil war then turbo-charged his rise to the top: 'In the first two years of the Civil War, Caesar twice deputed Antony to serve as his chief representative in Italy during prolonged periods of absence.

---

10 Welch (1995: 184), with further bibliography. She proceeds to offer the following character sketch of Mark Antony: 'Bluff good humour, moderate intelligence, at least a passing interest in literature, and an ability to be the life and soul of a social gathering all contributed to make him a charming companion and to bind many important people to him. He had a lieutenant's ability to follow orders and a willingness to listen to advice, even (one might say especially) from intelligent women. These attributes made Antony able to handle some situations very well. There was a more important side to his personality, however, which contributed to his political survival. Antony was ruthless in his quest for pre-eminence'.

11 Cicero covers these chapters of Antony's career in *Phil.* 2.48: see below.

Caesar did so first in April 49 when he set out for Spain to do battle with Pompey's legions. From April until Caesar's return in December, Mark Antony was granted pro-praetorian power by Caesar and entrusted with administering the whole of Italy, although at the time Antony was only a tribune of the plebs... A year later, in 48–47 Antony's powers were even more sweeping. As Caesar's *magister equitum* during Caesar's extended absence in Egypt and Asia Minor, Mark Antony exercised control over all of Italy and Rome until Caesar returned in September 47'.[12] In the following years, he was busy raising much needed cash for Caesar by 'liquidating Pompey's assets by resale' — a 'complex financial enterprise' which he managed to carry off with aplomb and handsome rewards from Caesar in the form of further political offices and advancement.[13]

In the year of Caesar's death, Antony was consul — but the assassination of his patron left him very much exposed: while he initially tried to reach a compromise with the conspirators and work towards a peaceful resolution of the simmering tensions between Caesarians and republicans, he soon came under pressure from Caesarian hard-liners, and in particular Caesar's adopted heir Octavianus, who eroded his support among the veterans and other loyalists by adopting a strident stance towards the conspirators. To rally support, shore up his base, and increase his influence, Antony began to pursue a much more confrontational approach that included pronounced pro-Caesarian measures of his own — which brought him into open conflict with Cicero and set the stage for the *Philippics*.

Cicero did manage to forge an alliance against Antony, consisting of a reluctant senate (under his leadership), the two (Caesarian) consuls of 43 (Aulus Hirtius and Gaius Vibius Pansa) and their armies, and Caesar's heir Octavianus (and his private army of Caesarian veterans); but his success was short-lived. By the summer of 43, Antony, Octavian, and Lepidus had formed their triumvirate and taken control of Italy. Cicero was one of the first — and certainly the most prominent — victim of their kill list. Despite their successful squashing of the republican opposition, the alliance between Antony and Octavian remained uneasy — and it ultimately broke down entirely in the late 30s BCE. In preparation for

---

12   Ramsey (2004: 162).
13   Ramsey (2004), with citations from 172.

the final showdown, Octavian picked up where Cicero left off: with a wholesale propaganda war against the character and (its failings) of his adversary.[14] At the centre of the effort stood the contention that Antony had lost his Roman ways and had fallen under the evil influence of the queen of Egypt, Cleopatra.[15] After Antony and Cleopatra lost the battle of Actium against Octavian (and his general Agrippa), they fled to Egypt and ended their lives. Here is Shakespeare's take (*Antony and Cleopatra* 4.15.52–70):

MARK ANTONY
The miserable change now at my end
Lament nor sorrow at, but please your thoughts
In feeding them with those my former fortunes,
Wherein I lived, the greatest prince o' th' world,
The noblest, and do now not basely die,
Not cowardly put off my helmet to
My countryman — a Roman by a Roman
Valiantly vanquished. Now my spirit is going.
I can no more.

CLEOPATRA
       Noblest of men, woo't die?
Hast thou no care of me? Shall I abide
In this dull world, which in thy absence is
No better than a sty? O see, my women,
The crown o' th' earth doth melt. My lord!
      [*Antony dies*]
O, withered is the garland of the war,
The soldier's pole is fall'n: young boys and girls
Are level now with men. The odds is gone,
And there is nothing left remarkable
Beneath the visiting moon.

For Shakespeare's Cleopatra, at least, Mark Antony was the world. As we stride into the Billingsgate that is *Philippic* 2, it is worth bearing in mind that hardly any politician in history has otherwise been treated more unfairly…

---

14   Scott (1933).
15   http://theconversation.com/the-fake-news-that-sealed-the-fate-of-antony-and-cleopatra-71287

1.3 The *Philippics*: Background, Dates of Composition, Corpus and Title

Quite a few historians argue, blessed with the benefit of hindsight, that the murder of Caesar simply arrested for a brief and bloody period of time the inevitable transformation of an oligarchic into an autocratic regime at Rome that had long been underway and was finally completed by Octavian. But for those living in the thick of things, the period after the Ides of March 44 was one of high crisis and contingency: everything was suddenly up in the air again, with all options on the table — a reconstituted *libera res publica*, centered in the senatorial aristocracy; a prolonged descent into civic bloodshed with uncertain outcome; the rise of another autocrat.[16]

Cicero, for one, was overjoyed at Caesar's assassination (even though he did not seem to have been partial to the conspiracy). But disillusion quickly set in. Antony's behaviour in particular started to grate on him — and he began to suspect him of trying to assume Caesar's mantle. Already in April, Cicero gloomily toyed with the idea of leaving Rome for Athens, to visit his son and sit out the year of Antony's consulship in self-imposed withdrawal from active politics (*Att.* 14.10.1 = 364 SB; 19 April 44). But soon after he had finally departed in the summer, he changed his mind and decided to return to Rome (*Att.* 16.7 = 415 SB; 19 August 44).[17] He arrived back in the capital on 31 August and, finding that the main item on the agenda for the senate meeting the following day was 'Honours for Caesar', sent in his apologies, claiming that he was too worn out by travel to attend. Antony, who was behind the motion of heaping further honours on the dead dictator, took this as a personal insult and furiously attacked Cicero in absentia during the meeting. Cicero replied at the senate meeting on the following day (2 September) with an oration that would become his *first Philippic* and constitutes a masterpiece of passive-aggressive insinuation.[18] Antony stewed on this over the next fortnight or so and then burst into a tirade against Cicero

---

16   Excellent accounts of this period include the incisive treatment by Gotter (1996), to which this entire commentary is much indebted, and (on a broader canvass) Osgood (2018).

17   See Ramsey (2001) for discussion of the circumstances.

18   Stevenson (2009), Usher (2010).

during the senate meeting on 19 September. *Philippic* 2 pretends to be a spontaneous riposte to Antony's vituperations (with Antony still on hand to be put on the spot — in fact, it was Cicero who was not present on the day!), but was actually composed and edited in the aftermath of the meeting. In *Philippic* 5, Cicero himself gives an account of the verbal sparring between himself and Antony in September 44 (5.19–20):[19]

Huc nisi venirem Kalendis Septembribus, fabros se missurum et domum meam disturbaturum esse dixit. Magna res, credo, agebatur: de supplicatione referebat. veni postridie: ipse non venit. locutus sum de re publica, minus equidem libere quam mea consuetudo, liberius tamen quam periculi minae postulabant. at ille homo vehemens et violentus, qui hanc consuetudinem libere dicendi excluderet ... inimicitias mihi denuntiavit; adesse in senatum iussit a. d. XIII Kalendas Octobris. ipse interea septemdecim dies de me in Tiburtino Scipionis declamitavit, sitim quaerens; haec enim ei causa esse declamandi solet. cum is dies quo me adesse iusserat venisset, tum vero agmine quadrato in aedem Concordiae venit atque in me absentem orationem ex ore impurissimo evomuit. quo die, si per amicos mihi cupienti in senatum venire licuisset, caedis initium fecisset a me; sic enim statuerat.

[If I did not come here on the Kalends of September (= 1 September) he said he would send workmen to vandalize my house. Important business was on the agenda, I seem to remember: discussion of a public thanksgiving! I came the following day (= 2 September): he himself didn't. I spoke on the commonwealth — less freely, for sure, than I am accustomed to, though more freely than his threats of danger warranted. Then this man of vehemence and violence, who wished to ban this custom of free speech, ... declared me his personal enmity and ordered me to be present in the senate on 19 September. Meanwhile he spent seventeen days declaiming about me in Scipio's villa at Tibur, seeking to work up a thirst — his usual reason for declaiming. When the day on

19   See also *Fam.* 10.2 = 341 SB (to Plancus, c. 19 September 44 BCE): *Meum studium honori tuo pro necessitudine nostra non defuisset si aut tuto in senatum aut honeste venire potuissem; sed nec sine periculo quisquam libere de re publica sentiens versari potest in summa impunitate gladiorum nec nostrae dignitatis videtur esse ibi sententiam de re publica dicere ubi me et melius et propius audiant armati quam senatores* ('As a friend I should not have failed to support the decree in your honour, had I been able to enter the Senate in security and dignity. But it is dangerous for any man of independent political views to move about in public when swords are drawn with complete impunity; and it does not seem to comport with my dignity to make a speech in a House where men-at-arms would hear me better and at shorter distance than members').

which he had ordered me to be present came, he entered the Temple of Concord with his bodyguard in battle formation and vomited from that foulest of mouths a speech against me in my absence. If my friends had allowed me to come to the senate on that day as I wished, he would have started his slaughter with me; that was his resolve.]

Cicero here mocks Antony's rigorous rhetorical exercises in the run-up to the rant he unleashed on 19 September. But at least Antony delivered his speech in person — unlike Cicero. While posturing as an impromptu response, *Philippic* 2 is, rather, a long-deferred *written* response, carefully drafted (and edited) over several weeks and (as far as we can tell) never orally performed in the senate.[20] Cicero attaches a draft of the oration to a letter to Atticus written on 25 October, wondering when (if ever) the moment for wider circulation might come (*Att.* 15.13 = 416 SB):

> orationem tibi misi. eius custodiendae et proferendae arbitrium tuum. sed quando illum diem cum tu edendam putes?

> [I am sending you the speech, to be kept back and put out at your discretion. But when shall we see the day when you will think proper to publish it?]

By 5 November 44, Atticus had read the speech and sent Cicero some comments, suggestions, and criticisms to which Cicero responded in turn.[21] Overall, then, as Sussman (1994: 54) puts it: 'the characterization of Antony was painstakingly premeditated and the speech itself is a consummate piece of craftsmanship'. At the same time, the long process of gestation also shows how difficult it was for Cicero to find a voice (and make it heard). Even the final product, if one reads between the lines of the invective bluster, shows up Antony as a frightfully powerful adversary, capable and competent in equal measure, a power broker of the first order — if perhaps no Julius Caesar. Indeed, 'maybe the only glove that C really lands on him is the easy shot of billing him as a JC clone, one helluva disappointment after the real thing'.[22]

---

20 The cited passage from *Philippic* 5 contains an implicit apology for this unusual practice: Cicero claims that had he been present, he would not have had the opportunity to reply since he would have been killed in cold-blood.

21 See *Att.* 16.11 = 420 SB: *nostrum opus tibi probari laetor; ex quo ἄνϑη ipsa posuisti, quae mihi florentiora sunt visa tuo iudicio...* — 'I am glad you like my work. You have quoted the very gems, and your good opinion makes them sparkle the brighter in my eyes...').

22 John Henderson, *per litteras.*

1.4 The Wider Corpus and the Title

Cicero finally disseminated the text more widely in late November or early December.[23] He was now fully committed to three interrelated objectives: to drag a reluctant senate into a military confrontation with Antony, whom he configured as the new tyrant-in-waiting; to act as self-appointed mentor of Octavian, who was courting Cicero as an influential establishment figure, and thereby ensure his support for the traditional order; and most importantly to restore the senatorial regime to power.

Over the next few months, Cicero weighed in with twelve more speeches against Antony.[24] On 20 December 44, he addressed both the senate (*Phil.* 3) and the people (*Phil.* 4) and did so again on 1 January 43 (*Phil.* 5, to the senate; *Phil.* 6, to the people). The remaining eight *Philippics* were all delivered in the senate: *Phil.* 7 (mid-January 43), *Phil.* 8 (4 February 43), *Phil.* 9 and 10 (both in early February 43), *Phil.* 11 (end of February 43), *Phil.* 12 (beginning of March 43), *Phil.* 13 (20 March 43), and *Phil.* 14 (21 April 43). All seem to have been published rapidly.[25] The last intervention occurred just after news had reached Rome of the battle of Forum Gallorum near Mutina (14/15 April 43). While the 'senatorial' alliance that Cicero helped put together against Antony won this encounter as well as a follow-up battle on 21 April at Mutina, the victories turned out to be Pyrrhic: soon after, Caesar Octavianus switched sides and Cicero was history.[26] By choosing *Philippics* as the label for his last oratorical efforts, he preternaturally seems to have known where he was heading.

The name *Philippics* alludes to the corpus of speeches that the Athenian orator Demosthenes (384–322 BCE) delivered against Philip II of Macedon (382–336 BCE), the father of Alexander the Great, who

---

23 See Hall (2002: 275, n. 6): 'While a written text of the speech was certainly being prepared in late October 44 (*Att.* 15.13.1–2; 15.13a.3; 16.11.1–2), the precise date of its circulation is not known. Early December seems plausible, given Antony's departure for Cisalpine Gaul at the end of November'.

24 Stroh (1982), followed by Manuwald (2008), argues that they form a cycle of twelve speeches in imitation of Demosthenes in their own right, to which *Philippic* 1 and 2 were later added.

25 Kelly (2008).

26 For a more detailed account of the historical context for each individual speech (and the nature of its intervention) see Manuwald (2007: 9–31: '2.1. Events in 44–43 BCE').

threatened to invade the Greek peninsula from the North and 'enslave' the Greek city-states, in particular Athens. He realized his ambitions after winning the battle of Chaeronea in 338 BCE, and Demosthenes' oratorical efforts against Philip acquired an iconic status as an eloquent stand on behalf of liberty against tyranny and oppression. In the 40s, Demosthenes more generally had become a prominent point of reference for Cicero's theorizing on oratory, and he began to think of himself as the Roman equivalent.[27] The label *Philippics* for the set of speeches against Antony deftly extended the affinities he felt with Demosthenes to the sphere of politics and helped to endow Cicero's endeavours with historical prestige. It suggests an analogy: just as Demosthenes fought for the freedom of the Greeks against Philip, the Macedonian tyrant, so Cicero was fighting for the freedom of the Romans against Mark Antony, the would-be tyrant of Rome.

When, precisely, he started to conceive of the speeches against Antony as a thematically unified set in conscious imitation of Demosthenes' resistance to Philip II is impossible to reconstruct; it certainly happened while the corpus was still evolving, but seemingly some time after the initial two interventions were first drafted. In a letter written to Cicero (*Brut.* 2.3.4 = 2 SB; 1 April 43), written after perusal of *Philippic* 5 and 7, Brutus praises Cicero for his spirit (*animus*) and his genius (*ingenium*) before signing off on the label *Philippics* that Cicero himself had proposed, half in jest (because of its potentially presumptuous implications): *iam concedo ut vel Philippici vocentur, quod tu quadam epistula iocans scripsisti* ('I am now willing to let them be called by the name of 'Philippics', as you jestingly suggested in one of your letters').[28] In the letter to Atticus that accompanied a draft of what would turn into *Philippic* 2, Cicero does not yet use the label, though one could argue that the speech already manifests a Demosthenic flavour: 'in the *Philippics*, beginning with the *Second Philippic*, one sees the first genuine attempt on Cicero's part to imitate Demosthenes' use of style and argumentation. After Antony's furious attack on him in the senate on 19 September, Cicero realized that reconciliation was not possible and that he was engaged in a death

---

27   Wooten (1983: 49).
28   See also *Brut.* 2.4.2 = 4 SB (Cicero to Brutus, 12 April 43): *haec ad te oratio perferetur, quoniam video delectari Philippicis nostris* ('The speech [= *Philippic* 11] will be sent to you, since I see you enjoy my Philippics').

struggle to preserve the only form of government in which he himself could function effectively (cf. *Letters to Friends*, I 12.2, 1). Moreover, Antony had attacked Cicero's whole career, as a politician, as an orator, and as a man; and Cicero realized that his reply had to be a defence of his entire life. Less than two years before, Cicero had put his hand to a Latin translation of Demosthenes' speech *On the Crown*. He had already come to think of himself, both as an orator and as a politician, in terms of Demosthenes'.[29]

You may want to ask yourself: does this analogy mean the speeches were pre-destined to make a posthumous hero out of Cicero (as they did of Demosthenes) but also doomed to seal permanent political failure? Though unlike Demosthenes', *Cicero's* Freedom Speech couldn't even turn up and make its Big Moment. Even within its own corpus, *Philippic 2* is unusual: 'the speech is in fact something of an <u>anomaly</u> within the collection as a whole. Its function as invective means that it contains little of the deliberate style of oratory found elsewhere in the *Philippics*; and with a total of 119 sections it is more than twice as long as any of the other speeches'.[30] See also Wooten (1983: 156): '... the primary aim of *Philippic* II is to establish firmly the character of the major participants in the conflict, very much like the first speech in the second action against Verres. As in this speech and as in Demosthenes' *Philippics* and *Olynthiacs*, narrative is used to discredit the character of the opponent. There is nothing in the speech about what actions should be taken to oppose Antony, nothing about Cicero's own political program, no rational analysis of the situation. Emotional appeals are used to

---

29 Wooten (1983: 50–51). (In his speech *On the Crown*, Demosthenes defended a fellow Athenian citizen Ctesiphon who had been dragged into court by Demosthenes' rival Aeschines for daring to propose that Demosthenes ought to be honoured with a civic crown for outstanding services to the city; Demosthenes used this occasion to justify his person and his politics.) NB: you might want to question Wooten's dogmatism: '...realized that...', 'Cicero realized...' — as if Cicero did not have any other options or might not have misjudged the situation. Likewise, imitation of his Greek models does not preclude emulation, not least in the area of hard-hitting verbal abuse. See Worman (2008: 321–22): 'Many of Cicero's most effective character assassinations rely on demonstrating that his opponents fail miserably in this bodily restraint. His extravagant portrait in the *Philippics* of Antony's appetitive outrages echoes in much more extreme form the excesses ... that Demosthenes attributes to his opponents, most particularly Aeschines but also Meidias, Androtion and, of course, Philip'.

30 Hall (2002: 275).

galvanize Cicero's supporters, and vilification of character is used to set the stage for the exposition of the specific proposals that Cicero would eventually make' (from the third *Philippic* onwards).

Its special status raises all sorts of questions: do the rest of the speeches step around or recycle it, only this time for real in the public spaces of the city? Has Cicero integrated *Philippic* 2 in with the rest or does it stick out like a surgically removed thumb? Might it be the dustbin for everything he didn't get into the rest — highlights too juicy to chuck away?

2. The *Second Philippic* as a Rhetorical Artifact – and Invective Oratory

As we have seen, then, *Philippic* 2 is anything but an impromptu outburst by an irate orator who had just been raked over the coals and ridiculed in front of his peers. It is, rather, a deliberate and highly *literary* act of retaliation, composed (and revised) over several weeks and released in cold blood at an opportune moment (when Antony was no longer present in Rome). Despite the craftsmanship, the overall structure of the speech, however, is deceptively simple and straightforward:

§§ 1–3: *exordium* [= preface, introduction]
§§ 3–41: Cicero's defence of himself
§§ 42–43: Transition (attack on Antony as orator)
§§ 44–114: Attack on Antony
§§ 115–119: *peroratio* [= conclusion]

After the exordium, Cicero responds to the abuse that Antony heaped on him in the speech of 19 September. We can gather from his rebuttal that Antony seems to have charged him with a lack of honour that manifested itself not least in his failure to live up to the obligations of friendship and his ingratitude towards Antony, who claimed to have saved Cicero's life (cf. *Phil*. 2.3–10). Cicero's consulship must have come in for ridicule — as well as the epic poetry he afterwards composed about it (cf. *Phil*. 2.11–20). Antony even seems to have found a way to blame Cicero for the death of Clodius, the outbreak of civil war, and the assassination of Caesar (cf. *Phil*. 2.21–36). And he mocked the low level of esteem in which (he claimed) Cicero was held in Roman society (cf. *Phil*. 2.40–42). After a lengthy rebuttal of this battery of charges and a brief transition, Cicero turns the tables on Antony: what Antony blamed on him, he now blames on Antony — and more. The speech concludes with a defiant peroration, in which Cicero expresses his unconditional commitment to weather the crisis of the commonwealth caused by Antony's perceived power grab — albeit by sacrificing his life for the sake of Rome's freedom.

Throughout, Cicero keeps his text aligned with the fiction that it is a spontaneous response to Antony's discourse.[31] In generic terms, *Philippic* 2 follows the conventions of oratory with a strong invective bent. Both of these terms — oratory and invective — are worth a closer look.

2.1 Oratory at Rome

The *orator*, operating in the domestic political sphere (*domi*), complemented the *imperator*, who was in charge of affairs outside the city (*militiae*). While military accolades, in particular the celebration of a triumph, outshone any other achievement, to be an esteemed public speaker was part of the portfolio of distinctions to which members of Rome's ruling elite aspired. Pliny's summary of the speech that Quintus Caecilius Metellus gave for his father Marcus in 221 BCE includes the assertion that dad could lay claim to the ten greatest and best achievements, which men with smarts spend their lives pursuing (Pliny the Elder, *Natural History* 7.139–40):[32]

> Q. Metellus in ea oratione quam habuit supremis laudibus patris sui L. Metelli pontificis, bis consulis, dictatoris, magistri equitum, xvviri agris dandis, qui primus elephantos ex primo Punico bello duxit in triumpho, scriptum reliquit decem maximas res optumasque in quibus quaerendis sapientes aetatem exigerent consummasse eum: voluisse enim primarium bellatorem esse, optimum oratorem, fortissimum imperatorem, auspicio suo maximas res geri, maximo honore uti, summa sapientia esse, summum senatorem haberi, pecuniam magnam bono modo invenire, multos liberos relinquere et clarissimum in civitate esse.

> [Quintus Metellus, in the speech that he delivered as the funeral oration of his father Lucius Metellus the pontiff, who had been consul twice, dictator, master of the horse and land-commissioner, and who was the first person who led elephants captured in the first Punic War in a triumph, has left it in writing that his father had achieved the ten greatest

---

31 Cf. Steel (2006: 59).
32 Cf. Pliny the Elder, *Natural History* 7.100: *Cato primus Porciae gentis tres summas in homine res praestitisse existimatur, ut esset optimus orator, optimus imperator, optimus senator* ('Cato of the Gens Porcia is deemed to have exemplified first the three supreme human achievements, excelling alike as orator, as general and as senator').

and highest objects in the pursuit of which wise men pass their lives: for he had made it his aim to be a most outstanding warrior, a supreme orator and a very brave commander, to be in charge of operations of the highest importance, to enjoy the greatest honour, to be supremely wise, to be deemed the most eminent senator, to obtain great wealth in an honourable way, to leave many children, and to achieve supreme distinction in the civic community.]

However, what exactly constituted a good public speaker remained controversial. Was (for instance) superior rhetorical skill more important than sound moral conviction? Under the influence of Greek rhetorical thought, the tension between technical proficiency and authoritative ethics acquired a cross-cultural complexion. When Cato the Elder (234–149 BCE) defined the orator as 'a good man who knows how to speak' (*vir bonus dicendi peritus*) he polemically asserted that the ability to coruscate with words was of secondary importance to the moral fiber of the speaker: no amount of sparkle, brilliance, and sophistication in the use of language can elevate a wordsmith to the status of an orator if he lacked proper ethics. In another adage — 'stick to the topic, the words will follow': *rem tene, verba sequentur* — Cato suggests that no formal training in rhetoric at all was needed to be a public speaker of substance.

To what extent he was representative of the first half of the second century BCE is difficult to determine, but by the late republic training in Greek and Latin rhetoric, including study trips to Greece, were part and parcel of an elite Roman education.[33] Still, Greek rhetorical theory and technique retained their potentially problematic quality in Roman oratorical practice. In Cicero's dialogue *On the Ideal Orator* (*de Oratore*), written in the mid-50s BCE, one of the characters, Antonius (the grandfather of Mark Antony) maintains that any semblance of learning is best avoided, especially in speeches addressed to a wider public. Cicero himself, throughout his life, was invested in rhetorical education and the figure of the ideal orator (*summus orator*), who in his view combined wisdom (*sapientia*) with eloquence (*eloquentia*) and was equally versed in the best that Greek culture had to offer (in both rhetoric and philosophy) as well as the ancestral traditions of Rome. (Indeed, the way he put it, the best insights of Greek philosophy, especially in matters

---

33 Corbeill (2007) offers a good account.

of ethics and statesmanship, were simply the articulation in discourse of what the Roman ancestors had previously realized and enacted in practice.) Even though Cicero argued that his engagement with Greek cultural resources happened in the spirit of imperial co-option and emulation, his 'intellectual' preferences rendered him vulnerable to scorn. In his *Anti-Cato*, a treatise written in response to Cicero's praise of the republican hero Cato the Younger (95–46 BCE), Caesar included a plea to the reader (Plutarch, *Life of Julius Caesar* 3.4):[34]

> And thus, at a later time, Caesar himself, in his reply to Cicero's *Cato*, begged that the discourse of a soldier not be judged by the standards of clever eloquence achieved by a *rhetor* who was naturally gifted and had plenty of free time to pursue his studies.

Caesar here brings into play the antithesis between himself, a man of action and of the army, and the 'born *rhetor*' Cicero. In Rome, the pinnacle of glory resided in military success, and Caesar thus implies that his antagonist, unlike himself, is a *vir non vere Romanus* ('not a genuine Roman man'). He tops his slyly offensive characterization of Cicero as a clever man of the word by suggesting that his own rise to power, which coincided with the cessation of republican politics, created the perfect condition for Cicero to do what he does best. With him in charge, Cicero had the necessary leisure to pursue his natural calling, which Caesar locates in the field of rhetoric and literature, rather than politics or the military. He thereby maliciously insinuates that Cicero's retirement from politics, while perhaps stripping him of the trappings of his Roman identity, has brought him back in touch with his true nature. The larger cultural polarity between the Roman doer and the Greek thinker gives added force to these polemics. In effect, Caesar's characterization of Cicero as a 'born' *rhetor* brands the former *pater patriae* and senatorial colleague as someone who is, in essence, a Greek. Shakespeare picks up on this, when he makes Cicero pretentiously *speak* Greek — and hence remains incomprehensible to an uneducated Roman like Casca, to whom everything Cicero said was, indeed, Greek.

Antony, too, was an orator of distinction, who received the traditional training of a member of Rome's ruling elite — and who also continued

---

34   The following is adapted from Gildenhard (2007: 39–40).

to hone his rhetorical talents through special tuition later in life.[35] In a letter to Q. Thermus (*Fam.* 2.18 = 115 SB, early May 50), Cicero himself refers to him and his two brothers as *summo loco natos, promptos, non indisertos* ('of the highest birth and no mean qualities of enterprise and eloquence') — not people one would want to cross needlessly. Antony certainly knew how to excite a crowd — as he proved when he delivered the funeral oration for Caesar.[36] This may well count as 'the apogee of Antony's oratory' for those with a soft spot for Shakespeare, who re-imagines the performance as follows (*Julius Caesar* 3.2.73–107):[37]

> Friends, Romans, countrymen, lend me your ears;
> I come to bury Caesar, not to praise him.
> The evil that men do lives after them;
> The good is oft interred with their bones;
> So let it be with Caesar. The noble Brutus
> Hath told you Caesar was ambitious:
> If it were so, it was a grievous fault,
> And grievously hath Caesar answer'd it.
> Here, under leave of Brutus and the rest –
> For Brutus is an honourable man;
> So are they all, all honourable men —
> Come I to speak in Caesar's funeral.
> He was my friend, faithful and just to me;
> But Brutus says he was ambitious;
> And Brutus is an honourable man.
> He hath brought many captives home to Rome
> Whose ransoms did the general coffers fill;
> Did this in Caesar seem ambitious?
> When that the poor have cried, Caesar hath wept:
> Ambition should be made of sterner stuff:
> Yet Brutus says he was ambitious;
> And Brutus is an honourable man.
> You all did see that on the Lupercal
> I thrice presented him a kingly crown,
> Which he did thrice refuse. Was this ambition?

---

35   For Antony as orator see Huzar (1982), Mahy (2013) and van der Blom (2016), Ch. 8: 'Career-making in a time of crisis: Marcus Antonius' oratory'.

36   See below § 91.

37   The quotation is from Huzar (1982: 650). She notes: 'Even more than the first compromising speeches to the Senate, this address wrenched popular sentiment from the claims of the tyrannicides to sympathy for Caesar, hence leadership for Antony'.

Yet Brutus says he was ambitious;
And, sure, he is an honourable man.
I speak not to disprove what Brutus spoke,
But here I am to speak what I do know.
You all did love him once, not without cause:
What cause withholds you then, to mourn for him?
O judgment! thou art fled to brutish beasts,
And men have lost their reason. Bear with me;
My heart is in the coffin there with Caesar,
And I must pause till it come back to me.

'Antony's Oration Over Caesar's Body', from: Edward Sylvester Ellis, *The Story of the Greatest Nations, from the Dawn of History to the Twentieth Century* (1900).[38]

Oratory is one of the main battlegrounds in *Philippics* 2. Cicero claims that Antony falls woefully short of the ideal, despite investing an enormous amount of money in substandard tuition. He mocks him for lack of

---

38   Image from Wikimedia, https://commons.wikimedia.org/wiki/File:The_story_of_
      the_greatest_nations,_from_the_dawn_of_history_to_the_twentieth_century_-_a_
      comprehensive_history,_founded_upon_the_leading_authorities,_including_a_
      complete_chronology_of_the_world,_and_(14777797442).jpg

natural ability and the hiring of second-rate teachers, who nevertheless get rewarded handsomely from the public purse. Put bluntly, he wants to shut him up for good.

2.2 Invective

Ancient rhetorical theory distinguishes three branches of oratory: *forensic* or *judicial* (employed in court, as part of a trial), *deliberative* (used to sway an audience on a matter of public policy; in Rome the two primary settings were the Forum and the senate), and *epideictic* (a ceremonial verbal display, often with the purpose of dispensing blame or praise — as in a funeral oration). This rough-and-ready grid is useful as a basic orientation — but does not get us all that far with such an idiosyncratic text as *Philippic* 2: a written pamphlet that pretends to be the record of an epideictic (or deliberative?) speech delivered in the senate, put into circulation to persuade other members of Rome's ruling elite to pursue a specific course of political action. To come to critical terms with this particular 'oration' it is arguably more promising to focus on the dominant 'mode of discourse', rather than the genre of oratory that Cicero chose for the occasion, i.e. invective. Invective is best defined by its primary purpose: character assassination through verbal abuse.[39] Invective speech operates across genres: as a means of discrediting opponents, it can (and does) occur in all three branches of oratory (as well as other literary forms: it is, for instance, prevalent in old comedy and satire, but also appears in other types of poetry and prose).

Invective's truth

Invective speech has a complex relationship with reality, especially in a culture without libel laws as that of ancient Rome. The principle 'anything goes' applied: as in contemporary 'roast comedy' any kind of insult and incrimination, however untrue, outrageous, or defamatory, was generally speaking fair game. Unlike contemporary roasting shows, however, the point of the abuse was to degrade the target for real — though (and here the roast parallel holds again), the most potent

---

39   On invective (often conceived in generic terms), see Nisbet (1961); Koster (1980); Ruffell (2003); Craig (2004); Powell (2006); Arena (2007a); Manuwald (2011).

form of abuse managed to combine hard-hitting humiliation with (a nasty sense of) humour. Thus in the speech on behalf of Caelius, which contains a similar invective assault as *Philippic* 2 (directed against Clodius' wife Clodia, who was a witness for the prosecution), Cicero distinguishes between boorish abuse and the urbane sophistication of a creative tongue-lashing. Those prosecuting his client, he suggests, are guilty of the former. By implication, he considered himself second to none in delivering the latter.[40] Cicero was fully cognizant of the important contribution the eliciting of laughter can make to effective communication — and had a reputation for his merciless mocking and poisonous (if entertaining) put-downs.[41] Indeed, 'murderous wit' is one of the qualities that Stockton identifies as hallmarks of Ciceronian invective — together with 'coarse raillery', 'pained incredulity', 'destructive logic', and 'moral fervour'.[42]

While much invective, then, is gleefully mendacious as it opts for the sleazy, the sensational, and the scandalous in its pursuit of vituperative s/laughter, it nevertheless operates under the pretence that it tells the truth. Invective discourse postures as a particular form of free speech — one that tears away veneers of respectability to expose and ridicule the hidden reality underneath. To some extent it is therefore pointless to enquire into the referential value of invective assertions designed not to give an accurate depiction of an individual's life or character, but to turn him into a kind of person you would not want to have in your community. Credibility in invective has little to do with checking facts or vetting evidence: a semblance of plausibility is all that is needed for even the most outrageous (and uproarious) insults to go forward: it is above all a creative, not primarily a representational mode of discourse. At the same time, invective mud sticks better if there is *some* connection with established facts. The abuse that Cicero attracted, for instance, tended to play off his relatively humble social background and place of origin (a new man from Arpinum), his actions as consul (the illegal executions of Roman citizens without trial), his endeavours to aggrandize himself, be it through the purchase of a magnificent villa

---

40 See *pro Caelio* 6, cited below 165.
41 His dialogue *On the Ideal Orator* contains a disquisition on humour in oratory (*de Orat.* 2.216–90). On Roman laughter see further Beard (2014).
42 Stockton (1971: 313), cited by Hall (2002: 293, n. 43).

on the Palatine, or through the insistent self-praise in his poetry.[43] So 'rather than saying that the truth of invective allegations is irrelevant, we may more accurately say that it is of secondary importance'.[44]

Even so, by flouting standards of discursive decency, feeding on preconceptions, and pandering to prejudices, invective generates its own reality in and through rhetoric. And it is up to the audience, i.e. *you*, whether you want to buy into it or rather insist on a quick 'fact check', so as not to succumb to 'fake news' and incendiary spin…

Invective's impact

Given the highly conventional and plainly imaginary elements of political invective in republican Rome, one may wonder to what extent verbal attacks, however vile and vitriolic, permanently dented anybody's reputation. Perhaps the consequences of unleashing aspersion upon an aristocratic peer happened to be relatively minor: a jeer and chuckle here, some rise in blood pressure and temporary irritation there, but overall a routine part of the political game, a ritual flyting exercise that consisted in the anodyne traffic of predictable insults that had the status of tired clichés and yawn-inducing commonplaces. The 'no hard feelings' attitude may well have prevailed in some cases. But to imply, as some scholars have done, that invective never did any significant damage arguably underestimates its ability to leave a mark on inner-aristocratic interactions. Its conventional nature does not exclude impact (not least since many blows in these verbal punch-ups were designed to land below the belt). As John Henderson (2006: 142–43) puts it:

> Invective is all about getting retaliation in first — pinch, punch, and no returns! Reliant on expected moves, and on their anticipation, this lobbing of rotten tomatoes is expressive behaviour, semi-un-trammelled by the constraints of 'proper conduct', and risking real enough social-political 'face' in the clubhouse of Roman prestige: the casement of epideictic braggadocio cushioned plenty, but nevertheless however playfully traded clichés could at (all) times land wounds, brand butts, kick ass.

---

43 For Cicero as target of invective himself see Arena (2007a) 153 and van der Blom (2014).
44 Craig (2004: 196).

How could a speaker know that he was not playing with fire — about to start a feud, go beyond the pale, or, indeed, sign his death sentence?[45] Language matters.

Invective's (dys-)function

By purporting to diagnose deviance, invective discourse illuminates the norms, values, and expectations of a civic community — as well as associated fears and anxieties. It stigmatizes difference and ostracizes those whom it perceives to fall short of community standards. As such, one could argue that invective had an important role to play in policing the boundaries of a civic community — as much recent scholarship has done, ably summarized by Arena:[46]

> Invective also had the potential to reshape and remodel the ethical and political code of society by expelling its deviant elements (or at least by trying to do so; see Ruffell 2003). As Corbeill (1996) argues, through his use of invective the orator acts as a definer of his society's moral code. Indeed, given Roman society's lack of canonical moral texts, invective had an important social function to play through its highlighting of virtue and vice. Although it was designed to humiliate the opponent in front of the community, invective also helped, through its enumeration of negative qualities, to shape examples of virtues (cf. e.g. *Rhet. Her.* 3.11).

True, a speaker will always portray his decision to abuse as being motivated by concerns for the community, civic welfare, and a commitment to the truth: anything else would be counterproductive. The target has to be shamed, ostracized, or indeed killed for the common good. But it is important to bear in mind that invective invents just as much as it represents: it is part of a struggle over the definition of reality. We should therefore not necessarily presuppose that invective is always functional, that such muscular managers of meaning as Cicero who define who is in and who is out do a service to their community in identifying 'deviant elements' within that ought to be expelled. In light of our earlier discussion, we should perhaps also entertain the possibility that invective brings deviance into being — and in doing so can be dysfunctional, insofar as it *aggravates* tensions and divisions within a

---

45   Compare and contrast Nisbet (1961) and Henderson (2006).
46   Arena (2007a: 154).

civic community. After all, character assassination is a mode of (verbal) warfare. As Icks and Shiraev (2014b: 1) put it in their introduction to a volume on this phenomenon:

> Throughout history, people have used the torch, the pitchfork, the bullet, the cannon, and (recently) the missile to damage, destroy, and kill. To protect themselves from attacks, people have built shields, armor, trenches, and fortresses, established military doctrines, and launched counterattacks. This book discusses attacks and defenses. Yet we have turned our attention to the destructive power of a different kind: words and images. Across countries and time, people have used images and words to harm, devastate, and completely destroy other people's reputation, status, and character.

Viewed in this light, invective becomes the rhetorical equivalent of civil warfare. Cicero's oratory arguably helped pave the way for an (even) 'nastier, more divided' Rome.

2.3 Cicero's Antony: Or How to Other a Peer

The 'identity' of a person is a composite and multifaceted phenomenon — despite the etymology of the term (*identitas* = 'the quality of being always the same'). Some aspects of who we are (or perceive ourselves to be) are generic (gender, ethnicity, nationality, legal status), others unique (family background, biography, or personal traits). Despite undeniable elements of continuity, our identity is under continual negotiation — both for ourselves and for others: indeed, identities are just as much a matter of self-perception as how we are perceived by others: and the two perspectives need not necessarily (indeed rarely do) fully coincide. Identities can be negotiated and challenged in discourse — and that is where invective rhetoric, and its potentially transformative power, comes in: it tries to strip the individual under attack of the positive aspects of their identity — of who they are in their own eyes and those of others.

The identity sapping of invective discourse can take various forms. In the *Philippics*, Cicero opts for a combination of remorseless ridicule and drastic demonization. Antony is a fool — but a dangerous one: to be laughed at, savagely, but then to be terminated. As Hall (2002: 288) observes, perhaps downplaying the demonizing that is also part of *Philippic* 2:

Antony is portrayed through this rhetoric of crisis as a violent, dangerous man who must be vigorously resisted. On other occasions, however, Cicero sets out to undermine Antony's moral and political authority through mockery. The most famous examples appear in the invective of *Philippic* 2, where the principal aim is to characterize Antony not as dangerous but as ridiculous; as a man of unparalleled *levitas*, quite unworthy of respect or admiration.

Antony is at the same time monstrous and malevolent, preposterous and pathetic. And at the heart of Cicero's verbal assault on Antony is a systematic 'othering' of his adversary, a transformation of a member of Rome's ruling elite, an aristocratic peer, into the veritable opposite:

Identity Facet	Historical Facts	Invective Fiction
Family pedigree	*nobilitas*	degenerate offshoot of a distinguished family
Degree of intelligence	high IQ, gifted political and military operator	doltish dim-wit (*stultus*)
Rhetorical ability	distinguished *orator*	a stammering failure (*balbulus*)
Habitual disposition	(by and large) sober (*sobrius*)	alcoholic (*vinolentus*) with emetic tendencies (*vomitator*)
Mental qualities and moral outlook	*compos mentis* | *vir bonus* | in (rational) control of his self	*furiosus*; creature of base instincts and appetites: gluttony, gambling, drinking, debauchery; *vir turpis*
Gender	Male (*vir*)	Effeminized / female (*cinaedus*; *meretrix*, *matrona*)
Ethnic background	*Romanus*	*barbarus*
Religious position / status	*augur*	perpetrator of impieties (*sacrilegus*)
Legal status	Roman citizen (*civis Romanus*)	external enemy (*hostis*)
Socio-political roles	*patronus* and *consul*	*tyrannus* / *rex*
Network of acquaintances	other members of Rome's ruling elite; clients	*latrones* ('brigands) and *lenones* ('pimps'), mime actors and mime actresses > scum
Species	*homo*	subhuman monster (*belua*)

Cicero questions Antony's morals, masculinity, and maleness (*vir, virtus*) by imagining a lurid past as toy-boy (*puer*) and male prostitute (*cinaedus, meretrix*). In sharp contrast to his role as *augur* (a priestly office), he charges him with the perpetration of impieties. Rejecting his identity as a Roman (*Romanus*), he highlights his affiliation with barbarians (*barbarus*). Instead of a sober senator exercising the self-control expected of a member of Rome's ruling elite, Antony comes across as a permanently intoxicated alcoholic (*vinolentus*), with strong emetic tendencies also in public (*vomitator*). Given the kind of person he is, the company he keeps is unsurprisingly equally depraved. He consorts with scum, 'attends birthday parties of professional clowns' (Hall 2002: 289 on *Phil.* 2.15), and has a love affair with the mime-actress Cytheris. Far from being a well-trained public speaker (*orator*), he is a linguistically challenged failure who stammers along (*balbulus*) and is stupid to boot (*stultus*). Yet, despite all of these personal failings, he is technically speaking consul, a high magistrate of the Roman people: in other words, he is an empowered pervert, whom Cicero identifies and outs not just as spitting counter-image of a member of Rome's ruling elite, but its mortal enemy. His verbal annihilation of Antony is not an end in itself: Cicero turns the skewering of the would-be tyrant who beleaguers the city with his soldiers into a rousing cry for (senatorial) freedom.

Much of Cicero's invective operates at the level of personal insults: Antony, he argues, is plain stupid and devoid of (oratorical) talent, but the focal point of his attack is an overall lack of self-control, which manifests itself in all areas where appetites are involved, in particular food, drink, and sex. Antony is a creature of base instinct, leading a life devoted to gluttony, gambling, drinking, and debauchery. A paradox emerges: a Roman man and magistrate ought to exercise legitimate power over others (the *potestas* of a *paterfamilias* and consul); but Antony is not even able to exercise power over himself. Cicero renders the paradox explicit at *Phil.* 6.4, where he mocks the notion that someone like Antony would listen to a senatorial embassy:

> Facile vero huic denuntiationi parebit, ut in patrum conscriptorum atque in vestra potestate sit, qui in sua numquam fuerit! quid enim ille umquam arbitrio suo fecit? semper eo tractus est, quo libido rapuit, quo levitas, quo furor, quo vinulentia; semper eum duo dissimilia genera

tenuerunt, lenonum et latronum; ita domesticis stupris, forensibus parricidiis delectatur, ut mulieri citius avarissimae paruerit quam senatui populoque Romano.

[He will no doubt readily obey this intimation, so as to submit to the conscript fathers and your power — a man who has never had himself in his power! For what has that man ever done on his own initiative? He has always been dragged where lust, where levity, where frenzy, where intoxication, has dragged him; two different classes of men have always held him in their grip, pimps and brigands. He so enjoys lecheries at home and murders in the forum that he would sooner obey a most avaricious woman than the senate and the Roman people.]

As this and other similar passages (not least from *Philippic* 2) are designed to illustrate, any ability Antony may have had to assert himself is severely compromised by base appetites, emotions, or character faults (sexual desire, fickleness, insanity, alcohol-addiction) and the ill-reputed company he keeps (pimps, brigands, a depraved wife). Since Antony is unable to exercise the requisite power (*potestas*) over his instincts and associates, he is unwilling to accept the legitimate power (*potestas*) of the senate and the people of Rome — instead, he remains beholden to the wrong people, a weak-kneed slave of his desires. Moreover, the depravity of Antony manifests itself in equal measure in the domestic sphere (in the form of acts of sexual transgressions: *stupra*) and the civic realm (murders in the forum: *parricidia*).

In Cicero's view, to have someone like Antony as consul (and, soon, pro-consul) poses an existential threat to the senatorial tradition of republican government. According to him, Antony has forfeited his right to be a member of Rome's ruling elite, indeed to be a part of Roman society or even the human species. The attack on the mainstays of Antony's identity — his status as *vir, nobilis, orator, augur, consul, civis Romanus* — culminates in Cicero's denial of his humanity. As Santoro L'Hoir (1992: 26) observes:

> Cicero fires his ultimate blast of vitriol in his glorious last stand against Antony. Like his predecessors Verres and Clodius, Antony is a *homo amentissimus* (*Phil.* 2.42; 5.37; cf. 3.2), and a *homo audacissimus* (2.78; 5.13; 6.2). He is, furthermore: *h. acutus* (2.28); *h. adflictus et perditus* (3.25); *h. detestabilis* (2.110); *h. impotentissimus* (5.42); *h. ingratissimus* (13.41); *h. nequam* and *nequissimus* (2.56; 61; 70; 78); *h. numquam sobrius* (2.81); *h. perditissimus* (5.13); *h. profligatus* (3.1); *h. sceleratus* (4.12); *h. simplex*

(2.111); *h. stupidus* (3.22); *h. turpissimus* (2.105); *h. vehemens et violentus* (5.19), among others. At one point, Antony ranks even lower than a *homo*: *Non est vobis res, Quirites, cum scelerato homine ac nefario, sed cum immani taetraque belua!* (*Phil.* 4.12: 'You have not now to deal, Romans, with a man merely guilty and villainous, but with a monstrous and savage beast').

Like his other adversaries (Verres, Catiline, Clodius, Piso and Gabinius, occasionally also Caesar) Cicero thus dehumanizes Antony. He casts him as a monstrous, amoral pervert, hell-bent on subverting Rome's social institutions and its political culture. He turns Antony into a repellent beast to instigate and rationalize drastic political action against him, turning him into an outlaw, foreigner, enemy, subhuman, who has lost the protection afforded by law, by his status as a Roman citizen, and by being human.

3. Why Read Cicero's *Second Philippic* Today?

'Classical' texts, or at least those we consider classical that have come to us from Greco-Roman antiquity, are texts that have managed to outlive the immediate historical context or even wider culture for which they were originally intended, attracting ever-new audiences down the ages. At times, such texts are simply read because they have been accorded the status of 'classical' at some point in the past. This, however, is a rather weak justification for continuing to read them — it might imply being in thoughtless thrall of choices that earlier generations have made for us. It is, therefore, always a good idea to ponder what makes the Greek or Latin text you have been asked to read (or happen to be reading: no need to stick to the syllabus) particularly relevant in the here-and-now. The following offers some suggestions of why at present *Philippic* 2 might be particularly good to think with.

3.1 Extremist Politics and the Rhetoric of Crisis

Philippic 2 bears witness to a desperately divided political community (and in particular its ruling elite), in which different interest groups struggled over the definition of facts and figures in increasingly polarized ways. At issue was, not least, the interpretation of Caesar and his assassination: was he a tyrant justly slain by a group of determined freedom fighters or a benefactor murdered by a bunch of treacherous ingrates? Or was there perhaps a middle way — the possibility of amnesty and reconciliation, rather than retaliation and further bloodshed? In this embittered battleground over the meaning of recent events, Cicero uses *Philippic* 2 to position himself as an extremist voice. In the first half of the speech he flatly denies the possibility of a middle ground when it comes to assessing the assassins (§§ 30–31). And in the second half (and the rest of the corpus) he opts for a 'rhetoric of crisis' that precludes compromise and furthers confrontation. As Wooten (1983: 58) explains:

> One of the most striking characteristics, therefore, of the rhetoric of crisis is the clarity and simplicity with which the orator views the situation that he faces. To him the contest is black and white, the struggle of good against evil; and what is at stake, he argues, is the very existence of the civilization that he is defending. He tries to convince the members of his audience that the history of their state has reached a fundamental crisis in which its very existence as they know it and everything that it represents are in danger. He then presents the situation as a clear choice between mutually exclusive and fundamentally opposed systems by means of what may be called the disjunctive mode.

Increasingly polarized political discourse, the attendant loss of a middle ground that cultivates commonly shared views and values as basis for compromise, and the rhetoric of crisis and existential emergency are phenomena that many political pundits also see on the rise in contemporary society and politics. One particularly intriguing question here again involves the power of rhetoric: to what extent does the language of crisis help produce — rather than react to — the problem it tries to fight?

3.2 Hate Speech

In a recent monograph on Cicero, Tahin draws a comparison between the public use of language in Greco-Roman antiquity and today:[47]

> It is crucial to state that a Greek or Roman orator was not bound by any modern standard of rationality, logic or rhetorical measure unless the circumstances of a particular case demanded it in order to win the case. Forms of argument (such as personal abuse, distortion or omission of facts, malicious slander, irrelevant details or sequences of narrative, logical *non sequitur*, counter accusations) which today are considered fallacious or inadmissible elements of reasoning in any rational discourse

---

47   Tahin (2016: 1).

(e.g. court hearings) were widely accepted tools of persuasion so long as they served the purposes of the orator.

The thought that we moderns live in a more enlightened and civilized age than the Greeks and the Romans is reassuring. And it is true that we possess libel laws. But recent developments may well prompt us to wonder about 'modern standards of rationality, logic or rhetorical measure', which may indeed be ruled out of court, but seem to thrive in the Bloggosphere and on Twitter — as well as more generally. The protocols of public discourse seem to have become more fluid in recent years, the boundary between the sayable and the unspeakable are shifting. We seem to have a heightened awareness of the fact that words can hurt, that there is a need for sensitive use of language and safe spaces, yet all the while crudity and extremism proliferate in public discourse, including the criminalization of adversaries: judges who come up with an inopportune ruling are labelled 'enemies of the people', politicians who beg to differ from the party line run the risk of being turned into 'traitors'.

Throw in the phenomenon of factoids and invented facts broadcast as news and parallels worth pondering between late-republican Rome and contemporary politics are not all that hard to come by, especially when it comes to abusive language (or hate speech). Invective blurs the distinction between truth and lies, reality and fiction. Much of what Cicero says in *Philippic* 2 is 'fake news' or malicious spin, served up in the service of a higher truth, a code of civic ethics. Does the end justify the means?

3.3 The Power of Eloquence and Post-Truth Politics

Cicero conceived of the *Philippics* as monumental oratory — his rhetorical testament as it were: 'Invoking the dangers he submits to as well as his contempt for death, a *Leitmotiv* in the *Philippics*, Cicero not only amplifies and dramatises the contemporary political situation, but he refashions it into the time-transcending narrative of a man desperately but resolutely fighting for his convictions. Thus Cicero ensures that his speeches would be read long after the conflict had been resolved and, more importantly, even in case Antony prevailed'.[48] While he failed in his efforts to restore republican freedom to the Roman commonwealth, he certainly succeeded in bequeathing his vision (of himself, of Antony, of the world) to posterity. What remains are his writings: they articulate an (arguably tragic) vision of resistance against (perceived) tyranny and constitute a type of political activism and civic commitment in a time of chaos, when constitutional safeguards and institutions, legal procedures and republican norms arguably no longer guaranteed the survival of the senatorial commonwealth. (What do you think: does Cicero take a courageous stance against tyranny here or is he a deluded and self-righteous warmonger who tries to rip Antony's heart out while shooting himself in the foot?)

As a (now classical) speech-act of universalizing import, *Philippic* 2 invites questions of a trans-historical nature: about the judgment of the author, the secrets of persuasive oratory, the power of spin, the divisive impact of hate-speech and its relation to physical violence, to name a few. Cicero was a master of (re-)defining reality — indeed inventing it — whenever the facts did not suit his purpose. In the *Philippics*, he generated a largely imaginary character portrait and corresponding *curriculum vitae* of Antony, which he embedded within a narrative on Roman politics to produce a moment of existential crisis, of bare survival, of life or death for each individual and the civic community at large — a favourite script of his, in which he invested throughout his career. The text to be studied is both a sensational exercise of dragging someone's reputation through the sewer and a fantastic illustration of how Cicero managed to make an impact on, indeed invent, reality through his rhetorical skills and the powers of his imagination. Cicero's approach in *Philippic* 2 thus arguably has certain affinities with contemporary variants of 'post-truth' politics, in which decency, respect for one's opponents, and cultivation of civilized language give way to polarizing abuse. In Cicero's case, the abuse has become classical — should it continue to inspire?

---

48   Scheidegger-Lämmle (2017: 34).

TEXT

     https://doi.org/10.11647/OBP.0156.03

§ 44: A Glance at Teenage Antony: Insolvent, Transgendered, Pimped, and Groomed

Visne igitur te inspiciamus a puero? sic opinor; a principio ordiamur. tenesne memoria praetextatum te decoxisse? 'patris', inquies, 'ista culpa est'. concedo. etenim est pietatis plena defensio. illud tamen audaciae tuae quod sedisti in quattuordecim ordinibus, cum esset lege Roscia decoctoribus certus locus constitutus, quamvis quis fortunae vitio, non suo decoxisset. sumpsisti virilem, quam statim muliebrem togam reddidisti. primo vulgare scortum; certa flagitii merces nec ea parva; sed cito Curio intervenit, qui te a meretricio quaestu abduxit et, tamquam stolam dedisset, in matrimonio stabili et certo collocavit.

Study Questions:

- Parse *visne*.
- Identify and explain the mood of *inspiciamus*.
- Identify and explain the mood of *ordiamur*.
- On what noun does the genitive *patris* depend?
- Parse *inquies*.
- Identify and explain the case of *audaciae tuae*.
- What did the *lex Roscia* stipulate? When was it passed?
- What noun does the adjective *virilem* modify?
- Who was Curio?

Stylistic Appreciation:

- How would you describe the overall tone Cicero adopts in this paragraph? Can you point to specific details in the text that epitomize it?
- What is the rhetorical effect of the word order in the sentence *etenim est pietatis plena defensio*?
- Discuss Cicero's choice of adverbs and adjectives in the second half of the passage, with an eye to the contrast between the seemingly banal (*certus, statim, certa, parva, cito, certo*) and the more elaborate (*virilem, muliebrem, vulgare, meretricio, stabili*).

Discussion Points:

- What's Cicero cooking up here (cf. *decoxisse, decoctoribus, decoxisset*) — or how does he construe a plot reminiscent of Peter Greenaway's *The Cook, the Thief, His Wife, & Her Lover* — with Antony performing in all four roles?
- Clothes make the wo/man: discuss the fashion-show staged in this paragraph (cf. *praetextatum, virilem* (sc. *togam*), *muliebrem togam, stolam*).
- Why is cross-dressing funny? Discuss with reference to contemporary takes, such as *Some Like it Hot*, *Tootsie*, or *The World According to Garp*.
- Can you think of more recent instances in which public figures are shamed for (alleged) misdemeanors in their youth? What's your take on this practice?

inspicio, -icere, -exi, -ectum	to examine, investigate, consider
opinor, -ari, -atus	to hold as an opinion, think, believe
ordior, -diri, -sus	to embark on, start, begin
praetextatus, -a, -um	being of an age to wear the *toga praetexta*
decoquo, -quere, -xi, -ctum	to boil down, waste away, squander; to be unable to pay debts; (intr.) to become insolvent
concedo, -dere, -ssi, -ssum	to go away, withdraw; to concede, grant
etenim (conj.)	and indeed; for
audacia, -ae, f.	daring, boldness, impudence, recklessness
sedeo, -ere, sedi, sessum	to sit, be seated
quattuordecim	fourteen
ordo, -inis, m.	row (of seats in a theatre), rank, standing order
decoctor, -oris, m. [decoquo + tor]	an insolvent person, defaulting debtor
quamvis	to any degree you like no matter how, however much
vitium, -i, n.	defect, fault, disadvantage
sumo, -mere, -mpsi, -mptum	to take up, put on (clothes etc.), seize
toga virilis	the toga worn by free male Roman upon reaching maturity
statim (adv.)	immediately, at once
toga muliebris	a toga worn by prostitutes and other stigmatized females prohibited from wearing the *stola*
reddo, -ere, -idi, -itum	to give back, restore, repay, render, deliver (w. predicate) to render, cause to turn out
vulgaris, -is, -e	common, ordinary, everyday
scortum, -i, n.	whore, prostitute, harlot
certus, -a, -um	fixed, settled, definite; certain, indisputable
flagitium, -(i)i, n.	shameful / disgraceful act; disgrace, infamy
merces, -edis, f.	payment for services rendered, wage, reward
cito (adv.)	quickly
meretricius, -a, -um	of, belonging to, or typical of a prostitute
quaestus, -us, m.	income, profit, occupation
abduco, -cere, -xi, -ctum	to lead away, carry off, remove; to attract away, entice away; divert
tamquam (conj.)	just as, (w. subj.) as though
stola, -ae, f.	garment for upper-class married women
stabilis, -is, -e	steady, lasting, permanent
colloco, -are, -avi, -atum	to put or set up, settle, establish, bestow

§ 45: Desire and Domesticity: Antony's Escapades as Curio's Toy-Boy

Nemo umquam puer emptus libidinis causa tam fuit in domini potestate quam tu in Curionis. quotiens te pater eius domu sua eiecit, quotiens custodes posuit ne limen intrares! cum tu tamen nocte socia, hortante libidine, cogente mercede, per tegulas demitterere. quae flagitia domus illa diutius ferre non potuit. scisne me de rebus mihi notissimis dicere? recordare tempus illud cum pater Curio maerens iacebat in lecto; filius se ad pedes meos prosternens, lacrimans, te mihi commendabat; orabat ut se contra suum patrem, si sestertium sexagiens peteret, defenderem; tantum enim se pro te intercessisse dicebat. ipse autem amore ardens confirmabat, quod desiderium tui discidi ferre non posset, se in exilium iturum.

Study Questions:
- What noun does the genitive *Curionis* depend on?
- What kind of ablative is *domu sua*?
- Parse *demitterere*.
- Explain the syntax of *quae* (*flagitia…*).
- Parse *scisne*. What kind of construction does it introduce?
- Parse *recordare*.
- Reconstruct the scenario presupposed in the *ut*-clause introduced by *orabat*.
- Explain the grammar and syntax of the phrase *sestertium sexagiens*.
- Parse *defenderem*.
- What kind of genitive is *tui discidi*?
- Parse *iturum*.

Stylistic Appreciation:
- Discuss the word order … *te pater eius*….
- Analyze how Cicero correlates and contrasts Curio father and Curio son in the second half of the paragraph (*recordare … se in exilium iturum*).
- Cicero here evokes a scenario (two young lovers prevented by an older guardian from carrying on their affair) familiar from New Comedy: can you identify stylistic and thematic touches reminiscent of the genre?

Discussion Points:
- How does Cicero construe the relationships between himself, Antony, Curio Junior, and Curio Senior?
- How would you describe the impact of Antony on the Curio household? (Start by picking out those terms that belong to the semantic field of 'household'.)
- Explore the nexus between 'family household' (overseen by a *paterfamilias*) and the 'commonwealth' (*res publica*) in Rome's cultural imaginary. What makes Cicero's portrayal of Antony's impact on the domestic situation in the Curio family so damning from a civic point of view?

nemo, inis, m. / f.	nobody, no one; as adj.: no
puer, -eri, m.	boy (here) slave boy
emo, emere, emi, emptum	to buy, purchase
libido, -inis, f.	desire, craving, sexual appetite, lust
causâ (abl., governing a gen.)	for the purpose of, for the sake of
quotiens (interr. or exclam.)	How many times? How many times!
domus, -us, f.	house
eicio, eicere, eieci, eiectum	to throw out, remove, expel
custos, -odis, m. and f.	guardian
limen, -inis, n.	threshold, doorstep
socia, -ae f.	a (female) partner, associate
cogo, -ere, coegi, coactum	to drive together, collect, summon, gather to compel, force, constrain
merces, -edis, f.	payment for services rendered, wage, reward
tegula, -ae, f.	a roof-tile
demitto, -ittere, -isi, -issum	to let fall, drop, make descend, lower
flagitium, -(i)i, n.	shameful / disgraceful act; disgrace, infamy
diu (comparative: *diutius*) (adv.)	for a long time, long
recordor, -ari, -atus	to call to mind, recollect
maereo, -ere	to be sad, mourn, grieve
lectus, -i, m.	bed, couch
prosterno, -ernere, -ravi, -ratum	to lay low, strike down, knock down to lay prostrate on the ground
commendo, -are, -avi, -atum	to commit / entrust someone (acc.) to (dat.)
sestertius, -i, m.	sesterce (a Roman coin)
(*decies centena milia*) *sestertium*	a hundred thousand sesterces
sexagiens (adv.)	sixty times
peto, -ere, -ivi / ii, -itum	to go for, seek out, seek to obtain, ask to sue for, lay claim to, demand
tantum, -i, (pron.)	so much
intercedo, -dere, -ssi, -ssum	to intervene; to exist between; oppose to intervene as guarantor, stand surety
confirmo, -are, -avi, -atum	to strengthen, make robust; to assert, declare
desiderium, -(i)i, n.	desire, longing; want, need; object of desire
discidium, -(i)i, n.	splitting, separation; divorce

§ 46: Family Therapy: Cicero as Counselor

Quo tempore ego quanta mala florentissimae familiae sedavi vel potius sustuli! patri persuasi ut aes alienum fili dissolveret; redimeret adulescentem, summa spe et animi et ingeni praeditum, rei familiaris facultatibus eumque non modo tua familiaritate sed etiam congressione patrio iure et potestate prohiberet. haec tu cum per me acta meminisses, nisi illis quos videmus gladiis confideres, maledictis me provocare ausus esses?

Study Questions:

- What kind of construction is *quo tempore*?
- What kind of ablatives are *familiaritate* and *congressione*?
- What norms and institutions does Cicero evoke with the formulation *patrio iure et potestate*?
- What are the swords that Cicero claims he and his audience see (cf. *illis quos videmus gladiis*)?
- What kind of conditional sequence does *nisi* introduce?
- What does Cicero refer to with *maledictis*?
- Parse *ausus esses*.

Stylistic Appreciation:

- Identify the stylistic features by which Cicero announces that he came to the rescue (*quo tempore … sustuli!*).
- The middle sentence of the paragraph begins and ends with *p*-alliteration: *patri persuasi … patrio iure et potestate prohiberet*. What (if anything) does Cicero thereby wish to emphasize?
- Analyze the rhetorical design of the *ut*-clause (*ut aes alienum … prohiberet*).

Discussion Points:

- What advice would you have given to Curio *pater* in this situation?
- To what extent (if at all) should parents be responsible for the extravagances of their offspring?

malum, -i, n.	trouble, distress, pain, hardship; harm, evil
florens, -ntis	flowering; prosperous, flourishing; distinguished
sedo, -are, -avi, -atum	to cause to subside; allay, relieve, mitigate
tollo, -ere, sustuli, sublatum	to pick up, raise, hoist; get rid of, remove
persuadeo, -dere, -si, -sum	(usually w. dat. of person) to persuade, prevail upon
aes alienum	debt
(cf. *aes, aeris,* n.	copper, bronze, brass)
dissolvo, -vere, -vi, -utum	to undo, dismantle, set free, clear up, pay
redimo, -imere, -emi, -emptum	to buy back, pay the cost of; rescue, save
praeditus, -a, -um (w. abl.)	endowed with, equipped / furnished with
res, rei, f.	property, wealth; thing, matter, material
res familiaris	private property, estate, patrimony
facultas, -atis, f.	ability, power, capacity, skill; (pl., as here) resources, means
familiaritas, -atis, f.	close friendship, intimacy
congressio, -onis, f.	meeting, encounter; sexual intercourse
memini, -inisse	to remember, pay heed to
patrius, -a, -um	paternal; ancestral
confido, -dere, -sus sum (w. dat.)	to put one's trust in, have confidence in
maledictum, -i, n.	insult, reproach, taunt
provoco, -are, -avi, -atum	to call out, stir up, challenge
audeo, -dere, -sus	to dare, venture, be bold

§ 47: Hitting 'Fast-Forward', or: How to Pull Off a *Praeteritio*

Sed iam stupra et flagitia omittamus: sunt quaedam quae honeste non possum dicere; tu autem eo liberior quod ea in te admisisti quae a verecundo inimico audire non posses. sed reliquum vitae cursum videte, quem quidem celeriter perstringam. ad haec enim quae in civili bello, in maximis rei publicae miseriis fecit, et ad ea quae cotidie facit, festinat animus. quae peto ut, quamquam multo notiora vobis quam mihi sunt, tamen, ut facitis, attente audiatis. debet enim talibus in rebus excitare animos non cognitio solum rerum sed etiam recordatio; etsi incidamus, opinor, media ne nimis sero ad extrema veniamus.

Study Questions:
- Parse *omittamus*.
- Parse *eo*.
- Parse *perstringam*.
- Explain the syntax of *quae* (*quae peto ut…*).
- What kind of ablative is *multo*?
- *ut facitis*: what is the meaning of *ut* here?
- Parse *incidamus*.

Stylistic Appreciation:
- Analyze the word order in the sentence *ad haec enim … festinat animus*.
- Analyze the design of the sentence *debet enim … recordatio*.

Discussion Points:
- What is a *praeteritio*? Why (and when) is it an effective rhetorical technique? Can you design your own on a topic of the day?
- What exactly is it that Cicero leaves unspoken? And is it decent to even ask this question?
- Why does Cicero claim that Antony's more recent misdeeds are better known to his audience than to himself?

iam (adv.)	now; by now, by then, already
stuprum, -i, n.	dishonour, shame; illicit sexual intercourse
flagitium, -(i)i, n.	shameful / disgraceful act; disgrace, infamy
omitto, -ittere, -isi, -issum	to let go of; withdraw from; abandon to leave out of account, pass over, omit
quidam, quaedam, quiddam	a certain person; a certain (undefined) thing
honeste (adv.)	honourably, with propriety, decently
liber, libera, liberum	free; licentious; showing lack of restraint
verecundus, -a, -um	modest, seemly, becoming
inimicus, -i, m.	personal adversary
audio, -ire, -ivi / ii, -itum	to hear; to listen to to hear said with respect to oneself
reliquus, -a, -um	left, remaining
perstringo, -ngere, -nxi, -ctum	to constrict, brush, graze, skirt, hug
miseria, -ae, f. (esp. pl.)	affliction, distress; trouble, woe
festino, -are, -avi, -atum	to act hurriedly, make haste, move quickly
attente (adv.)	carefully, with concentration
excito, -are, -avi, -atum	to cause to move, rouse, stir, provoke
cognitio, -onis, f.	the act of getting to know; investigation
recordatio, -onis, f.	recollection
etsi (conj.)	even if, although (introducing main clause) and yet
incîdo, -dere, -di, -sum [*in + caedo*]	to cut open, sever, break up, cut short
not to be confused with: *incido, -ere, -i, incasum* [*in + cado*]	to fall (into), rush upon, arise, occur
nimis (adv.)	to an excessive degree, too much, unduly
sero (adv.)	late, tardily; too late
extremum, -a, um	situated at the end, last remaining

§ 48: Antony Adrift

Intimus erat in tribunatu Clodio qui sua erga me beneficia commemorat;
eius omnium incendiorum fax, cuius etiam domi iam tum quiddam molitus
est. quid dicam ipse optime intellegit. inde iter Alexandriam contra senatus
auctoritatem, contra rem publicam et religiones; sed habebat ducem Gabinium,
quicum quidvis rectissime facere posset. qui tum inde reditus aut qualis? prius
in ultimam Galliam ex Aegypto quam domum. quae autem domus? suam enim
quisque domum tum obtinebat nec erat usquam tua. domum dico? quid erat
in terris ubi in tuo pedem poneres praeter unum Misenum, quod cum sociis
tamquam Sisaponem tenebas?

Study Questions:

- What case is *Clodio*? How does it fit into the syntax of the sentence?
- What is the antecedent of *qui*?
- What are Antony's *beneficia* towards Cicero?
- What is the verb of the clause *eius omnium incendiorum fax*?
- What is the antecedent of *cuius*?
- Parse *domi*.
- Identify and explain the mood of *dicam*.
- Parse *senatus*.
- What is the verb of the sentence *inde iter … et religiones*?
- What kind of accusative is *Alexandriam*?
- Parse *qui* (*tum inde reditus*).
- What is the verb of the question *qui tum inde reditus aut qualis?*
- What are the verbs in the sentence *prius in ultimam Galliam ex Aegypto quam domum*?
- Explain the mood of *poneres*.
- Where is Sisapo?

Stylistic Appreciation:

- Quite a few sentences in this paragraph lack a verb: what is the rhetorical effect of these elisions?
- Analyze the rhetorical design of *contra senatus auctoritatem, contra rem publicam et religiones*.
- *quid dicam? – qui … reditus aut qualis? – quae autem domus? – quid erat in terris?*: the paragraph teems with rhetorical questions: why does Cicero opt for this device here?
- Explore the rhetorical effect of such indefinite pronouns as *quiddam*, *quidvis*, and *quisque*.

intimus, -a, -um (w. dat.)	(of friends) most intimate, closest
tribunatus, -us, m.	the office of tribune; tribuneship
erga (prep. + acc.)	towards, for, to
beneficium, -(i)i, n.	service, kindness, favour
commemoro, -are, -avi, -atum	to recall, mention, relate; place on record
incendium, -(i)i, n.	destructive fire, conflagration
fax, facis, f.	torch, firebrand (fig.) a person that starts mischief
quidam, quaedam, quiddam	a certain person; a certain (undefined) thing
molior, -iri, -itus	to labour, make efforts, strive, set in motion
intellego, -gere, -xi, -ctum	to understand, realize, discern
inde (adv.)	from there, thence; next
religio, -onis, f.	supernatural feeling of constraint; religious scruple, fear, or awe
habeo, -ere, -ui, -itum (w. double acc.)	to have someone acting in a certain capacity
quicum	= *cum quo*
quivis, quaevis, quidvis (pron.)	anyone, anything
reditus, -us, m.	the act of coming back, return
prius (adv.)	at an earlier time, previously, before
obtineo, -inere, -inui, -entum	to maintain, keep up; to govern, hold to secure, gain
usquam (adv.)	in any place, anywhere
pedem ponere (*in* + abl.)	to set foot (in)

Discussion Points:

- *cuius domi – quam domum – quae autem domus? – suam domum – nec erat … tua* [sc. *domus*] *– domum dico*: what is Cicero trying to achieve with his relentless focus on the home / household? How does this emphasis relate to the 'imperial geography' that his references to Alexandria, Gaul, and Spain evoke?

§ 49: Credit for Murder

venis e Gallia ad quaesturam petendam. aude dicere te prius ad parentem tuam
venisse quam ad me. acceperam iam ante Caesaris litteras ut mihi satis fieri
paterer a te: itaque ne loqui quidem sum te passus de gratia. postea sum cultus a
te, tu a me observatus in petitione quaesturae; quo quidem tempore P. Clodium
approbante populo Romano in foro es conatus occidere, cumque eam rem tua
sponte conarere, non impulsu meo, tamen ita praedicabas, te non existimare,
nisi illum interfecisses, umquam mihi pro tuis in me iniuriis satis esse facturum.
in quo demiror cur Milonem impulsu meo rem illam egisse dicas, cum te
ultro mihi idem illud deferentem numquam sim adhortatus. quamquam, si in
eo perseverares, ad tuam gloriam rem illam referri malebam quam ad meam
gratiam.

Study Questions:

- What is the sense of *ad* in the gerundive phrase *ad quaesturam petendam*?
- Parse *aude*.
- Parse *paterer*.
- Explain the grammar and syntax of *quo* (*quidem tempore*).
- What construction is *approbante populo Romano*?
- What does the *-que* in *cumque* link?
- Parse *conarere*.
- Parse *interfecisses* and explain the tense and mood.
- What does *rem illam* refer to?
- Identify and explain the mood of *dicas*.
- What kind of clause does *quamquam* introduce?

Stylistic Appreciation:

- Analyze the rhetorical design of the *cum*-clause *cumque eam rem tua sponte conarere, non impulsu meo*.
- Analyze how Cicero brings personal pronouns and possessive adjectives into play in this paragraph (*te*; *parentem tuam*; *mihi* … *a te*; *ne loqui quidem sum te passus*; … *sum cultus a te*, *tu a me observatus* …; *tua sponte conarere, non impulsu meo*; … *te non existimare* …; *mihi pro tuis in me iniuriis*; *impulsu meo*; *te ultro mihi idem illud deferentem*; *ad tuam gloriam* … *ad meam gratiam*).

Discussion Points:

- The paragraph is stuffed full with technical terms to do with socio-political relations in republican Rome such as *satis facere, gratia, colo, observare*, as well as practices that smoothed the economy of friendship and patronage, such as letters of recommendation (cf. *acceperam iam ante Caesaris litteras*). How does Cicero get invective mileage out of this idiom?

quaestura, -ae, f.	quaestorship
peto, -ere, -ivi / ii, -itum	to make for, resort to, seek (to obtain); (here) to be a candidate for, seek (office)
prius … quam … / priusquam	before
accipio, -ipere, -epi, -eptum	to receive, acquire, get
litterae, -arum, f.	a letter
satis facere, -ere, feci, factum	to meet a person's needs or desires (w. dat.) to make amends, give attention to
ne … quidem	not even
gratia, -ae, f.	favour, goodwill, kindness, gratitude; influence
colo, -ere, -ui, cultum	to cultivate, farm, look after, adorn, worship to pay attention to, cultivate the friendship of
observo, -are, -avi, -atum	to observe, watch; pay attention to, respects
petitio, -onis, f.	an attack, request, claim; candidature
conor, -ari, -atus	to make an effort, attempt, endeavour
occido, -dere, -di, -sum	to kill, slaughter; ruin
(spons), spontis, f.	will, volition
sponte mea (tua, sua)	of my (your, one's) own will, voluntarily
impulsus, -us, m. [*impello*]	shock, thrust; incitement to action, prompting
praedico, -are, -avi, -atum	to make known, declare, announce
demiror, -ari, -atus	to be utterly astonished at, to wonder
ultro (adv.)	in addition, of one's own accord
defero, -rre, detuli, delatum	to convey, bring; to entrust, confer (here) to present for acceptance, offer
adhortor, -ari, -atus	to give encouragement to, urge on
quamquam	(introducing a main sentence) to be sure, however, at any rate
persevero, -are, -avi, -atum	to persist in; continue
refero, -rre, rettuli, relatum + ad	(here) to assign to

§ 50: With Caesar in Gaul: Profligacy and Profiteering

quaestor es factus: deinde continuo sine senatus consulto, sine sorte, sine lege
ad Caesarem cucurristi. id enim unum in terris egestatis, aeris alieni, nequitiae
perditis vitae rationibus perfugium esse ducebas. ibi te cum et illius largitionibus
et tuis rapinis explevisses, si hoc est explere, haurire quod statim effundas,
advolasti egens ad tribunatum, ut in eo magistratu, si posses, viri tui similis esses.

    accipite nunc, quaeso, non ea quae ipse in se atque in domesticum decus
impure et intemperanter, sed quae in nos fortunasque nostras, id est in universam
rem publicam, impie ac nefarie fecerit. ab huius enim scelere omnium malorum
principium natum reperietis.

Study Questions:

- What construction is *perditis vitae rationibus*?
- What kind of genitives are *egestatis, aeris alieni,* and *nequitiae*? On what noun
  do they depend?
- Explain the syntax of *perfugium*.
- Explain the syntax of *te* (*ibi te cum…*)
- Explain the syntax of the two infinitives *explere* and *haurire*. What case are
  they in?
- What construction does *ducebas* govern?
- Who does *viri tui* refer to?
- What kind of ablative is *scelere*?
- Parse *reperietis*.

Stylistic Appreciation:

- What is the effect of the absence of connectives in the opening sentences
  (*quaestor … ducebas*), in particular the two asyndetic tricola *sine senatus
  consulto, sine sorte, sine lege* and *egestatis, aeris alieni, nequitiae … profugium,*
  and the polysyndeton in the following *cum*-clause (*ibi te cum et illius
  largitionibus et tuis rapinis explevisses*) and the rest of the paragraph (*in se atque
  in domesticum decus; impure et intemperanter; in nos fortunasque nostras; impie
  ac nefarie*)?
- What does the hyperbaton *id enim unum … perfugium* enact?
- Analyze the rhetorical design of Cicero's transition from a focus on
  domesticum decus to one on *universa res publica*.

Discussion Points:

- What image of Caesar do you get from this paragraph? To what extent is it
  historically accurate?
- What is the *scelus* that Cicero refers to at the end of the paragraph? Why does
  he call it the source of all evils?
- How does Cicero entwine the personal and the political here?

quaestor, -oris, m.	quaestor (a Roman magistrate)
facio, -ere, feci, factum	to do, make, construct, produce
	(here) to appoint to an office
continuo (adv.)	forthwith, immediately
senatûs consultum	decree of the senate
sors, -rtis, f.	lot, appointment, allocation
	sphere of duty assigned by lot
egestas, -atis, f.	extreme poverty, need, destitution
aes alienum	debt
(cf. *aes, aeris,* n.	copper, bronze, brass)
nequitia, -ae, f.	moral worthlessness, profligacy, vice
perdo, -ere, -idi, -itum	to ruin, destroy, dissipate, waste
ratio, -onis, f.	(here) 'guiding principle'
perfugium, -(i)i, n.	refuge, shelter, sanctuary
duco, -cere, -xi, -ctum	(here) to consider, believe, think
largitio, -onis, f.	largess, gift; bribe, dole
rapina, -ae, f. [rapio + ina]	plunder
expleo, -ere, -evi, -etum	to fill up, satisfy, make good,
	carry to completion, achieve
haurio, -rire, -si, -stum / -ritum	to draw, scoop up; drink, imbibe
	to consume, absorb
effundo, -undere, -udi, -usum	to pour out, shed, discharge, expend, use up
advolo, -are, -avi, -atum	to fly towards, approach swiftly
egens, -ntis	poverty-stricken, needy, indigent
quaeso (-ere)	(in 1st pers. parenthesis) I ask / implore you
	please
decus, -oris, n.	high esteem, honour, glory
	honourable / seemly behaviour, dignity
impure (adv.) [impurus + e]	foully, vilely, infamously
intemperanter (adv.) [intemperans + ter]	without self-control or restraint
	excessively, violently
universus, -a, -um	the whole of, entire; universal
impie (adv.) [impius + e]	disrespectful (of the gods)
nefarie (adv.) [nefarius + e]	wickedly, foully, monstrously
principium, (i)i, n. [princeps + ium]	start, origin, founding
nascor, -i, natus	to be born, come into being, arise
reperio, -ire, repperi, -tum	to find by looking, discover

§ 78: Caesar's Approach to HR, or Why Antony Has What it Takes

Et domi quidem causam amoris habuisti, foris etiam turpiorem, ne L. Plancus praedes tuos venderet. productus autem in contionem a tribuno pl. cum respondisses te rei tuae causa venisse, populum etiam dicacem in te reddidisti. sed nimis multa de nugis: ad maiora veniamus.

C. Caesari ex Hispania redeunti obviam longissime processisti. celeriter isti redisti, ut cognosceret te, si minus fortem, at tamen strenuum. factus es ei rursus nescio quo modo familiaris. habebat hoc omnino Caesar: quem plane perditum aere alieno egentemque, si eundem nequam hominem audacemque cognorat, hunc in familiaritatem libentissime recipiebat.

Study Questions:

- Parse *domi* and *foris*.
- Explain the syntax of *te* (… *respondisses te rei tuae…*).
- What is the verb in the sentence *sed nimis multa de nugis*?
- Identify and explain the mood of *veniamus*.
- Parse *redeunti* and explain its syntax.
- Parse *isti*.
- Whom does *ei* refer to?
- What is the antecedent of *quem*?
- What is the verb of the relative clause introduced by *quem*?
- Parse *cognorat*.

Stylistic Appreciation:

- How does design enhance sense in the sentence *factus es ei rursus nescio quo modo familiaris*?
- Cicero must want to have himself say *-isti … isti … -isti* this way — so why?

Discussion Points:

- What kind of principles (moral, utilitarian, any) do you apply in choosing your friends? What do you think of Caesar's approach?
- Can we (ever) tell from what they write to each other if any Romans were what *we*'d like to think of as friends? (E.g. Cicero and … Atticus?)

causa, -ae, f.	judicial proceedings, trial; case, cause; an alleged reason or extenuating plea; excuse, pretext; a ground (of action), (good) reason
foris (adv.)	out of doors, outside; away from home
turpis, -is, -e (adj.)	offensive, loathsome; shameful, disgraceful
praes, -dis, m.	one who acts as surety or security
vendo, -ere, -idi, -itum	to sell; to dispose of; to promote the sale of
produco, -cere, -xi, -ctum	to bring forth, lead out; to bring before a public meeting; to present; to extend in time, draw out
contio, -onis, f.	a public meeting, assembly; public speech
dicax, -acis (adj.)	having a ready tongue, witty
reddo, -ere, -idi, -itum	to give back, restore, render; to pay; bring about, produce
nugae, -arum, f. pl.	trifles, frivolities
obviam (adv.)	in the way, towards, against, to meet
procedo, -dere, -ssi, -ssum	to go / move forward, advance, come forth
strenuus, -a, -um	active, vigorous, keen, energetic
rursus (adv.)	backwards; once again
nescio quo modo	in some (strange / unaccountable) way; somehow or other
familiaris, -is, -e	of or belonging to one's household; closely associated by friendship, intimate; well-known, familiar; (as noun) friend
omnino (adv.)	in every respect, absolutely, altogether
plane (adv.)	plainly, clearly, distinctly
perditus, -a, -um	debilitated, broken, ruined, bankrupt; morally depraved
aes alienum	debt
egens, -ntis	poverty-stricken, needy, indigent
nequam (indeclinable)	having no value, useless; morally worthless, depraved
familiaritas, -atis, f.	close friendship, intimacy
libenter (adv.)	with pleasure, willingly, gladly

§ 79: The Art of Nepotism

His igitur rebus praeclare commendatus iussus es renuntiari consul et quidem cum ipso. nihil queror de Dolabella qui tum est impulsus, inductus, elusus. qua in re quanta fuerit uterque vestrum perfidia in Dolabellam quis ignorat? ille induxit ut peteret, promissum et receptum intervertit ad seque transtulit; tu eius perfidiae voluntatem tuam ascripsisti. veniunt Kalendae Ianuariae; cogimur in senatum: invectus est copiosius multo in istum et paratius Dolabella quam nunc ego.

Study Questions:

- How does *qua* fit into the syntax of the sentence?
- What kind of clause does *quanta* introduce? What noun does *quanta* modify? What case is it in?
- What kind of genitive is *vestrum*?
- What kind of *ut*-clause is *ut peteret*?
- What is the accusative object of *peteret, intervertit,* and *transtulit*?
- How do *promissum et receptum* fit into the sentence?
- Who does *eius* [in the phrase *eius perfidiae*] refer to?
- Parse *copiosius* and *paratius.*
- What kind of ablative is *multo*?

Stylistic Appreciation:

- What might *praeclare commendatus* be dripping with?
- Why might Cicero rely on a rhetorical question (… *quis ignorat?*) when invoking the notoriety of Caesar's and Antony's perfidy towards Dolabella?
- Analyze the rhetorical design of *invectus est … quam nunc ego.*

Discussion Points:

- Discuss the implications of the passives in the passage (*iussus es; renuntiari; est impulsus, inductus, elusus; cogimur*).
- What kind of picture does Cicero draw of Caesar's coterie here? How does he position himself (and the rest of the senators) within Caesar's universe?

praeclare (adv.)	very clearly; very well; with conspicuous merit or success
commendo, -are, -avi, -atum	to entrust, commit; to bring to the favourable notice of, to recommend
renuntio, -are, -avi, -atum	to take / send back a message, report; to announce; to proclaim
quidem (particle)	certainly, indeed, at any rate; and what is more
queror, -ri, -stus (*de*)	to complain, protest, grumble
nihil, n. (indecl.)	nothing (used adverbially) in no respect, not at all
impello, -ellere, -uli, -ulsum	to strike or beat against; assail to impel along, push forward, urge on
induco, -cere, -xi, -ctum	to lead to, bring to, induce, prevail on
eludo, -dere, -si, -sum	to deceive, trick, fool; to avoid or escape from; baffle; elude
perfidia, -ae, f.	faithlessness, treachery, falsehood
peto, -ere, -ivi / -ii, -itum	to seek, reach out for, go for, aim at to be a candidate for, seek (a magistracy) to stand for election
promitto, -ittere, -isi, -issum	to send forth; to promise, guarantee
recipio, -ipere, -epi, -eptum	to admit (to shelter), receive; to accept to regain, recover
interverto, -tere, -si, -sum	to embezzle, tamper with; cancel, revoke
transfero, -ferre, -tuli, -latum	to carry or convey, transport to transfer (from one person to another) to translate
ascribo, -bere, -psi, -ptum	to write in addition; to enrol, enlist to reckon as belonging to, assign, ascribe to attribute
kalendae, -arum f. pl.	the first day of the month, the Calends
cogo, -ere, coegi, coactum	to drive together, round up to bring together, assemble, muster to summon, convene to compel, force, constrain
inveho, -here, -xi, -ctum	to carry / bring in; import; to ride into attack (pass.) to attack with words, inveigh (against)
copiose (adv.)	abundantly, copiously (rhet.) with a wealth of words and arguments, eloquently
parate (adv.)	in a state of readiness, after due preparation

§ 80: Antony Augur, Addled and Addling

Hic autem iratus quae dixit, di boni! primum cum Caesar ostendisset se, priusquam proficisceretur, Dolabellam consulem esse iussurum — quem negant regem, qui et faceret semper eius modi aliquid et diceret — sed cum Caesar ita dixisset, tum hic bonus augur eo se sacerdotio praeditum esse dixit ut comitia auspiciis vel impedire vel vitiare posset, idque se facturum esse asseveravit. in quo primum incredibilem stupiditatem hominis cognoscite.

Study Questions:
- What is the subject accusative and the verb of the indirect statement introduced by *ostendisset*?
- Explain the syntax of *Dolabellam*.
- Explain the syntax of *quem*.
- Why are *faceret* and *diceret* in the imperfect subjunctive?
- What kind of clause does *ut* introduce?
- Explain the syntax of *id*.
- What does the *-que* after *id* link?
- Explain the syntax of *quo*.

Stylistic Appreciation:
- Analyze the rhetorical design of the exclamation *Hic autem ... di boni!*
- What is the rhetorical effect of the parenthesis *quem negant ... et diceret*?

Discussion Points:
- What role and function did 'religious objections' play in the political culture of the Roman republic? Can you think of possible advantages of involving the gods in this way in political decision-making?
- Compare and contrast the appeals to the divine sphere in ancient Rome with the ways in which the supernatural is brought into play in contemporary politics.

iratus, -a, -um	angry, enraged, furious
primum (adv.)	first
ostendo, -dere, -di, -tum / -sum	to show, display; to make clear to make known, disclose (a fact / opinion)
priusquam (conj.)	before
proficiscor, -icisci, -ectus	to set out, depart
nego, -are, -avi, -atum	to say (that … not), deny
semper (adv.)	always, all the time; at all times, invariably
augur, -uris, m.	augur
sacerdotium, -(i)i, m.	priesthood
praeditus, -a, -um (w. abl.)	endowed / provided (with); possessed (of)
comitium, -ii, n.	the place for assemblies
comitia (pl.)	a (voting) assembly
auspicium, -(i)i, n.	auspices; omen the right to take auspices; augural powers
impedio, -ire, -ivi / -ii, -itum	to restrict the movement of; obstruct, hinder
vitio, -are, -avi, -atum	to cause faults / defects in, spoil, harm, impair to invalidate (because of some technical fault)
assevero, -are, -avi, -atum	to assert emphatically, declare, affirm

§ 81: Compounding Ignorance through Impudence

Quid enim? istud quod te sacerdoti iure facere posse dixisti, si augur non esses et consul esses, minus facere potuisses? vide ne etiam facilius. nos enim nuntiationem solum habemus, consules et reliqui magistratus etiam spectionem. esto: hoc imperite; nec enim est ab homine numquam sobrio postulanda prudentia. sed videte impudentiam. multis ante mensibus in senatu dixit se Dolabellae comitia aut prohibiturum auspiciis aut id facturum esse quod fecit. quisquamne divinare potest quid viti in auspiciis futurum sit, nisi qui de caelo servare constituit? quod neque licet comitiis per leges et si qui servavit, non comitiis habitis sed priusquam habeantur, debet nuntiare. verum implicata inscientia impudentia est: nec scit quod augurem nec facit quod pudentem decet.

Study Questions:
- Explain how *istud* fits into the syntax of its sentence.
- Parse *sacerdoti*.
- What do you need to supply to complete the *ne*-clause (*vide ne…*)?
- Whom does Cicero have in mind when he says *nos* (*nos enim…*)?
- What is the difference between *nuntiatio* and *spectio*?
- Parse *esto*.
- Explain the syntax of *hoc* and *imperite*.
- Identify and explain the case of *viti*.
- What kind of ablative is *comitiis* (*quod neque licet comitiis per leges…*)?
- What construction is *comitiis habitis*?

Stylistic Appreciation:
- How does Cicero generate a sense of ridicule at Antony's supposed stupidity and a sense of outrage at his impudence in this paragraph?

Discussion Points:
- Explore the ways in which Cicero draws on Rome's civic religion to expose Antony as supposedly ignorant. Then ask yourself whether Antony did not know very well exactly what he was doing.

sacerdotium, -(i)i, n.	priesthood
ius, iuris n.	law, code
augur, -uris, m.	augur
minus (compar. adv.)	(as a mild neg.) not (so) very, not fully
nuntiatio, -onis, f.	the announcement (by an augur) of the signs he had observed
magistratus, -us, m.	magistracy; magistrate
spectio, -onis, f.	the act / the right of observing omens
imperite (adv.)	in an ignorant or unskilful manner
sobrius, -ia, -ium	sober
postulo, -are, -avi, -atum	to ask for, demand; expect
prudentia, -ae, f.	wisdom, sagacity, intelligence
impudentia, -ae, f.	shamelessness, effrontery, impudence
mensis, -is, m.	month
comitia, -orum, n. pl.	voting assembly
prohibeo, -ere, -ui, -itum	to keep off, hold at bay; prevent, stop, forbid
auspicium, -(i)i, n.	augury; omen; augural powers; auspices
quisquam, quicquam (pron.)	any (single) person, anyone (at all)
divino, -are, -avi, -atum	to practise divination; to foresee
vitium, -(i)i, n.	defect, fault, shortcoming / unfavourable augury; augural impediment
de caelo servare	to watch the sky
constituo, -uere, -ui, -utum	to set up, establish, decide, decree, resolve
licet, -ere, -uit / -itum est	it is permitted; one may
implico, -are, -avi / -ui, -atum / -itum	to fold or twine about itself; entwine, enfold / to intertwine, involve, entangle
inscientia, -ae, f.	ignorance
pudens, -ntis	behaving properly; decent
decet, -ere, decuit	(impers.) it is right, proper, fitting

§ 82: Antony Galloping after Caesar Only to Hold his Horses

Itaque ex illo die recordamini eius usque ad Idus Martias consulatum. quis umquam apparitor tam humilis, tam abiectus? nihil ipse poterat; omnia rogabat; caput in aversam lecticam inserens, beneficia quae venderet a collega petebat. ecce Dolabellae comitiorum dies. sortitio praerogativae; quiescit. renuntiatur: tacet. prima classis vocatur, renuntiatur. deinde, ita ut assolet, suffragia; tum secunda classis. quae omnia sunt citius facta quam dixi.

Study Questions:
- Parse *recordamini*. What is its accusative object?
- What noun does *eius* depend on?
- Parse *Idus*.
- What is the verb in the sentence *quis … abiectus*?
- Explain the tense and mood of *venderet*.

Stylistic Appreciation:
- What is the point of the hyperbaton *eius … consulatum*?
- In the second half of the passage (*ecce … dixi*), how does Cicero rhetorically re-enact what he claimed was an extremely smooth and quick dispatch of proceedings?

Discussion Points:
- What associations do you think Cicero wanted to invoke with the image of Antony sticking his head into the rear end of Caesar's litter (*caput in aversam lecticam inserens*)?
- How's your grasp of Roman voting assemblies? Can you explain what the technical terms in this passage mean (*sortitio praerogativa, renuntiatur* (2x), *prima classis, suffragia, secunda classis*)?

recordor, -ari, -atus	to call to mind, give one's thoughts to
usque (ad)	all the time (up to), right (until)
Idus, -uum, f. pl.	Ides
Martius, -a, -um	of or belonging to Mars; of March
umquam (adv.)	at any time, ever
apparitor, -oris, m.	an attendant on a magistrate; lictor, servant, clerk
humilis, -is, -e	low, low down; humble, lowly submissive, abject, ignoble, mean
abiectus, -a, -um	dejected, downcast; humble, commonplace groveling, subservient
rogo, -are, -avi, -atum	to ask, to ask for, request; to ask approval for
caput, -itis, n.	head
aversus, -a, -um	having the back turned, facing in the opposite direction; situated at the back
lectica, -ae, f.	a litter
insero, -ere, -ui, -tum	to put or thrust in, insert, introduce
beneficium, -(i)i, n.	service, kindness; favour
vendo, -ere, -idi, -itum	to sell; betray for money
collega, -ae, m.	a colleague
ecce (interjection)	See! Behold! Look! Lo and behold!
sortitio, -onis, f.	lottery, allocation by lot
praerogativus, -a, -um	(of a *centuria*) appointed by lot to vote first
quiesco, -ere, quievi, quietum	to repose, rest; to take no action, stand by, do nothing
renuntio, -are, -avi, -atum	to proclaim (the results of)
taceo, -ere, -ui, -itum	to be silent, say nothing
classis, -is, f.	one of the five classes into which the Roman citizens were divided on the basis of property
assoleo, -ere	to be a customary accompaniment to be usual, go with (impers.) it is usual, the custom is
suffragium, -(i)i, n.	a vote, resolution
(sex) suffragia	a group of six out of the eighteen equestrian *centuriae*

§ 83: Antony's Fake Auspices

Confecto negotio bonus augur — C. Laelium diceres — 'alio die' inquit. o impudentiam singularem! quid videras, quid senseras, quid audieras? neque enim te de caelo servasse dixisti nec hodie dicis. id igitur obvenit vitium quod tu iam Kalendis Ianuariis futurum esse provideras et tanto ante praedixeras. ergo hercule magna, ut spero, tua potius quam rei publicae calamitate ementitus es auspicia; obstrinxisti religione populum Romanum; augur auguri, consul consuli obnuntiasti. nolo plura, ne acta Dolabellae videar convellere, quae necesse est aliquando ad nostrum collegium deferantur.

Study Questions:
- What construction is *confecto negotio*?
- Who was C. Laelius?
- Identify and explain the tense and mood of *diceres*.
- Identify and explain the case of *impudentiam singularem*.
- Parse *servasse*.
- What kind of ablative is *tanto*?
- What noun does *magna* modify?
- What kind of ablative is *calamitate*?
- Explain the syntax of *plura*.
- What kind of clause does *ne* introduce?

Stylistic Appreciation:
- Analyze the rhetorical design of *quid videras, quid senseras, quid audieras?*
- What is the point of the hyperbaton *magna … calamitate*?
- What stylistic device is Cicero playing with in *augur auguri, consul consuli obnuntiasti*?

Discussion Points:
- How sincere do you think Cicero was when he conjured the prospect of divine punishment because of Antony's alleged abuse of the auspices? And is 'sincerity' a useful category for discussing rhetoric involving the divine sphere?

conficio, -icere, -eci, -ectum	to do, perform, accomplish; carry out to bring to completion, finish off, conclude
impudentia, -ae, f.	shamelessness, effrontery, impudence
singularis, -is, -e	specific, peculiar, special, single; remarkable
sentio, -tire, -si, -sum	to feel, discern, recognize, have experience of
obvenio, -enire, -eni, -entum	to come up, to fall to; to happen, occur, arise; to present itself
vitium, -(i)i, n.	defect, fault, shortcoming unfavourable augury; augural impediment
provideo, -idere, -idi, -isum	to see in advance, see beforehand; foresee
praedico, -cere, -xi, -ctum	to say beforehand; to give warning of, foretell
hodie (adv.)	today, at the present time, now; yet, still
hercule (interjection)	by Hercules!
calamitas, -atis, f.	disaster, misfortune, ruin, calamity
ementior, -iri, -itus	to falsify, mispresent, fabricate, invent
obstringo, -ngere, -nxi, -ctum	to constrict, constrain, confine to place under an obligation; to bind (w. abl.) to involve, implicate in
religio, -onis, f.	religious awe (here) breach of religious protocol; religious pollution
obnuntio, -are, -avi, -atum	to announce (unfavourable omens) to impede civic procedures
actum, -i, n.	act, deed, transaction; decrees; written record of events
convello, -ellere, -elli, -ulsum	to tear up, dislodge; shake, batter; nullify
aliquando (adv.)	at some time or other; one day; ever
collegium, -(i)i, n.	a college or board of priests
defero, -rre, detuli, delatum	to carry, convey, bring to refer for decision (to), put (before)

§ 84: On to the Lupercalia...

Sed arrogantiam hominis insolentiamque cognoscite. quamdiu tu voles, vitiosus consul Dolabella; rursus, cum voles, salvis auspiciis creatus. si nihil est cum augur eis verbis nuntiat quibus tu nuntiasti, confitere te, cum 'alio die' dixeris, sobrium non fuisse; sin est aliqua vis in istis verbis, ea quae sit augur a collega requiro.

   sed ne forte ex multis rebus gestis M. Antoni rem unam pulcherrimam transiliat oratio, ad Lupercalia veniamus. non dissimulat, patres conscripti: apparet esse commotum; sudat, pallet. quidlibet, modo ne faciat quod in porticu Minucia fecit. quae potest esse turpitudinis tantae defensio? cupio audire, ut videam ubi campus Leontinus appareat.

Study Questions:

- Parse *cognoscite*.
- Parse *voles* (*quamdiu ... voles*; *cum voles*).
- Explain the use of *cum* (*cum voles*).
- Explain the syntax of *ea*.
- How does *augur* fit into the syntax of its sentence?
- What are the Lupercalia?
- Parse *veniamus*.
- What happened in the *porticus Minucia*?
- What's up with the *campus Leontinus*?

Stylistic Appreciation:

- Cicero here alternates between addressing the senate, engaging Antony, speaking in the first person plural, and adopting the point of view of a participant observer. What is the rhetorical effect of these variations in perspective?
- What are the devices Cicero uses to create a vivid (and visceral) description of Antony's reaction to his mentioning of the Lupercalia?

Discussion Points:

- How does Cicero bring the theme of augural manipulation to a close and segue into the following topic?

arrogantia, -ae, f.	haughtiness, insolence, pride, conceit
insolentia, -ae, f.	unfamiliarity; extravagance; insolence, arrogance
quamdiu (interr. and rel. adv.)	(interr.) for how long? (rel.) for what length of time, as long as
vitiosus, -a, -um	flawed, defective; faulty, unsound
rursus (adv.)	backwards, once again on the other hand, contrariwise
creo, -are, -avi, -atum	to procreate; bring into being; produce to appoint
salvus, -a, -um	safe, secure, unharmed, intact, unimpaired
nuntio, -are, -avi, -atum	to report, convey, deliver, announce
confiteor, -fiteri, -fessus sum	to admit (the truth / commission of); reveal
requiro, -rere, -sivi / -sii, -situm	to try to find, seek; ask / enquire about
vis, vis, f.	strength, power, force; (of words) meaning, significance, general sense
forte (adv.)	by any chance
transilio, -ire, -ui	to leap or spring across; to pass over, skip
dissimulo, -are, -avi, -atum	to conceal, disguise; pretend not to notice
patres conscripti	senators
appareo, -ere, -ui, -itum	to be seen / visible; to appear; to be plain
commotus, -a, -um	excited, nervous; angry, annoyed
sudo, -are, -avi, -atum	to sweat, perspire
palleo, -ere, (-ui)	to be pale / bloodless; to pale
quilibet, quaelibet, quidlibet	whoever / whatever you please
modo ut (ne)	only provided that (… not)
porticus, -us, f.	portico, colonnade
turpitudo, -inis, f.	indecency, disgrace, shamefulness

§ 85: *Vive le roi! Le roi est mort*

Sedebat in rostris collega tuus amictus toga purpurea, in sella aurea, coronatus. escendis, accedis ad sellam — ita eras Lupercus, ut te consulem esse meminisse deberes — diadema ostendis. gemitus toto foro. unde diadema? non enim abiectum sustuleras, sed attuleras domo, meditatum et cogitatum scelus. tu diadema imponebas cum plangore populi; ille cum plausu reiciebat. tu ergo unus, scelerate, inventus es qui, cum auctor regni esses eumque quem collegam habebas dominum habere velles, idem temptares quid populus Romanus ferre et pati posset.

Study Questions:

- Parse *amictus*.
- What are the verbs in the sentences *gemitus toto foro* and *unde diadema*?
- Explain the case of *domo*.
- How does *meditatum et cogitatum scelus* fit into the syntax of the sentence?
- What aspect(s) of the imperfect are in play in *imponebas* and *reiciebat*?
- Parse *scelerate*.
- How does *dominum* fit into the syntax of the sentence?
- Parse *idem*. How does it fit into the sentence?
- Why is *temptares* in the subjunctive?
- Why is *posset* in the subjunctive?

Stylistic Appreciation:

- Discuss Cicero's use of tenses (present, imperfect, pluperfect) in this paragraph.

Discussion Points:

- Do you find Cicero's account of the incident entirely plausible? What do you think happened in the Roman forum on 15 February 44 BCE — and why?

rostrum, -i, n.	snout, muzzle, beak; ship-beak
rostra (pl.)	speaker's platform
amicio, -cire, -cui / -xi, -ctum	to cover, clothe, dress
purpureus, -a, -um	purple
sella, -ae, f.	seat, stool, chair
coronatus, -a, -um	adorned with wreaths, garlanded
escendo, -dere, -di, -sum	to ascend, go up
accedo, -dere, -ssi, -ssum	to draw near, approach, go to
Lupercus, -i, m.	a priest taking part in the Lupercalia
diadema, -atis, n.	ornamental headband, diadem, crown
ostendo, -dere, -di, -tum / -sum	to show, display; disclose; demonstrate
gemitus, -us, m.	groaning, moaning
unde (interr. adv.)	from what place? where… from? whence?
abicio, -cere, -eci, -ectum	to throw away; discard; throw down (w. *ad pedes*) to throw oneself at the feet of
tollo, -ere, sustuli, sublatum	to pick up, lift, hoist; raise to get rid of, remove, eliminate
affero, -rre, attuli, allatum	to bring with one, deliver, fetch; serve to confer, bestow (on), put forward
meditor, -ari, -atus	to think about constantly, contemplate to intend, devise, plan, think out
cogito, -are, -avi, -atus	to think, ponder, consider; to prepare for, plan, contemplate
scelus, -eris, n.	crime, villainy
impono, -onere, -osui, -ositum	to place / put / lay on; confer
plangor, -oris, m.	the action of beating; lamentation
plausus, -us, m.	clapping of hands in approval; applause
reicio, -icere, -ieci, -iectum	to throw, drive back; to refuse to accept, rebuff, reject
sceleratus, -a, -um	accursed; ill-starred; unfortunate (of persons) accursed because of criminal acts
invenio, -enire, -eni, -entum	to encounter, come upon, meet to find, come across, discover
auctor, -oris, m.	agent, advocate, supporter; originator, author, founder
tempto, -are, -avi, -atum	to test, try out, attempt, investigate
patior, -ti, -ssus	to be subjected to, experience, undergo, suffer

§ 86: Antony as Willing Slave and Would-Be King-Maker

At etiam misericordiam captabas: supplex te ad pedes abiciebas. quid petens? ut servires? tibi uni peteres, qui ita a puero vixeras ut omnia paterere, ut facile servires; a nobis populoque Romano mandatum id certe non habebas. o praeclaram illam eloquentiam tuam cum es nudus contionatus! quid hoc turpius, quid foedius, quid suppliciis omnibus dignius? num exspectas dum te stimulis fodiamus? haec te, si ullam partem habes sensus, lacerat, haec cruentat oratio. vereor ne imminuam summorum virorum gloriam; dicam tamen dolore commotus: quid indignius quam vivere eum, qui imposuerit diadema, cum omnes fateantur iure interfectum esse qui abiecerit?

Study Questions:

- Explain Cicero's use of the imperfects *captabas* and *abiciebas*.
- What kind of *ut*-clause is *ut servires*?
- What kind of subjunctive is *peteres*?
- Parse *paterere*. What kind of *ut*-clauses are *ut omnia paterere* and *ut facile servires*?
- Identify and explain the case of *hoc* (*quid hoc turpius…?*).
- Identify and explain the case of *sensus*.
- What is the antecedent of the relative pronoun *qui* (*qui abiecerit*)?

Stylistic Appreciation:

- Analyze the rhetorical design of *haec te … oratio*.

Discussion Points:

- At the end of the paragraph, Cicero argues that Antony deserves to be dead — indeed, ought to have been killed for his attempt to crown Caesar king. In what scenarios (if any) do you endorse capital punishment as a justified response to politically motivated actions?

misericordia, -ae, f.	pity, compassion, pathos
capto, -are, -avi, -atum	to try to get hold of, grasp at; seek, aim at to go in for, aspire after, try to win over
supplex, -icis	suppliant
abicio, -cere, -eci, -ectum	to throw away; discard; throw down (w. *ad pedes*) to throw oneself at the feet of
servio, -ire, -ivi / -ii, -itum	to serve as slave, wait on, labour for to be politically subject, act in subservience
patior, -ti, -ssus	to be subjected to, experience, undergo, suffer
mandatum, -i, n.	order, instruction, commission
contionor, -ari, -atus	to deliver a public speech
turpis, -is, -e	offensive, foul, loathsome; shameful, degrading, disgraceful
foedus, -a, -um	offensive, foul, loathsome; hideous, unclean, repugnant, monstrous shameful, disgraceful, vile
supplicium, -(i)i, n.	reparation; punishment; penalty
exspecto, -are, -avi, -atum	to wait for, await; look forward to, hope for
dum (conj.)	as long as, while; until, until such time as
stimulus, -i, n.	goad, prick, spur
fodio, -dere, fodi, fossum	to pierce, prick, prod, jab; dig
sensus, -us, m.	sense; understanding, self-awareness
lacero, -are, -avi, -atum	to tear, rend, mangle; shatter, batter, torture to cause mental anguish, vex, harass
cruento, -are, -avi, -atum	to stain with blood, to cause to bleed, wound
imminuo, -uere, -ui, -utum	to diminish
indignus, -a, -um	unworthy, unmerited; unseemly, shameful scandalous, shocking

§ 87: Historical Precedent Demands Antony's Execution

At etiam ascribi iussit in fastis ad Lupercalia C. Caesari dictatori perpetuo M. Antonium consulem populi iussu regnum detulisse, Caesarem uti noluisse. iam iam minime miror te otium perturbare; non modo urbem odisse sed etiam lucem; cum perditissimis latronibus non solum de die sed etiam in diem bibere. ubi enim tu in pace consistes? qui locus tibi in legibus et in iudiciis esse potest, quae tu, quantum in te fuit, dominatu regio sustulisti? ideone L. Tarquinius exactus, Sp. Cassius, Sp. Maelius, M. Manlius necati ut multis post saeculis a M. Antonio, quod fas non est, rex Romae constitueretur?

Study Questions:

- Parse *ascribi.*
- What are the *fasti*?
- Who is the subject of the first sentence (*At etiam ... noluisse*)?
- How does *uti* fit into the syntax of the sentence?
- Explain the syntax of *odisse* and *bibere.*
- Parse *consistes.*
- Explain the grammar of *qui* (*locus...*).
- What is the antecedent of *quae*?
- What case is *Romae*?

Stylistic Appreciation:

- Analyze the style of the proposed inscription *C. Caesari ... uti noluisse.*
- What is the rhetorical effect of Cicero's *m*-ing in *iam iam minime miror*?

Discussion Points:

- What we seem to capture here is Antony's (and Caesar's) version in retrospect of what happened at the Lupercalia. How does it differ from Cicero's?

ascribo, -bere, -psi, -ptum	to add in writing, insert; enrol, enlist, assign
fasti, -orum, m. pl.	list of festivals; calendar; list of consuls
perpetuo (adv.)	continuously; without limit in time, permanently
iussus, -us, n.	bidding, command
defero, -rre, detuli, delatum	to carry, convey, bring; transfer, hand over to entrust; confer, award, grant
utor, uti, usus	to use, avail oneself of, exercise, employ
iam (adv.)	now, by now
minime (superlative adv.)	least; least of all, to a minimal degree (= a negative) by no means, not at all
otium, -(i)i, n.	freedom from business, leisure time domestic peace
perturbo, -are, -avi, -atum	to throw into confusion, upset, disrupt to agitate, perturb, stir up
odi, -isse, osum	to hate, dislike, have an aversion to
perditus, -a, -um	debilitated, broken; ruined, desperate; morally depraved
latro, -onis, m.	mercenary; brigand, robber, bandit
consisto, -sistere, -stiti	to stop, halt, stand still to find a home, settle; reside, live
tollo, -ere, sustuli, sublatum	to pick up, lift, hoist; raise to get rid of, remove, eliminate
dominatus, -us, m.	absolute rule, lordship, dominion
regius, -a, -um	royal, regal; despotical
ideo (adv.)	for that reason, therefore
exigo, -igere, -egi, -actum	to drive out, force out, eject to achieve, complete; spend time, complete to demand, require
neco, -are, -avi, -atum	to put to death, kill
fas (indecl.), n.	what is right / permissible by divine law
constituo, -uere, -ui, -utum	to set up, place, establish; decree, decide

§ 88: Antony on the Ides of March

Sed ad auspicia redeamus; de quibus Idibus Martiis fuit in senatu Caesar acturus. quaero: tum tu quid egisses? audiebam equidem te paratum venisse, quod me de ementitis auspiciis, quibus tamen parere necesse erat, putares esse dicturum. sustulit illum diem Fortuna rei publicae. num etiam tuum de auspiciis iudicium interitus Caesaris sustulit? sed incidi in id tempus quod eis rebus in quas ingressa erat oratio praevertendum est. quae tua fuga, quae formido praeclaro illo die, quae propter conscientiam scelerum desperatio vitae, cum ex illa fuga beneficio eorum qui te, si sanus esses, salvum esse voluerunt, clam te domum recepisti!

Study Questions:

- Parse *redeamus*.
- What kind of ablative is *Idibus Martiis*?
- Parse *fuit … acturus*.
- Identify and explain the tense and the mood of *egisses*.
- Explain the syntax of *te* and *me*.
- Parse *incidi*.
- What case is *eis rebus*?
- Parse *formido*.

Stylistic Appreciation:

- Discuss Cicero's use of the future (perfect) and the subjunctive in this paragraph.
- What are the stylistic features that Cicero uses to capture Antony's flight from the senate house after Caesar's murder (*quae tua fuga … recepisti!*)?

Discussion Points:

- Reconstruct the events — and the likely motivations and psychology of the main actors — in the wake of Caesar's assassination. Why did the conspirators only kill Caesar and not also his main supporters?

ago, agere, egi, actum	to drive, bring, move
agere de	to deal with, to make a matter of business
equidem (particle)	(w. first pers. sg.) I for my part; indeed, in truth
pareo, -ere, -ui, -itum	to submit to, obey
tollo, -ere, sustuli, sublatum	to pick up, lift, hoist; raise to get rid of, remove, eliminate
interitus, -us, m.	violent death, extinction
incido, -ere, -i, incasum	to fall or drop into, to impinge on; to enter inadvertently into, come upon to present itself, arise, occur
ingredior, -di, -ssus	to go into, enter upon, commence, embark on
praeverto, -tere, -ti, -sum	to urge on firstly; to attend to firstly (w. dat.) to give precedence to (over)
fuga, -ae, f.	flight, fleeing, rout; exile, banishment
formido, -inis, f.	fear, terror, alarm; religious dread, awe
conscientia, -ae, f.	complicity, awareness of, (guilty) conscience
desperatio, -onis, f.	abandonment of hope, despair
cum (conj.) + indicative	when
beneficium, -(i)i, n.	service, kindness; favour
clam (adv.)	secretly, under cover
recipio, -ipere, -epi, -eptum	to admit to shelter, welcome, receive (refl.) to turn back, withdraw, retire

§ 89: No Compromise with a Public Enemy!

O mea frustra semper verissima auguria rerum futurarum! dicebam illis in Capitolio liberatoribus nostris, cum me ad te ire vellent ut ad defendendam rem publicam te adhortarer, quoad metueres, omnia te promissurum; simul ac timere desisses, similem te futurum tui. itaque cum ceteri consulares irent redirent, in sententia mansi: neque te illo die neque postero vidi neque ullam societatem optimis civibus cum importunissimo hoste foedere ullo confirmari posse credidi. post diem tertium veni in aedem Telluris et quidem invitus, cum omnis aditus armati obsiderent.

Study Questions:
- What case is *auguria*?
- Why might *dicebam* be in the imperfect?
- Explain the syntax of *me* (*cum me ad te ire vellent*).
- What kind of clause is *ut ... adhortarer*?
- Parse *desisses*.
- How is *tui* to be construed?
- Parse *mansi*.
- What days does Cicero refer to with *illo die, postero* [*die*] and *post diem tertium*?
- Where was the temple of Tellus?

Stylistic Appreciation:
- Analyze the rhetorical design and the ideological punch of *neque ... credidi*.

Discussion Points:
- Was Cicero correct in thinking that any compromise with Antony was bound to fail?

frustra (adv.)	to no purpose, in vain, without avail
verus, -a, -um	real, true; grounded in truth, well-founded
liberator, -oris, m.	liberator
quoad (interr. and rel. adv.)	to the degree that, as far as; while up to the time that, until
metuo, -ere, -i, metutum	to regard with fear, be afraid of, fear
simul atque / ac	as soon as, the moment that
desino, -inere, -(i)i, -itum	to leave off, desist, finish, stop, cease from
similis, -is, -e	similar, like (w. gen. or dat.) (*sui / sibi*) constant, unchanged
consularis, -is, -e	of or proper to a consul (as noun) former consul
maneo, -ere, -si, -sum	to remain, persist, continue, abide by to remain fixed
societas, -atis, f.	partnership, fellowship, society close relationship
importunus, -a, -um	unfavourable, troublesome, oppressive
foedus, -eris, n.	formal agreement, treaty, bond, tie
aedes, -is, f.	room, apartment; (pl.) house, abode; temple, sanctuary
aditus, -us, m.	approach, entry; access
armatus, -i, m.	an armed man, soldier
obsideo, -idere, -edi, -essum	to occupy; besiege, blockade, lay siege to to beset, assail, press

§ 90: Antony's Finest Hour

Qui tibi dies ille, M. Antoni, fuit! quamquam mihi inimicus subito exstitisti, tamen me tui miseret quod tibi invideris. qui tu vir, di immortales, et quantus fuisses, si illius diei mentem servare potuisses! pacem haberemus, quae erat facta per obsidem puerum nobilem, M. Bambalionis nepotem. quamquam bonum te timor faciebat, non diuturnus magister offici; improbum fecit ea quae, dum timor abest, a te non discedit, audacia. etsi tum, cum optimum te multi putabant me quidem dissentiente, funeri tyranni, si illud funus fuit, sceleratissime praefuisti.

Study Questions:
- Explain the syntax of *qui*.
- Parse *miseret*.
- Parse *invideris*.
- What kind of conditional sequence does Cicero use with *fuisses – potuisses*?
- What noun does *ea* modify?
- What construction is *me quidem dissentiente*? What is the force of *quidem*?
- Parse *funeri*.

Stylistic Appreciation:
- How does design reinforce sense in the sentence *quamquam bonum … audacia*?

Discussion Points:
- Do you agree with Cicero that the republican commonwealth and peace could have been restored had Antony continued to collaborate with the senate?

subito (adv.)	suddenly, unexpectedly
exsto, -are, exstiti	to stand out, exist, be found
misereo, -ere, -ui	to feel / show compassion, have pity
me miseret + gen.	I am moved to pity / feel sorry for
invideo, -idere, -idi, -isum	to look at askance, regard with ill will or envy
obses, -idis, m. / f.	hostage; surety, pledge, guarantee
nepos, -otis, m. / (f.)	a grandson, descendant
diuturnus, -a, -um	lasting for a long time, permanent, long-lived
officium, -(i)i, n.	duty, obligation
improbus, -a, -um	morally unsound, unprincipled, rascally shameless, insolent, rude
audacia, -ae, f.	boldness, daring; impudence, effrontery
etsi (conj.)	even if, although (introducing a main clause) and yet
dissentio, -tire, -si, -sum	to differ in opinion, disagree, dissent
funus, -eris, n.	funeral rites or ceremonies; funeral dead body, corpse; death
scelerate (adv.)	with heinous wickedness, atrociously
praesum, -esse, -fui	to be in charge (of), be in control (of)

§ 91: Antony as Dr Jekyll and Mr Hyde

Tua illa pulchra laudatio, tua miseratio, tua cohortatio; tu, tu, inquam, illas faces incendisti, et eas quibus semustilatus ille est et eas quibus incensa L. Bellieni domus deflagravit. tu illos impetus perditorum et ex maxima parte servorum quos nos vi manuque reppulimus in nostras domos immisisti. idem tamen quasi fuligine abstersa reliquis diebus in Capitolio praeclara senatus consulta fecisti, ne qua post Idus Martias immunitatis tabula neve cuius benefici figeretur. meministi ipse de exsulibus, scis de immunitate quid dixeris. optimum vero quod dictaturae nomen in perpetuum de re publica sustulisti: quo quidem facto tantum te cepisse odium regni videbatur ut eius omnem propter proximum dictatorem metum tolleres.

Study Questions:
- What is the verb of the opening sentence (*Tua ... cohortatio*)?
- How does *et eas ... et eas* fit into the sentence?
- What does the *et* after *perditorum* link?
- What kind of construction is *quasi fuligine abstersa*?
- What kind of ablative is *reliquis diebus*?
- Parse *senatus*.
- What noun does *qua* modify? What case is it in?
- Parse *Idus*.
- *neve*: what does the enclitic conjunction *-ve* link?
- Why is *dixeris* in the subjunctive?
- What is the main clause in the sentence *optimum vero ... sustulisti*?
- What noun does the genitive *dictaturae* depend on? What kind of genitive is it?
- Explain the syntax of *quo* (*quo quidem facto*).
- What kind of genitive is *regni*?
- What kind of clause does *ut* (*ut eius omnem...*) introduce?
- What does *eius* refer back to?

Stylistic Appreciation:
- Analyze the design of the opening sentence (*Tua ... cohortatio*).
- What is the rhetorical effect of the anaphoric *tu, tu, inquam*?

Discussion Points:
- Why was the funeral of Caesar such a charged moment?

laudatio, -onis, f.	panegyric; (funerary) eulogy; funeral oration
miseratio, -onis, f.	compassion, pity; expression of grief
cohortatio, -onis, f.	exhortation, encouragement
fax, -cis, f.	torch, firebrand
incendo, -dere, -di, -sum	to set on fire, kindle; incite, stir up, inflame, provoke
sem(i)ustilo, -are	to half-burn, scorch
deflagro, -are, -avi, -atum	to destroy by fire, burn down
impetus, -us, m.	onset, thrust, attack, violence violent mental impulse, urge
repello, -ere, reppuli, repulsum	to drive back, repel, fend off, deter
immitto, -ittere, -isi, -issum	to cause to go, send (against), direct
quasi	as it were
fuligo, -inis, f.	soot
abstergeo, -gere, -si, -sum	to wipe clean, remove, wipe off
senatûs consulta	decrees of the senate
immunitas, -atis, f.	exemption, immunity
tabula, -ae, f.	a flat piece of wood, board, plank a writing tablet, record; bronze plate
-ve (enclitic)	or
beneficium, -(i)i, n.	service, kindness; favour
figo, -gere, -xi, -xum	to drive in, fix in, insert (nails etc.) to fasten up; post up for public information, to promulgate
exsul, -lis, m.	a banished person, exile
tollo, -ere, sustuli, sublatum	to pick up, lift, hoist; raise to get rid of, remove, eliminate
proximus, -a, -um	nearest, adjacent, close immediately preceding, last, most recent immediately following, next

§ 92: Selling the Empire

Constituta res publica videbatur aliis, mihi vero nullo modo, qui omnia te gubernante naufragia metuebam. num igitur me fefellit, aut num diutius sui potuit esse dissimilis? inspectantibus vobis toto Capitolio tabulae figebantur, neque solum singulis venibant immunitates sed etiam populis universis: civitas non iam singillatim, sed provinciis totis dabatur. itaque si haec manent, quae stante re publica manere non possunt, provincias universas, patres conscripti, perdidistis, neque vectigalia solum sed etiam imperium populi Romani huius domesticis nundinis deminutum est.

Study Questions:
- What noun does *omnia* modify?
- What construction is *te gubernante*?
- Parse *sui*.
- What construction is *inspectantibus vobis*?
- Parse *venibant*.
- What construction is *stante re publica*?

Stylistic Appreciation:
- Analyze the dramatic trajectory of the first sentence (*constituta … metuebam*).

Discussion Points:
- Explore the political and financial relationships between Rome and its (conquered) provinces in late-republican times. To what extent does the paragraph here foreshadow the realities of the principate?
- Cicero accuses Antony of something akin to treason. Was he a 'traitor of the people'? Who *is* a traitor of the people?

constituo, -uere, -ui, -utum	to set up, establish, decree, decide, arrange
guberno, -are, -avi, -atum	to guide the course of, steer; direct, govern
naufragium, -(i)i, n.	shipwreck; disaster, calamity, ruin; wreckage
fallo, -lere, fefelli, -sum	to deceive, trick, mislead; disguise
diutius (compar. adv.)	longer
inspecto, -are, -avi, -atum	to look at, watch; (intr.) to look on
singuli, -ae, -a (pl.)	each one of, every single; individual, single (masculine pl. form used as noun) individuals
universus, -a, -um	whole, entire
veneo, -ire, -ii, (-itum)	to be sold
civitas, -atis, f.	community; the rights of a citizen, citizenship
singillatim (adv.)	one by one, singly, separately
vectigal, -alis, n.	revenue; income
nundinae, -arum, f. pl.	a market-day; a market or fair
deminuo, -uere, -ui, -utum	to lessen, diminish; curtail, impair

§ 100: Further Forgeries and a Veteran Foundation

Sed ad chirographa redeamus. quae tua fuit cognitio? acta enim Caesaris pacis causa confirmata sunt a senatu; quae quidem Caesar egisset, non ea quae egisse Caesarem dixisset Antonius. unde ista erumpunt, quo auctore proferuntur? si sunt falsa, cur probantur? si vera, cur veneunt? at sic placuerat ut ex Kalendis Iuniis de Caesaris actis cum consilio cognosceretis. quod fuit consilium, quem umquam advocasti, quas Kalendas Iunias expectasti? an eas ad quas te peragratis veteranorum coloniis stipatum armis rettulisti?

o praeclaram illam percursationem tuam mense Aprili atque Maio, tum cum etiam Capuam coloniam deducere conatus es! quem ad modum illinc abieris vel potius paene non abieris scimus.

Study Questions:

- Identify and explain the mood of *redeamus*.
- How does *quae ... Antonius* fit into the syntax of the sentence?
- Identify and explain the mood of *egisset* and *dixisset*.
- What kind of construction is *quo auctore*?
- Parse *veneunt*.
- Identify and explain the case of *percursationem*.
- What kind of ablative is *mense Aprili atque Maio*?
- Identify and explain the case of *Capuam*.
- Parse *abieris*.

Stylistic Appreciation:

- Discuss the design and rhetorical force of the question *quae tua fuit cognitio?*
- How does design reinforce theme in the sentence *acta enim Caesaris ... dixisset Antonius?*

Discussion Points:

- Why does Cicero use a string of rhetorical questions to attack Antony's handling of Caesar's state papers?
- How does Cicero manage the transition from one topic (Caesar's *acta*) to the next (Antony's journey and doings in Southern Italy)?

chirographum, -i, n.	one's handwriting; document, manuscript
cognitio, -onis, f.	the act of getting to know, comprehension study, investigation, inquiry
actum, -i, n.	act, deed, transaction
erumpo, -umpere, -upi, -uptum	to burst forth, spring out / up
profero, -ferre, -tuli, -latum	to bring forth; to put on show, display to give voice to, utter, express to produce (documents) in evidence; publish
veneo, -ire, -ii, (-itum)	to be sold
placeo, -ere, -ui or -itus	to be pleasing / acceptable to; seem good to be resolved or agreed on (by)
consilium, -(i)i, n.	debate, discussion, deliberation advice, counsel deliberative or advisory body; council decision; intention; deliberate action
advoco, -are, -avi, -atum	to call upon, summon, call together, convoke
exspecto, -are, -avi, -atum	to wait for, expect
peragro, -are, -avi, -atum	to travel through, traverse
veteranus, -a, -um	mature (as noun) veteran
colonia, -ae, f.	settlement, colony
stipo, -are, -avi, -atum	to compress, press tight (w. abl.) to surround with, fill, cram, stuff
percursatio, -onis, f.	a rapid journey
deduco, -cere, -xi, -ctum	to lead away from, remove, bring back to establish, settle
illinc (adv.)	from that place, thence
abeo, -ire, -ii, -itum	to go away, depart; pass away
potius (adv.)	rather, more exactly, on the contrary
paene (adv.)	almost, all but, practically

§ 101: Revels and Remunerations

Cui tu urbi minitaris. utinam conere, ut aliquando illud 'paene' tollatur! at quam nobilis est tua illa peregrinatio! quid prandiorum apparatus, quid furiosam vinulentiam tuam proferam? tua ista detrimenta sunt, illa nostra: agrum Campanum, qui cum de vectigalibus eximebatur ut militibus daretur, tamen infligi magnum rei publicae vulnus putabamus, hunc tu compransoribus tuis et collusoribus dividebas. mimos dico et mimas, patres conscripti, in agro Campano collocatos. quid iam querar de agro Leontino? quoniam quidem hae quondam arationes Campana et Leontina in populi Romani patrimonio grandiferae et fructuosae ferebantur. medico tria milia iugerum: quid si te sanasset? rhetori duo: quid si te disertum facere potuisset? sed ad iter Italiamque redeamus.

Study Questions:

- How does *Cui* fit into the syntax of the sentence?
- Parse *minitaris*.
- What kind of clause does *utinam* introduce?
- What does *'paene'* refer (back) to?
- Parse *conere* and explain the mood.
- Parse *apparatus*.
- How do you reconcile the relative pronoun *qui* (nominative masculine singular, referring back to *agrum Campanum*) with a first person plural verb (*putabamus*)?
- Identify and explain the tense and mood of *querar*.
- Parse the adjectives *Campana* and *Leontina*. What noun do they modify?
- Parse *sanasset* and explain the tense and mood.
- Parse *rhetori*.
- What noun needs to be supplied after *duo*?

Stylistic Appreciation:

- What might the homoioteleuton in *quid furiosam vinulentiam tuam proferam* emphasize?
- Discuss the positioning of deictic and pronominal adjectives in *tua ista detrimenta sunt, illa nostra*.

Discussion Points:

- Can you think of more recent instances in history where individuals benefitted financially from close association with powerful politicians? (Put differently, to what extent is kleptocracy a universal?)

minitor, -ari, -atus	(intr. w. dat.) to use threats (against)
utinam	if only
conor, -ari, -atus	to attempt, endeavour
quam	how
nobilis, -is, -e	renowned, famous, celebrated
peregrinatio, -onis, f.	travel abroad, foreign travel
prandium, -(i)i, n.	midday meal
apparatus, -us, m.	preparation; display, pomp, sumptuousness instruments, equipment
furiosus, -a, -um	frenzied, raving mad; wild, uncontrolled
vinulentia, -ae, f.	fondness for wine excessive wine consumption, intoxication
profero, -ferre, -tuli, -latum	to bring forth; show, display; produce to make known, public, disclose
detrimentum, -i, n.	material reduction; harm, damage, loss
ager, agri, m.	piece of land, country, region; soil, terrain
vectigalis, -is, -e	(of land etc.) yielding taxes; subject to taxes
eximo, -imere, -emi, -emptus	to take out, extract; get rid of, banish to remove (from); set free, exempt
infligo, -gere, -xi, -ctum	to knock or dash (against), to inflict
compransor, -oris, m.	table-companion
collusor, -oris, m.	playmate, fellow gambler
divido, -idere, -isi, -isum	to separate, divide (up), split, share out
mimus, -i, m.	an actor in mimes; a mime
mima, -ae, f.	an actress performing in mimes
colloco, -are, -avi, -atum	to put or set in a particular place; to put up, place, settle
queror, -ri, -stus (*de*)	to regret, complain, grumble, protest
quoniam (conj.)	seeing that … now, since, because
quondam (adv.)	formerly; in the future, some day
aratio, -onis, f.	the action of ploughing; estate of arable land
patrimonium, -(i)i, n.	property, possession, estate
grandifer, -era, -erum	yielding large crops
fructuosus, -a, -um	fruitful, productive; rewarding, lucrative
fero, -re, tuli, latum	(here) to have on or in it, contain
medicus, -i, m.	doctor, physician
mille (indecl. n. and adj.)	a thousand
milia, -ium (pl.)	thousand
iugerum, -i / -is, n.	pl. acres, an expanse of farmland
sano, -are, -avi, -atum	to cure, heal, restore to health
rhetori, -oris, m.	teacher of rhetoric, rhetorician
disertus, -a, -um	eloquent; skillfully expressed

§ 102: Antony Colonized a Colony!

Deduxisti coloniam Casilinum, quo Caesar ante deduxerat. consuluisti me per litteras de Capua tu quidem, sed idem de Casilino respondissem: possesne, ubi colonia esset, eo coloniam novam iure deducere. negavi in eam coloniam quae esset auspicato deducta, dum esset incolumis, coloniam novam iure deduci: colonos novos ascribi posse rescripsi. tu autem insolentia elatus omni auspiciorum iure turbato Casilinum coloniam deduxisti, quo erat paucis annis ante deducta, ut vexillum tolleres, ut aratrum circumduceres; cuius quidem vomere portam Capuae paene perstrinxisti, ut florentis coloniae territorium minueretur.

Study Questions:
- Parse *Casilinum* and explain its case. Where is Casilinum located?
- Identify and explain the mood of *respondissem*.
- Why is *posses* in the imperfect subjunctive?
- Explain the syntax of *auspicato*.
- Parse *rescripsi*.
- What construction is *omni auspiciorum iure turbato*?
- What kind of ablative is *paucis annis*.
- Explain the syntax of *cuius*. What noun does it refer back to?
- What kind of clause are *ut … tolleres* and *ut … circumduceres*?

Stylistic Appreciation:
- Discuss the design of the opening sentence (*Deduxisti … deduxerat*).
- After *consuluisti*, '*tu quidem*' is technically speaking unnecessary — why does Cicero add it nevertheless?

Discussion Points:
- Do you find it plausible that Antony consulted Cicero on a religious technicality to do with his settlement policy?

deduco, -cere, -xi, -ctum	to lead away from, remove, bring back
	to establish, settle
consulo, -ere, -ui, -tum	to consult, take counsel
auspicato (adv.)	after taking the auspices; auspiciously
incolumis, -is, -e	undamaged, unimpaired, intact
ascribo, -bere, -psi, -ptum	to add in writing, insert; enroll, enlist, assign
rescribo, -bere, -psi, -ptum	to write in response
insolentia, -ae, f.	unfamiliarity; lack of moderation
	insolence, arrogance
elatus (ppp. of *effero*)	raised above; exalted; sublime
vexillum, -i, n.	military standard
aratrum, -i, n.	a plough
circumduco, -cere, -xi, -ctum	to lead round, go round
vomer, -eris, m.	ploughshare
perstringo, -ngere, -nxi, -ctum	to brush, graze, skirt
florens, -ntis	flowering, flourishing, prosperous; powerful
minuo, -uere, -ui, -utum	to reduce in size or extent, make smaller
	to weaken, detract

§ 103: Antony's Enrichment Activities

Ab hac perturbatione religionum advolas in M. Varronis, sanctissimi atque integerrimi viri, fundum Casinatem. quo iure, quo ore? 'Eodem', inquies, 'quo in heredum L. Rubri, quo in heredum L. Turseli praedia, quo in reliquas innumerabiles possessiones'. et si ab hasta, valeat hasta, valeant tabulae modo Caesaris, non tuae, quibus debuisti, non quibus tu te liberavisti. Varronis quidem Casinatem fundum quis venisse dicit, quis hastam istius venditionis vidit, quis vocem praeconis audivit? misisse te dicis Alexandriam qui emeret a Caesare; ipsum enim expectare magnum fuit.

Study Questions:
- On what noun does the genitive *M. Varronis* depend?
- Parse *inquies*.
- On what noun do the genitives *heredum* (2x) depend?
- Identify and explain the tense and mood of *valeat* and *valeant*.
- What are the antecedents of *quibus* (2x)?
- Parse *venisse*.
- Identify and explain the case of *Alexandriam*.
- Identify and explain the mood of *emeret*.

Stylistic Appreciation:
- Analyze the design of the sentence *Varronis quidem … audivit?*

Discussion Points:
- How does Cicero play off Caesar against Antony in this paragraph?

perturbatio, -onis, f.	disturbance, upheaval; confusion, disorder
advolo, -are, -avi, -atum	to fly towards; hasten towards to swoop on, snatch eagerly at
sanctus, -a, -um	(religious) sacrosanct, inviolate, sacred (moral), scrupulous, upright, blameless virtuous
integer, -gra, -grum	fresh, undecided; whole, complete, untouched morally unblemished, upright
fundus, -i, m.	bottom, base; basis, foundation a country estate, farm; homestead
Casinas, -atis (adj.)	of Casinum
os, oris, n.	face, countenance, expression
heres, -edis, m. (f.)	heir, successor
praedium, -(i)i, n.	a landed property, estate, land
hasta, -ae, f.	spear, javelin spear stuck in the ground at a public auction
reliquus, -qua, -quum	the rest of, remaining
innumerabilis, -is, -e	countless
possessio, -onis, f.	occupancy, possession; seizure, control (pl.) a holding, estate
valeo, -ere, -ui, -itum	to be powerful, be well, have force to have legal authority, be valid, apply
debeo, -ere, -ui, -itum	to be under an obligation to pay, owe to to be indebted for (I) ought, should
libero, -are, -avi, -atum	to free, release from, discharge, fulfil, cover
veneo, -ire, -ii, (-itum)	to be sold
venditio, -onis, f.	the action / process of selling, sale
praeco, -onis, m.	announcer; auctioneer
emo, -emere, emi, emptum	to buy, purchase; win over; procure

§ 104: *Animal House*

Quis vero audivit umquam — nullius autem salus curae pluribus fuit — de fortunis Varronis rem ullam esse detractam? quid? si etiam scripsit ad te Caesar ut redderes, quid satis potest dici de tanta impudentia? remove gladios parumper illos quos videmus: iam intelleges aliam causam esse hastae Caesaris, aliam confidentiae et temeritatis tuae. non enim te dominus modo illis sedibus sed quivis amicus, vicinus, hospes, procurator arcebit. at quam multos dies in ea villa turpissime es perbacchatus! ab hora tertia bibebatur, ludebatur, vomebatur. o tecta ipsa misera, 'quam dispari domino' — quamquam quo modo iste dominus? — sed tamen quam ab dispari tenebantur! studiorum enim suorum receptaculum M. Varro voluit illud, non libidinum deversorium.

Study Questions:
- Parse *nullius*.
- Identify and explain the case of *curae* and *pluribus*.
- What kind of clause is *ut redderet*?
- How does *satis* fit into the syntax of the sentence?
- Parse *remove*.
- Parse *intelleges*.
- Identify and explain the case of *illis sedibus*.
- What kind of accusative is *multos dies*?

Stylistic Appreciation:
- What are the stylistic devices Cicero uses to underscore the disgraceful conduct of Antony and his mates at Varro's villa?
- What work is the tragic quote doing here?

Discussion Points:
- What would *you* do as a lodger in Varro's villa?

umquam (adv.)	at any time, ever
salus, -utis, f.	personal safety, immunity from harm, well-being, security
curae, -ae, f.	anxiety, worry, care, distress; concern
fortuna, -ae, f.	fortune (pl.) wealth, property
detraho, -here, -xi, -ctum	to detach, strip off, remove, take away
satis (indecl. noun / adv.)	enough, sufficient; sufficiently, adequately
removeo, -overe, -ovi, -otum	to move back / away, remove, set aside
gladius, -(i)i, m.	sword
parumper (adv.)	for a short while, for a moment
confidentia, -ae, f.	assurance, self-confidence; audacity, temerity
temeritas, -atis, f.	recklessness, thoughtlessness, boldness
sedes, -is, f.	a place to sit, seat; dwelling, house
quivis, quaevis, quodvis	any that you please
vicinus, -a, -um	situated close at hand (as noun) neighbour
hospes, -itis, m.	guest, visitor; host
procurator, -oris, m.	occupant, manager, keeper
arceo, -ere, -ui	to prevent from approaching, keep away, repulse; hinder, stop
turpis, -is, -e	offensive, loathsome, foul, repulsive; morally repugnant, disgraceful
perbacchor, -ari, -atus	to carouse or revel through
vomo, -ere, -ui, -itum	to be sick, vomit; discharge
tectum, -i, n.	roof, ceiling; house, dwelling
dispar, -aris	unequal, dissimilar (in character)
receptaculum, -i, n.	repository
deversorium, -(i)i, n.	lodging

§ 105: *Animal House*: The Sequel

Quae in illa villa antea dicebantur, quae cogitabantur, quae litteris mandabantur! iura populi Romani, monumenta maiorum, omnis sapientiae ratio omnisque doctrinae. at vero te inquilino — non enim domino — personabant omnia vocibus ebriorum, natabant pavimenta vino, madebant parietes, ingenui pueri cum meritoriis, scorta inter matres familias versabantur. Casino salutatum veniebant, Aquino, Interamna: admissus est nemo. iure id quidem; in homine enim turpissimo obsolefiebant dignitatis insignia.

Study Questions:

- What does the -*que* after *omnis* link?
- What construction is *te inquilino*?
- Parse *salutatum*.
- Identify and explain the case of *Casino, Aquino,* and *Interamna*.

Stylistic Appreciation:

- Discuss the stylistic devices Cicero uses to hail Varro's learning.
- Discuss the stylistic devices Cicero uses to lambast Antony's depravity.

Discussion Points:

- Compare and contrast Cicero's depiction of Antony's conduct in Varro's villa in §§ 104–05 with contemporary frat-boy comedies such as *Animal House*: what is (or isn't) funny — and why?

mando, -are, -avi, -atum	to hand over, deliver, consign to commit to (writing / memory), entrust
doctrina, -ae, f.	instruction; learning
inquilinus, -i, m.	tenant, lodger
persono, -are, -ui / -avi, -atum	to make a loud / pervasive noise, to make resound
ebrius, -a, -um	intoxicated, drunk
nato, -are, -avi, -atum	to swim; (w. abl.) to be drenched / inundated
pavimentum, -i, n.	floor, surface, pavement
madeo, -ere	to be wet / sodden
paries, -etis, m.	wall
ingenuus, -a, -um	native; free-born; honourable
meritorius, -a, -um	let out for a price, hired
scortum, -i, n.	prostitute
obsolefacio, -facere, -feci, -factum	to make common, degrade
insigne, -is, n.	mark of rank, status, identity, honour distinction

§ 106: Antony Cocooned

Cum inde Romam proficiscens ad Aquinum accederet, obviam ei processit, ut est frequens municipium, magna sane multitudo. at iste operta lectica latus per oppidum est ut mortuus. stulte Aquinates: sed tamen in via habitabant. quid Anagnini? qui cum essent devii, descenderunt ut istum, tamquam si esset consul, salutarent. incredibile dictu + sed cum vinus + inter omnis constabat neminem esse resalutatum, praesertim cum duos secum Anagninos haberet, Mustelam et Laconem, quorum alter gladiorum est princeps, alter poculorum.

Study Questions:
- Parse *ei*: whom does the pronoun refer to?
- Who is the subject of *processit*?
- What is a *municipium*?
- What is the meaning of *ut* in *ut mortuus*?
- Explain the syntax of *qui* (*qui cum essent devii*).
- What is the significance of Cicero's use of the imperfect subjunctive in *tamquam si esset consul*?
- NB: We don't know why the text here has become garbled beyond restoration (to date). It doesn't happen often in Cicero's classic speeches.
- Parse and explain the syntax of *esse resalutatum*.
- On what noun does the genitive *poculorum* depend?

Stylistic Appreciation:
- What stylistic devices does Cicero use in his portrayal of Antony's alleged mistreatment of locals on his journey back to Rome?

Discussion Points:
- Discuss the implications of Cicero challenging Antony's status as consul (cf. *tamquam si esset consul*).

accedo, -dere, -ssi, -ssum	to draw near, approach, reach
obviam (adv.)	in the way / path of, so as to meet
procedo, -dere, -ssi, -ssum	to go / move forward, come forth, advance
frequens, -ntis	densely packed, crowded, populous
municipium, -(i)i, n.	municipality, community
sane (adv.)	certainly, truly (qualifying adjs. or advs.) very, decidedly, quite (w. concessive force) admittedly, certainly, to be sure
multitudo, -inis, f.	large number, large quantity, multitude population, the common people, the masses
operio, -ire, -ui, -tum	to shut, close, cover (from sight), conceal
habito, -are, -avi, -atum	to live in, inhabit, dwell
devius, -a, -um	out-of-the-way, remote; turning aside
tamquam (conj.)	in the same way as, just as (w. conditional clause) just as (if)
saluto, -are, -avi, -atum	to greet, hail, salute; to call on to pay respects
consto, -are, -iti	to stand together, take up a position
constat	a decision is taken it is apparent / plain it is an established fact, it is known
resaluto, -are, -avi, -atum	to return the greeting of
praesertim (adv.)	above all, first and foremost, especially
praesertim cum	(causal) especially since, seeing that (adversative) although in spite of the fact that
alter … alter …	the one … the other …
princeps, -ipis, m.	master, expert, chief man; person in charge
poculum, -i, n.	drinking-vessel, cup, bowl

§ 107: Symbolic Strutting after Caesar

Quid ego illas istius minas contumeliasque commemorem quibus invectus est in Sidicinos, vexavit Puteolanos, quod C. Cassium et Brutos patronos adoptassent? magno quidem studio, iudicio, benevolentia, caritate, non, ut te et Basilum, vi et armis, et alios vestri similis quos clientis nemo habere velit, non modo illorum cliens esse. interea dum tu abes, qui dies ille collegae tuo fuit, cum illud quod venerari solebas bustum in foro evertit! qua re tibi nuntiata, ut constabat inter eos qui una fuerunt, concidisti. quid evenerit postea nescio — metum credo valuisse et arma; collegam quidem de caelo detraxisti effecistique non tu quidem etiam nunc ut similis tui, sed certe ut dissimilis esset sui.

Study Questions:
- Identify and explain the mood of *commemorem*.
- Locate the Sidicini and the town of Puteoli on a map.
- Who were C. Cassius and the (two) Bruti?
- Who was Basilus?
- Parse *adoptassent* and explain the mood.
- What construction is *qua re tibi nuntiata*?
- Explain the syntax of *qua*.
- Parse *evenerit* and explain the mood.

Stylistic Appreciation:
- What stylistic features help to underscore Cicero's spitting contempt in *illas istius minas contumeliasque commemorem*?

Discussion Points:
- Why would the Sidicini and the inhabitants of Puteoli side with the liberators?
- What does patronage of local communities by leading Roman aristocrats entail?
- What episode does Cicero refer to when he talks about the destruction of the 'tomb' by Antony's colleague Dolabella?

minae, -arum, f.	threats, menaces
contumelia, -ae, f.	insult, indignity, affront
commemoro, -are, -avi, -atum	to recall, mention, relate
inveho, -here, -xi, -ctum	to carry / bring in; import; to ride into attack (pass.) to attack with words, inveigh (against)
vexo, -are, -avi, -atum	to agitate, buffet; damage; attack constantly; to harass, trouble
patronus, -i, m.	patron; advocate
adopto, -are, -avi, -atum	to select, secure; adopt
studium, -(i)i, n.	earnest application, zeal, ardour; enthusiasm, eagerness devotion, goodwill, support
iudicium, -(i)i, n.	exercise of judgement; decision favourable opinion, esteem
benevolentia, -ae, f.	goodwill, benevolence, friendliness
caritas, -atis, f.	dearness, high price; love, affection, esteem
veneror, -ari, -atus	to worship, adore; pay homage to
bustum, -i, n.	funeral pyre; grave-mound, tomb
everto, -tere, -ti, -sum	to turn upside down; overturn; ruin
unâ (adv.) *unâ esse*	in one body, together; at the same time to be present
concido, -ere, -i	to collapse, fall; to die or be killed
evenio, -enire, -eni, -entum	to come out, emerge; to happen, come about
metus, -us, m.	fear
valeo, -ere, -ui, -itum	to be powerful, have strength to be well
detraho, -here, -xi, -ctum	to remove; to pull or force down to pull down, demolish

§ 108: Swords Galore, or: Antony's Return to Rome

Qui vero inde reditus Romam, quae perturbatio totius urbis! memineramus Cinnam nimis potentem, Sullam postea dominantem, modo Caesarem regnantem videramus. erant fortasse gladii, sed absconditi nec ita multi; ista vero quae et quanta barbaria est! agmine quadrato cum gladiis sequuntur, scutorum lecticas portari videmus. atque his quidem iam inveteratis, patres conscripti, consuetudine obduruimus. Kalendis Iuniis cum in senatum, ut erat constitutum, venire vellemus, metu perterriti repente diffugimus.

Study Questions:
* What kind of accusative is *Romam*?
* Parse *totius*.
* Explain the grammar and sense of *agmine quadrato*.
* How do you account for the genitive in the phrase *scutorum lecticas*?
* What construction is *his … inveteratis*?
* Identify and explain the case of *Kalendis Iuniis*.

Stylistic Appreciation:
* Analyze the design of the sentence *memineramus … videramus*.
* Identify the stylistic devices that Cicero employs to contrast a bad past with a worse present in this paragraph.

Discussion Points:
* How do you think Antony would have advertised his return to Rome?

inde (adv.)	from that place, thence, from there
	from that time, from then on; next, then
reditus, -us, m.	return
perturbatio, -onis, f.	physical disturbance, agitation, upheaval
	disorder, disruption
nimis (adv.)	to an excessive degree, too much, unduly
potens, -ntis	having or exercising power over, powerful
dominor, -ari, -atus	to exercise sovereignty, act as despot, rule
modo (adv.)	just, only (now); recently
fortasse (adv.)	it may be, possibly, perhaps
absconditus, -a, -um	hidden, concealed; covert, disguised
barbaria, -ae, f.	the foreign world, uncivilized people
	barbarousness, brutality
agmen, -inis, n.	stream, current; mass, multitude, throng
	an army on the march, column
quadro, -are, -avi, -atum	to square up, to form a rectangular shape
agmen quadratum	an army marching in a rectangle, the baggage
	in the midst (= ready for any enemy attack from any direction);
	'hollow square formation'
scutum, -i, n.	shield
lectica, -ae, f.	a litter
porto, -are, -avi, -atum	to transport, convey; to carry, bear
invetero, -are, -avi, -atum	to become old or established;
	to make / become customary
consuetudo, -inis, f.	habit, custom
obduresco, -escere, -ui	to become hard, harden;
	to become hardened / callous
metus, -us, m.	fear
perterreo, -ere, -ui, -itum	to frighten greatly, terrify
repente (adv.)	without warning, suddenly; in an instant,
	all at once
diffugio, -ugere, -ugi	to run away, flee; scatter, disperse

§ 109: Playing Fast and Loose with Caesar's Legislation

At iste, qui senatu non egeret, neque desideravit quemquam et potius discessu nostro laetatus est statimque illa mirabilia facinora effecit. qui chirographa Caesaris defendisset lucri sui causa, is leges Caesaris easque praeclaras, ut rem publicam concutere posset, evertit. numerum annorum provinciis prorogavit; idemque, cum actorum Caesaris defensor esse deberet, et in publicis et in privatis rebus acta Caesaris rescidit. in publicis nihil est lege gravius; in privatis firmissimum est testamentum. leges alias sine promulgatione sustulit, alias ut tolleret promulgavit. testamentum irritum fecit, quod etiam infimis civibus semper obtentum est. signa, tabulas, quas populo Caesar una cum hortis legavit, eas hic partim in hortos Pompei deportavit, partim in villam Scipionis.

Study Questions:

- Identify and explain the case of *senatu*.
- Why is *egeret* in the (imperfect) subjunctive?
- What is the antecedent of *qui*?
- Identify and explain the case of *lucri sui*.
- What kind of clause is *ut rem publicam concutere possit*?
- What kind of ablative is *lege*?
- What is the antecedent of *quod*?
- Identify and explain the case of *infimis civibus*.

Stylistic Appreciation:

- In this paragraph, we get a cascade of main clauses, with the verbs in the perfect tense: *desideravit – laetatus est – effecit – evertit – prorogavit – rescidit – sustulit – promulgavit – fecit – deportavit*. What is the rhetorical effect? And what does the principle, stated in the present tense halfway through the paragraph (*in publicis nihil est lege gravius; in privatis firmissimum est testamentum*), add to the overall design and rhetorical impact?

Discussion Points:

- Is Cicero here making mountains out of molehills?

egeo, -ere, -ui	to need, want, require; to lack, be devoid of
desidero, -are, -avi, -atum	to long for, desire; to stand in need of, require to feel / notice the absence of, miss
potius (adv.)	rather, on the contrary; by preference
discessus, -us, m.	absence (from), departure, going away
laetor, -ari, -atus	to rejoice, be glad, be delighted (in)
statim (adv.)	immediately, at once, without delay
mirabilis, -is, -e	causing wonder, remarkable, extraordinary
facinus, -oris, n.	deed, act, event; misdeed, crime, outrage
chirographum, -i, n.	one's handwriting; document, manuscript
lucrum, -i, n.	material gain, profit
concutio, -tere, -ssi, -ssum	to shake, agitate; distress, upset
everto, -tere, -ti, -sum	to turn upside down; overturn; ruin
prorogo, -are, -avi, -atum	to extend (a term of office) be added, prolong, keep going
rescindo, -indere, -idi, -issum	to remove by hewing, split, break open to cancel, revoke, rescind, annul
gravis, -is, -e	heavy, ponderous; stern, harsh grave, serious, earnest, weighty oppressive, troublesome
testamentum, -i, n.	will, testament
promulgatio, -onis, f.	official proclamation (of a proposed law)
promulgo, -are, -avi, -atum	to make known (the terms of a proposed law) to make widely known, publish
irritus, -a, -um	not ratified or valid, null and void; ineffectual
infimus, -a, -um	lowest in position most undistinguished, humblest, lowest
obtineo, -inere, -inui, -entum	to maintain, keep up, persist in to govern, hold, retain control of to cover, extend over to secure, gain, obtain, sustain one's claim to
signum, -i, n.	mark; sign, emblem; statue
tabulae, -ae, f.	(here) painting
una cum + abl.	together with
hortus, -i, m.	garden
lego, -are, -avi, -atum	to send as an envoy to dispose of by legacy, bequeath
partim … partim… (adv.)	in part … in part…
deporto, -are, -avi, -atum	to bring, convey, transport

§ 110: Caesar: Dead Duck or Deified Dictator?

Et tu in Caesaris memoria diligens, tu illum amas mortuum? quem is honorem maiorem consecutus erat quam ut haberet pulvinar, simulacrum, fastigium, flaminem? est ergo flamen, ut Iovi, ut Marti, ut Quirino, sic divo Iulio M. Antonius. quid igitur cessas? cur non inauguraris? sume diem, vide qui te inauguret: collegae sumus; nemo negabit. o detestabilem hominem, sive quod tyranni sacerdos es sive quod mortui! quaero deinceps num hodiernus dies qui sit ignores. nescis heri quartum in circo diem ludorum Romanorum fuisse, te autem ipsum ad populum tulisse ut quintus praeterea dies Caesari tribueretur? cur non sumus praetextati? cur honorem Caesaris tua lege datum deseri patimur? an supplicationes addendo diem contaminari passus es, pulvinaria contaminari noluisti? aut undique religionem tolle aut usque quaque conserva.

Study Questions:

* In the phrase *in Caesaris memoria,* what kind of genitive is *Caesaris?*
* Explain the grammar of *quem* (*quem is honorem…*).
* Parse *inauguraris.*
* Parse *sume.*
* Identify and explain the case of *destestabilem hominem.*
* How is *mortui* to be construed?
* Explain the syntax of the sentence *quaero … ignores.*

Stylistic Appreciation:

* What is the tone of the initial question (*Et tu … mortuum*)?
* Discuss the rhetorical force and arrangement of *pulvinar, simulacrum, fastigium, flaminem.* (Make sure you know what each of these items refers to.)
* Analyze the design of *est ergo flamen, ut Iovi, ut Marti, ut Quirino, sic divo Iulio M. Antonius.*
* Cicero shows a notable preference for asyndeton in this paragraph. Why?
* What figure of thought does Cicero use in *sive quod tyranni sacerdos es sive quod mortui* and *aut undique religionem tolle aut usque quaque conserva?* Why is it effective?

Discussion Points:

* Cicero here blasts Antony for inconsistency in his attitude towards Caesar. What might account for such 'qualified devotion' to the dead dictator on Antony's part?

diligens, -ntis	careful, attentive, diligent, scrupulous
consequor, -qui, -cutus	to go or come after, follow; to bring about, achieve, reach; (intr.) to succeed
pulvinar, -aris, n.	a cushioned couch for the statue of a god
simulacrum, -i, n.	likeness, image, statue
fastigium, -i, n.	tip, apex; top, summit a rigged or pointed roof, pediment, gable
flamen, -inis, m.	a *flamen* (a specially appointed priest)
cesso, -are, -avi, -atum	to hold back from, desist; be inactive
inauguro, -are, -avi, -atum	to consecrate by augury for a priesthood
sumo, -mere, -mpsi, -mptum	to take (up), to adopt
detestabilis, -is, -e	detestable, execrable, abominable
deinceps (adv.)	in succession, in turn; after that, next
num (interrogative particle)	introducing a question implying a negative answer (introducing indirect questions) whether by any chance
hodiernus, -a, -um	of or belonging to this day
hodiernus dies	this day
ignoro, -are, -avi, -atum	to be ignorant or unaware of, fail to recognize
nescio, -ire, -ivi / -ii, -itum	not to know, to be unaware of
heri (adv.)	yesterday
fero, -rre, tuli, latum	(here) to propose to (*ad*)
praeterea (adv.)	in addition to that, as well, besides
tribuo, -uere, -ui, -utum	to grant, bestow, award; allocate, devote
praetextatus, -a, -um	wearing the *toga praetexta*
desero, -ere, -ui, -tum	to forsake, leave, abandon; part company
patior, -ti, -ssus	to be subjected to, undergo, experience to suffer, put up with, tolerate, allow
supplicatio, -onis, f.	the offering of propitiation to a deity; thanksgiving
contamino, -are, -avi, -atum	to defile, pollute, befoul; corrupt to render ritually unclean, profane, desecrate
undique (adv.)	from all sides or directions
usque quaque (adv.)	everywhere, in every possible respect, wholly

§ 111: A Final Look at Antony's Illoquence

Quaeris placeatne mihi pulvinar esse, fastigium, flaminem. mihi vero nihil istorum placet: sed tu, qui acta Caesaris defendis, quid potes dicere cur alia defendas, alia non cures? nisi forte vis fateri te omnia quaestu tuo, non illius dignitate metiri. quid ad haec tandem? exspecto enim eloquentiam. disertissimum cognovi avum tuum, at te etiam apertiorem in dicendo. ille numquam nudus est contionatus: tuum hominis simplicis pectus vidimus. respondebisne ad haec, aut omnino hiscere audebis? ecquid reperies ex tam longa oratione mea cui te respondere posse confidas?

Study Questions:
- Parse *vis*.
- What kind of ablative are *quaestu* and *dignitate*?
- What is the verb in the sentence *quid ad haec tandem?*
- How does the genitive phrase *hominis simplicis* fit into the sentence?
- What is the antecedent of *cui*?

Stylistic Appreciation:
- Cicero here blasts Antony for his lack of eloquence. What ensures that he does so eloquently?

Discussion Points:
- Explore the role of ancestors in Roman culture — and political oratory. Who was Antony's *avus*?

pulvinar, -aris, n.	a cushioned couch for the statue of a god
fastigium, -i, n.	tip, apex; top, summit a rigged or pointed roof, pediment, gable
flamen, -inis, m.	a *flamen* (a priest specially appointed for a specific divinity)
cur (adv.)	(interr.) for what reason / purpose, why (relative) on account of which
curo, -are, -avi, -atum	to watch over, look after, care for, attend to
forte (adv.)	by chance, perhaps
fateor, -eri, fassus	to concede, admit, acknowledge, confess
quaestus, -us, m.	gainful occupation, profit, income, gain
metior, -iri, mensus (*metitus*)	to measure, mark off, estimate, gauge
tandem (adverb)	after all; at last
disertus, -a, -um	dexterous or skilled in speaking, eloquent
cognosco, -oscere, -ovi, -itum	to get to know, find out; to find to be
avus, -i, m.	grandfather; ancestor
etiam (particle)	still, yet, even now; even, actually
apertus, -a, -um	open; uncovered, unveiled, bare, naked open-hearted, frank
numquam (adv.)	at no time, never; not in any circumstances
nudus, -a, -um	naked
contionor, -ari, -atus	to deliver a public speech, address a meeting
simplex, -icis	simple, basic, plain, artless, simple-minded
pectus, -oris, n.	breast, chest; soul, mind, personality
omnino (adv.)	in every respect, absolutely, altogether; at all, in any degree, in any circumstances
hisco, -ere	to open, gape, open the mouth to speak
audeo, -dere, -sus	to have a mind, be prepared, intend to dare, venture
ecquis, ecquid	is there anyone who? is there anything that?
reperio, -ire, repperi, -tum	to find, discover, light upon; make up, devise

§ 112: The Senate Under Armour

Sed praeterita omittamus: hunc unum diem, unum, inquam, hodiernum diem, hoc punctum temporis, quo loquor, defende, si potes. cur armatorum corona senatus saeptus est, cur me tui satellites cum gladiis audiunt, cur valvae Concordiae non patent, cur homines omnium gentium maxime barbaros, Ituraeos, cum sagittis deducis in forum? praesidi sui causa se facere dicit. non igitur miliens perire est melius quam in sua civitate sine armatorum praesidio non posse vivere? sed nullum est istud, mihi crede, praesidium: caritate te et benevolentia civium saeptum oportet esse, non armis.

Study Questions:
- Parse *praeterita*.
- Identify and explain the mood of *omittamus*.
- Parse *inquam*.
- Parse *Concordiae*. What does it refer to?
- Who are the Ituraeans?
- Explain the syntax of *perire*.
- What kind of ablatives are *caritate* and *benevolentia*?

Stylistic Appreciation:
- Analyze the design and the rhetorical force of the accusative objects of *defende*.
- Discuss the rhetorical power of the sequence of rhetorical questions introduced by *cur* (4x).

Discussion Points:
- Do you agree with Cicero that the best 'bodyguard' a statesman can have is the devotion and benevolence he inspires among his fellow-citizens?

praeteritus, -a, -um	past, bygone, former
omitto, -ittere, -isi, -issum	to let go off, release; discontinue to leave out of account, disregard to ignore, omit mention of, pass over
punctum, -i, n.	a small hole, prick, sting
punctum temporis	a moment, instant
armatus, -i, m.	an armed man, soldier
corona, -ae, f.	wreath, garland, crown a circle (of bystanders), spectators a ring (of soldiers)
saepio, -ire, -si, -tum	to surround with a hedge, fence round, enclose, encircle
satelles, -itis, m.	one of a bodyguard, henchman, attendant partisan, supporter, accomplice
valvae, -arum, f. pl.	a double door, a folding door
pateo, -ere, -ui	to be open; to be visible; to extend
sagitta, -ae, f.	arrow
praesidium, -(i)i, n.	means of security, defence, protection; bodyguard, escort
miliens (adv.)	a thousand times
pereo, -ire, -ii (-ivi), -itum	to vanish, disappear; to perish, die
caritas, -atis, f.	love, affection, esteem
benevolentia, -ae, f.	goodwill, benevolence, friendliness

§ 113: The *Res Publica* Has Watchers!

Eripiet et extorquebit tibi ista populus Romanus, utinam salvis nobis! sed quoquo modo nobiscum egeris, dum istis consiliis uteris, non potes, mihi crede, esse diuturnus. etenim ista tua minime avara coniunx, quam ego sine contumelia describo, nimium diu debet populo Romano tertiam pensionem. habet populus Romanus ad quos gubernacula rei publicae deferat: qui ubicumque terrarum sunt, ibi omne est rei publicae praesidium vel potius ipsa res publica, quae se adhuc tantum modo ulta est, nondum reciperavit. habet quidem certe res publica adulescentis nobilissimos paratos defensores. quam volent illi cedant otio consulentes; tamen a re publica revocabuntur. et nomen pacis dulce est et ipsa res salutaris; sed inter pacem et servitutem plurimum interest. pax est tranquilla libertas, servitus postremum malorum omnium non modo bello sed morte etiam repellendum.

Study Questions:
- Explain the construction *utinam salvis nobis*.
- Parse *egeris*.
- Why does Cicero call Antony's wife Fulvia *minime avara*?
- Parse *volent*.
- Identify and explain the mood of *cedant*.
- What kind of genitive is *pacis*?
- What kind of genitive is *malorum omnium*?
- What kind of ablatives are *bello* and *morte*?

Stylistic Appreciation:
- What makes the first two sentences (*Eripiet … diuturnus*) 'a brilliant opening to a passage of high rhetoric'? (Lacey 1986: 240).
- With the phrase *gubernacula rei publicae* Cicero brings the well-known metaphor of the 'ship of state' into play (with *gubernacula* as metonym for the ship): what does the metaphor contribute to his rhetorical agenda?

Discussion Points:
- Who are the political agents in this paragraph? Can you bring them into systematic correlation?
- Do you agree with Cicero that slavery is worse than death?
- What do *you* think freedom consists in?

eripio, -ipere, -ipui, -eptum	to seize, pull, tear from; snatch (away)
extorqueo, -quere, -si, -tum	to remove with a twist, wrench away to obtain by force; dislocate
salvus, -a, -um	safe, secure, unharmed; intact, undamaged still alive, existing, surviving, extant

ago, agere, egi, actum + *cum*	(here) to transact business (with), treat
consilium, -(i)i, n.	debate, discussion, deliberation, advice deliberative or advisory body; council decision; intention; deliberate action
utor, -i, usus	to use, employ, engage in
diuturnus, -a, -um	lasting for a long time, durable, lasting
avarus, -a, -um	greedy, avaricious, rapacious; miserly, mean
coniunx, -ugis, m. / f.	partner in marriage, spouse, husband / wife
contumelia, -ae, f.	insulting language or behaviour; affront
describo, -bere, -psi, -ptum	to represent, draw, describe
pensio, -onis, f.	a payment (of money), instalment
gubernaculum, -i, n.	steering-oar; the helm of the ship of state
defero, -rre, detuli, delatum *deferre ad*	to carry, convey, bring; transfer to entrust (something) to, put into the hands of
ubicumque (adv.)	in whatever place, wherever; in any place whatever
adhuc (adv.)	up to the present time, as yet, so far
tantum modo	only, merely, only just
ulciscor, -cisci, -tus	to inflict retribution / take revenge on to take vengeance on behalf of, avenge
nondum (adv.)	not yet
recipero, -are, -avi, -atum	to recover, regain, get back; restore, revive
adulescens, -ntis, m. / f.	a youthful person, young man or woman
paratus, -a, -um [ppl. of *paro*]	ready to hand, available; prepared, ready
cedo, -dere, -ssi, -ssum	to withdraw, go away, retire, depart to give in, yield, submit
otium, -(i)i, n.	leisure, relaxation; idleness; a state of public tranquility or peace
consulo, -ere, -ui, -tum	to consult, take counsel about, decide upon (intr. w. dat.) to consult the interests of, take thought for, look after
revoco, -are, -avi, -atum	to call upon to return, summon back, recall
salutaris, -is, -e	salutary, wholesome, promoting life / health
servitus, -utis, f.	servitude, bondage, slavery
intersum, -esse, -fui	to lie between, intervene to constitute a difference, be different, differ to make a difference, be significant
postremus, -a, -um	last, final; most recent (of an evil) extreme, worst
malum, -i, n.	trouble, distress, pain, hardship; evil, wickedness; harm, damage
repello, -ere, reppuli, repulsum	to push or thrust away, drive back, repel to fend off, deter, spurn, reject

§ 114: Caesar's Assassination: A Deed of Unprecedented Exemplarity

Quod si se ipsos illi nostri liberatores e conspectu nostro abstulerunt, at exemplum facti reliquerunt. illi quod nemo fecerat fecerunt. Tarquinium Brutus bello est persecutus, qui tum rex fuit cum esse Romae licebat; Sp. Cassius, Sp. Maelius, M. Manlius propter suspicionem regni appetendi sunt necati: hi primum cum gladiis non in regnum appetentem, sed in regnantem impetum fecerunt. quod cum ipsum factum per se praeclarum est atque divinum, tum expositum ad imitandum est, praesertim cum illi eam gloriam consecuti sint quae vix caelo capi posse videatur. etsi enim satis in ipsa conscientia pulcherrimi facti fructus erat, tamen mortali immortalitatem non arbitror esse contemnendam.

Study Questions:
- Who was Tarquinius?
- What case is *Romae*?
- Who were Sp. Cassius, Sp. Maelius, and M. Manlius?
- Explain the construction *regni appetendi*.
- In the phrase *in regnum appetentem* does the preposition *in* govern the noun *regnum* or the participle *appetentem*?
- What noun does the genitive phrase *pulcherrimi facti* depend on?
- What word does the partitive genitive *fructus* depend on?

Stylistic Appreciation:
- How does Cicero differentiate the recent from the distant past?
- Consider Cicero's use of the verb *facere* in this paragraph: *exemplum facti — fecerat — fecerunt — (impetum) fecerunt — ipsum factum — (in ipsa conscientia) pulcherrimi facti*. Why does he insist so much on 'deed' and 'done'?
- Why is *mortali immortalitatem* 'an effective use of *adnominatio*' (Ramsey)?

Discussion Points:
- In what ways is the murder of Caesar particularly glorious?
- What does immortality consist of for Cicero in this paragraph?
- How would you justify tyrannicide?

conspectus, -us, m.	sight, view; appearance, look
aufero, -rre, abstuli, ablatum	to carry or fetch away, remove, take away withdraw
persequor, -qui, -cutus	to follow persistently, pursue, press hard to seek requital or restitution for, seek out
licet, -cere, -uit / -itum est	it is permitted, one may (w. subjunctive) although
propter (prep. + acc.)	because of, for the purpose of, on account of
suspicio, -onis, f.	suspicion, mistrustful feeling; a faint indication, suggestion
regnum, -i, n.	kingship, tyranny; kingdom
appeto, -ere, -ivi / -ii, -itum	to try to reach, stretch out for; desire, seek
neco, -are, -avi, -atum	to put to death, kill
impetus, -us, m.	onset, thrust, attack; violent impulse, urge
cum ... tum...	(here) not only, as well as
praeclarus, -a, -um	radiant, brilliant, magnificent, glorious
divinus, -a, -um	divine, godlike

expono, -onere, -osui, -ositum
     exponere ad
	to expose; to put on show, display
	     to expose to

§ 115: Looking for the Taste of (Genuine) Glory…

Recordare igitur illum, M. Antoni, diem quo dictaturam sustulisti; pone ante oculos laetitiam senatus populique Romani, confer cum hac nundinatione tua tuorumque: tum intelleges, quantum inter lucrum et laudem intersit. sed nimirum, ut quidam morbo aliquo et sensus stupore suavitatem cibi non sentiunt, sic libidinosi, avari, facinerosi verae laudis gustatum non habent. sed si te laus adlicere ad recte faciendum non potest, ne metus quidem a foedissimis factis potest avocare? iudicia non metuis? si propter innocentiam, laudo; sin propter vim, non intellegis, qui isto modo iudicia non timeat, ei quid timendum sit?

Study Questions:
- Parse *recordare*.
- Parse *senatus*.
- What noun governs the genitive *tuorum*?
- Parse *intelleges*.
- Why is *intersit* in the subjunctive?
- Parse *quidam*.
- What kind of dative is *ei*?

Stylistic Appreciation:
- Analyze the rhetorical craftsmanship of *sed nimirum … non habent*.
- What is the effect of the asyndetic paratactic opening sequence (three imperatives — *recordare, pone, confer* — followed by *tum intelleges*)?

Discussion Points:
- What does *vera laus* consist in for Cicero?
- What is a stronger motivation for ethical conduct: desire for praise or fear of punishment?

recordor, -ari, -atus	to call to mind, recollect
laetitia, -ae, f.	joy, gladness, pleasure; delight
confero, -rre, contuli, collatum	to bring, take, carry, convey to bring together; to compare
nundinatio, -onis, f.	the action of trading or trafficking
quantum (adv.)	how much; to what extent
lucrum, -i, n.	material gain, profit
laus, -dis, f.	praise, commendation; renown; praiseworthiness, excellence
nimirum (particle)	without doubt, evidently, presumably
quidam, quaedam, quoddam	a particular, a certain
morbus, -i, m.	disease, illness, sickness, infirmity
sensus, -us, m.	capacity to perceive by the senses; sensation feeling
stupor, -oris, m.	numbness, stupefaction, dullness
suavitas, -atis, f.	pleasantness, charm
cibus, -i, m.	food, nutriment
libidinosus, -a, -um	arbitrary, capricious; lustful, licentious
avarus, -a, -um	greedy, avaricious
facinerosus, -a, -um	criminal, wicked
gustatus, -us, m.	the act of tasting; the sense of taste
adlicio, -icere, -exi, -ectum	to entice, attract, lure; to attract to, win over
foedus, -a, -um	offensive, foul, loathsome; hideous, unclean, repugnant, monstrous shameful, disgraceful, vile
avoco, -are, -avi, -atum	to call / summon away, turn aside, avert to dissuade
innocentia, -ae, f.	freedom from guilt, innocence uprightness, blamelessness, integrity

§ 116: Caesar You Are Not!

Quod si non metuis viros fortis egregiosque civis, quod a corpore tuo prohibentur armis, tui te, mihi crede, diutius non ferent. quae est autem vita dies et noctes timere a suis? nisi vero aut maioribus habes beneficiis obligatos quam ille quosdam habuit ex eis a quibus est interfectus, aut tu es ulla re cum eo comparandus. fuit in illo ingenium, ratio, memoria, litterae, cura, cogitatio, diligentia; res bello gesserat, quamvis rei publicae calamitosas, at tamen magnas. multos annos regnare meditatus, magno labore, magnis periculis quod cogitarat effecerat; muneribus, monumentis, congiariis, epulis multitudinem imperitam delenierat; suos praemiis, adversarios clementiae specie devinxerat. quid multa? attulerat iam liberae civitati partim metu, partim patientia consuetudinem serviendi.

Study Questions:
- Parse *ferent*.
- Identify and explain the case of *dies et noctes*.
- What kind of ablative is *ulla re*?
- What kind of accusative is *multos annos*?
- Parse *cogitarat*.

Stylistic Appreciation:
- What is the rhetorical effect of Cicero's penchant for asyndetic enumerations in this paragraph? (See esp. *ingenium, ratio, memoria, litterae, cura, cogitatio, diligentia* and *muneribus, monumentis, congiariis, epulis,* but also *magno labore, magnis periculis* and *suos praemiis, adversarios clementiae specie*.)
- What are your thoughts on Cicero's repeated use of the attribute *magnus*? (*res ... at tamen magnas, magno labore, magnis periculis*)?
- After concluding two sentences with the verb (*effecerat*; *delenierat*), why does Cicero depart from standard word order in the last sentence and lead with the verb (*attulerat*)?

Discussion Points:
- Does Cicero get his assessment of Caesar right?
- What accounts for the rise of autocratic demagogues? Are they born or made?

metuo, -ere, -i, metutum	to regard with fear, be afraid of, to fear
egregius, -ia, -ium	outstanding, excellent, pre-eminent
prohibeo, -ere, -ui, -itum	to keep off, hold at bay; prevent, preclude
timeo, -ere, -ui	(intr.) to experience fear, be afraid (w. dat.) to be afraid (on behalf of) (w. *ab, unde*) to fear harm (from)

beneficium, -(i)i, n.	service, kindness; favour
obligo, -are, -avi, -atum	to tie up, secure, place under obligation
interficio, -ficere, -feci, -fectum	to do away with, put to death, kill; destroy
ingenium, -(i)i, n.	natural disposition, temperament; inherent quality or character mental powers, natural abilities, talent
ratio, -onis, f.	the act of reckoning, calculation; reason
littera, -ae, f.	letter (of the alphabet)
litterae (pl.)	letter, missive, dispatch literary works, writings; literary activities scholarship, erudition, culture
cura, -ae, f.	anxiety, worry, care; serious attention, zeal the administration, charge, command (of)
cogitatio, -onis, f.	reflection, thought
diligentia, -ae, f.	carefulness, attentiveness, assiduity
quamvis (adverb)	to any degree you like; no matter how (w. subjunctive) however (w. indicative) although
calamitosus, -a, -um	wretched, unfortunate, ill-starred causing disaster, disastrous, calamitous
meditor, -ari, -atus	to think about constantly, contemplate
munus, -eris, n.	function, task; duty; gift, tribute, token
monumentum, -i, n.	statue, trophy, building; monument
congiarium, -(i)i, n.	a quantity (of wine, oil, money) distributed as a gift gratuity, largesse, donation
epulum, -i, n.	a public feast, banquet
imperitus, -a, -um	lacking experience, ignorant, untutored
delenio, -ire, -ii, -itum	to soothe down, mollify, cajole; bewitch
clementia, -ae, f.	clemency, leniency
species, -ei, f.	spectacle, sight; appearance, look, display assumed appearance, veneer (*specie* + gen.) under the specious cover / on the pretext of
devincio, -cire, -xi, -ctum	to tie fast, bind; subjugate; oblige
affero, -rre, attuli, allatum	to bring with one, deliver, fetch; add, confer (+ acc. and dat.) to bring (a condition) about (for / upon)
partim ... partim... (adv.)	partly ... partly...
patientia, -ae, f.	endurance, hardiness; forbearance, tolerance apathy, passivity
consuetudo, -inis, f.	usage, custom, habit, convention
servio, -ire, -ivi / ii, -itum	to serve, wait on, be the servant of to be subservient, be subject to servitude

§ 117: Once Burnt Lesson Learnt!

Cum illo ego te dominandi cupiditate conferre possum, ceteris vero rebus nullo modo comparandus es. sed ex plurimis malis quae ab illo rei publicae sunt inusta hoc tamen boni est quod didicit iam populus Romanus quantum cuique crederet, quibus se committeret, a quibus caveret. haec non cogitas, neque intellegis satis esse viris fortibus didicisse quam sit re pulchrum, beneficio gratum, fama gloriosum tyrannum occidere? an, cum illum homines non tulerint, te ferent?

Study Questions:
- What kind of ablatives are *cupiditate* and *ceteris … rebus*?
- What are the subject and the verb of the sentence starting *sed ex plurimis malis…*?
- What kind of ablative is *ab illo*?
- Parse *inusta*.
- What does the genitive *boni* depend on?
- Explain the syntax of *satis*.
- What kind of ablatives are *re*, *beneficio*, and *fama*?
- Parse *ferent*.

Stylistic Appreciation:
- What do the stylistic devices on display here, such as alliteration or asyndetic tricola, contribute to the tone of the passage?

Discussion Points:
- Do you share Cicero's view of tyrannicide?
- 'We don't get fooled again'. This passage is often thought to be the nub of the whole speech. Does it read that way?

dominor, -ari, -atus	to exercise sovereignty, act as a despot, rule
inuro, -rere, -ssi, -stum	to burn, scorch; to make / imprint by burning to impress indelibly, brand on
disco, -ere, didici	to acquire knowledge of, learn, get to know
credo, -ere, -idi, -itum	to commit, entrust; trust, rely on to give credence to, believe
committo, -ittere, -isi, -issum	to bring together, join, connect; entrust to
caveo, -ere, cavi, -tum	to take precautions, be aware, take care (w. acc. or *ab* + abl.) to guard against, beware of
pulcher, -chra, -chrum	pleasing, beautiful; excellent, fine morally beautiful, honourable, noble
beneficium, -(i)i, n.	service, kindness; favour
gratus, -a, -um	grateful, thankful; welcome, popular
gloriosus, -a, -um	boastful, vainglorious; glorious, illustrious
occîdo, -dere, -di, -sum	to cause the death of, kill, slaughter

§ 118: Here I Stand. I Can Do Naught Else

Certatim posthac, mihi crede, ad hoc opus curretur neque occasionis tarditas exspectabitur. respice, quaeso, aliquando rem publicam, M. Antoni; quibus ortus sis, non quibuscum vivas, considera. mecum, ut voles: redi cum re publica in gratiam. sed de te tu videris; ego de me ipse profitebor. defendi rem publicam adulescens, non deseram senex: contempsi Catilinae gladios, non pertimescam tuos. quin etiam corpus libenter obtulerim, si repraesentari morte mea libertas civitatis potest, ut aliquando dolor populi Romani pariat quod iam diu parturit!

Study Questions:
- What tense is *curretur*?
- Why are *ortus sis* and *vivas* in the subjunctive?
- Parse *considera*.
- How are we to construe *mecum*?
- Parse *voles*.
- Parse *redi*.
- Parse *videris*.
- Parse *defendi*.
- Parse *obtulerim* and explain the mood.

Stylistic Appreciation:
- What is the rhetorical effect of the impersonal passive *curretur*?
- How does Cicero pile pressure on Antony?

Discussion Points:
- What do you think of Cicero's self-promotion, i.e. that he has led a life devoted to selfless service to the state?
- Would you sacrifice your life for the welfare of the state?
- What do you make of Cicero's birth imagery?

certatim (adv.)	with rivalry, in competition, emulously
posthac (adv.)	from this time, from now on, hereafter
occasio, -onis, f.	convenient or favourable circumstances; the right or appropriate moment
tarditas, -atis, f.	slowness, delay
exspecto, -are, -avi, -atum	to wait for, await, expect
respicio, -icere, -exi, -ectum	to look round, look back; to turn one's thoughts or attention to to take notice of, heed
quaeso, -ere	to ask for, pray for, request
aliquando (adv.)	at some time or other; sometimes (in commands) now at last
orior, -iri, -tus	to rise, emerge, arise; to come into existence, be born (of persons) to be born (of), be descended (from)
gratia, -ae, f.	favour, goodwill, kindness, friendship
in gratiam redire	to become reconciled
profiteor, -iteri, -essus	to state openly, declare, avow to promise, guarantee, lay claim to
defendo, -dere, -di, -sum	to ward off, fend off; defend, protect
desero, -ere, -ui, -tum	to forsake, leave, abandon; part company
contemno, -nere, -psi, -ptum	to regard with contempt, despise
pertimesco, -escere, -ui	to become very scared of
quin etiam (adv.)	yes, and...; and furthermore
libenter (adv.)	with pleasure, willingly, gladly
offero, -rre, obtuli, oblatum	to put in the path of, expose to; to present, provide, supply; offer
repraesento, -are, -avi, -atum	to give immediate effect to; to present to view, manifest to bring back into the present, revive
pario, -ere, peperi, partum	to give birth to, bear, produce, bring forth
parturio, -ire, -ivi	to be on the point of giving birth; be in labour to be pregnant with

§ 119: Give Me Liberty or Give Me Death!

Etenim si abhinc annos prope viginti hoc ipso in templo negavi posse mortem immaturam esse consulari, quanto verius nunc negabo seni! mihi vero, patres conscripti, iam etiam optanda mors est, perfuncto rebus eis quas adeptus sum quasque gessi. duo modo haec opto, unum ut moriens populum Romanum liberum relinquam — hoc mihi maius ab dis immortalibus dari nihil potest — alterum ut ita cuique eveniat ut de re publica quisque mereatur.

Study Questions:

- What kind of accusative is *annos … viginti*?
- Parse *consulari* and *seni* and explain how they fit into the syntax of the sentence.
- What kind of ablative is *quanto*?
- What kind of dative is *mihi*?
- Parse *perfuncto* and explain how it fits into the sentence.
- Identify and explain the case of *hoc* (*mihi maius*).

Stylistic Appreciation:

- Discuss the effect of the numerous reiterations of the same word (*negavi / negabo*; *mortem immaturam / mors*; *optanda … est / opto*; *cuique / quisque*) in the final paragraph.
- Explore Cicero's pregnant use of the letter '*m*' in this paragraph (*mortem immaturam*; *mihi* [… *optanda*] *mors* [*est*]; *moriens*; *mihi maius* [*ab dis*] *immortalibus*). How does sound reinforce sense?

Discussion Points:

- Did Cicero reap what he sowed?
- Should Antony have got the message?

abhinc (adv.)	back from the present, ago
prope (adv.)	near, nearby; close; almost
viginti (indeclinable)	twenty
nego, -are, -avi, -atum	to say (that … not); deny
immaturus, -a, -um	unripe, immature; premature, untimely
consularis, -is, -e	of or proper to a consul (as noun) former consul, a man of consular rank
vere (adv.)	really, truly; correctly, truthfully
senex, -is, m.	an old man
opto, -are, -avi, -atum	to desire, pray for
perfungor, -gi, -ctus	to carry through / discharge one's part (in perfect + abl.) to have finished one's part, be done (with)
adipiscor, -ipisci, -eptus	to overtake, catch up with, arrive at, attain to obtain, acquire, achieve, win, secure
gero, -rere, -ssi, -stum	to bear, carry; perform; conduct
modo (adv.)	not more than, only, just
evenio, -enire, -eni, -entum	to come out, emerge (w. dative) to fall by lot, be allotted (to); happen to

mereo, -ere, -ui, -itum
   mereri bene / male (de) (deponent)
   mereri (de)
	to earn, procure, gain; deserve
	   to deserve well / ill of,
	   to behave (towards)

quisque, quaeque, quidque	each

COMMENTARY

 https://doi.org/10.11647/OBP.0156.04

§ 44: A Glance at Teenage Antony: Insolvent, Transgendered, Pimped, and Groomed

Since OCR invites us to parachute right into the middle of *Philippic 2*, here is a quick orientation of where exactly in the text we are when we reach § 44: after his opening statement (§§ 1–2) and his rebuttal of Antony's attack on him (§§ 3–41), Cicero spends the following two paragraphs inveighing against his adversary's skills as a public speaker, with particular reference to Antony's oratorical efforts in the period immediately after Caesar's assassination. This transitional section (§§ 42–43) helps to set up the second main part of the speech, which begins here in § 44: it features a prolonged and systematic assault on Antony. This portion is of prodigious length (§§ 44–114) and will bring us right up to the concluding peroration (§§ 115–19). Still, Cicero alleges at the end of § 43 that in detailing Antony's depravities he will proceed selectively, so as to have something in reserve for future jousts (*nec enim omnia effundam, ut, si saepius decertandum sit, ut erit, semper novus veniam*). Shortage of subject matter won't be a problem: after all, Antony's vices and misdeeds are legion (*quam facultatem mihi multitudo istius vitiorum peccatorumque largitur*).

One theme that offers continuity across §§ 40–44 is 'inheritance and bankruptcy'. Cicero concludes his self-defence by debunking Antony's slur that bequests do not come his way (§ 40: *hereditates mihi negasti venire*), before noting, at the beginning of § 42, that this line of attack is a bit rich coming from someone like Antony who refused to accept his father's estate because it was loaded with debts (*quamquam hoc maxime admiratus sum, mentionem te hereditatum ausum esse facere, cum ipse hereditatem patris non adisses*). Antony senior died debt-ridden around 71 BCE, when Antony junior was eleven or twelve years old, and Cicero chooses this shameful loss of family fortune as the point of departure for his obloquy in § 44. It enables him to suggest that Antony comes from a disreputable branch of the *gens Antonia* and lacks filial *pietas* on top (since he chose to disown his father). And it dovetails nicely into his main line of attack in the opening paragraph, Antony's shockingly disgraceful sex-life, including the willingness to earn money as a male prostitute before ending up as Curio's toy-boy.

Moment in time: This and the following three paragraphs (45–47) detail, or allude to, events that allegedly (! Cicero freely mixes fact and fiction) took place in the late 70s and early to late 60s BCE.

Visne igitur te inspiciamus a puero?: Cicero began the previous paragraph with a direct address to his wider (imaginary) audience (43: *at quanta merces rhetori data est! audite, audite, patres conscripti, et cognoscite rei publicae vulnera* — 'But what a fee was given to Antony's teacher in rhetoric! Hear, hear, senators, and learn about the wounds inflicted on the commonwealth!'). By contrast, he opens § 44 with a rhetorical question addressed specifically to Antony, who is also imagined in attendance: *vis* is the 2nd person singular of *volo, velle*, attached to which is the enclitic interrogative particle *-ne*. Verbs of will and desire are followed either by an accusative-plus-infinitive (*visne … nos te inspicere …?*) or a subordinate clause introduced by *ut* or *ne* — though 'when the idea of Wishing is emphatic, the simple Subjunctive, without *ut*, is employed' (Gildersleeve and Lodge 347). This is the construction here. In the English translation, an infinitive might be a good way of linking *vis* and *inspiciamus*: 'would you like us to examine you…?'

igitur: the conjunction here serves to introduce the promised topic: Antony's depravity (see *OLD* s.v. 4): 'So then'.

a puero: *puer* means 'boy', and the ablative phrase indicates a point of origin in time, i.e. 'from boyhood'.

Extra information:
The precise reference of Roman age-terms is often difficult to determine. In his dialogue *Cato Maior de Senectute* 33, Cicero outlines the 'race-course of life' as involving the following four stages:

- the weakness of childhood (*infirmitas puerorum*): c. 3–16 (following infancy?)
- the fierceness of youth (*ferocitas iuvenum*): c. 17–30
- the seriousness of settled age (*gravitas constantis aetatis*): c. 30s and 40s
- the maturity of old age (*senectutis maturitas*): c. 50s–

For further details, see Parkin (2003) and Cokayne (2003).

sic opinor: *sic* here means 'yes' and *opinor* in response to a question 'I think so'. Cicero answers his own rhetorical question with a colloquial affirmation that gives his discourse a snarky flavour: he clearly relishes the prospect of going through Antony's imaginary *CV*.

a principio ordiamur: *ordiamur* is an exhortative subjunctive ('Let us…'). The hiatus here, i.e. the collocation of vowels at the end of one word (*principi-o*) and the beginning of another (*o-rdiamur*), is unusual: in good prose style, 'the juxtaposition of the same long vowels should be avoided' (Kirchner 2007: 191). One is therefore left wondering whether Cicero here deliberately breaches stylistic conventions, perhaps to feign distaste at the material he is about to delve into. The phrase *a principio* reiterates and fortifies *a puero* in a mock-serious tone designed to suggest meticulous attention to detail, reminiscent of the *Sound-of-Music* principle 'Let's start at the very beginning, a very good place to start' or Lewis Carroll, *Alice in Wonderland*: '"Begin at the beginning", the King said, very gravely, "and go on till you come to the end: then stop"'. (And — nice irony — it must have been the cue for OCR to jump in here!)

tenesne memoria praetextatum te decoxisse?: another rhetorical question held in the 2nd person singular, again with the verb (*tenes*) upfront and the enclitic interrogative particle -*ne* tagged on. *tenes … memoria* (= *meministi*) introduces an indirect statement with *te* as subject accusative and the intransitive *decoxisse* as verb. ‖ *decoquo* is a culinary term, meaning 'to diminish the volume of a liquid by boiling (*coquo*) it down (*de*)'. Metaphorically, it was used to refer to squandering resources (the Latin equivalent to our 'to burn through money') as well as the outcome thereof: 'to become insolvent', which is its meaning here. The waste of Antony's patrimony and its toxic consequences are key themes in the paragraph, reinforced through lexical repetition: see *decoctoribus*, *decoxisse*. ‖ *praetextatum* stands in predicative position to *te*: 'when you (still) wore the *toga praetexta*', i.e. 'when you were a boy'. Cicero's use of *praetextatus* as age-label (rather than *puer, iuvenis,* or *adulescens*) prepares the ground for the sartorial satire to follow.

'patris', inquies, 'ista culpa est': Cicero imagines Antony's response to the charge of bankruptcy to be a 'It's all me dad's fault'. *inquies* is 2nd person singular future indicative active. ‖ The sentence well illustrates the power of dramatic word order. Stripped of rhetorical amplification, the Latin might read: *culpam esse patris dicet* ('He will say that it is the fault of his father'). Instead of any such bland and boring pronouncement, Cicero offers up a rhetorical gem. To start with, we get an instance of so-called *sermocinatio* or 'dialogue', as Cicero switches from direct address (*visne*...?) to impersonation:[1] he acts out what he imagines to be Antony's reply to the charge of insolvency. The use of direct (instead of indirect) speech adds drama to the occasion and also enables Cicero 'to perform Antony'. It further conveys the impression that Antony is under cross-examination, and what he (according to Cicero) comes up with in a moment of stress is not pretty: in a shocking act of shameless disloyalty, he blames his father. The exposed position of the genitive *patris*, further emphasized by the inset *inquies*, enacts Antony's willingness to leave his father hung out to dry, to deflect responsibility from himself.

patris: Rome's political culture, with its emphasis on the emulation of forebears and commitment to the preservation of ancestral customs (*mores maiorum*), was much invested in the figure of the father and the notion of paternal discipline (*patria potestas*), in particular their role in transmitting standards of behaviour and adherence to social norms across the generations. Cicero here intimates that Antony, lacking a proper father figure, was set adrift early on with disastrous consequences. His biological father, the disreputable Marcus Antonius Creticus, was strikingly unsuccessful as a military commander, had a nasty reputation for large-scale provincial exploitation, and died in bankruptcy. And his stepfather, Publius Cornelius Lentulus Sura, joined Catiline's conspiracy and was among those executed by Cicero in

---

1   For the technique of impersonation see *Rhetorica Ad Herennium* 4.65; *Silva Rhetoricae,* http://rhetoric.byu.edu/: 'Speaking dramatically in the first person for someone else, assigning language that would be appropriate for that person's character (and for one's rhetorical purpose)'.

63 BCE. (In § 14, Cicero explicitly blames Antony for choosing Lentulus as role model rather than a morally more upright relative; cf. also § 17.)

ista culpa: there is a hidden agenda in Cicero's use of the demonstrative pronoun *ista*. It implies a sense of relief, coupled with an admission of guilt, on Antony's part: *in this particular instance*, he is able to shift the blame onto someone else, and does so gladly even if it amounts to a betrayal of his progenitor; yet the over-emphatic demonstrative suggests a guilty conscience — a nervous awareness that further charges are bound to stick. In a mere five words, Cicero thus sketches out a nuanced character profile of Antony: fretting, disloyal, guilty, stupid.

concedo: *concedo* means something like 'granted' and is designed to surprise: why does Cicero concede a point to the opponent? But as we read on, it becomes apparent that the quasi-conciliatory tone in fact prepares the way for a sucker punch:

etenim est pietatis plena defensio: *etenim* sets up the sarcastic quip that Cicero only lets him off the hook since Antony anyway impales himself: his imaginary line of defence (shifting blame onto his father) manifests a shocking lack of *pietas*. Cicero again uses extraordinary word order to highlight the key lexeme: just as *patris*, the genitive *pietatis* takes pride of place. The correlated fronting of both *patris* and *pietatis* (words further linked by alliteration) energizes Cicero's sarcasm stylistically. (Contrast the 'unmarked' variant: *etenim defensio est plena pietatis*.) Antony here violates a fundamental Roman value: 'the father / son relationship was bilateral in nature, including devotion and affection on the part of the sons and consideration and respect on the part of the fathers. The Latin word *pietas*, used to describe moral and social duty of both sons and fathers, encapsulated this dual set of emotional obligations' (Cantarella 2003: 286).

etenim: the conjunction is used for 'adding something in explanation or corroboration of what has been said or implied' (*OLD* s.v.).

plena: for *plenus* + genitive see Gildersleeve & Lodge 239: 'Of adjectives of *Fulness*, with the Genitive, only *plenus*, *repletus*, *inops*, and *inanis* are classical and common; … *Plenus* occurs very rarely with the Abl. in Cicero and Caesar, more often in Livy'.

**illud [est] tamen audaciae tuae quod sedisti in quattuordecim ordinibus,
cum esset lege Roscia decoctoribus certus locus constitutus, quamvis
quis fortunae vitio, non suo decoxisset**: the main verb of the sentence
(*est*) is understood. *audaciae tuae* is a genitive of characteristic. The
substantive *quod*-clause (in the indicative: Cicero claims to be reporting a
fact) elaborates on — and stands in apposition to — *illud*. The subsequent
cum- and *quamvis*-clauses explain why Cicero objects to Antony having
taken a seat in the theater in the front fourteen rows. At Rome, 'seating
arrangements at the games were a reflection and reaffirmation of the
social hierarchy' (Edwards 1993: 111), and in 67 BCE the tribune of
the people Lucius Roscius Otho passed the *lex Roscia theatralis*, which
reserved the first fourteen rows (the *quattuordecim ordines*) behind the
orchestra in the Roman theatre for the 'knights' (*equites*) — a social rank
based in part on the assessment of wealth, i.e. property and possessions
worth at least 400,000 sesterces. (We play the same games of privilege,
eg John Lennon at the Royal Variety Performance, 'For our last number
I'd like to ask your help. Would the people in the cheaper seats clap your
hands? And the rest of you, if you'll just rattle your jewelry'.) Roscius'
law stipulated that those whose fortune dipped below this level lose the
privilege of special seating — even if (as Cicero goes on to stress in the
quamvis-clause) the insolvency was not their fault, but a stroke of bad
luck. See further Rawson (1987: 102).

audaciae tuae: *audacia* ('recklessness'), which might be a useful quality
in battle, 'is exclusively negative in Cicero's works' (McDonnell 2006:
59). *audax* and *audacia* are common slurs in Cicero's political invective,
referring generally 'to those who oppose the *boni* with disregard for the
law' (Grillo 2015: 124), with reference to Wirszubski (1961) and Weische
(1966: 28–33), and Cicero, *de Inventione* 1.5); yet 'the intensive application
within [the second speech against Catiline] associates them specifically
with the conspirators' (Hutchinson 2005: 185). In *Philippic* 2, Cicero
comes back to the thematic link between Catiline and *audacia* right away,
calling Antony 'more reckless than Catiline' (*audacior quam Catilina*)
in the programmatic opening paragraph. *audacia* remains a hallmark
of Antony throughout the speech: see §§ 4 (*o incredibilem audaciam*), 9
(*audaciae tuae*), 19 (Antony takes pride in his *audacia*, though certain of
his seemingly reckless acts should rather be ascribed to his stupidity),
43 (*homo audacissime*), 64 (Antony's *audacia* tops that of everyone else),

68 (*o audaciam immanem*), 78 (*nequam hominem audacemque*), 90 (*audacia*). Here we might capture a sly dig at Antony's stepfather (see above on *patris*), who passed on his wicked disposition to his impressionable charge. Words 'of the *audeo, audax, audacia* family' also occur frequently in Roman comedy to refer to improper or outrageous behaviour: see Sussman (1998: 117, n. 8). The two frames of reference — political invective and comedy — are clearly not mutually exclusive.

decoctoribus certus locus constitutus: this is the first of three instances of the attribute *certus, -a, -um* in the paragraph, all mockingly alliterated. (In addition to *decoctoribus certus locus constitutus*, see *certa ... merces* and *cito Curio ... in matrimonio ... certo collocavit* below.) The collocation *certus locus* would seem to imply that Roscius' law, on top of depriving the insolvent of the privilege to sit with their rank, allocated them to a special area (of shame?), though our sources are silent on what that area might have been.

quamvis quis fortunae vitio, non suo [vitio] **decoxisset**: the law did not differentiate between those who became insolvent owing to circumstances beyond their control such as parental mismanagement (= *fortunae vitio*, where *fortuna* means something akin to 'bad luck') and those who were personally responsible for their family's loss of wealth.

sumpsisti virilem, quam statim muliebrem togam reddidisti: after dealing with one instance of teenage delinquency, Cicero moves on to the moment when Antony came of age, which in Rome was marked by the ritual change of the *toga praetexta* (the boyhood *toga*) for the *toga virilis* (the manhood *toga*). Cicero's syntax suggests that Antony instantly perverted the garment — turning it into something suitable for a person the exact opposite of a man with citizenship status, i.e. a woman (*mulier*) for sale (as the next sentence shows): the noun that *virilem* modifies, i.e. *togam*, which also serves as antecedent to the relative pronoun *quam*, has been sucked into the relative clause to keep close company with *muliebrem*: 'you assumed the toga of manhood, which you instantly turned into the outfit worn by female prostitutes'. This is humiliation not by cross-dressing but by trans-gendering: 'Accusations of men wearing women's clothing are a well-attested form of invective and there are repeated examples of this within Cicero's speeches. In this passage, however, it is not that Antony has made himself effeminate by wearing women's clothes, he has instead worn the *toga muliebris* and so has become a *scortum*, a prostitute' (Dixon 2014: 302). (In fact, Cicero puts it the other way around, claiming that Antony as soon as he came of age, prostituted himself and thereby transformed his brand-new *toga virilis*, which ought to have been a badge of pride, into a *toga muliebris*, a mark of shame.) 'Woman' is a common aspersion in the hyper-masculine, testosterone-fuelled world of Roman politics, which often coincides with charges of sexual licentiousness: in one of his speeches against Verres (2.2.192), for instance, Cicero suggests that it is impossible to find a man lazier and more cowardly, more a man among women and a contemptible woman among men than his adversary (*homo inertior, ignavior, magis vir inter mulieres, impura inter viros muliercula proferri non potest*); and in the speech on his house (*de Domo sua* 139), his archenemy Clodius is said to have violated religious sensibilities by being a woman among men and a man among women (*contra fas et inter viros saepe mulier et inter mulieres vir*). Interestingly enough, Curio Pater is supposed to have quipped about Caesar that he was 'every woman's man and every man's woman' (Suetonius, *Life of Julius Caesar* 52.3: *omnium mulierum virum et omnium virorum mulierem*).

primo [eras] **vulgare scortum**: the original meaning of *scortum* is 'leather' or 'hide', but it is also a word for both male and female prostitute from Plautus onwards, presumably on account of a fantasised connection between the working of leather and sexual intercourse: see Adams (1983), who also notes that *scortum* was a more pejorative term than *meretrix*.[2] So *scortum vulgare* = 'a whore — and a common one to boot'. (In fact, the underlying idea might be that the *scortum* is like an 'old boot', supposedly worn 'hard' — and worn out — by too much sex.) The practice of prostitution carried a heavy social stigma in republican Rome and included 'the exclusion of prostitutes and pimps from the senatorial order, the equestrian order, the roll of judges (*album iudicum*), the decurionate, and the army' — as well as a host of other civic disabilities (McGinn 1998: 26). The accusation of prostitution is a standard topos of political invective: 'Not surprisingly, prostitutes

---

2   See further Strong (2016), esp. 11: 'While Roman texts sometimes used *scortum* and
      meretrix interchangeably, *scortum* has a much stronger association with prostitutes
      of low status…'

provided fuel for the fires of Roman invective, both in the courtroom and out, and an accusation of prostitution was a handy weapon to use against both male and female opponents' (Williams 2010: 36). Cicero liked the slur. In the *pro Caelio*, he turns Clodia into a quasi-prostitute. In the speech on his house (*Dom.* 49), he calls her brother Clodius a *scortum populare* ('everybody's favourite slut') and in the speech for Sestius (*Sest.* 39) a *scurrarum locupletium scortum* ('a whore for rich idlers'). See also *in Catilinam* 2.6, where Cicero implies homoerotic bonds between Catiline and his fellow-revolutionaries. Many prostitutes, male or female, were slaves — a connection Cicero does not fail to make: see the subsequent paragraph.

primo: an adverb ('initially').

certa [erat] **flagitii merces nec ea** [merces erat] **parva**: having joined the oldest profession in the world in the attempt to restore the family's fortune, Antony (so Cicero suggests) made himself sexually available at a fixed rate (*certa … merces*), which amounted to a considerable sum (*nec ea parva*). The lexeme *merces* hints at the etymologically related term *meretrix* ('woman who earns, paid woman', from *mereo* 'to receive one's wage', 'earn', or, more specifically, 'to earn money by prostitution'); cf. also *a meretricio quaestu* in the following sentence.

flagitii: *flagitium* means 'disgrace', 'infamy' and can also refer to outrageous behaviour, esp. (as here) to a disgraceful act of sexual misconduct (*OLD* s.v. 4c). Cicero associates Antony with *flagitium* at various points throughout the oration: see §§ 24, 45, 47, 57, 58, 76 (+ 15 and 35 for the adjective *flagitiosus*).

sed cito Curio intervenit, qui te a meretricio quaestu abduxit et, tamquam stolam dedisset, in matrimonio stabili et certo collocavit: The blow-by-blow (cf. *statim, primo, cito*) of Cicero's 'travesty' reaches its coup de grâce: Curio comes to the rescue (*intervenit* is highly ironic), collecting (or 'abducting') Antony from plying his trade in Rome's red-light district and making an honest wo/man out of him: the *stola* was the garb worn by legally married Roman matrons. The elements of this scenario are easy to parallel in New Comedy: 'Like the young lover in numerous Roman comedies, Curio rescues his beloved from the threat of a life of prostitution to make her his wife' (Edwards 1993: 64).

Curio: C. Scribonius Curio (c. 84–49 BCE) is a curious character and constant companion throughout the first half of the speech (see §§ 3, 4, 11, 45–46, 48, 50–51, 58). Born just a couple of years before Antony, he became quaestor in 54, tribune of the people in 50, and praetor in 49, before dying in the same year fighting on Caesar's side against King Juba I (a supporter of Pompey) in North Africa. Like his father he was well-connected and a reasonably talented orator, being in cahoots with, or entertaining friendly relations with, such varied characters as Antony, Clodius (whom he supported in the context of the Bona Dea scandal), and Caesar (quite belatedly, after years of opposition, persuaded, it seems, by a handsome financial reward). In a letter to Atticus from 13 February 61, in which he details resistance against the senatorial effort to pass a bill against Clodius on account of his religious transgression at the Bona Dea festival, Cicero refers to 'the whole Catilinarian gang with little Miss Curio at their head' (*Att.* 1.14.5 = 14 SB: *totus ille grex Catilinae duce filiola Curionis*). Despite the fact that Cicero did not always see eye to eye with Curio *filius* or Curio *pater* (for whom see § 45 below), he entertained friendly relations with the family, the occasional bust-up notwithstanding (Cicero's letters *ad Familiares* 2.1–7 are addressed to Curio Junior).

Cicero drops hints about the relationship between Antony and Curio from the end of the exordium onwards. In response to Antony's accusation that Cicero turned his back on him after an initial phase of support, Cicero rejects the idea that young Antony was ever under his influence: however salutary that may have been, Curio would not have tolerated any such interference (*Phil.* 2.3):

> at enim te in disciplinam meam tradideras — nam ita dixisti — domum meam ventitaras. ne tu, si id fecisses, melius famae, melius pudicitiae tuae consuluisses. sed neque fecisti nec, si cuperes, tibi id per C. Curionem facere licuisset.

> [You had given yourself over to my instruction (as you put it), had frequented my house. If indeed you had done so, you would have taken better care of your reputation and your virtue. But you neither did so nor, had you wished, would Gaius Curio have let you.]

As Shackleton Bailey (1982: 219) points out, we are here dealing with 'a hit at Antony's subservience to a possessive lover'. This opening gesture to their smutty affair (as filthy as fabricated) finds full elaboration in §§ 44–46.

qui te a meretricio quaestu abduxit: *meretricius quaestus* is synonymous with *flagitii merces* in the previous sentence. *abducere* can imply seduction: Cicero relishes the paradox that Curio 'seduces' Antony the 'seductress' away from his métier of seduction.

tamquam stolam dedisset: *tamquam* introduces a comparative clause, in which Cicero is speaking figuratively and counterfactually (hence the subjunctive): 'as though he had given you a *stola*', i.e. 'as if he had turned you into an honourable woman'.

in matrimonio stabili et certo collocavit: at the moment Antony is supposed to become a *vir*, he loses the plot of growing up. His period as a free-lance prostitute segues into a 'stable' love affair with one particular suitor that resembles a proper marriage, thus completing the process of transforming Antony from fledgling man to full-blown woman.

By construing *collocare* with *in* + ablative, Cicero tweaks the standard idiom *in matrimonium collocare* = 'to give in marriage' (*OLD* s.v. 9). Here the meaning of *collocare* is rather 'to put / place (into a situation or condition)': *OLD* s.v. 7. Part of the fun here is that he describes the relationship with full irony as a proper marriage rather than using another term that would have flagged up the perverse nature of the liaison, such as *matrimonium iniustum*, a union in which the partners wanted to be married but lacked *conubium*, i.e. 'the capacity to marry legally', or *concubinatus*, partners living together but with one or both lacking the desire to be married (see Treggiari 1991: 49–52 or Hersch 2010: 19–22). The repetition of *certus* reinforces the irony: Antony has moved from selling his sexual favours for a *fixed* price tag to a *firm* and stable marriage (though, as the next paragraph shows, his mercenary motives remained very much alive).

* * *

Digging Deeper: Fashion and Fornication in Late-Republican Rome

In his opening salvo, Cicero traces Antony's transition from childhood to wo/manhood via a series of references to Roman dress, which he correlates with hints at various sexual depravities. To appreciate the invective punch in the story he tells about this formative period of Antony's life, we thus need to take a closer look at 'fashion' and 'fornication' in late-republican Rome.

Fashion

The first item on display in Cicero's fashion show is unisex child-wear (... *praetextatum te* ..., a reference to the *toga praetexta*, worn by citizen children of both sexes), before gender-specific teenage attire gets showcased: the garment of manhood, the *toga virilis*, makes an all-too-brief appearance, with Antony, seemingly still half in déshabillé, dropping it again to dress himself up in truly grown-up finery, the *toga muliebris* or prostitute's outfit. After this excursion into the *haute couture* of the demi-monde, the show concludes with a return to respectability (of sorts): in his final appearance on Cicero's catwalk Antony sports fashion suited for a properly married woman, the *stola*.

As we do today, the Romans used attire to assert and promote values and distinctions — not least of age, gender, social rank, and civic status. As Edmondson (2008: 22) explains:

> Roman citizens, therefore, both male and female, were marked by their entitlement to wear what was construed as distinctively Roman civic dress, or, to use Suetonius' term, *habitus patrius et civilis* (*Calig.* 52.1; cf. *Tib.* 13.1). By wearing the *toga* or *stola* on civic occasions, they demonstrated their membership in a defined and bounded community, the *gens Romana*; they laid claim to a shared Roman identity and the cultural traditions with which each of these garments was invested. Roman public dress helped to delineate precisely what it meant to be Roman.

This is especially true since the use of the *toga* was restricted to Roman citizens: 'the right to wear the toga was withheld by law from non-citizens, foreigners as well as slaves, rendering it an exclusive badge of citizenship and the sartorial manifestation of Roman identity' (George 2008: 95). In Virgil's *Aeneid*, Jupiter famously calls the Romans 'masters of the world and the people who wear the toga' (1.286: *Romanos, rerum dominos gentemque togatam*). The outfit thus included and excluded. And despite Augustus' edict that all citizens are to wear the *toga* when visiting the Forum (Suetonius, *Life of Augustus* 40.5), we ought not to imagine that the garment erased (rather than reinforced) social distinctions also *within* Rome's civic community:

> Togas, like the Romans who wore them, were not created equal; citizenship at Rome did not entail membership in an undifferentiated collective, but in a highly stratified social system in which elements on visible display such as dress assumed enormous significance. As a powerful cultural symbol, the toga was a means to an end whose significance varied according to status. The wealthy embraced its positive connotations of civic engagement, or moral righteousness, and, more fundamentally, of Roman identity as part of their social entitlement. Other status groups, clients and others, who profited less easily from it, could regard the toga more realistically, without the roseate glow of social privilege (George 2008: 107).

In order to see how Antony manages to pervert the signifying codes of Roman dress in Cicero's sartorial satire, we need to have a look at the ideologies woven into the fabric of all the garments that Cicero parades before us. For each was designed to broadcast a specific meaning and message about its wearer.[3]

(i) The *toga praetexta*

Cicero's first gesture to dress comes in the form of the age-label *praetextatum* ('while you wore the *toga praetexta*', i.e. 'while you were still a boy'). The prepubescent dress was unisex, or, to put this differently, boys too wore purple:

---

3   Further bibliography includes Heskel (1994), esp. 140–41 on *Phil.* 2.44: Vout (1996), who encourages us to 'think about the toga not as a **garment** but as a **cultural symbol**'; Dyck (2001); Olson (2003); the papers collected in Cleland, Harlow, and Llewellyn-Jones (2005); Davies (2005); and the papers collected in Harlow and Nosch (2014). For a recent, sophisticated study of body, dress, and identity in ancient Greece, see Lee (2015), and for a trailblazing modern take on 'the language of clothes' see Lurie (1981/2000), a Pulitzer Prize winning publication 'about a subject everyone is obsessed with — especially those who claim they aren't' (as it says on the cover) — or Jennifer Baumgartner, *You Are What You Wear: What Your Clothes Reveal About You*, Da Capo Press, 2012.

> Roman boys and girls were distinguished from adult Roman citizens
> by their wearing of a purple-bordered toga (the *toga praetexta*). Such
> *togae praetextae* marked children out early as members of the Roman
> civic body and helped to socialize them into the traditions of their
> community, but interestingly did not differentiate them by gender.
> Before puberty their incipient Romanness, their membership in the
> *gens togata*, was much more crucial than whether they were male or
> female (Edmondson 2008: 26).

Children were not the only ones who wore the *toga praetexta*; it was also
the garment of those with special responsibilities for the (religious) well-
being of the commonwealth (generals, magistrates, some priests and
priestesses) and other social groups when involved in the performance
of certain sacrifices. The garment therefore possessed a 'sacral
aura' — which extended to its use by children, protecting them from
any kind of (polluting) sexual overture: 'the *toga praetexta* functioned
as an insignia of free-birth and free condition (*insignia ingenuitatis et
libertatis*) to advise adults to avoid any expression of sexuality of any
kind toward or around the child' (Sebesta 2005: 115), who goes on to
explain the sacred protection that the garment was meant to extend to
its wearer (116):

> That the *praetexta* indicated a special social category is shown by its
> etymological meaning 'woven first / woven before'. This etymology
> derives from the weaving technique required by the warp-weighted
> loom originally used by the Romans. ... As the verb *praetexere* is used
> in the sense of protecting and defending ..., so the *praetexta* denoted
> the weaving of a religious garment, as well as protecting the act of its
> weaving from religious pollution by warning by-standers to refrain from
> sacrilegious words, gestures, or activity.

(ii) The *toga virilis*

Around the age of sixteen or seventeen, i.e. after reaching sexual
maturity, a Roman male would undergo a ritual exchange of clothing
that signified his entry into adulthood:

> The ritual exchange of the *bulla* [sc. the protective amulet of the freeborn
> boy] and *toga praetexta* for the *toga virilis* was a defining moment in the
> life of a freeborn Roman boy as it marked the end of his boyhood and the
> beginning of his adult years. In setting aside the *bulla* and *praetexta*, the
> boy divested himself of the symbols of his boyhood, which represented a

degree of venerability and vulnerability as well. Donning the *toga virilis*, he assumed a new identity, his white toga communicating his achievement of adulthood with its attendant freedoms (Dolanksy 2008: 58).

As its attribute suggests, the *toga vir-ilis* marked its wearer as a *vir*, a lexeme that has a range of meanings. Most basically, it refers to an 'adult male', but it can also mean 'husband' or 'soldier': 'The term also designates a position of authority and responsibility: the adult is enfranchised, while the child (or slave) is not; the man rules his wife in the household; the soldier is the defender of the safety of the state. In short, the term evokes more than mere gender' (Gunderson 2000: 7). Gunderson goes on to cite Maria Wyke (1994: 136): 'In the practices of the Roman world, the surface of the male body is thus fully implicated in definitions of power and civic responsibility'.

Nothing is further removed from the image of the *vir* as an independent agent performing roles of responsibility within the household (as *paterfamilias*) and the commonwealth (as patron, magistrate, general, or senator) than the pathic passivity of a professional prostitute, which Cicero claims Antony became when reaching adulthood. Arguably, Cicero's invective here taps into deep-seated Roman anxieties that 'growing up' can go awry as he homes in on a key moment in the journey of an upper-class Roman youth from boyhood to adulthood: upon assuming the *toga virilis*, he would have started a period of 'apprenticeship' in civic life under the guidance of an older male, often a close friend of the family, the so-called *tirocinium fori*. But the charge was potentially vulnerable (or perceived to be vulnerable) to sexual power-play that would compromise his status and reputation as a *vir*, though it is important to emphasize that the Romans did not evolve practices of homoerotic bonding *à la Grecque* (see further below on fornication). As Stroup (2010: 143) explains:

> Cicero's acerbic reference to the *toga muliebris* — the 'woman's toga' prescribed for registered prostitutes [NB: that is uncertain: see below] — hints at the pathic connotations that might have accompanied any ritual training of the young by the old .... The goal of this passage, and indeed the whole of the *Philippics*, is to destroy Antony's character by any means necessary. But this is no empty vituperation: the harsh innuendo of the *tirocinium* joke would fall flat did it not capitalize on an already deeply embedded social understanding of the act as one that, if bungled, could effectively 'unmake' the men it sought to produce.

In the *pro Caelio*, Cicero struggles mightily with the problem that the defendant, a former protegé of his, had (so far) not really turned out the way he was supposed to given Cicero's educational influence.

(iii) The *toga muliebris*

Cicero pretends that Antony, right after doffing the *toga praetexta* for the *toga virilis*, turned it into a *toga muliebris*, which here clearly refers to a garment associated with prostitutes. Given that *Philippic* 2.44 is our 'earliest clear and explicit testimony that the prostitute's hallmark was a *toga*' (McGinn 1998: 159) it is not easy to reconstruct the cultural norms and practices that enabled this invective punch — since it is difficult to judge how much can be built on the Ciceronian evidence. As McGinn goes on to say, 'the point of the remark concerning the *muliebris toga* assumes the exclusive identification of the wearing of the "female" toga with prostitutes' (159). A note of caution is in order here: 'Given Cicero's masterful use of Roman Comedy in his rhetoric, his reference to the prostitute's *toga* does not rule out comic usage as the source of the practice but proves nothing by itself' (159–60). Further (if later) evidence that associates prostitutes with the wearing of the *toga* includes Horace, *Satires* 1.2.61–63 and 80–82 (see the discussion in Gowers (2012: 104–05); cf. Dixon (2014: 302–04) for a slightly more skeptical view of the evidence), Tibullus 3.16.3–4, and Martial 2.39 (with Vout 1996: 215). But it remains unclear, especially for Cicero's times, to what extent the donning of a (darkened?) *toga* by prostitutes — as Dixon (2014: 302–04) notes, a rather impractical garment in which to ply their trade — was a social norm (or even legally enforced) or rather proverbial (akin to the idiom 'to wear the trousers').

(iv) The *stola*

If Roman boys when coming of age exchanged the *toga praetexta* for the *toga virilis* and entered public life, Roman girls had no such career prospects. For them, the defining watershed in their transition from childhood to adulthood was getting married (often in their early teens) — a change of status that also coincided with a change in clothes, the donning of the so-called *stola*: 'The *stola* indicated that the wearer was married in a *iustum matrimonium* (a legal marriage between two citizens) and was therefore a mark of honor, a way to distinguish sexual and social rank in broad fashion' (Olson 2008: 27). As Edmondson (2008: 24) explains, 'the dress of the matron was designed to shield its wearer both physically and morally from the prying gaze of disreputable males who might impugn her chastity'. The dress carried associations of chastity — Antony has stopped whoring around town, now that he has become Curio's lawfully wedded wife.

Fornication

Historically speaking, Greek and Roman attitudes to sexual matters have often been a significant source of embarrassment for classical educators and scholars alike, to the point that they often gingerly sidestepped or even censored the evidence. Over the past few decades, however, the rich visual and verbal legacy of ancient erotics has become a vibrant field of study, sweeping away the inhibitions of earlier centuries. First impulses for serious scholarly study of the historical nature of sexual experience came from feminist thought and practice in the 1960s and 1970s. Then, in 1976, the French savant Michel Foucault published the first instalment of his multi-volume *History of Sexuality* (*The Will to Knowledge / La volonté de savoir*) with a focus on the institutional and discursive construction of sexual experience in the early modern period. Foucault argued that sexuality is not a given, something one is born with; rather sexualities get formed within specific cultural contexts. Sexual preferences (and prejudices) thus emerge at least in part as the product of socio-historical and cultural circumstances. This means, among other things, that seemingly identical acts may have radically different meanings from one culture to the next — as well as within any one culture. An early case study of this phenomenon was *Greek Homosexuality* (first published in 1978) by the British Hellenist Kenneth Dover. He showed that the Greeks cultivated certain forms of (male) same-sex desire that defy our categorical distinction between 'homosexuality' and 'heterosexuality'. The volumes by Foucault and Dover became landmark publications, not least since other scholars soon intertwined the works and thereby amplified their arguments. Dover's work was also one of the inspirations behind Michel Foucault's second and third volumes of his *History of Sexuality*, which appeared in 1984 and looked at Greek texts from the fifth-century BCE and the early imperial period (2/3rd century CE). Foucault is particularly keen on highlighting discontinuities between ancient and modern ways of construing the sphere of the erotic (including such categories as sex and gender, sexual preferences, sexual practices, and associated discourses of morality and desire etc.).[4]

For some time, ancient Rome played second fiddle as scholars focused on the Greek experience; but from the 1990s onwards a series of studies by Amy Richlin and Craig Williams (among others) began to redress the balance.[5] As Martha Nussbaum (2010: xiii) puts it:

> First published in 1999, Craig Williams' *Roman Homosexuality* does for the Romans what Dover did for the Greeks. ... Williams argues convincingly that for Romans over quite a long period spanning the republic and the early empire, same-sex desire was regarded as perfectly ordinary and unproblematic — for males. ... A freeborn Roman male would be expected in the normal course of things to desire other males and to act on this desire — in contexts carefully restricted by the status of the parties. Sex (on the part of males) with male (and female) slaves or prostitutes was seen as unproblematic, even for married men — though wives at times complained. Sex with freeborn males, by contrast, was strongly discouraged. Thus same-sex acts typically involved asymmetrical power relations.

The same principle of historical specificity applies — which means that the Roman approaches to erotic experience differed in important ways from those found in ancient Greece (and our own). Thus no culture of pederasty developed in Rome that revolved around the relationship between a young freeborn male and an older male companion; but like the Greeks, the Romans tended to associate masculinity quite forcefully with performing penetration (which entailed the inverse corollary, i.e. the shameful loss of masculinity if one suffered penetration).[6]

When Cicero impugns Antony as Curio's toy boy (or lawfully married wife), he thus draws on his culture's normative preconceptions

---

4   Further readings include Thorp (1992), Weeks (1991) (2001), Davidson (1998) (2001) (2007).

5   See Richlin (1983/1992) (1991) (1992b) (1993) and Williams (1999/2010), further Edwards (1993), the papers in Hallet and Skinner (1997), Clarke (1998), Skinner (2005), Langlands (2006), Vout (2013), and Chrystal (2015).

6   On penetration see e.g. Richlin (1992) xviii and, more recently, Kamen and Levin-Richardson (2015). For the notion of masculinity in contemporary culture, see for instance the papers in Adams and Savran (2002) and Whitehead and Barrett (2001).

about gender (masculinity) and sexual experience, casting his opponent as the lowest of the low: a man who revels in the role of passive partner in homoerotic encounters (the Greek term for this is *cinaedus*), which suggests that he has lost any claim to being a man: 'The ultimate degradation of the passive partner lies in equating not only his behavior but also his sex to that of a woman; later in the same speech, Curio is described as Antonius' husband (*vir*; *Phil.* 2.50)'.[7] Cicero's focus on what Antony does with his body has a political discontent. Throughout the speech, he pushes an analogy between the physical body and the social body: a depraved individual, who indulges in a repulsive lifestyle and detestable practices will infect the body politic, the civic community conceived as a corporeal entity:

> This charge, which would read as libellous in our own culture, offers Cicero a way to insult and explain simultaneously. His portrayal of Antony as decadent and soft is tied inextricably to what Cicero sees as his moral and political failings. *Mollitia* is not an excuse, but an analysis: surely a man this degenerate and wrong-headed must desire to engage in the worst of sexual depravities. His status as *cinaedus* is deftly tied to lack of piety and financial profligacy (Manwell 2010: 115).[8]

Cicero was not the only one who pandered to such prejudices: Antony and his brother Lucius accused Octavian of the same thing (prostituting himself to Julius Caesar and Aulus Hirtius).[9]

---

7   Corbeill (1996: 149). See also Edwards (1993: 64).
8   See further Langlands (2006: 306): 'Antony allowed himself to come under the influence of the very worst kind of men, with the inevitable consequences for his sexual and then civic development'. Kelly (2014) explores the portrayal of Antony (and his questionable but also alluring masculinity) in modern popular culture, in particular the cinema.
9   Suetonius, *Life of Augustus* 68–69.

§ 45: Desire and Domesticity: Antony's Escapades as Curio's Toy-Boy

At the end of the previous paragraph, we left Antony seemingly safely 'married' to a contemporary of his, young Curio, who is said to have transformed the scoundrel from a disreputable prostitute into a honourable wife. But this touching scene of domestic bliss is not destined to last as Cicero moves on to explore the corrosive impact of the 'marriage' on the Curio-family. Two interrelated semantic fields dominate the paragraph: sexual passion (*libidinis causa, hortante libidine, flagitia, amore ardens, desiderium*); and 'the Roman household'. The latter includes references to architectural features (*limen, per tegulas*), ways and means of exit (*eiecit*) and entry (*intrares, demitterere*), and furniture (*in lecto*). More importantly, Cicero relies on the household as an ideological institution: it is the place of residence of the Roman *familia*, with the *paterfamilias* as *dominus* exercising his *patria potestas*, i.e. the (legal) power he held over the other members of his household, such as wife, children (cf. *filius*), or slaves (cf. *puer*). The *patresfamilias* are in many ways the domestic analogues to the senators (called *patres conscripti*) in the civic sphere; and breakdown of domestic discipline and dissolute morals at home were thought to impact on the fitness to perform public duties in the service of the commonwealth.

Cicero already lamented Antony's pollution of hallowed property through sexual mischief in the opening portion of the speech, when he portrayed him as 'wallowing in every kind of vice in a virtuous house [that of Pompey the Great, which Antony acquired when it was put up for sale after Pompey's defeat and death in 48 BCE], exhausted by drink and debauchery' (*Phil.* 2.6: ... *cum omnis impuritates pudica in domo cotidie susciperes vino lustrisque confectus*). In § 45, we get the youthful prelude to this more recent outrage. The scenario Cicero conjures up features plot elements of romantic New Comedy, suitably blackened, with the youthful libertine (Curio Junior) and his lover (Antony) running foul of Curio Senior, who, playing the strict father familiar from the comic stage, repeatedly chucks his son's homeboy out of the house — to no avail. Antony keeps climbing straight back in over the roof, fired up by lust and lucre, and finally causes the *paterfamilias* to undergo a psychological breakdown that reduces him to a whimpering wretch unwilling to get out of bed.

And who is called upon to clean up the mess? Cicero himself. When the time came for Curio Junior to fess up that he also stood surety for Antony for the sweet sum of six million sesterces that he in turn needed to secure from his father, he turned to Cicero for support, confessing his undying love for Antony in the process. As Campanile (2017: 58) puts it:

> Soon we find ourselves right in the middle of a comedy: there is the golden-hearted prostitute who falls in love, a free-born maiden of noble and important origins forced by poverty into this trade (Mark Antony), along with the young tearaway who wants to marry her (Curio); then there is the *durus pater* (Curio Senior), who fails to comprehend how all this could have befallen his son and reacts violently, putting the 'maiden' out of the door (still Mark Antony), and then barring it with guards. ... The only thing missing here is a *mitis senex* who might act as a go-between. And sure enough he soon appears: Cicero, the old family friend who arrives on the scene and tries to make everyone see sense in order to restore peace to the family.

With Antony, then, (Greek) literature has come to (Roman) life — though despite Cicero's protestation that he has first-hand knowledge of the wayward affair, we should not take the sordid picture he paints of the Curio household at face value.

Likewise, the presence of 'comic scripts' ought not to be misconstrued to mean that we are just dealing with light-hearted fun. While the plot might derive from the genre of comedy, acting it out for real is highly scandalous (however entertaining). Antony compromises the integrity of the household as an architectural unit, threatens the relationship that forms the backbone of a Roman aristocratic family, i.e. that between father and son, and perverts the values that define Roman domestic life and discipline. Already in his youth, he emerges as an agent of destruction of anything sound and moral in Roman society. His infiltration of the Curio household results in its disintegration. He is a repugnant and toxic individual, morally unfit to be involved in affairs of state. The paragraph is both uproariously funny and deeply disturbing.

Nemo umquam puer emptus libidinis causa tam fuit in domini potestate quam tu [fuisti] **in** [potestate] **Curionis**: *puer* here has the technical sense of 'slave-boy', as Cicero compares Antony's 'marriage' to Curio to that of a boy bought for the single purpose of sexual gratification. *tam* and *quam* correlate the comparison; Cicero can afford to be elliptical in the *quam*-clause since the missing verb (*fuisti*) and noun (*potestate*) are easily supplied from what precedes. ‖ Slaves, considered property under Roman law, were almost entirely at the mercy of their masters, subject to physical punishment, sexual exploitation, torture, and execution. 'Neither society nor the law recognized slaves as legal persons: they belonged to their master, who could use them for his own sexual needs or hire them out for the pleasure of others' (Fantham 2011: 118) or, as Cantarella (1992: 99) puts it, 'the Roman *paterfamilias* was an absolute master, … he exercised a power outside any control of society and the state. In this situation why on earth should he refrain from sodomising his houseboys?' Within his invective agenda, the invitation to compare the relationship between Antony and Curio to the situation of a sex-slave does three things: it emasculates Antony (transforming him from a *vir* back into a *puer*); it relocates him from the highest to the lowest stratum of Roman society, turning a *civis* into a *servus*; and it reinforces the idea that he was the passive partner in the relationship. In the course of the paragraph, Cicero ups the ante: Antony and Curio are both animated by passion (*libido*) for each other; and Antony is as much enslaved to Curio financially and physically, as Curio is to Antony emotionally.

nemo ... puer: *nemo* is here used as an adjective modifying *puer* ('no slave-boy').

libidinis causa: the post-positive preposition *causâ* governs the genitive. The phrase is to be construed with the participle *emptus*: normal word order would be *puer libidinis causa emptus*. *libido* is inherently negative: it designates (excessive) lust and conveys the impression that whoever experiences it is in thrall to his sexual desires — rather than keeping such urges under control with his rational self.

in domini potestate: the reference here is to *patria potestas* of the *paterfamilias* or *dominus*. The legal power a Roman father had over his household was virtually absolute, including the so-called *ius vitae necisque* ('the power over life and death'). We need not — indeed should not — imagine that all Roman fathers were brutal authoritarians, ready to punish their offspring harshly at the slightest transgression. Real life is always more complex than ideological constructs, institutional norms, and legal arrangements. Nevertheless, the scope for drastic action existed and gave Cicero a frame of reference. Paternal discipline and filial obedience are at the heart of the Roman *domus* or *familia*, which was thought to form the backbone of the Roman commonwealth (the *res publica*).

quotiens te pater eius domu sua eiecit, quotiens custodes posuit ne limen intrares! cum tu tamen nocte socia, hortante libidine, cogente mercede, per tegulas demitterere: Cicero begins with two main clauses in asyndeton marked by anaphora (*quotiens ... eiecit, quotiens ... posuit*), followed by a negative purpose clause (*ne ... intrares*) and a temporal *cum*-clause (*cum ... demitterere*), which does not introduce a new topic but fleshes out the circumstances of the action given in the main clause, here with an adversative sense (cf. *tamen*), hence the subjunctive (Kühner-Stegmann II, 342; and cf. *Phil.* 13.19: *ingressus est urbem quo comitatu vel potius agmine! cum dextra sinistra gemente populo R. minaretur dominis, notaret domos, divisurum se urbem palam suis polliceretur* 'He entered the city, and with what a following, or rather line of battle! when, amid the groans on right and left of the Roman people, he threatened householders, marked their houses, and openly promised to portion out the city among his supporters').

pater eius: Curio Senior (or Curio *pater*) was born around 125 BCE, held the consulship in 76 (when Cicero was a candidate for the quaestorship), and celebrated a triumph probably four years later, in the wake of his proconsulship in Macedonia (75–72 BCE). Cicero praises him in his *pro lege Manilia* (delivered in 66) as one of four *consulares* supportive of the bill that would give Pompey the command against Mithridates (*Man.* 68). A passage in Cicero's dialogue *Brutus* (280) seems to suggest that Curio handed over responsibility for the training of his son in oratory to Cicero (McDermott 1972: 402) in the late 60s — just when relations hit a rough spot since Curio led the defence of Clodius who stood accused of disrupting the festival of the Bona Dea disguised in women's clothes. Cicero attacked the defendant together with his advocate in the senate in 61, in an invective speech entitled *in Clodium et Curionem*, and a written version of it leaked out inopportunely in 58, much to Cicero's consternation: he was in exile at the time and could ill afford to alienate a possible ally in his pitch for a recall (see Crawford 1984: 9–10). Despite the contretemps, Curio came to support Cicero's return to Rome and also proved himself a staunch opponent of Caesar before dying in 53 — though his death at least ensured that he did not have to witness his son joining Caesar in the run-up to the civil war (though might also have enabled it). For the most part, he comes across as a principled disciplinarian in our sources — very much in contrast to his extravagant and spendthrift offspring. But irrespective of his actual character, the role he plays here is that of a stock figure from New Comedy — the stern father vainly trying to impose discipline upon a wayward son.

domu sua eiecit: *domu sua* is an ablative of separation with *eiecit*. (Remember that *domus* is a fourth declension noun of feminine gender; the ablative singular is either *domo* or (as here) the archaic *domu*.)

nocte socia, hortante libidine, cogente mercede: Cicero uses three ablative phrases to specify how and why Antony managed to circumvent the measures of Curio Senior to keep him out of his house: he used the cover of darkness (*nocte socia*), egged on as he was by lust (*hortante libidine*) and the need for money (*cogente mercede*). Cicero varies the asyndetic tricolon, moving from a nominal ablative absolute consisting of two nouns (the non-existent participle of *sum, esse* needs to be supplied) in the first colon to present participles (*hortante, cogente*) and nouns (*libidine, mercede*) in the second and third.

hortante libidine, cogente mercede: note that Antony (according to Cicero) prostitutes himself for personal pleasure as well as material gain: he is in desperate financial straits, but also urged on by depraved lust.

per tegulas demitterere: *demitterere* is the alternative 2nd person singular imperfect subjunctive passive form of *demitto* (= *demittereris*), here perhaps best taken in a middle sense ('you let yourself down through the roof', trans. Shackleton Bailey). The scenario brings to mind a comparable scene in Terence's *Eunuch* where a mythological painting is described as follows (584–89, Chaerea speaking):

> ibi inerat pictura haec, Iovem
> quo pacto Danaae misisse aiunt quondam in gremium imbrem aureum.
> egomet quoque id spectare coepi; et, quia consimilem luserat
> iam olim ille ludum, impendio magis animus gaudebat mihi,
> deum sese in hominem convortisse atque in alienas tegulas
> venisse clanculum per impluvium fucum factum mulieri.

[There was the following painting: it depicted the story of how Jupiter sent a shower of gold into Danae's bosom. I began to look at it myself, and the fact that he had played a similar game long ago made me all the more excited: a god had turned himself into human shape, made his way by stealth on to another man's roof, and come through the skylight to play a trick on a woman (trans. Barsby).]

Barsby (1999: 197) explains the architecture involved: 'the *atrium* of a Roman house had a rectangular opening in the roof (*compluuium*) and a similarly shaped basin underneath to catch rainwater (*impluuium*)' — and it is this opening through which we ought to imagine Antony climbing back in.

quae flagitia domus illa diutius ferre non potuit: *quae* is a connecting relative (= *ea*). Cicero personifies the household (*domus illa*). ‖ It is not easy to see how this sentence fits into the argument, especially since its elimination would provide a much more seamless transition between the image of Antony entering secretly through the roof and Cicero's explication why he is so remarkably well informed about these shenanigans (*scisne...*). In addition, the claim *ferre non potuit* remains strangely inconsequential.

scisne me de rebus mihi notissimis dicere?: a reader might wonder how Cicero knows all these intimate details, and he preempts any skepticism by explaining how he acquired inside knowledge of what was most likely a freely invented (or at the very least richly embellished) scenario.

recordare tempus illud cum pater Curio maerens iacebat in lecto: *recordare* is the second person singular present imperative passive form of the deponent *recordor*, with *tempus illud* as accusative object. The phrase sets up a temporal *cum*-clause (in the indicative). *maerens* is a circumstantial participle ('grief-stricken'), correlating thematically and syntactically with *lacrimans* in the following sentence.

filius se ad pedes meos prosternens, lacrimans, te mihi commendabat: after Cicero has reduced Curio Senior to a state of emotional wretchedness, he turns his attention to the son. As noted above, *Brutus* 280 suggests that Curio had become part of Cicero's entourage in the late 60s BCE or as McDermott (1972: 402) puts it: 'Curio *filius* seems to have served a *tirocinium fori* with Cicero at about the time he was serving a *tirocinium libidinis* with Antonius'. He dates the interview mentioned here to 61 BCE or thereabouts: 'Plutarch's account of Antonius' association with Curio and Clodius (*Ant.*, 2, 3–4) and Antonius' departure for the east in 58 suggest a date for this interview not far from the time of the trial of Clodius' (401). *filius* correlates with *pater*, the son is in tears like his father (*lacrimans*, a circumstantial participle, correlates with *maerens*), and both father and son are prostrate (*iacebat in lecto* ~ *se ad pedes meos prosternens*). Through his penchant for submission, Antony paradoxically managed to lay low both Curiones as well: the elder lies in bed, sick with disgust; the younger lies at Cicero's feet, pleading on behalf of his chum.

Ancient supplications were highly formalized involving the following four steps: (i) an approach to a person or place; (ii) a gesture of submission on the part of the suppliant (such as throwing oneself at the feet or grasping the knees of the person to be supplicated); (iii) the verbal request; (iv) the response of the *supplicandus* (see Naiden 2006: 4). Within this standard pattern, we may note two interesting tweaks. First, Cicero had a choice of how to phrase the gesture of supplication; and with *se ad pedes meos prosternens* he opted for an extreme form of abjection used elsewhere of defeated enemies asking for mercy (*OLD* s.v. *prosterno*

3b). And secondly, Curio's plea comes in two parts: first, he commends Antony to Cicero's care (*te mihi commendabat* — a formulation perhaps reminiscent of New Comedy: see Sussman (1998: 124, with n. 30); and secondly, he asks for Cicero's assistance in pumping his dad for the six million sesterces which he gave to Antony (*orabat ut...*). This is touching: clearly, what is foremost on Curio Junior's mind is the well-being of his beloved, which he feels is most secure in Cicero's keeping — only after taking care of Antony does he worry about himself and the looming confrontation with his father.

lacrimans: a circumstantial participle ('in tears'), analogous to *maerens* above. Welling up can be a powerful emotive gesture, and tears drop copiously not least in those rhetorical contexts (such as law courts or pleas for mercy on the battlefield) in which the performer is trying to elicit sympathy and pity. In and of itself, public weeping is thus not necessarily effeminizing: in Livy and elsewhere, many a Roman father resorts to crying to generate support for their accused sons (see 1.26.12, 8.33.23 with de Libero 2009: 212). Yet Curio Junior throwing himself at Cicero's feet while crying him a river on behalf of Antony seems preposterously OTT.

orabat ut se contra suum patrem, si sestertium sexagiens peteret, defenderem: the *ut* after *orabat* ('a verb of beseeching') introduces a final object clause; *se*, the third-person singular reflexive pronoun and accusative object of *defenderem*, as well as the possessive adjective *suum*, refer to Curio Junior, the subject of the principal clause. Curio calls on Cicero's help because he anticipates a massive bust-up with his dad in case he has to come clean on how much money he stood surety for on Antony's behalf. Apparently, he had not cleared this with his father beforehand — a risky move: in Rome, all family-wealth belonged to the *paterfamilias*, and Curio *pater* could have decided to let Antony hang out to dry when asked by his son to stump up for his lover's debts.

si sestertium sexagiens peteret: at issue are six million sesterces. The full phrase, in regular order, would be: *sexagiens* (60 times) *centena millia* (100,000) *sestertium* (of sesterces). The omission of *centena millia* is unremarkable; but numerical adjectives such as *sexagiens* usually precede the noun they modify since they tend to carry emphasis (Allen

& Greenough 598b). Why, then, has Cicero here inverted the usual word order? Arguably, the *si*-clause is focalized via Curio Junior, who tries to hide the embarrassingly large sum at issue (*sexagiens*) by tugging it in behind the noun (*sestertium*): a sly piece of characterization.

tantum enim se pro te intercessisse dicebat: *dicebat* introduces an indirect statement with *se* (i.e. Curio) as subject accusative and *intercessisse* as infinitive. *intercedo* here means 'to intervene as guarantor' 'stand surety' (*OLD* s.v. 4b) with *tantum* (referring back to *sestertium sexagiens*) as the accusative of the sum guaranteed. *se pro te* correlates antithetically with *se contra suum patrem* in the previous sentence: Curio's loyalties rest with his lover rather than his father, a clear violation of filial *pietas*.

ipse autem amore ardens confirmabat, quod desiderium tui discidi ferre non posset, se in exilium iturum: *confirmabat* introduces an indirect statement with *se* as subject accusative and *iturum* (sc. *esse*) as (future) infinitive (from *eo, ire*). Curio's confessions continue: hopelessly infatuated with Antony (the *a*-alliteration in *autem amore ardens* gives mock-acoustic expression to his passionate yearning), he claims to be unable to bear a state of separation: if Antony were to go into exile to avoid punishment for defaulting on his debts, he would join him. *ardens* is another circumstantial participle: Curio is 'on fire with love'. (Livy uses the same phrase to capture Sextus Tarquinius' mental state before his rape of Lucretia.) Overall, the relationship between Antony and Curio is difficult to classify: both are on fire with passionate love (*libido*), though Antony also seems to be receiving significant financial compensation for services rendered — which in turn is difficult to reconcile with his condition of enslavement.

quod desiderium tui discidi ferre non posset: a very condensed expression. Curio said that he would be unable to bear 'the overwhelming longing (sc. for you, Antony) caused by your sudden or forcible separation'. *tui discidi* is an objective genitive dependent on *desiderium*. *discidium* can also refer to the 'estrangement of lovers' or 'divorce' (*OLD* s.v. 2b) and thereby continues the marriage-metaphor of the previous paragraph. Cicero construes an inversion of the usual scenario where an exile feels *desiderium patriae*: Curio is so enthralled to Antony that he would gladly give up his *patria* and suffer 'social death' in exile as long as he can be around his chum.

Extra information:

Libido and *flagitium* are unequivocally negative terms. But burning passion (cf. *amore ardens*) and passionate longing (cf. *desiderium*) for an absent friend are not per se inappropriate feelings in the context of male-male relationships in late-republican Rome. In fact, Cicero had used much the same idiom half a decade earlier to express his sentiments about Pompey, after deciding not to follow him out of Italy on his flight from Caesar when civil war broke out (*Letter to Atticus* 9.10.2 = 177 SB):

> Amens mihi fuisse a principio videor et me una haec res torquet quod non omnibus in rebus labentem vel potius ruentem Pompeium tamquam unus manipularis secutus sim. vidi hominem xiiii Kal. Febr. plenum formidinis. illo ipso die sensi quid ageret. numquam mihi postea placuit nec umquam aliud in alio peccare destitit. nihil interim ad me scribere, nihil nisi fugam cogitare. quid quaeris? sicut ἐν τοῖς ἐρωτικοῖς alienat quod immunde, insulse, indecore fit, sic me illius fugae neglegentiaeque deformitas avertit ab amore. nihil enim dignum faciebat quare eius fugae comitem me adiungerem. nunc emergit amor, nunc desiderium ferre non possum, nunc mihi nihil libri, nihil litterae, nihil doctrina prodest. ita dies et noctes tamquam avis illa mare prospecto, evolare cupio.

> [I think I have been out of my senses from the start, and the one thing that tortures me is that I have not followed Pompey like any private soldier in his drift or rather plunge to disaster. I saw him on 17 January, thoroughly cowed. That very day I realized what he was at. Thereafter he was never to my liking. He went on blundering now here now there. Meanwhile not a line to me, not a thought except for flight. In short, just as *en choses d'amour*, anything uncleanly, uncouthly, unsuitably done alienates, so the ugliness of his flight and discourtesy turned me from my affection. Nothing in his conduct seemed to deserve that I should join him as his companion in flight. But now my affection comes to the surface, the sense of loss is unbearable, books, writing, philosophy are all to no purpose. Like Plato's bird I gaze out over the sea day and night, longing to take wing.]

Despite the erotic terminology, there is nothing sexual about Cicero's sentiments — he is using the idiom to convey the depth of his affection and attachment to a person, about whose character and policy-decisions he was profoundly conflicted, in a way that was conventional in Roman epistolary discourse: see Williams (2012: 222) on the language of *amor, desiderium*, and burning as conventional expressions in the letters.

§ 46: Family Therapy:
Cicero as Counselor

After the delusional image of marital stability that concluded § 44, matters fell apart in § 45: Curio *pater* and Curio *filius* have both been reduced to tears, even though the reasons for their emotional incontinence differ drastically: the former is laid low by a bout of depression at his inability to check his son's self-destructive infatuation with Antony (a case of senile dementia), the latter wails at Cicero's feet in an effort to protect his beloved (call it penile dementia). For the day of reckoning appears nigh: if Curio *pater* were to refuse to pick up the bill, both young men might end up in exile. It is worth noting that not all of the problems that the Curio family faces are down to the lurid sex-appeal of Antony who has clearly addled the mind of Curio Junior. When *patria potestas* breaks down, all hell tends to break loose, and Curio Senior is in clear need of a guide who can tell him what to do: Cicero to the rescue!

In § 46, Cicero features himself as a steady and competent counselor to sort out what is frankly an over-emotional and quite unnecessary mess, created by the inability of the father to deal adequately with Antony. All he needs to do is reassert paternal authority — and Cicero tells him how best to go about it. He offers Curio Senior a lesson in paternal discipline, combining a measure of kindness (paying off his son's debts) with a measure of severity (laying down the law on future relations with Antony, which essentially amounts to imposing a restraining order). He emboldens the Elder Curio to take an approach to the problem that is both generous and tough-minded, grounded in the best of Roman common sense, a tough but pragmatic approach that combines *disciplina* with what one may label *humanitas* (sympathy with the plight of fellow-humans, in this case a son who has temporarily lost his ways under the sinister influence of Antony) to shore up his *familia*. Following up on Curio Junior's desperate pleading, he convinces the father to settle the debt of his son, however feckless he may have been (and thus enable him to grow up into a viable member of Rome's civic community), but also to exercise his paternal powers to shut down any further contact between Curio Junior and Antony. The individual left out in the cold is Antony.

In sum: under the influence of Antony, the two Curios have failed to maintain the demeanor expected of those who belong to Rome's ruling elite. In the last sentence of the paragraph, Cicero seamlessly pivots from Antony's personal failings to his political crimes: he conjures a fearsome display of military force, designed to intimidate Cicero and his audience as part of the speech's setting. Cicero here offers a representative snapshot of Antony's corrosive impact on the fabric of Rome's ruling elite and society at large. In nuce, this is the scenario that Cicero conjures for the speech as a whole: what Antony does to the Curio household, he is currently doing to the *res publica*. The analogy to Curio Senior is the senate. Cicero came to the rescue once; he offers to do so again — in fact does so with this very speech. Cicero advocates the same approach now, which he advised then: to reassert (senatorial) *auctoritas* and close ranks against the subversive, revolutionary madman.

Quo tempore ego quanta mala florentissimae familiae sedavi vel potius sustuli!: *quo* is a connecting relative pronoun (= *eo*); *quo tempore* an ablative of time. The adjective *quanta* (modifying *mala*) is exclamatory: 'how many evils did I...' *florentissimae familiae* is either genitive (depending on *mala*) or dative. Cicero systematically alliterates here (*quo – quanta; florentissimae – familiae; sedavi – sustuli*). The pair of verbs forms a climax: after the mild *sedavi*, Cicero, throwing modesty to the winds (*vel potius*: ah, what the heck!), decides to boast that he sorted their problems (*sustuli*), period.

florentissimae familiae: the superlative seems somewhat exaggerated. The Scribonii Curiones were a relatively new presence within the ranks of Rome's ruling elite: the first to reach the consulship was Curio *pater*; and by the time Cicero wrote *Philippic* 2, the family had again disappeared into oblivion.

patri persuasi ut aes alienum fili dissolveret; redimeret adulescentem, summa spe et animi et ingeni praeditum, rei familiaris facultatibus eumque non modo tua familiaritate sed etiam congressione patrio iure et potestate prohiberet: Cicero continues with an alliterative jingle (*patri persuasi*), as he prevails upon Curio Senior to do two things (though he uses a tricolon to spell them out): to pay off his son's debt (*dissolveret*) — and thereby rescue the young man from (financial) ruin (*redimeret*); and to cut off any further contact with Antony (*prohiberet*). The asyndetic juxtaposition of *dissolveret* and *redimeret* (*redimeret* and *prohiberet* are linked by the -*que* after *eum*) signals stylistically that they form one idea (action – outcome), as does the overall chiastic structure of the first two cola:

> A₁ *aes alienum*
>
> B₁ *fili*
>
> C₁ *dissolveret,*
>
> C₂ *redimeret*
>
> B₂ *adulescentem summa spe et animi et ingeni praeditum*
>
> A₂ *rei familiaris facultatibus*

> A = debt and resources to pay it off;
> B = Curio Junior, as *filius* and talented *adulescens*;
> C = payment of debt and personal redemption

Overall, the *ut*-clause moves from past transgressions to their cancellation for the present (*dissolveret, redimeret*) and advice on how to avoid further problems in the future (*prohiberet*).

patri persuasi: in classical Latin *persuadere* takes the dative.

aes alienum: literally, '(copper or bronze) money (*aes*) borrowed from another person (*alienum*)', hence 'debt'.

adulescentem: Curio was in his early twenties at the time, but Roman age markers are imprecise (see above 132–33) and *adulescens* fits in well with the touches from New Comedy that Cicero sprinkles throughout these paragraphs.

summa spe et animi et ingeni praeditum: the alliterated phrase *summa spe* is an instrumental ablative governed by *praeditum*. *spes* here refers to Curio's future prospects — 'endowed with exceptional potential'. *et ... et...* connects the two genitives *animi* and *ingeni*. *animus* refers to his (bold) spirit, i.e. such qualities as energy and daring; *ingenium* is his creative imagination, more specifically his oratorical talent.

rei familiaris facultatibus: literally 'with the resources of the family's wealth'

non modo tua familiaritate, sed etiam congressione: *familiaritas* refers to a strong (political) friendship, with connotations of affection and intimacy: Grillo (2015: 262), citing Hellegouarc'h (1963: 70); *congressio* is more hands-on: it refers to an actual encounter and can carry connotations of sexual congress. Both nouns are ablatives of separation with *prohiberet*.

patrio iure et potestate: the power of the Roman *paterfamilias* (the so-called *patria potestas*), which included the *ius vitae necisque*, was virtually unlimited in conception, though in practice tightly hedged by societal norms and expectations: see above 150. Cicero here conjures up all three concepts in slightly unorthodox formulations. It is not entirely clear what his recommendation added to Curio Senior's earlier attempts to bar Antony from entering the house (detailed in the previous paragraph), though the implication might be that Curio had so far abstained from exercising his full power as *paterfamilias* (had behaved, in other words, like one of the Greek fathers in New Comedy). He now is advised to increase the threat level: instead of just keeping Antony away, he is encouraged to threaten his son with drastic consequences if he violates the paternal prohibition.

haec tu cum per me acta meminisses, nisi illis quos videmus gladiis confideres, maledictis me provocare ausus esses?: the sentence begins with a *cum*-clause, which is followed by a conditional sequence. The logic here is not entirely obvious, as one step seems to have been elided. Cicero seems to be asking: 'when you remember ..., would you have dared to…?', while also supplying the answer: '[no, you would not have] — if you could not trust in those swords'.

haec tu cum … meminisses: standard word order would be *cum haec … meminisses*. Cicero places the accusative object (*haec*) and the (strictly speaking unnecessary) second personal pronoun (*tu*) in front of the conjugation (*cum*).

per me acta: Usually, Latin uses *a / ab* + ablative to express agency with passive verbs, but *per* + acc. is also a possibility, especially when the sense is 'through the instrumentality of' (*OLD* s.v. 15). Cicero succeeded in prevailing upon Curio Senior and was therefore instrumental in ensuring the payment of Curio Junior's debt, his ensuing redemption, and the imposition of the non-contact policy with regard to Antony. (This is what *haec … acta* refer to, rather than the act of persuasion.)

nisi … confideres, … ausus esses?: Cicero addresses a question to Antony cast as mixed conditional sequence with the protasis in the imperfect subjunctive and the apodosis in the pluperfect subjunctive. (The form *ausus esses* is pluperfect passive subjunctive, but *audeo*, you will recall, is a so-called 'semi-deponent', i.e. has active forms, with active meanings, in the present system and passive forms, with *active* meanings, in the perfect system.) He pairs a past counterfactual scenario (Antony would not have dared to challenge him) with a scenario in the present that he *imagines* as *real* — for Antony's threatening demeanor towards Cicero, see the next note.

illis quos videmus gladiis: Cicero here caters to the conceit that he is delivering an actual oration (rather than publishing a pamphlet) and conjures the scenario that Antony and his armed henchmen surround the speaker's platform, threatening physical violence. The hyperbaton *illis … gladiis*, further amplified by the placement of the antecedent after the relative clause, nicely enhances the shock-value of *gladiis*. The scene is reminiscent of the opening of the *pro Milone*.

maledictis: the term refers us back to the exordium, where Cicero claims that Antony provoked him without cause with verbal abuse (§ 1: … *ultro me maledictis lacessisti*). By calling Antony's verbal attacks *maledicta*, Cicero implicitly discredits Antony's qualities as a public speaker (a theme running throughout *Philippic* 2). See *pro Caelio* 6, where Cicero first distinguishes between *male dicere* and *accusare* and then outlines two different modes of *male dicere* — one dull and abusive, the other witty:

> aliud est male dicere, aliud accusare: accusatio crimen desiderat, rem ut definiat, hominem ut notet, argumento probet, teste confirmet; maledictio autem nihil habet propositi praeter contumeliam; quae si petulantius iactatur, convicium, si facetius, urbanitas nominatur.
>
> [abuse is one thing, accusation is another. Accusation requires ground for a charge, to define a fact, to mark a man, to prove by argument, to establish by testimony. The only object of slander, on the other hand, is to insult; if it has a strain of coarseness, it is called abuse; if one of wit, it is called elegance.]

All Antony has to offer is slander (*maledictio*); there is no substance to anything he says, and as the rest of the speech makes clear, Antony uses 'abusive language' (*convicium*) without any redeeming wit — in contrast to Cicero, who is known for his *urbanitas*, and the New Comic scenario he unfolds in §§ 44–46 indeed combines *maledictio* and *urbanitas* brilliantly. Etymologically, *maledictis* also picks up *quanta mala* from the beginning of the paragraph, keeping Antony in close company with evil things.

§ 47: Hitting 'Fast-Forward', or: How to Pull Off a *Praeteritio*

After wrapping up his opening anecdote in his imaginary biography of Antony, Cicero continues with a transitional paragraph that lays out his approach to the rest of the material. As in § 43, he stresses that he has to leave out a lot. Some of the stuff that Antony got up (or down) to is simply beyond the pale: the sort of X-rated material no person with any sense of decency would be able to put into words. And there is also a feeling of urgency: Cicero is loath to linger too long on Antony's youthful depravities in his hurry to get to his conduct during the civil wars, which is of greater relevance in the here-and-now (even though it is also more familiar to his audience — or so Cicero claims). The paragraph is therefore highly reflexive in outlook, as Cicero comments explicitly on some of the moral and rhetorical considerations and contextual coordinates (such as the purported degrees of familiarity of his audience with different aspects of his subject matter) that shape his discourse.

The technical terms for gesturing to material without treating it fully are *occultatio* ('obfuscation') or *praeteritio* ('a passing by and over'; *paralipsis* in Greek). An excellent ancient discussion of this useful ploy can be found in the so-called *Rhetorica ad Herennium*, a rhetorical treatise written in the early first century BCE (4.37):

> *Paralipsis / Praeteritio* occurs when we say that we are passing by, or do not know, or refuse to say that which precisely now we are saying, as follows: 'Your boyhood, indeed, which you dedicated to intemperance of all kinds, I would discuss, if I thought this the right time. But at present I advisedly leave that aside. This too I pass by, that the tribunes have

reported you as irregular in military service. Also that you have given satisfaction to Lucius Labeo for injuries done him I regard as irrelevant to the present matter. Of these things I say nothing, but return to the issue in this trial'. Again: 'I do not mention that you have taken monies from our allies; I do not concern myself with your having despoiled the cities, kingdoms, and homes of them all. I pass by your thieveries and robberies, all of them'. This figure is useful if employed in a matter which is not pertinent to call specifically to the attention of others, because there is advantage in making only an indirect reference to it, or because the direct reference would be tedious or undignified, or cannot be made clear, or can easily be refuted. As a result, it is of greater advantage to create a suspicion by *Paralipsis / Praeteritio* than to insist directly on a statement that is refutable.

Compare the more recent discussion found in Farnsworth (2011: 166–67):

The usual purposes that the device serves include these: a. To gain credit—though not too much—for discretion or propriety while still setting loose an indiscretion or impropriety. ... b. To leave the substance of a sentiment, or a piece of it, to the listener's imagination, and so enhance its force. The fantasy of what the complete version of the thought would have been may be more powerful than a plain statement of it. ... c. To limit debate over a controversial utterance by offering it as only half-said; when the speaker denies fully saying it, he hopes to make a rebuttal seem uncalled for, and to assign himself a relaxed burden of proof. ... d. Amusement. The paradox inherent in a good use of *praeteritio* can be a source of humor and charm, at least when it does not take itself too seriously.

All four aspects identified by Farnsworth are in play in our passage: (*a*) Cicero comes across as a paragon of propriety (his commitment to verbal restraint stands in explicit contrast to Antony's sexual and rhetorical incontinence) by not delving into the sordid details of his adversary's sex life, while at the same time cashing in on the allure of scandal with his lurid insinuations of unspeakable filth. (*b*) He thereby invites the audience to indulge their imagination — not least in conjuring up and putting together the organs and orifices he passes over in silence: any scenario they can think of, however lewd, Antony is bound to have acted out. The result is insinuation porn, which enables him to keep his mouth squeaky clean and the minds of his audience satisfyingly dirty. (*c*) Given that Cicero here operates with artistic license rather than sound empirical evidence, the mode of intimation renders him less vulnerable

to the objection that he is making it all up. (*d*) He also benefits from the
humour inherent in the 'gossip's trope' — which he combines with a
serious message:

> Cicero has just told an unusually gross (but plausible) lie about Antony's
> sexual habits as a young man. The decorum, the tact, and the modesty
> of the speaker, compounded with the hint that this sort of material is
> endless, are audacious and funny, but the sexual depravity is presented
> as being only a prelude to perversions of the political intelligence, a
> theme which again offers inexhaustible material. Here moral indignation
> is coupled with decorum — it is the perfection of *gravitas*. Or rather, it is
> *gravitas* mimed, a droll imitation of the real thing, an action designed to
> irritate the victim and amuse the audience, for if *praeteritio* is not urbane,
> casual, mocking or witty — as it always is when Cicero has his wits and
> his nerve — it is nothing.[10]

Throughout *Philippic* 2, Cicero uses the sexual as code for the political.
According to the logic that leopards don't change their spots, Antony's
erotic escapades prefigure his behaviour in civic life: there is no reason to
assume that someone who so conspicuously lacks the virtues expected
of a Roman statesman in his youth miraculously acquired them later on.
As Cicero goes on to argue, the juvenile delinquent indeed grew up into
an uninhibited creature of inordinate appetites who lusts after drink
and sex, money and power — the more the better. Antony is not just a
menace to morals but to society at large.

Sed iam stupra et flagitia omittamus: *iam* ('now') refers to this particular
moment in Cicero's discourse: the time has come to move on from
Antony's youthful depravities. *omittamus* is an exhortatory subjunctive
('Let us...'), introducing a rather lengthy *praeteritio*.

stupra et flagitia: while the term *stuprum* can be applied to label any
shameful conduct, without specific reference to sexual practices, for
the most part (including here) it refers to 'the offense consisting in the
violation of the sexual integrity of freeborn Romans of either sex' (such
as pederasty or adultery) (Williams 1999: 96). He goes on to point out
that the concept is implicated in how Roman society was set up: 'At
stake here is the fundamental distinction between freeborn and slave,
which in turn bolsters the self-identifying practices of the freeborn by

---

10   Johnson (1969: 173). For *occultatio* in Cicero see further Usher (1965).

promoting the ideal of the physical inviolability of the free Roman citizen' (106). *flagitium*, which Cicero already used in §§ 44 and 45, also has a more general meaning ('any shameful act that causes infamy and disgrace'), but here specifically evokes forms of sexual transgression.[11]

sunt quaedam quae honeste non possum dicere: *quaedam* is neuter plural and antecedent of *quae* ('there are certain things that…'). Cicero engages in the conceit of self-censorship, in apparent deference to standards of decency: the implication is that the (undefined) things Antony did are literally 'unspeakable' for any honourable member of Roman society. Self-censorship can be a serious problem when it enforces a code of silence over actual abuse of power; here it is a posture designed to titillate the (salacious) imagination of his audience (that includes *me — and you!*) with unspecified acts of sexual transgression on Antony's part and at the same time highlight his own good sense and finely tuned sensibilities of what is and what is not acceptable to put into words in civil society. He thereby signals concern over public morality: it is a question of taste and decency to veil Antony's more outrageous sexual escapades in a shroud of silence.

The question of course arises: what does Cicero pass over in silence? Scholars suspect that the reference here is to oral intercourse. This was a difficult area for the public orator (unlike a poet such as Catullus), insofar as he would involve himself in a performative contradiction were he to talk about it: he would, in a sense, befoul his own mouth by putting filth into words. Corbeill (1996: 105) identifies 'the two principal rhetorical considerations that characterize Roman invective involving sexual practices and the *os*' as follows: 'First, the orator must limit himself to double entendres, vague references that allow him to cast aspersions on an opponent while maintaining his own dignity as a public speaker. Second, the orator cannot directly accuse his more prominent opponents of improper social and sexual activity'. And with this in mind Richlin (1983/1992: 15) answers the question 'what can he be leaving out?' as follows: 'Without giving a graphic description of Antony's intercourse with the younger Curio, he has implied that it was habitual and passionate. The ultimate insult was to accuse someone of indulgence in oral intercourse, and presumably Cicero means to imply

---

11   For the semantics of *flagitium* see Thomas (2007: 179–214).

this for Antony. But the weight of the sentence is on the neat paradox, "You have done things that a man of good morals cannot even name", and on the contrast between Cicero, who is *honestus* and *verecundus*, and Antony, who is not'. Antony knows no boundaries — neither for himself nor for others. Cicero by contrast exercises restraint and abides by the protocols of public discourse: he prefers playing coy to being gratuitously gross. Internal self-regulation is a prized attribute in a Roman aristocrat — and precisely what Antony lacks.

honeste: the adverb here refers to 'moral integrity'; it is a key concern of Cicero's (late) philosophy. See in particular his *On Duties* (*de Officiis*).

tu autem eo liberior [*es*] **quod ea in te admisisti quae a verecundo inimico audire non posses**: the main verb (*es*) has to be supplied. The basic meaning of *liber* is 'free', i.e. possessing the social and legal status of a free man, as opposed to a slave; but it can also refer specifically to 'free speech', either in a positive sense ('outspoken', 'frank', 'candid') or in a negative sense ('showing lack of restraint'). This is the meaning of the comparative *liberior* here: Cicero refers back to the verbal abuse (see on *maledicta*, above 165) Antony showered on him and relates it back to his enemy's sexual track-record: in light of what has gone *into* Antony's mouth, the filth that comes *out* of it hardly surprises.

eo: an ablative of respect ('in this regard').

quod ea in te admisisti: *quod* is causal here: Cicero explains why Antony can be more outspoken when it comes to verbal abuse than he is. Not that Cicero is particularly reticent — though he continues in the mode of double entendre that enables him to have his cake and eat it:

> The phrase 'allowed to be done to yourself' (*in te admisisti*), with its apparently neutral overtones, seems to continue Cicero's pose of discreet reticence. But other occurrences of the verb *admitto* indicate that Cicero is further incriminating Antonius at the very moment he claims to be exercising discretion. This verb 'was the technical term for the bringing of one animal to the other (usually the male to the female)'; more significantly, *admitto* can refer euphemistically to a pimp allowing his prostitute access to a man. The portrayal of Antony pimping for himself as a young male whore coincides with imagery Cicero employed earlier in the speech (2.44–45)' (Corbeill 1996: 106, with quotation and reference to Adams 1982: 206–07).

This is a rather complicated (though quite plausible) scenario, but the invective punch here might also be much more straightforward. The basic meaning of *admitto* is 'to allow to enter' (also in the specific sense of allowing enemies to enter into, with *in* + acc.), and Cicero might again refer to the fact that Antony gave up his corporal inviolability as a male citizen by allowing his bodily orifices to be penetrated.

quae a verecundo inimico audire non posses: Antony's lewd behaviour is such that he could not hear about it even from a personal enemy (*inimicus*) if that enemy has any sense of shame (*verecundia*). *audire* here means 'to hear said with respect to oneself': *OLD* s.v. 5. Cicero rephrases *non possum dicere* from the previous sentence in chiastic order, shifting from speaking to listening.

a verecundo inimico: the phrase harks back to the exordium: Cicero began the speech by pondering why Antony had decided to make him his personal enemy (*inimicus*) and reached the conclusion that each *hostis* (public enemy) of the *res publica* in recent memory also happened to be his personal enemy (*inimicus*).

sed reliquum vitae cursum videte, quem quidem celeriter perstringam: Cicero invites his readers (addressed directly with the imperative *videte*: another sop to the fiction that Cicero is delivering an oration) to take a bird's eye view of the rest of Antony's biography. This invitation to synoptic autopsy serves as counterpoint to the relative clause where he announces that he will cover the following years quickly (*celeriter*) and superficially (*perstringere* is here used figuratively in the sense of 'barely scratching the surface'). The particle *quidem* has a concessive sense ('admittedly').

perstringam: first person singular future indicative active.

ad haec enim quae in civili bello, in maximis rei publicae miseriis fecit, et ad ea quae cotidie facit, festinat animus: standard word order would be *animus ad haec, quae... et ad ea, quae... festinat*. There might be an element of enactment in the unusual placement of the subject (*animus*) at the very end of the sentence: the *animus* has indeed 'hurried on', even overtaking the verb (*festinat*). The alliterated sequence of verb — *fecit : facit : festinat* — also generates an impression of speed.

(Note how *festinat* also recapitulates the vowels of the previous two verbs.)

quae in civili bello, in maximis rei publicae miseriis fecit: *in maximis rei publicae miseriis* stands in apposition to, and glosses, *in civili bello*. The reference is to the conflict between Caesar and the senate, initially with Pompey as leading general, that broke out in 49 and lasted until c. 46 BCE. Traditionally, the lexeme *bellum* referred to a properly declared state of war with another people. *bellum civile* ('civil war') is a paradoxical phrase that brings together the sphere known as *militiae*, where *bellum* refers to violent confrontation with a foreign enemy, and the civic sphere of domestic and more or less peaceful politics (*domi*); it emerged in the last century of the republic to capture the suicidal in-fighting that broke out among Rome's ruling elite from c. 133 BCE onwards (see Introduction 9–10). In a political culture much invested in *consensus* and *concordia* (at least according to Cicero), civil war is indeed 'the greatest of all evils' (note the plaintive alliteration *maximis … miseriis*.

quae peto ut, quamquam multo notiora vobis quam mihi sunt, tamen, ut facitis, attente audiatis: *quae* is a connecting relative (= *ea*), picking up *haec* and *ea* from the previous sentence. Syntactically, it is the accusative object of *audiatis*, i.e. it belongs into the first *ut*-clause (dependent on *peto*): 'as far as these matters are concerned, I ask that you listen to them attentively — as you do now — even though they are much better known to you than to me'. It is not entirely clear what periods Cicero has in mind and why he insists on stressing that Antony's conduct during these times is significantly better known to his audience than to himself. He 'perhaps refers to his absences from Rome and Italy during the Civil War and after Caesar's death' (Denniston 1926: 126–27), i.e. 7 June 49–autumn 48 and 7 April–31 August 44. It is rather unlikely (*pace* Ramsey 2003: 230) that he is also referring to his stay in Brindisi from autumn 48–autumn 47, after he had been pardoned by Caesar and was permitted to return to Italy but not to Rome, because he spent those excruciating months under the direct jurisdiction of Antony. In fact, his implicit claim to have been absent (unlike others) at least until after Pharsalus and the death of Pompey subtly reinforces his credentials as a republican resistance fighter, glossing over his early return to Caesar-occupied Italy in the autumn of 48, well before the hot phase of the civil war was over.

multo: an ablative of the degree of difference with the comparative *notiora*, literally 'more well known *by much*'.

ut facitis: a parenthetical comment on the conduct of his imaginary audience. It lessons the force of the exhortation: Cicero simply asks his audience to continue to do what they are anyway already doing.

debet enim talibus in rebus excitare animos non cognitio solum rerum sed etiam recordatio: the word order is again highly wrought. Stripped of rhetorical manipulation the sentence might run: *in talibus enim rebus non solum cognitio sed etiam recordatio rerum animos excitare debet*. The reshuffle involves an inversion of the usual sequence subject – verb, with the verb here placed up front; the anastrophe of the preposition *in* (*in talibus rebus > talibus in rebus*); and the inverted order of *excitare animos*. The design is therefore just as 'excited' as Cicero wants the minds of his audience to be; and it ensures that the emphasis falls heavily on the very last word of the sentence: *recordatio*. Cicero here tries to counter the well-known phenomenon that the motivating force of anger fades over time: something that triggers an acute emotion of being wronged at the first instance of recognition and the willingness to lash out and do something about the injustice suffered might not do so years after the fact. Conventional wisdom and consolatory literature even hold that painful experiences may over time turn into pleasant memories: *forsan et haec olim meminisse iuvabit*, as Virgil's Aeneas has it 'perhaps it will one day be pleasing to remember even these hardships' (*Aeneid* 1.203). Cicero has to argue the opposite: he dredges up stuff from history and tries to render it relevant for present purposes, by generating a sense of outrage at the recollection of both Antony's past and present misdeeds.

excitare animos: what can easily get lost in stereotypical images of the Romans as emotionally controlled is the fact that emotions are an important part of politics in general and public oratory in particular. In his philosophical writings, Cicero often endorses the proto-Stoic figure of the completely impassionate, rational agent; but in rhetorical contexts he recognizes the productive force and overriding importance of emotions. A good speaker will rouse his audience not just with arguments but also with emotive appeals to adopt a particular outlook or course of action.

non cognitio solum rerum, sed etiam recordatio: Cicero has a certain fondness for abstract nouns, not least in his philosophical writings, but also in his speeches. *cognitio* denotes 'the act of getting to know', i.e. refers to those matters that Cicero's audience is as of yet unfamiliar with and learns through his discourse; *recordatio* means 'recollection' and thus refers to matters already known to his audience — he only needs to trigger their memory. The genitive *rerum* stands *apo koinou*, i.e. goes with both nouns.

etsi incidamus, opinor, media ne nimis sero ad extrema veniamus: when *etsi*, as here, introduces a main clause it has the sense of 'and yet', limiting the preceding sentence (Gildersleeve & Lodge 391). But this causes difficulties: the preceding sentence refers to material Cicero intends to cover in depth, i.e. Antony's behaviour in the run-up to, and during, the civil war and, more recently, in the aftermath of Caesar's assassination. One would therefore have expected an affirmative, rather than a concessive link-up.

incidamus ... media: without indication of vowel length, many of the forms of *incîdo* (from *in* + *caedo*, with a long *-i*; basic meaning: to cut), and *incido* (from *in* + *cado*, with a short *-i*; basic meaning: to fall) are indistinguishable. Here Cicero is saying: 'Let's cut the middle part (*media*: neuter acc. plural) short', referring to the period from c. 58–50 BCE, to be covered briefly in §§ 48–50a.

ne nimis sero ad extrema veniamus: *ne* introduces a negative purpose clause ('lest'). Like *media*, *extrema* is an adjective used as a noun, in the neuter accusative plural — 'the last, i.e. most recent, matters' in line with his preference for vague generic neuter pronouns throughout this (transitional) paragraph: *quaedam; ea; haec enim quae...; ea quae...; quae... notiora.*

§ 48: Antony Adrift

§§ 48–50a are devoted to Antony's public career in the 50s BCE. At the opening of § 48, we are in Rome and the year is 58: Antony, Cicero claims, became a bosom friend of Clodius, who was tribune of the people at the time (about to drive Cicero into exile and burn down his house…) as well as married to Antony's future wife Fulvia. The couple offered Antony excellent opportunities to pursue his imputed revolutionary and sexual passions: Cicero casts him as Clodius' principal firebrand in the city while engaging in some marital foreplay in his home. After his stint as catalyst for Clodius' incendiary actions that — according to Cicero — saw conflagrations across the capital, he has Antony drift off to the edges of the empire in search of some work experience abroad, without changing the company he keeps. In 57–55, we find him in the entourage of Aulus Gabinius, one of the consuls of 58, and hence (according to Cicero) co-responsible for Cicero's exile. (He let him know about it in the *in Pisonem*, an invective attack on the other consul of 58, Lucius Calpurnius Piso, though Cicero reserves sufficient spite for Gabinius as well.) And in 54, Antony ends up with Caesar's forces in Gaul. If we read between the lines of Cicero's invective, what emerges is an impressive record of foreign service, which suggests that Antony proved adept at navigating the opportunities offered by Rome's system of imperial exploitation, helped along, no doubt, by family connections. In Cicero's account, of course, Antony comes across as a rootless scoundrel, unanchored and adrift, a piece of human dross without a proper home, floating about at the edges of the world: Cicero's invective GPS tracks Antony to the farthest reaches of Roman power, from the South-East (Alexandria) to the North-West (Gaul), with a notional footprint in Italy (Misenum) that Cicero combines with a gesture to the far West (Sisapo in Spain): anywhere but R/Home. In line with the logic of fast-forward, the account is of course highly selective: Cicero focuses on those moments that lend themselves to negative comment, while omitting others that constitute less amenable targets for abusive jeers.

Intimus erat in tribunatu Clodio qui sua erga me beneficia commemorat: *intimus*, used as superlative of *interior*, means 'furthest from the outside', 'most remote', 'inmost' and, with specific reference to friends, 'most intimate', 'closest'. Placed up front for emphasis and standing in predicative position to the (implied) subject of the sentence, it is to be construed with the dative *Clodio*: 'He, who recalls favours he has done me, was Clodius' most intimate chum during his tribuneship'. Cicero suppresses any hint of what may have been the real motive behind Antony's association with Clodius: 'Antony may have been drawn to Clodius by a desire to avenge the death of his stepfather P. Lentulus, who had been executed by Cicero (§ 17), or the connection with Clodius may have come about through the younger Curio, Antony's close friend (§§ 44–45), who led demonstrations on Clodius' behalf in 61 when he was charged with sacrilege in the Bona Dea affair' (Ramsey 2003: 230). There is arguably a suggestion of contagion and pathology here — intimacy ensures that Clodius' revolutionary zeal rubs off on Antony. According to Plutarch, *Life of Antony* 2.4, the association was short-lived and Antony, smelling a change of winds, took himself off to Greece for military service and training in oratory:

ὁ δὲ βραχὺν μέν τινα χρόνον τῇ Κλωδίου τοῦ θρασυτάτου καὶ βδελυρωτάτου τῶν τότε δημαγωγῶν φορᾷ πάντα τὰ πράγματα ταραττούσῃ προσέμιξεν ἑαυτόν· ταχὺ δὲ τῆς ἐκείνου μανίας μεστὸς γενόμενος, καὶ φοβηθεὶς τοὺς συνισταμένους ἐπὶ τὸν Κλώδιον, ἀπῆρεν ἐκ τῆς Ἰταλίας εἰς τὴν Ἑλλάδα, καὶ διέτριβε τό τε σῶμα γυμνάζων πρὸς τοὺς στρατιωτικοὺς ἀγῶνας καὶ λέγειν μελετῶν.

[Then Antony allied himself for a short time with Clodius, the most audacious and low-lived demagogue of his time, in the violent courses which were convulsing the state; but he soon became sated with that miscreant's madness, and fearing the party which was forming against him, left Italy for Greece, where he spent some time in military exercises and the study of oratory.]

As Pelling (1988: 119) notes, τῇ ... φορᾷ ... προσέμιξεν ἑαυτόν, which literally means 'mingled himself in with the (destructive) impulses of Clodius' is a 'very striking phrase' — and, with its innuendo of untoward physical intimacy, arguably picks up on *intimus* (and the following sentence) in Cicero, who was one of Plutarch's sources. Unlike Plutarch, Cicero does not specify how long Antony and Clodius 'mingled', which suggests that Plutarch was right in saying that it was not for long.

qui sua erga me beneficia commemorat: the antecedent of *qui* is the implied subject of *erat* (*is*), so the subject of the relative clause is Antony as well (not Clodius). Cicero here returns to one of his sorest points: Antony's accusation of ingratitude in the speech that triggered *Philippic* 2. The basis for this claim was an episode in 48 BCE, when Antony was Caesar's Master of the Horse, which included responsibility for keeping followers of Pompey out of Italy. After Pharsalus, Cicero just wanted to go home and managed to receive permission from Caesar, perhaps facilitated by his son-in-law Dolabella — but only as far as Brindisi in Southern Italy where he spent several miserable months under the jurisdiction of Antony. He lets rip on the situation early on in the speech, disputing that not having been killed by a bandit should count as a kindness (*beneficium*): 'what kind of benefaction is it to abstain from an atrocious crime?' (§ 5: *Quale autem beneficium est quod te abstinueris nefario scelere?*). In §§ 59–60, he returns to the issue in a similar vein. Still, that he should be beholden to Antony in this moment of extreme vulnerability must have festered with Cicero: see Wistrand (1978: 49, n. 6): 'It was also an awkward question whether Cicero owed Antony gratitude for sparing his life at Brundisium, cf. Dio 46,22,5. The answer that Cicero gives (*Phil.* 2,3,5f. and 2,24,59f.) is ambiguous. He maintains that he had been grateful, but declares on the other hand that Antony's mercy — like the mercy Caesar had shown — had been a *beneficium latronum*'. In § 48 Cicero tries to counterbalance any favours received against the most vicious blow to his self(-esteem) and his career, his banishment from Rome in 58 BCE, which Clodius engineered. Anyone on intimate terms with the mastermind of his exile, so Cicero here asserts, has by definition forfeited any claim to a superior position in the economy of favours and services.

eius omnium incendiorum fax [erat], **cuius etiam domi iam tum quiddam molitus est**: the main verb (*erat*) needs to be supplied. *fax* stands in predicative position to the implied subject (Antony): 'he was the firebrand of all the conflagrations of him'. *eius* refers to Clodius and is the antecedent of the relative pronoun *cuius*, a possessive genitive dependent on the locative *domi*: '... of him in whose house he [sc. Antony] ... put into motion a humpin' sumpin''.

eius omnium incendiorum fax: *fax*, literally 'torch' or 'firebrand', also has a figurative sense, denoting 'a person or thing that starts mischief, rouses passions, enthusiasm, etc.' (*OLD* s.v. 8). *incendium* can similarly be used figuratively, to refer to outbreaks of (political) violence: see *OLD* s.v. 3. Cicero developed a wide-ranging idiom of abuse to target Clodius as a scourge of Rome, 'firebrand' being one of his favourites. Here Antony becomes the catalyst, the initial spark that caused *all* of Clodius' 'conflagrations'. *fax* comes with connotations of revolutionary chaos that destroys the city (and, on the conceit that Rome is coextensive with the world, the universe at large). Given the real threat of large-scale fires in urban centres, it is a metaphor with a particularly visceral punch, tapping into darkest fears. Cicero here contrives to make Antony responsible for unleashing Clodius on Roman society, simply on the grounds that he could be found in his entourage while Clodius held the office of tribune in 58 BCE (the year Cicero was forced into exile). The *incendia* Cicero refers to here thus surely include that of his house, stormed, looted, and burnt to the ground by Clodius' troopers once he had left the city.

cuius etiam domi iam tum quiddam molitus est: Cicero is back to his game of sexual double entendres via vague, yet pregnant, neuter pronouns: *quiddam molitus est* ('he put something in motion') refers to adultery with Clodius' wife Fulvia. Fulvia (c. 80–40 BCE) had, as Cicero spitefully put it, a 'triumvirate' of husbands:[12] Clodius (sometime before 58–52 BCE, when Clodius was killed in a street fight; Scribonius Curio (yes, none other than Antony's buddy from the previous paragraphs)

---

12   See *Att.* 16.11.1 = 420 SB. As Shackleton Bailey (1967: 300) notes, 'the point of the jest is the implication that Antony and Curio were Fulvia's *viri* in effect during Clodius' lifetime' — in other words, they were her men both simultaneously and successively.

from 51 until Curio's death in 49 BCE; and finally Antony, whom she married in 46 BCE. With *iam tum* ('already back then') Cicero nastily implies that Antony jumped the queue: instead of waiting his turn, he had it on with Fulvia already in 58.

Extra information:
If you want to learn more about Fulvia, who by all accounts must have been an extraordinary woman, start with Ann R. Raia's & Judith Lynn Sebesta's entry on Fulvia in *Philippic* 2 in their *Online Companion to the Worlds of Roman Women*: https://www2.cnr.edu/home/sas/araia/Fulvia.html. See also Babcock (1965) and Hallett (2015). Brennan (2012: 357) suggests that the funeral Fulvia staged after the death of Clodius inspired Antony's approach to the funeral of Caesar: 'After Clodius met a violent death at the hands of his political rival Milo in 52 BCE, Fulvia stage-managed his funeral in a manner that would be remembered and revisited in years to come. Fulvia's success at whipping Rome's populace into a frenzy — so much so that they carried her husband's corpse into the Senate house and burned it down as a pyre — was not lost on Mark Antony after Caesar's assassination in 44 BCE'.

quid dicam ipse optime intellegit: *quid dicam* is an indirect question, hence the subjunctive. Cicero again refrains from spelling matters out, preferring to deal in dark hints; and Antony as the culprit is of course supposed to be in the know.

inde iter Alexandriam [fecit] **contra senatus auctoritatem, contra rem publicam et religiones**: the main verb of the sentence is again elided but easily supplied from context; *iter* is a verbal noun implying movement (Pinkster 2015: 1043) and governs the accusative of direction *Alexandriam*. Cicero operates in fast-forward mode, skipping over details in Antony's biography, such as rhetorical studies in Greece and (distinguished) military service with Gabinius in Syria (58–56), which yield no invective returns. Instead he homes in on an event in 55 that enables him to portray Antony as acting against the interests of the commonwealth and violate principles of Rome's civic religion.

The point at issue was the succession to the throne of Egypt. In 58, king Ptolemy XII Auletes (the father of Cleopatra VII, Antony's future lover), who had bought his way to the kingdom of Egypt during Caesar's consulship in 59, got kicked out of the country by the people and went to Rome to bribe himself back onto the throne. Many members of Rome's ruling elite licked their chops at the prospect of restoring him to power — cashing in on his bribes and acquiring military glory in the process. In late 57, the senate initially decided to entrust the task to Publius Lentulus Spinther, the governor-elect of Cilicia, but in January 56 a prophetic utterance was discovered in Rome's collection of Sibylline oracles that threw a wrench in the works: it predicted danger for the commonwealth should the restoration happen by violent means. The senate thereupon cancelled its earlier decree. After much inconclusive manoeuvring, Gabinius, to whom Ptolemy had turned for help as a Roman proconsul in the area with a well-trained fighting force at hand, went all Nike and just did it in 55. According to Plutarch, a decisive voice in convincing the hesitant proconsul to grab the opportunity even without any official endorsement from the senate was Antony (*Life of Antony* 3): 'After this, Ptolemy tried to persuade Gabinius by a bribe of ten thousand talents to join him in an invasion of Egypt and recover the kingdom for him. But the greater part of the officers were opposed to the plan, and Gabinius himself felt a certain dread of the war, although he was completely captivated by the ten thousand talents. Antony, however, who was ambitious of great exploits and eager to gratify the request of Ptolemy, joined the king in persuading and inciting Gabinius to the expedition'.

The affair was hardly a decade old, and Cicero could limit himself to the barest allusion (*Alexandriam*). To what extent Antony's alleged involvement would have been common knowledge is another question. But he was part of the campaign, which sufficed Cicero to single out three forms of defiance in an unbalanced tricolon, around the anaphora of *contra*: against the authority of the senate (*senatus auctoritas*); against the commonwealth (*res publica*); and against the protocols that regulated Rome's interaction with the divine sphere (*religiones*).

senatus auctoritatem: *senatus* is genitive singular.

sed habebat ducem Gabinium, quicum quidvis rectissime facere posset: the antecedent of *quicum* (the relative pronoun in the ablative + the preposition *cum* here used as a postpositive enclitic) is *Gabinium*. Antony is the subject of *habebat* and *posset* (a consecutive subjunctive). The pronoun *quidvis*, the accusative object of *facere*, means, literally, 'anything you want' (from *quid* + *vis* — from *volo*). The sentence drips with irony, not least in light of the fact that the affair had nasty repercussions for Gabinius, who was put on trial on the triple charge of (*a*) *maiestas* (high treason) for leaving his province without senatorial approval and in defiance of the Sibylline Oracles; (*b*) *repetundae* (extortion of money, including the bribe he had accepted from Ptolemy); (*c*) *ambitus* (illegal means of canvassing for the consulship). The third charge was eventually dropped; of the first he was acquitted; but, despite Cicero's (!) defence (yes, Pompey, an ally of Gabinius, had ways and means of twisting our orator's arms at the time), he was found guilty of extortion and had to go into exile.

rectissime: Mayor (1861: 98) deftly glosses the deeply ironic superlative as 'without the least risk of being called to account'.

qui tum inde reditus [erat] **aut qualis? prius in ultimam Galliam ex Aegypto** [iit] **quam domum** [rediit]: the repetition of *inde*, the renewed suppression of the verb, and the rhetorical question combine to convey an impression of haste: Cicero is speeding through Antony's biography — just as Antony is speeding across the Near East and Western Europe. Both *qui* and *qualis* are interrogative adjectives modifying *reditus* — a construction difficult to replicate in English: 'And then what next (*tum inde*)? His homecoming — what was it like?' Cicero answers his own question, again in staccato form with the verbs elided. After his successful Egyptian venture, Antony, in 54, went to join Caesar on his campaign in Gaul before returning to Rome.

in ultimam Galliam: 'to furthest Gaul' — rather accurate, while also conveniently extreme: in 54 BCE Caesar had to contend with an uprising of the Belgian chieftain Ambiorix.

quae autem domus [erat]?: as Mayor (1861: 99) notes, the *autem* here has a corrective force: Cicero finished the previous sentence with the idiomatic expression *domum redire* ('to return home'), in which *domum* figures generically to indicate a place rather than a specific property. Cicero now builds on this, asking, 'Actually, what was that home you returned to anyway?'

suam enim quisque domum tum obtinebat nec erat usquam tua [sc. domus]: the answer to his own rhetorical question revolves around a temporal watershed signaled by the adverb *tum*: back in the 50s, i.e.

before the property confiscations and redistributions that happened in the wake of the civil war that broke out in 49, of which Antony was a major beneficiary, acquiring the former property of Pompey the Great (see §§ 62, 64, 103 and above 150–51), each person (*quisque*) had their own house (*suam… domum*) — and yours, Antony (a sudden shift from third to second person), did not exist (*nec erat usquam tua*).

domum dico? quid erat in terris ubi in tuo pedem poneres praeter unum Misenum, quod cum sociis tamquam Sisaponem tenebas?: Cicero has one more go: 'Do I keep saying "home"?', now extending his frame of reference from Rome to elsewhere in Italy or indeed the entire world (*in terris*). Apparently, in the wake of his father's bankruptcy, Antony's family lost all of its property, except a place at Misenum, a promontory in Campania, which he owned jointly with others. In a society in which the aristocratic *domus* constituted an important symbol of social status and family lineage, the lack of a family home renders Antony unfit for public service: 'Of course, still today the size and elegance of a house are thought to symbolize status, but the nature of Roman public life dictated that the domus be of markedly greater importance, as implied by some malicious remarks about Roman leaders. Among other things for which Antony is ridiculed in the *Second Philippic*, Cicero includes the fact that Antony had no *domus* of his own even before Caesar's confiscations, when nearly everyone had his own house'.[13]

ubi in tuo [fundo / praedio] **pedem poneres**: after *in tuo*, one could supply a noun such as *fundus* ('country estate') or *praedium* ('landed property', 'estate'), but in many ways the bare neuter pronoun is the more attractive option: 'Could you set your foot on any place on earth you could call yours…?' The alliteration *pedem poneres* is onomatopoetic, the subjunctive potential.

---

13   Saller (1994: 89). The 'even' in the last sentence strikes an odd note insofar as it implies that Antony could have lost his home during the confiscations: the exact opposite was the case, of course: he bought Pompey the Great's house at auction! Cicero makes much of this 'outrage' elsewhere in the speech, inveighing against Antony's lack of *domus* here and his wrongful 'domestication' there. For the house as an important site of identity politics in late republican Rome see further Clarke (1991), Wallace-Hadrill (1994), Hales (2009) (2013) and Hölkeskamp (2014).

Misenum: *Misenum*, the antecedent of *quod*, should here be understood in the sense of *villam Misenensem*: see Shackleton Bailey (1986: 63, n. 46). He explains: 'If Misenum had been a town in its own right an adjectival form would have been used'.

tamquam Sisaponem: *Sisaponem* stands in apposition to *quod*: 'which you own jointly with partners in the same way (*tamquam*) as Sisapo [sc. is owned]. The reference is to a place in Spain (Hispania Baetica) where cinnabar (vermilion) was mined. The mines were in the possession of a corporation, so no individual was an exclusive owner. Lacy (1986: 193) detects various overtones: the place was a complete backwater in the middle of nowhere, notoriously difficult to reach; the association is of 'the common dosshouse of a group of partners, not a family home with gods'; and 'cinnabar dealers were notorious cheats'. And at any rate, what is quite all right in the case of mines (co-ownership) is a disgrace in the case of private property. As Denniston (1926: 128) suggests, we may conjecture that 'Antony had made over a portion of his property at Misenum, or conceded certain rights over it, to his creditors; and that consequently he was a mere partner in his own property'. In addition, the reference to Spain completes Cicero's geopolitical sweep, from the farthest East and South (Egypt) to the farthest North (Belgium) to the farthest West (Spain). In the 50s, Antony is adrift in the world, a notional exile, without any place in Rome and hardly a foothold in Italy — precisely what Cicero would like him to become again.

§ 49: Credit for Murder

At the end of the previous paragraph, we left Antony with Caesar in furthest Gaul (54 BCE). Now we have moved on a year: in the summer or fall of 53, Antony returned to Rome to stand for election to the quaestorship. His quest for public office coincided with the hot phase of street brawling between the gangs of Clodius and Milo that ended with the former dead and the latter exiled for his murder. Antony's role in all of this was marginal at best, but Cicero had his reasons for dwelling on the affair. Antony seems to have blamed him for Clodius' death — a charge Cicero already rebutted at length in the first half of the speech (2.21–22). § 49 completes the argument by turning the tables on Antony: the one with Clodius' attempted murder on his *CV* is Antony, not Cicero. Cicero is at pains to point out yet again that he has no blood on his hands: he has no wish to take credit for any attempt on Clodius' life, whether it failed (as was the case with Antony's) or succeeded (Milo's). There may also have been secondary considerations for returning to Clodius: from the very beginning of the speech, where Cicero imputes to Antony the (perverse) wish to appear more insane than the former tribune (2.1: … *furiosior quam Clodius viderere*) the two keep company. Any mention of Clodius inevitably also brings to mind Clodius' spouse Fulvia, who went on to marry Curio after Clodius' death and then, after Curio died in the civil wars, became Antony's wife in 46 BCE (see above 178–79): she, too, is a major target of invective abuse throughout the speech.

Chronology: the precise moment of Antony's return to Rome, his activities in the run-up to his election as quaestor, and indeed the year of his quaestorship, are not easy to determine from our (seemingly conflicting) sources. As Linderski and Kaminska-Linderski point out:

'We do not know exactly when Antonius left Gaul and returned to Rome *ad quaesturam petendam* but it was in the period of armed clashes between Milo and Clodius who were canvassing respectively for the consulship and the praetorship. As the consuls for 53 were elected only in July or August of that year, the electoral *comitia* for 52 could only have been summoned, at the earliest, late in August or in September, and Antonius cannot have come to Rome long before that date' (1974: 216).[14] In their reconstruction of what happened, 'Antonius came to Rome in 53 with a clear plan to obtain the quaestorship of 52', but then changed his plans: 'The Clodius affair caused him to withdraw his candidature for 52 and to stand for 51. On his election in the summer or autumn 52 he hurried to Caesar without waiting for an appropriate *senatus consultum*' (223) (see further on § 50 below). Set out schematically, we are dealing with the following likely chronology:[15]

Late August / September 53

Antony returns to Rome with the intention to stand for the quaestorship

Autumn / Winter 53

Antony gets embroiled in the street-fighting around Clodius and his gang and on one occasion almost kills Clodius; he decides to postpone standing for the quaestorship

18 January 52 + aftermath

Clodius gets killed by Milo's slaves in a street brawl | this is followed by popular unrest; Pompey is declared *consul sine collega*

April 52

Trial of Milo, with Cicero acting on behalf of the defence and Antony as a member of the prosecution

---

14 See further Gruen (1974: 339), on Antony's role in the prosecution of Milo as one of the *subscriptores*: 'Antonius' relations with Clodius had fluctuated — not surprisingly, in view of the latter's vagaries. But, after Clodius' death, he was prepared to take his part. A former cavalry officer under Gabinius and soon to join Caesar in Gaul, Antonius may have been acting in the interests of the triumvirs — and certainly *in his own*'.

15 Based on Linderski and Kaminska-Linderski (1974) and Ruebel (1979).

Summer / Autumn 52

Antony gets elected to the quaestorship for 51 and right away returns to
Caesar in Gaul, without waiting for the passing of the senatorial decree on
the assignment of the quaestors to specific provinces, the *Senatus Consultum
de provinciis quaestorum* (Cicero picks up on this in § 50: see below)

5 December 52

The tenure of Antony's quaestorship begins

Favours and (political) friendships: much in § 49 involves key social
protocols that governed aristocratic interaction in republican Rome.
Friendship networks and patronage-relations were a big part of how
the Roman elite exercised power, resulting in an economy of favours
and services received and rendered, frequently with shifting alliances.
In order to be a successful patron, it helped to be on good terms with
as many other members of the ruling elite as possible. And it often
happened that people who disliked each other and had significant run-
ins saw themselves helping each other and collaborating at the request of
a third party. In the 50s, the triumvirs, and Caesar in particular, twisted
Cicero's arm, forcing him to lend his support to individuals he deemed
repulsive and despicable, such as Gabinius. One of the favours that
Caesar asked of Cicero was reconciliation with Antony. Cicero obliged
(no choice), but here pretends that Antony, on account of the favour he
received from Cicero at Caesar's behest, i.e. support in his candidacy for
the quaestorship, tried to return it by having a shot at killing Clodius,
one of Cicero's arch-enemies.

venis e Gallia ad quaesturam petendam: Cicero switches to the present
tense (*venis*) for vividness. *ad* here expresses purpose: '(in order)
to stand as candidate for the quaestorship'. *petere* is a technical term
for 'seeking to obtain a specific magistracy', 'being a candidate for',
'standing for election to': *OLD* s.v. 9. If the chronology suggested above
is correct, Antony started his canvassing campaign in 53 (for tenure in
52), but — for whatever reason — was not elected (and did not stand as
a candidate?) until 52 (and assumed office in 51). Cicero, in his summary
approach to those years, is unconcerned with such niceties.

aude dicere te prius ad parentem tuam venisse quam ad me [venisses]: *aude*, the imperative singular of *audeo*, to dare, governs the supplementary infinitive *dicere*, which introduces an indirect statement with *te* as subject accusative and *venisse* as infinitive. This is followed by a temporal clause introduced by *quam* (set up by *prius*). (The conjugation *priusquam* ('before') may be written as two words (*prius quam*), which — as here — may be separated by intervening words: see *OLD* s.v.) Cicero elides the verb of the *priusquam*-clause, but it can easily be supplied from context. Cicero dares Antony to deny that after his prolonged absence from Rome he knocked at Cicero's door to enlist help in a bid for the quaestorship before calling on his mother Julia (note that *tuam*, modifying the gender-neutral *parentem*, is feminine: Antony's father had already died).

acceperam iam ante Caesaris litteras ut mihi satis fieri paterer a te: itaque ne loqui quidem sum te passus de gratia: to smoothe the ground, Caesar anticipated the meeting between Antony and Cicero by sending Cicero a letter (*litteras — litterae* is a plural noun), requesting that he respond positively to Antony's efforts to make amends for his earlier hostility. Cicero obliged Caesar to the extent that he waived off Antony's attempt to explain himself and re-establish friendly relations.

Extra Information: a republic of letters[16]
You might wonder about this 'politics by letter' we capture in this paragraph — it looks kind of seedy, doesn't it; a special variant of nepotism by which influential members of the ruling elite fixed things in the dark corridors of power, away from the public limelight — the ancient equivalent to a special 'phone call' in modern times, which happens to be more important than merit or interview performance in determining (say) the outcome of a job search. The fact is, the volume of correspondence that flowed to and from Rome in late-republican times was significant and constituted an important medium for doing politics. Members of Rome's oligarchy performed their role as patrons via an economy of favours granted and received, and the letter proved an ideal format to make personal requests or issue recommendations (i.e. requests on behalf of others). It offered an intuitive medium of interaction for a ruling elite that had much invested in the cultivation of networks grounded in 'friendship', tactical and

---

16   The following is adapted from Gildenhard (2018).

otherwise.[17] The tropes routinely invoked to characterize friendship tend to be similar to the commonplaces employed to describe ideal epistolary dialogue: most obviously, friendship and epistolary ideology are much invested in the mirror-effect that assimilates the interacting parties (friends, senders and receivers) to one another. Many of the concerns and values of the senatorial elite (face, status, obligations; a commitment to oligarchic equality; consensual politics; cultivation of friendly relations through care and courtesy, including the investment of time) found congenial articulation in and through the writing of letters and manifest themselves in the 'politics of politeness' that defined epistolary discourse among Roman aristocrats.[18]

Letter-writing in republican Rome thus reflected and helped to sustain the rule of a senatorial elite, enacting a set of aristocratic values that resonated with key principles of republican government. Yet the practice of elite letter-writing also stood in latent tension to public procedures and civic institutions of the commonwealth, owing to the tendency of the genre to 'personalize politics'. And one power broker, who also happened to be a particularly gifted and active pen pal, ultimately managed to destroy the oligarchic equilibrium that sustained the senatorial tradition of republican government, not least through his strategic use of epistolary communication. As John Henderson and Josiah Osgood have shown, Caesar exercised his stranglehold on Roman politics during his decade-long absence from Rome while on campaign in Gaul in the 50s BCE, not least through an active correspondence with key associates in the capital.[19] A special gift for multi-tasking and discursive speed enabled him to produce a steady stream of letters. In addition, already in the 50s, he seems to have innovated in how he organized his staff, instituting a special position for a high-ranking secretary reminiscent of a practice known from the royal courts of the Hellenistic period.[20] And the importance of long-distance communication did not lessen during the years of civil warfare: during the five-year period between his crossing of the Rubicon in January 49 and his assassination on the Ides of March 44, Caesar was only sporadically present in Rome.

ut mihi satis fieri paterer a te: literally 'that I allow [*paterer* = 1st person singular imperfect subjunctive passive of the deponent *patior*, introducing an indirect statement] that attention be given [*satis fieri* or *satisfieri*: present infinitive passive of *satisfacere*] by you [*a te*: ablative of

---

17   A sample of landmark publications on the phenomenon of Roman friendship includes Saller (1982), Brunt (1988b), White (1993), Konstan (1997), Verboven (2002), Burton (2011), and Williams (2012). For the letter-format as an enactment of friendship see Trapp (2003: 40–41).
18   Hall (2009).
19   Henderson (2007), Osgood (2009).
20   See Malitz (1987).

agency] to me [*mihi*]'. Differently put: 'Caesar asked me not to send you packing when you'd come knocking at my door'.

itaque ne loqui quidem sum te passus de gratia: the main verb is *passus sum*; it introduces an indirect statement with *te* as subject accusative and *loqui* (framed by *ne... quidem*: 'not even') as infinitive. *de gratia* goes with *loqui*. Literally: 'Therefore I allowed you not even to speak about [re-establishing] friendly relations', i.e. because he had already granted the request on the basis of Caesar's letter, though in English the negation in *ne... quidem* is perhaps best used with *passus sum*: 'Therefore I did not even allow you to speak about...'. The hyperbaton between *loqui* and *de gratia* is expressive of the lack of need to put the request for renewed friendship into words. Likewise, the word order *sum te passus* seems to smother Antony, as Cicero generates the impression that he is a plaything in the diplomatic relations of more important statesmen, such as Caesar and himself.

postea sum cultus a te, tu a me observatus [es] in petitione quaesturae: the imperfect balance of personal pronouns (there is no *ego* corresponding to *tu*) might hint at the fact that the ensuing period of collaboration rested on shaky foundations — as do the two passive verbs (*sum cultus*; *observatus*), which are chiastically positioned around the two ablatives of agency (*a te* :: *a me*).

quo quidem tempore P. Clodium [approbante populo Romano] **in foro es conatus occidere, cumque eam rem tua sponte conarere, non impulsu meo, tamen ita praedicabas, te non existimare, nisi illum interfecisses, umquam mihi pro tuis in me iniuriis satis esse facturum**: a potentially confusing sentence: the main clause (underlined) consists of two parts linked by the *-que* after *cum*: *quo quidem tempore P. Clodium ... in foro es conatus occidere* and *tamen ita praedicabas*. The *cum*-clause functions as bridge between the two segments of the main clause: *eam rem* refers back to Antony's attempt to kill Clodius; and the adversative sense of *cum* ('even though') sets up *tamen ita praedicabas*. *praedicabas* governs an indirect statement with *te* as subject accusative and *existimare* as infinitive, which in turn governs an indirect statement with an understood *te* as subject accusative and *satis esse facturum* as verb. This last indirect statement also functions as apodosis of a conditional sequence, with *nisi illum interfecisses* as protasis: 'It was just at that time that, with the approval of the Roman people, you attempted to kill Publius Clodius in the Forum, and, although you attempted that deed at your own initiative, and not at my instigation, you still professed that you thought that, except by killing him, you could never make amends for your wrongs against me'.

quo quidem tempore P. Clodium … in foro es conatus occidere: *quo* is a connecting relative (= *eo*). The moment in time indicated by the ablative of time *quo… tempore* (qualified by the particle *quidem*: Antony's support of Cicero is the exception, not the rule) is suitably vague, but falls in the autumn of 53 BCE, i.e. shortly after Antony's return from Gaul. Cicero had already mentioned the incident in his speech in defence of Milo (*pro Milone* 40).

approbante populo Romano: an ablative absolute; whatever approval from the people Cicero claims for Antony's failed attack on Clodius' life, the populace felt outraged over Clodius' death at the hands of Milo.

cumque eam rem tua sponte conarere, non impulsu meo: the verb of the concessive *cum*-clause is *conarere*, the alternative 2nd person singular imperfect subjunctive passive of the first-conjugation deponent *conor, conari* (= *conareris*). It is framed by the contrastive chiasmus (a) *tua* (b) *sponte* :: *non* (b) *impulsu* (a) *meo*. Cicero insists that he did not instigate Antony in any way to try to kill Clodius; his emphasis on Antony deciding by himself to make an attempt on Clodius' life sets up the following sentence where Cicero rebuts Antony's claim that he put Milo onto it.

pro tuis in me iniuriis: Cicero now gives an account of the rationale for Antony's failed attempt at homicide, which runs something as follows: (*a*) in the past Antony inflicted grievous *iniuriae* on Cicero; (*b*) now Cicero nevertheless does his best to help Antony out, if at the behest of Caesar; (*c*) Antony feels that he has accumulated such an amount of social debt — consisting of favours from Cicero compounded by his earlier mistreatment of him — that, he feels, he can only repay it by murdering Cicero's personal enemy Clodius. It is not entirely clear, however, what these *iniuriae* are; and there is indeed no evidence for personal enmity between Cicero and Antony until after the outbreak of civil war in 49, i.e. long after Clodius' actual demise. Cicero, it seems, plays fast and loose with chronology, most likely (as the subsequent sentence makes clear) in response to Antony's charge that it was he who egged on Clodius' actual killer, Milo (and was also the brain behind the assassination of Caesar) — the éminence grise, in other words, who does not shy away from instigating murder to suit his political turns.

in quo demiror cur Milonem impulsu meo rem illam egisse dicas, cum te ultro mihi idem illud deferentem numquam sim adhortatus: Cicero picks up on the previous antithesis *tua sponte – non impulsu meo* to reiterate his rebuttal of Antony's charge that he incited Milo to murder Clodius (cf. 2.21, cited above). Given that Cicero never made any move to encourage Antony along those lines even though Antony freely volunteered his services, it makes no sense to assume that he tried to incite Milo. The sense of both the *cum*-clause and of the participle *deferentem* (modifying *te*, the accusative object of *sim adhortatus*) is concessive: '*even though* I never encouraged you *despite the fact* that you offered that same deed (just like *rem illam* above and below, *idem illud* refers to the killing of Clodius) to me of your own accord'.

in quo: a connecting relative (= *in eo*): 'in this affair'.

demiror: Cicero uses the composite (*de-miror*) for emphasis: 'I am *utterly* baffled…'

cur Milonem impulsu meo rem illam egisse dicas: *cur* introduces an indirect question (hence the subjunctive). *dicas* governs an indirect statement with *Milonem* as subject accusative, *egisse* as infinitive and *rem illam* (= the killing of Clodius) as object accusative.

quamquam, si in eo perseverares, ad tuam gloriam rem illam referri malebam quam ad meam gratiam: *quamquam* here introducing a main clause, elaborating on the previous point that Cicero never gave any encouragement to Antony's homicidal plans and certainly would not have wished to take credit for the killing had he succeeded. The moods and tenses of the conditional sequence (imperfect subjunctive in the protasis: *perseverares*; imperfect indicative in the apodosis: *malebam*, from *malo, malle* — 'prefer') reflect the fact that Cicero is looking at the possibility of Antony's managing to kill Clodius from a past point of view: 'in case you persevered, I preferred that the deed be assigned to your glory rather than my influence' (see Gildersleeve and Lodge 383). *gratia* here refers to the influence over Antony that Cicero acquired by supporting his candidacy for the quaestorship — doing away with Clodius is thus Antony's idea of returning a favour, a murderous expression of misconceived gratitude, which Cicero gracefully declines, preferring Antony to take full credit for the deed. As Griffin and Atkins (1991: xlv–xlvi) explain: '*Gratia* draws its meaning from the social network of friendships and other relationships bound by exchange of services. Someone who is in a position to grant benefits or give assistance has *gratia* in that he has influence or the potential to command gratitude. Someone who has already granted someone else a benefit has *gratia* in that, according to the public code, he deserves gratitude'. The key here is that there is a coercive element to *gratia*: someone who has received a favour is in 'debt' and expected to reciprocate to balance the sheets.

rem illam: yet another reference to the murder of Clodius, following on from *eam rem*, *rem illam* and *idem illud*.

§ 50: With Caesar in Gaul: Profligacy and Profiteering

In § 47 Cicero announced that he intends to treat the portion of Antony's biography that falls in-between his depravities as a teenager and the role he played in the civil war cursorily: *ad haec enim quae in civili bello, in maximis rei publicae miseriis fecit, et ad ea quae cotidie facit, festinat animus.* Barely three paragraphs later, we reach this moment. The first half of § 50 (*quaestor es factus... viri tui similis esses*) traces Antony's return to Caesar in Gaul after his election to the quaestorship in the autumn of 52 and his return to stand for election to another magistracy, the tribuneship. Antony succeeded in getting himself elected and entered office on 10 December 50. A few weeks later, on 10 January 49, Caesar crossed the Rubicon with his army.

Cicero gets much invective mileage out of Antony's role in plunging Rome into civil war. To prep his readers properly, he pauses portentously for an impassioned address to his senatorial audience (*accipite nunc, quaeso... reperieties*). The address, which makes up the rest of the paragraph, introduces a lengthy assessment of a decision Antony made as a tribune of the people in the increasingly convulsive negotiations over Caesar's status (and his demands) that preceded the outbreak of war. When Antony and some of his colleagues in office, who had used their position as tribunes to represent Caesar's interests, including the veto of certain senatorial measures designed to rein in the strongman, felt that their safety had become compromised, they fled Rome to join Caesar at Ravenna. This offered Caesar the perfect pretext to initiate hostilities — he could spin his aggression as motivated by the desire to safeguard the constitutional rights of the tribunes of the people, i.e. to defend republican traditions against the tyrannical exercise of power by an oligarchic clique around Pompey. In §§ 51–55 (not part of the set text) Cicero dwells at length on this momentous action by the pro-Caesarian tribunes, and in particular Antony, turning Antony into the ultimate cause of Rome's collapse into civil conflict and constitutional chaos.

quaestor es factus: deinde continuo sine senatus consulto, sine sorte, sine lege ad Caesarem cucurristi: after his election, Antony 'almost immediately' (*continuo*) returned to Caesar in Gaul. Cicero represents the departure as an outrageous breach of constitutional protocols: the asyndetic tricolon, reinforced powerfully by the triple anaphora of the preposition *sine* (further enhanced by the alliteration with *senatus* and *sorte*) gives the impression that Antony trampled upon tradition in his rush from the city. This was not the case. To understand Cicero's spin here requires some understanding of the procedure that governed the assignment of elected quaestors to provinces. As Linderski and Kaminska-Linderski (1974: 221) explain, quaestors could be assigned directly to a specific province by senatorial decree (*senatus consultum*); allocation of the remaining ones would happen by lot (*sorte*) on the date of their entry into the office. They accordingly reconstruct the events in 51 as follows:

- Autumn 52: Antony gets elected to the quaestorship; Caesar requests that he be assigned to him.

- Shortly after the election: Antony leaves Rome to join Caesar in Gaul, assuming, rightly, that his assignment to Caesar by senatorial decree is a mere formality.

- Shortly after his departure: the senate passes a *senatus consultum* that indeed ratifies Antony's assignment to Caesar's provinces. (See Linderski and Kaminska-Linderski (1974: 220–21): 'Cicero does not say that such a decree was not passed | at all; indeed the implication is that it was in fact carried out but only after Antonius had already left the city').

- 5 December 52: those quaestors as yet unassigned are distributed to provinces by lot.

The sentence thus offers a brilliant illustration of Cicero's gift for spin, i.e. the ability to twist unobjectionable facts and harmless truths into invective, without lying outright. Antony did indeed rush to Caesar *sine senatus consulto* [Cicero simply fails to mention that such a decree was supplied shortly thereafter], *sine sorte* [true, of course, but utterly unobjectionable: Antony had no need to wait for the *sortitio provinciarum* since he was about to be assigned a province by senatorial decree], and *sine lege* [a vague phrase that is technically true, gives the impression of constitutional outrage, but does not really apply in any meaningful way to the case at hand]. What was 'a minor constitutional impropriety' (Antony leaving Rome without waiting for the official passing of the senatorial decree, which anyway 'was a matter of administrative routine': Linderski and Kaminska-Linderski 1974: 221) gets turned into eloquent outrage at Antony's alleged depravity.

continuo: the temporal adverb is worth pausing over: 'The word is commonly rendered as "immediately"; Cicero, however, … uses it often to indicate that between two closely connected events no other event occurred bearing upon them. Thus the length of time indicated by *continuo* may vary considerably, as is also true of other similar expressions like *mox* and *nuper*. The exact meaning of the passage would be that in the period of time between Antonius' election and his departure from Rome no decree of the senate was passed concerning the quaestorian provinces and no *sortitio provinciarum* took place' (Linderski and Kaminska-Linderski 1974: 220).

senatus consulto: *senatus* (a fourth declension noun) is genitive singular, depending on *consulto*.

sine sorte: for sorting out the lot in republican Rome, see Rosenstein (1995).

sine lege: 'without any legal justification' (Linderski and Kaminska-Linderski, 1974: 220, n. 37).

ad Caesarem cucurristi: the passage here anticipates another, more consequential flight to Caesar — on the eve of civil war in January 49 BCE. Cicero will shortly shift his focus from the domestic to the civic sphere, using (Antony's two flights to) Caesar as a bridge.

id enim unum in terris egestatis, aeris alieni, nequitiae perditis vitae rationibus perfugium esse ducebas: the pronoun *id* has a somewhat vague reference ('being in Gaul with Caesar'), as Cicero continues his geopolitical vilification of Antony from the previous paragraph. In § 48, we encountered Antony adrift, without a moral or geographical centre, and here we get more of the same. Caesar's headquarters are the only place on earth able to afford Antony protection against the consequences of his vices and profligacy. *ducere* here has the sense 'to consider, believe, think, reckon' (*OLD* s.v. 30) and governs an indirect statement with *id unum* as subject accusative, *esse* as infinitive, and *perfugium* as predicative complement.

id… unum: *unum* modifies *id* in predicative attribution; English here prefers the adverb rather than the adjective: 'this alone' rather than 'this one' (see Gildersleeve & Lodge 204–06).

in terris: *terra* in the plural can refer, as here, to 'the earth with all that it contains, the known or inhabited world' (*OLD* s.v. 9).

egestatis, aeris alieni, nequitiae … perfugium: the *OLD* s.v. *perfugium* 2a lists this passage as an example of *perfugium* being construed with genitives that indicate the items that receive protection, but that doesn't sound quite right. It's not that Antony wishes to protect his penury, debt, and moral worthlessness — quite the contrary, as the next sentence makes clear. The genitives are better understood as qualities or circumstances that require Antony to seek protection. (See e.g. *Div.* 2.150: *perfugium videtur omnium laborum ac sollicitudinum esse somnus* — 'Sleep is regarded as a refuge from every toil and care'.)

egestatis: the lexeme *egestas* ('extreme poverty', 'destitution') carries opprobrium. The late-antique commentary on Virgil that goes under the name *Servius Auctus* notes a propos *Georgics* 1.146: *peior est egestas, quam paupertas: paupertas enim honesta esse potest, egestas enim turpis est* ('*egestas* is worse than *paupertas*: for *paupertas* can be honourable, *egestas* is shameful'). Unsurprisingly, Cicero exploits its pejorative connotations for his invective agenda: 'The word *egestas* has a bad odour in the public orations of Cicero…; for him and his aristocratic audiences it denoted one of the prime causes of political radicalism' (Jocelyn 1967: 398). In the speech *de Provinciis Consularibus*, for instance, he vilifies the *scelus*, *cupiditas*, *egestas*, *audacia* of the two consuls of 58, Piso and Gabinius (43). See also *Philippic* 2.62: *cogebat egestas*.

nequitiae: *nequitia* is a catch-all term applied to persons of bad moral fiber ('worthlessness') that manifests itself in such characteristics as idleness (in this sense it becomes a calling card of the elegiac lover), negligence, vileness, profligacy, or wickedness. (In his *Tusculan Disputations* 3.17–18, Cicero defines *nequitia* as the antonym of *frugalitas* and offers a faux-etymological explication of the term.)

perfugium: in his *Bellum Civile* (if not before), Caesar fashioned himself as offering a place of safety to those in distress. At *Bellum Civile* 1.6, he notably writes of events in early January 49, i.e. just before the outbreak of the civil war: *profugiunt statim ex urbe tribuni plebis seseque ad Caesarem conferunt*: 'instantly, the tribunes of the people fled from the city and went to Caesar'. One of the tribunes was of course Antony. See also Sallust, *Bellum Catilinae* 54.3, in his contrastive comparison of Caesar and Cato: *Caesar dando sublevando ignoscundo, Cato nihil largiundo gloriam adeptus est. in altero miseris perfugium erat, in altero malis pernicies* ('Caesar gained glory by giving, helping, and forgiving; Cato by never stooping to bribery. One was a refuge for the unfortunate, the other a scourge for the wicked'). For Sallust, both Caesar's support for the wretched (those who had fallen on hard times without their fault) and Cato's uncompromising attitude towards evil-doers seem positive qualities; Cicero is less forgiving. For him, the *perfugium* that Caesar offers to someone like Antony discredits the future dictator as well. Later on in the speech, he makes the point explicitly, in language that recalls the present passage (§ 78): *habebat hoc omnino Caesar: quem plane perditum aere alieno egentemque, si eundem nequam hominem audacemque cognorat, hunc in familiaritatem libentissime recipiebat* ('This was entirely Caesar's way: when a man was utterly ruined by debt and in want, if he recognised in that man an audacious rascal, he most willingly admitted him into his friendship').

perditis vitae rationibus: Cicero uses the expression *perdita ratio* (as antonym to *bona ratio*) at *in Catilinam* 2.25, in the sense of 'reckless (*perdita*) guiding principle' (*ratio*): see Dyck (2008: 159). Here the meaning seems to be: 'after you have ruined any (possibility for a) normal way of life'. (See *OLD* s.v. *ratio* 13: *ratio vitae* ~ 'a plan or pattern of life', i.e. a way of life that conforms to rational and socially acceptable principles).

ibi te cum et illius largitionibus et tuis rapinis explevisses, si hoc est explere, haurire quod statim effundas, advolasti egens ad tribunatum, ut in eo magistratu, si posses, viri tui similis esses: the period begins with a temporal *cum*-clause (*ibi te cum... explevisses*), attached to which is a *si*-clause that segues into a *quod*-clause (*si hoc est... effundas*); then comes the main clause (*advolasti egens ad tribunatum*), followed by a purpose clause introduced by *ut*; embedded therein is another *si*-clause (*si posses*). Cicero keeps Antony in constant motion: in his frenetic profligacy, the wastrel somehow manages to gorge himself rich in Gaul through Caesar's munificence and his own criminal exploitations only to instantly regurgitate all of his newfound wealth and fly back to the capital in the same state of disgraceful penury in which he left it (an 'achievement' marked by the figura etymologica *egestatis ... egens*).

illius largitionibus: like its near synonym *liberalitas*, *largitio* ('generosity'), the noun to the adjective *largus* ('munificent, bountiful, lavish') and the deponent *largior, -iri, -itus* ('to give generously, bestow, lavish', but also 'to give presents corruptly, engage in bribery') could be used in both a positive and a negative sense. A generous spirit, perhaps even the open-handed distribution of personal wealth among the less fortunate, are in principal praiseworthy qualities, but in late-republican Rome (and elsewhere), the bestowal of largesse by powerful members of the ruling elite among peers and subordinates also constituted a form of expenditure with an obvious political motivation: it generated ties that bound the recipients into an economy of services via an ethics of reciprocity. And no-one was more adept in buying in personal loyalty than Caesar. His 'generosity to his lieutenants and troops ... was notorious in his own day, naturally arousing suspicions among his peers and rivals' (Pelling (2011: 214), with reference to Cic. *Att.* 7.11.9 (130), 8.14.1 (164), *Fam.* 7.13.1 (36), *Phil.* 2.50 and 116, and Catullus 29.3). In some places, Cicero differentiates between positive *liberalitas* and negative *largitio*, while conceding that in practice it is often impossible to tell the two apart: see e.g. *On the Ideal Orator* (*de Oratore*) 2.105: *de ambitu raro illud datur, ut possis liberalitatem atque benignitatem ab ambitu atque largitione seiungere* — 'in cases involving bribery at elections it is rarely possible to distinguish open-handedness and generosity from bribery and corruption'). But in his *On Duties* (*de Officiis*), Cicero condemns *liberalitas* in the sense of the unfettered use of resources: to build up networks of friends grounded in material obligations is a proto-tyrannical feature corrosive of oligarchic equality within Rome's senatorial elite. (A third term of similar semantic range as *liberalitas* and *largitio*, i.e. *munificentia*, 'seems to have escaped any connotations of bribery, even though it often pertains to gifts of significant proportions made by the politically powerful': Forbis 1996: 34. See further Coffee 2016: 82–85).

Extra information:
Catullus 29 offers a 'no-holds barred' critique of the sleaze economy by which Rome's generals (in this case Pompey and Caesar) bled dry conquered people not least to subsidize revolting, if loyal, underlings at Rome (in this case Mamurra, whom Catullus elsewhere calls 'Rome's greatest dick'). Note the reference to *sinistra liberalitas* in line 15.

tuis rapinis: one of the 'perks' of being in cahoots with a successful general was the opportunity to profit from imperial exploitation through plunder and booty (which of course also funded the *largitio* of the commander).

si hoc est explere, haurire quod statim effundas: *hoc est* = *id est*, with the infinitive *explere* as predicative complement, which is then glossed in apposition by *haurire quod statim effundas*: 'if this is what is meant by *explere* ("to stuff oneself full"), namely to gulp down (*haurire*) what one then instantly regurgitates'.

ut in eo magistratu, si posses, viri tui similis esses: Curio, Antony's 'husband' (that's the meaning of *viri tui*, a little splatter of invective bile in the spirit of 2.44–47), preceded him in the tribuneship, holding it in 50 BCE.

accipite nunc, quaeso, non ea quae ipse in se atque in domesticum decus impure et intemperanter [fecit], sed quae in nos fortunasque nostras, id est in universam rem publicam, impie ac nefarie fecerit: the sentence is not easy to construe given that we have a relative clause that lacks a verb (*non ea quae... intemperanter*), followed by an indirect question (*quae... fecerit*). Some scholars have detected an anacoluthon here, i.e. an unexpected discontinuity of syntactical structure: see Ramsey (2003: 309). But as Roland Mayer (2005: 200) has shown, the syntax can be made to work without us needing to suppose a change of construction: '*Accipite* governs two objects, first *ea quae* ..., then an indirect question, which grammatically considered is a noun-clause. That the relative clause implicitly borrows its indicative verb, *fecit*, from the subjunctive verb of the indirect question, *fecerit*, is certainly nonchalant, but the syntax of the sentence has not gone off the rails'. Quite the contrary: the relative clause and the indirect question correlate Antony's disastrous personal track-record in the domestic sphere (just covered) with his calamitous impact on the commonwealth (about to come into focus). Cicero here makes use of 'the powerful idea that a man's public behaviour will be all of a piece with his conduct in the private sphere': Treggiari (1997). Analogous design aids the (climactic) transition: in both subordinate clauses, Cicero uses pleonastic phrasing to specify the target of Antony's brutish and brutalizing behaviour (*in se atque in domesticum decus ~ in nos fortunasque nostras*) and indicate its nature (*impure et intemperanter ~ impie ac nefarie*), given further coherence by anaphora (quadruple use of the preposition *in* + accusative) and alliteration (see underlining).

in se atque in domesticum decus: see Thomas (2007: 96): 'In connection with *a se*, *domesticum decus* sets out the stakes of Antony's behaviour for those who keep his company: even such a *florentissima familia* as the Curiones (*Phil.* 2.46) risks a loss of social esteem. Such fear is the reason why *domesticum decus* designates "domestic honour", that is, the exact opposite of *dedecus* ("shame"). The loss of *decus* has an important role to play: it is one of the consequences of Antony's political monstrosity, which is at the core of the second *Philippic*'.[21]

impure et intemperanter: the basic meaning of *impurus* is 'unclean', 'filthy', 'foul' and is a standard epithet that Cicero attaches to his enemies. See e.g. *in Catilinam* 2.23: *in his gregibus omnes aleatores, omnes*

---

21   'Coordonné à *se*, *domesticum decus* exprime l'enjeu de la conduite d'Antoine pour son entourage, qui risque de ne plus mériter la considération générale alors qu'il s'agit d'une *florentissima familia* (2, 46). Cette crainte fait que *domesticum decus* désigne ainsi l' "honneur domestique", soit l'exact inverse de *dedecus*. La perte du decus a son importance car elle est un des effets de cette monstruosité politique d'Antoine sur laquelle est centrée la seconde *Philippique*'.

adulteri, omnes impuri impudicique versantur. It can — but does not have to — have religious connotations (see e.g. Cic. *Dom.* 104: *quam* (sc. *religionem*) *tu impurissime taeterrimeque violasti*). Here it sets up the climactic use of *impie* in the indirect question — just as *intemperanter* prepares the ground for *nefarie.* (Cicero also uses it of Antony at *Phil.* 1.12.)

in nos fortunasque nostras: 'against us and our fortunes', with *fortunae* carrying the sense of 'prosperous living conditions'

id est in universam rem publicam: *universa res publica* means 'the whole / entire commonwealth' and often figures as the catch-all frame of reference that concludes the enumeration of more specific items that form part of the public sphere (here *nos* and *fortunae nostrae*). Ramsey (2003: 235) suggests that '*id est* is here corrective, equivalent to *uel potius* ['or rather']', but the sense is arguably stronger if one takes *id est* as a simple specification: it would then cater to the deeply engrained habit of Rome's senatorial elite to identify their own well-being with that of the *res publica* as a whole. For a more elaborate example see *in Catilinam* 4.24 (the final paragraph of the speech, addressed to the people): *quapropter de summa salute vestra populique Romani, de vestris coniugibus ac liberis, de aris ac focis, de fanis atque templis de totius urbis tectis ac sedibus, de imperio ac libertate, de salute Italiae, de universa re publica decernite diligenter, ut instituistis, ac fortiter* ('With the care, therefore, and the courage that you have displayed from the beginning, take your decision upon the salvation of yourselves and of the Roman people, upon your wives and children, your altars and hearths, your shrines and temples, the buildings and homes of the entire city, your dominion and your freedom, the safety of Italy and upon the whole Republic').

impie ac nefarie: the two terms reiterate and intensify *impure et intemperanter*: 'impure' has become 'impious'; and 'reckless' has been upgraded to 'blasphemous'. (*nefarie* derives from *nefas*, which means 'an offence against divine law, an impious act, sacrilege'.) Antony now is a full-blown religious criminal.

ab huius enim scelere omnium malorum principium natum [esse] **reperietis**: *ab scelere* is an ablative of origin with *natum*: 'you will find that the beginning of all evils arose from the crime of this man!'

§ 78: Caesar's Approach to HR, or Why Antony Has What it Takes

In March 45, Antony left Narbo in Southern Gaul for a surprise visit to Rome that caused some consternation in the city, not least because the reasons for his arrival in the capital remained unclear. Some feared that he had come as a henchman of Caesar, perhaps to prepare the ground for reprisals or even proscriptions. Cicero comments on the situation in a letter to Atticus (12.19.2 = 257 SB, 14 March 45), mentioning that Balbus and Oppius, two of Caesar's chief lieutenants, wrote to him with reassurances that Antony's sudden appearance in Rome was nothing to worry about. In the event, Antony felt obliged to announce publicly that he arrived on personal business and not at the behest of Caesar. In §§ 77–78a, Cicero elaborates on what this 'personal business' consisted in, suggesting that Antony desired to tell his wife Fulvia that he had stopped seeing his mistress; and that he was still struggling to service his debts and wanted to prevent the selling of his sureties. (He only mentions the latter when he speculates about Antony's motives for the surprise visit in a letter to Atticus 12.18a.1 = 256 SB: ... *sed tamen opinor propter praedes suos accucurrisse* — '... but I imagine he has hurried up to save his sureties'.)

Much of Cicero's account — especially Antony's confession of love to his wife Fulvia — is held in a low, comic key, and Cicero himself dismisses the affair, after emphasizing how much grievance and upset it caused to everyone else in Rome and Italy, as trifles (*nugae*) — a mere warm-up act for far more serious matters (*maiora*). The set text picks up halfway through § 78, when Antony (we are now in the summer of 45) left Rome again to meet Caesar on his way back from Spain, where he squashed the last republican resistance. Cicero alleges that there had been a cooling off in their relationship (§§ 71–77), but Antony's 'credentials' (bankruptcy and moral depravity) were such that Caesar was overjoyed to re-establish friendly terms and make Antony the renewed beneficiary of his patronage. The paragraph thus also contains yet another scathing indictment of Caesar's malign politics of friendship. It is important to note, however, that the estrangement between Caesar and Antony in 46–45 BCE (and hence also the reconciliation) is a malicious fiction put into circulation by Cicero to desparage Antony. Once we discount his invective aspersions all the evidence points to continuing excellent relations between Caesar and one of his most trusted lieutenants, who was in charge of liquidating Pompey's assets during this period, a challenging task designed to raise much needed cash for Caesar's military operations.[22]

Et domi quidem causam amoris habuisti, foris etiam turpiorem [causam habuisti], **ne L. Plancus praedes tuos venderet**: literally, 'and at home indeed you had the excuse of love', with *amoris* as a genitive of definition, though a more natural idiom in English would be to say 'you had love as an excuse'. *causam* also has to be supplied with *turpiorem*. The comparative makes it clear that 'love' is no excuse at all, but a disgraceful motivation; its only redeeming feature is that there are even worse. *foris* plays off *domi*, *etiam* plays off *quidem*.

domi: a locative.

foris etiam turpiorem: *causam* and *habuisti* need to be supplied from the previous clause.

L. Plancus: Lucius Munatius Plancus was one of the six or eight 'city prefects' (*praefecti urbi*) to whom Caesar entrusted public business before his departure for Spain late in 46 BCE. He happened to be in charge of debt management, fulfilling a function usually performed by the *praetor urbanus*. He began his career as a legate of Caesar in 54, held the consulship in 42, and continued to do well under Augustus, being appointed censor in 22. In January, 27 BCE, it was Plancus who

---

22 See Ramsey (2004).

proposed the motion that the senate confer the *cognomen* Augustus on Caesar Octavianus. See further Watkins (1997) and Nisbet-Hubbard (1970: 90–94).

praedes tuos: in §§ 71–74 Cicero generates the impression that Caesar increasingly leaned on Antony to make him pay up for the property of Pompey which he had acquired at auction — which Antony struggled to do. Upon his departure for Spain, Caesar extended the deadline for payment (§ 74), but then, according to the scenario supposed here, nevertheless instructed Plancus to sell the property of those who had stood surety for Antony (*praedes tuos*) to recover the money.

productus autem in contionem a tribuno pl. cum respondisses te rei tuae causa venisse, populum etiam dicacem in te reddidisti: the sentence starts with a *cum*-clause (the conjunction is much delayed), into which the perfect participle *productus* belongs. The verb of the *cum*-clause, *respondisses*, introduces an indirect statement with *te* as subject accusative and *venisse* as infinitive. The verb of the main clause (*reddidisti*) takes an accusative object (*populum*) and a predicate (*dicacem*): 'to render something / someone such and such'.

productus autem in contionem a tribuno pl[ebis]: only elected officials had the right to convene a public assembly (*contio*) and permit private citizens to speak to the people. Most likely, Antony asked the tribune to convene the meeting, but through the passive construction and the choice of verb (*respondisses*) Cicero makes it out as if Antony was asked by the tribune to justify his actions in front of the people.

rei tuae causa: we are likely dealing with another scurrilous double entendre here, with *res tua* referring to Antony's 'junk'. See Barr (1981: 422–23):

> The question at once arises, can *res* = *membrum virile* be attested elsewhere? I believe it can. Cicero, in *Philippic* 2,77f., describing Marcus Antonius' hasty return from Narbo in 45 to the great alarm of Italy and the city of Rome, relates how Antonius, with elaborate precautions, presented himself to his wife Fulvia and effected a tearful reconciliation. Two reasons for Antonius' return are put forward by Cicero: *et domi quidem causam amoris habuisti, foris etiam turpiorem ne L. Plancus praedes tuos venderet* (78). When Antonius in a *contio* is challenged by a tribune

to explain his conduct, the unfortunate wording of his reply evidently afforded the populace an opportunity to exercise its wit: *productus autem in contionem a tribuno plebis cum respondisses te rei tuae causa venisse, populum etiam dicacem in te reddidisti* (78). J. D. Denniston in his edition of the speech (Oxford, 1926) *ad loc.* thinks the joke consists in the fact that Antonius notoriously had no *res* ('property') to speak of. What made the people *dicax* at Antonius' expense, however, was surely not his endowment in respect of property, but in another respect suggested by the ambiguity of *res*, and Cicero, unwilling to let the joke rest there, underlines the point in the neat innuendo of the formula of transition that immediately follows: *sed nimis multa de nugis: ad maiora veniamus!* (78).

dicacem: *dicax*, from a morphological point of view the combination of the verb stem *dic-* + *ax*, refers to the ability to deliver witty (and often cutting) repartee. It is associated with urban sophistication from Plautus onwards. See *Truculentus* 682–83: *iam postquam in urbem crebro commeo,* | *dicax sum factus* ('Now that I come into the city often, I have become witty'). But essentially *populus dicax* is a paradox: refinement and sophistication tend to be the preserve of an exclusive elite, fostering a culture of aesthetic distinctions grounded in (educational) privilege. It's the same as saying a snail will make you look speedy — by comparison.

in te: 'at your own expense'.

sed nimis multa de nugis: ad maiora veniamus: in the first clause, Cicero omits the verb (*dico / dicimus*: 'but [I am talking] too much about trivialities') and follows this up with a self-exhortation (*veniamus* is an exhortative subjunctive): the ellipsis is appropriate at a moment when Cicero cuts himself short: brevity is a virtue. *multa* (a reference to quantity) and *de nugis* (a reference to quality) set up *ad maiora*, the implication being that what Cicero has to say about the more important matters will be spot-on.

multa: accusative neuter plural, the accusative object of the implied verb.

C. Caesari ex Hispania redeunti obviam longissime processisti: the adverb *obviam* often governs a dative, here *C. Caesari*, modified by the present participle *redeunti*: 'you went out further than anyone else (*longissime*: adverb in the superlative) to meet (*obviam*) Caesar on his way back from Spain'.

celeriter isti redisti, ut cognosceret te, si minus fortem, at tamen strenuum: *isti* and *redisti* are the contracted 2nd person singular perfect indicative active forms of *eo, ire* and *redeo, redire* (= *iisti rediisti*). *ire redire* is an idiomatic phrase meaning 'to pass to and fro, come and go': *OLD* s.v. *eo* 1g. *ut* introduces a purpose clause; its verb (*cognosceret*) takes *te* as accusative object, which is modified by *fortem* and *strenuum* in predicative position: '... that he might discern you as — if not brave — yet still full of energy'. Cicero himself of course engaged in a significant amount to toing and froing during the 40s, both when civil war first broke out in 49, then in the summer of 44, when he left Rome for Greece, only to return soon thereafter. In fact, *Philippic* 1 begins with an extensive explanation of his movements (a *consilium et profectionis et reversionis meae* — a slightly more elevated idiom than *ire redire*): see *Phil.* 1.1 and 6–11.

fortem... strenuum: at least since Cato the Elder (e.g. at *de Agricultura* 4: *ex agricolis et viri fortissimi et milites strenuissimi gignuntur*: 'from farmers the bravest men and the most valiant soldiers are sprung'; see further Cornell (2013: 87), *fortis atque strenuus* are two positive qualities that work in unison — the former referring to a mental disposition, the latter to the physical ability to act on it. The attributes recur together in other writers (such as Sallust) and elsewhere in Cicero, so their disjunction here through the somewhat 'precious' differentiation *si minus – at tamen* puts a mocking spin on standard idiom. Given that Cicero strips Antony of any claim to bravery (he did not participate in the campaign in Spain), his solicitous rush to meet the victorious general appears particularly preposterous.

factus es ei rursus nescio quo modo familiaris: the sentence might baffle at first sight (unsurprisingly, since it is meant to convey bafflement) because of the unusual word order and all sorts of seemingly complicated little fill-words in between the alliterated (and inverted) frame *factus... familiaris*, but is actually fairly straightforward. Antony is the (implied) subject: 'you became (*factus es*) a friend (*familiaris*) to him (*ei*) again (*rursus*) I don't know how / in some way or other (*nescio quo* *modo)'*. Or, less literally: 'Somehow you managed to weasel your way back into Caesar's friendship'.

habebat hoc omnino Caesar: *habet hoc* = 'has this characteristic'. Commentators compare Cicero, *in Pisonem* 81 and Horace, *Sermones* 1.3.3. Ramsey (2003: 275) suggests that *moris* (the genitive of *mos*) has to be understood as part of a colloquial expression meaning 'this was Caesar's way', i.e. 'he had this trait'. The adverb *omnino* ('certainly') drips with irony.

quem plane perditum aere alieno egentemque, si eundem nequam hominem audacemque cognorat, hunc in familiaritatem libentissime recipiebat: Cicero here uses one verb (*cognorat*: the syncopated third person singular pluperfect active of *cognosco* = *cogno|ve|rat*) for both the relative clause introduced by *quem* (the antecedent is *hunc*) and the *si*-clause: 'whom he found to be obviously bankrupt and destitute — if the same person was [known to him as] a morally worthless and reckless human being — this man he received with the greatest delight into his circle of friends'.

The Ethics and Politics of Friendship in Caesar's World

Two related aspects are worth a closer look here: (i) the kinds of characters who were attracted to Caesar; (ii) Caesar's willingness to extend 'friendship' to anyone on strictly utilitarian principles, irrespective of their 'moral worth'.

(i) Cicero dissed half of Caesar's supporters (just like those of Catiline in the 60s) as belonging into a basket of deplorables already before the outbreak of the civil war (*Letter to Atticus* 7.3.5 = 126 SB, written 9 December 50):

> verum tamen haec video, cum homine audacissimo paratissimoque negotium esse, omnis damnatos, omnis ignominia adfectos, omnis damnatione ignominiaque dignos illac facere, omnem fere iuventutem, omnem illam urbanam ac perditam plebem, tribunos valentis addito Q. Cassio, omnis qui aere alieno premantur, quos pluris esse intellego quam putaram (causam solum illa causa non habet, ceteris rebus abundat).

[All the same I see this much: we are dealing with a man who fears nothing and is ready for anything. All persons under legal sentence or censorial stigma, and all who deserve the one or the other, are on his side, so are pretty well all the younger people, all the desperate city rabble, some sturdy Tribunes, Q. Cassius now included, all the debt-ridden, who I find are worth more than I supposed! — Caesar's side lacks nothing but a cause, all else they have in abundance.]

He was not alone in this assessment. The Caesarian loyalist Caelius, who was also on friendly terms with Cicero, also noted Caesar's appeal to those who had little or nothing to lose. In a letter to Cicero, written on 8 August 50, he predicts that 'all who live in present fear and small hope for the future will rally to Caesar' (*Fam.* 8.14.3 = 97 SB).

(ii) Caesar himself seems to have welcomed all and sundry with open arms into his networks of associates. An anecdote transmitted by Suetonius nicely captures his endorsement of a 'friendship-above-all-else attitude' (*Life of Julius Caesar* 72):

Amicos tanta semper facilitate indulgentiaque tractauit... iam autem rerum potens quosdam etiam infimi generis ad amplissimos honores prouexit, cum ob id culparetur, professus palam, si grassatorum et sicariorum ope in tuenda sua dignitate usus esset, talibus quoque se parem gratiam relaturum.

[His friends he always treated with pronounced kindness and consideration. ... Moreover, when he was already in power, he raised some friends of the humblest background to the highest positions, and when he was blamed for it, openly declared that if he had used the help of brigands and murderers in defending his rank and standing, he would have repaid such men too in the same way.]

Caesar certainly offered those who would have struggled to assert themselves in a system dominated by established aristocratic families unprecedented opportunities for career advancement. But his reliance on 'upstarts' may in part have been due to the fact that members of the traditional ruling elite refused to cooperate:[23]

Caesar's shift toward autocracy was in good part due to the refusal of many Republicans to admit defeat. Cicero had accepted Pharsalus

---

23   Watkins (1997: 43).

in 48 as decisive. Had more leading senators done the same, even if reluctantly, and cooperated with Caesar, they might have saved much of their ancestral state and their own role in it. Instead, they had rallied in Africa and seen their cause defeated again. Within a few months the remnants had regrouped in Spain — with the same results. No senatorial general could defeat Caesar, no senatorial army could best his. The obstinate refusal to accept the verdict of the battlefield and to work with Caesar while they could still nudge him toward retention of the traditional forms of the *res publica* compelled him to rely on his subordinate officers rather than members of the old nobility. Precisely this goes far to explain the rise of men like Plancus who would not have reached the highest offices in the state had there not been a dearth of candidates from illustrious families.

What would you have done in their stead? Would you have accepted that Caesar had trumped the old system and engaged with his regime as the new normal — not least in view of the personal benefits to be derived from playing ball with the potentate? Or would you have withdrawn your services as a matter of principle?

§ 79: The Art of Nepotism

After his victory in the civil war, Caesar, while nominally upholding republican traditions, effectively exercised autocratic powers and could determine whom to reward when with what position in the state. As Denniston (1926: 144) puts it: 'After the victory of Munda the senate voted Caesar, among other honours, the right to appoint the magistrates. Outwardly he declined the privilege, but by "recommending" certain persons to the people for election he accepted the substance of it (Dio, xliii 45, 1; Suet. *Iul.* 41)'. This distribution of favours did not always happen without friction among his faithful. Cicero here homes in on a tussle between Antony and Dolabella over appointments to the consulship for 44 BCE. Despite the fact that both benefitted from Caesar's patronage, the two had a fractious history: in 47, Antony clamped down violently on Dolabella's attempt to push through a debt cancellation, and there were also rumours (picked up by Cicero in § 99) that Dolabella had committed adultery with Antony's then-wife Antonia.[24] Cicero dwells at length (§§ 79–84a) on this contretemps between Antony and Dolabella. Dolabella, despite being his former son-in-law, remained a puzzle for Cicero: 'Before the end of April Cicero had already reason to believe that Antony and Dolabella were hand in glove (*Att.* 14.14.4 = 368 SB; 28 or 29 April: rumour of an extended provincial command for both consuls). And on 9 May, in the very midst of his rhapsodies about the overturned pillar, he accuses Dolabella of sharing with Antony the spoils from the temple of Ops (*Att.* 14.18.1 = 373 SB). Cicero's unbalanced and volatile

---

24   On the clash between Antony and Dolabella in 47 BCE, see further Welch (1995).

temperament is strikingly illustrated by the correspondence of the first half of May, which shows clearly that he did not know what to make of Dolabella'.[25]

In order to understand what happened, we need to distinguish between *consules ordinarii*, i.e. the two consuls who were initially elected and took office at the beginning of the year, and *consules suffecti*, i.e. 'substitute consuls' who replaced the elected consuls if they died or were otherwise incapacitated during their time in office. (Even being a suffect consul was a great honour, though people thought Caesar made a mockery of it when the consul Quintus Fabius Maximus died on 31 December 45 BCE and he appointed Gaius Caninius Rebilus as suffect consul for the last few remaining hours of the year.)

For the consulship of 44 BCE, Cicero implies the following timeline:

Sometime in 45:

Caesar promises the two consulships for 44 to Antony and Dolabella.

Antony manages to prevail upon Caesar to change his mind, break his promise to Dolabella, and take up the second consulship himself.

As consolation prize, Caesar designates Dolabella *consul suffectus* upon his departure for Parthia (scheduled for 18 March), when he would have stepped down from his consulship.

This irritates Antony, who announces that he would try to thwart Dolabella's election. (The date when Caesar designated Dolabella as *consul suffectus* remains vague — though in § 81 Cicero implies that it happened some time ago: Antony made his objections known 'many months before' (*multis ante mensibus*) the actual election.)

January 44:

An irritated Dolabella expresses his annoyance with Antony in a speech to the senate.

Mid-March:

During the election of Dolabella to the suffect consulship, Antony voices religious objections

---

25   Denniston (1926: 165–66).

14 March:

Caesar gets murdered.

17 March:

Antony accepts Dolabella as his colleague in the consulship.

It is not entirely straightforward to sift facts from fiction here. Sometime in 45 BCE, Caesar indeed must have decided that Antony and himself should be the *consules ordinarii* for 44, with Dolabella becoming a *consul suffectus* upon his departure for the campaign against Parthia. Likewise, there is no reason to doubt that Antony vigorously opposed the plan to make Dolabella suffect consul. Conversely, however, there is no evidence to corroborate Cicero's assertion that Caesar initially designated Dolabella as one of the two *consules ordinarii* and then, at the advice of Antony, changed his mind. This vacillation, which makes Caesar look feeble and Antony treacherous, is most likely a Ciceronian construct. He milks it for all it is worth, at seemingly excessive length (§§ 79–84a), partly to drive a wedge between the two prominent Caesarians who jointly held the consulship at the time Cicero composed *Philippic* 2, partly because it enables him to suggest that Antony's conduct has been at variance with Rome's civic religion, out of ignorance and/or impudence.

His igitur rebus praeclare commendatus iussus es renuntiari consul et quidem cum ipso: the subject of the sentence is Antony, whom Cicero continues to address directly. After the past participle *commendatus* (modifying an implied *tu*), we get the main verb in the passive (*iussus es*) followed by a passive infinitive (*renuntiari*), yielding the somewhat contrived 'you were ordered to be declared (elected) consul' — instead of the far more straightforward 'Caesar ordered you to be declared (elected) consul'. The two passives constitute a sly dig at the obfuscated agent, i.e. Caesar. By turning Antony into the passive subject of Caesar's act of ordering, rather than the (more natural) subject accusative of an indirect statement, Cicero manages to convey syntactically the utter lack of transparency in the way Caesar and his favourites wielded their power, not least in filling offices (such as the consulship).

renuntiari: *renuntiare* is a technical term of Rome's political culture, referring to the act of announcing (or rather re-porting) the results of an election by the presiding magistrate in the voting assemblies (the *comitia* and the *concilium plebis*). The prefix *re-* captures the fact that the magistrate reported *back* to the assembly what the people in the assembly had themselves decided in casting their votes; compare and contrast *pro-nuntiare*, which refers to acts of announcing a decision to somebody *not* involved in making it.[26] In order to fully appreciate the sarcasm and outrage at Caesar's and Antony's perversion of the appointment process to Rome's highest magistracy that Cicero packs into this sentence, a few words on the practice of *renuntiatio* (= the presiding magistrate announcing the results of the consular elections for the following year) is in order. The opening of Cicero's *pro Murena* affords a good example of what this moment traditionally meant (or could be taken to mean) (*Mur.* 1):

> Quae precatus a dis immortalibus sum, iudices, more institutoque maiorum illo die quo auspicato comitiis centuriatis L. Murenam consulem renuntiavi, ut ea res mihi fidei magistratuique meo, populo plebique Romanae bene atque feliciter eveniret, eadem precor ab isdem dis immortalibus ob eiusdem hominis consulatum una cum salute obtinendum, et ut vestrae mentes atque sententiae cum populi Romani voluntatibus suffragiisque consentiant, eaque res vobis populoque Romano pacem, tranquillitatem, otium concordiamque adferat.

> [On that day, judges, on which, after taking the auspices, I announced Lucius Murena's election as consul to the centuriate assembly, I prayed to the immortal gods according to the custom and tradition of our ancestors that his event should bring good fortune to myself, the reliable discharge of my office and to the people and the plebs of Rome. Today I address the same prayer to those same immortal gods to preserve the consulship and at the same time the welfare of the same man, that your minds and your verdict may concur with the wishes and the votes of the Roman people and that this concurrence may bring peace, tranquillity, calm, and harmony to yourselves and to the Roman people.]

Cicero embeds recall of the moment in which he announced the outcome of the consular elections for 62 BCE within a past and present prayer.

---

26   See Kunkel (1995: 182).

The agents and institutions involved include: the immortal gods (and their goodwill towards the commonwealth), ancestral customs, the voting assemblies, the presiding consul, the consular elections and the consulship (Rome's highest magistracy) itself, the Roman people and their popular will as expressed in (free) elections, and civic welfare, peace, and domestic harmony guaranteed by proper civic procedures and divine benevolence. *Renuntiatio* guarantees annalistic continuity as the reigning consuls announce their successors, a handing over of power crucial for the functioning of a political culture grounded in oligarchic equality, managed not least by means of annual elections to public office. The act occurred on a tribunal marked out as a sacred precinct (*templum*).[27] By contrast, in Caesar's Rome, this hallowed ritual, which constituted an essential element of the senatorial tradition of republican government, has become a perverse manifestation of Caesar's power and cronyism. The dictator remained committed to the constitutional forms and procedures of the republican commonwealth, such as *renuntiatio*, but his control of the proceedings and the personnel rendered them meaningless charades.

his... rebus: the instrumental ablative phrase sums up the catalogue of Antony's vices (or, from Caesar's point of view, virtues) detailed in the previous sentence, i.e. being in debt, impoverished, worthless, and reckless. *res* is here perhaps best understood in the sense of 'qualities'.

praeclare commendatus: clearly dripping with irony. For such sarcastic use of *praeclare*, see also *Phil*. 7.3.

et quidem cum ipso: 'and what's more with himself [*ipso* refers to Caesar] as your colleague'. The particle *quidem* here sets up a further heightening of the sense of outrage Cicero is trying to generate. The fact that Antony managed to weasel himself into the consulship is particularly obnoxious since Caesar continued to monopolize one of the two high magistracies. See *OLD* s.v. *quidem* 5 (adding a reinforcement or afterthought): 'And what is more', 'and — at that', often preceded by *et*.

---

27   Kunkel (1995: 85, n. 111); he also argues that before the official *renuntiatio* the successful candidates swore an oath to do with the execution of his office: 93 n. 146.

nihil queror de Dolabella qui tum est impulsus, inductus, elusus: Publius Cornelius Dolabella was the one-time husband of Cicero's daughter Tullia, whom he married in the summer of 50 but divorced in November 46, when Tullia was already pregnant with their second child. She died from the consequences of childbirth at Dolabella's house in February of 45, plunging Cicero into deep despair. His letters from this period are stricken with grief — a good %age of it in mourning the Republic and his own status in it — to the point that many of his correspondents exhorted him to pull himself together.[28] This personal experience resonates in *nihil queror de Dolabella*: it is not that he has any particular sympathy for his former son-in-law. This, however, does not change the fact that he was made the innocent butt of Antony's ability to pull strings with Caesar. The asyndetic tricolon of verbs that conclude the relative clause re-enacts the way in which he was jerked around and made a fool of.

nihil: the indeclinable neuter noun *nihil* ('nothing') is here used adverbially. See *OLD* s.v. 11: 'in no respect', 'not at all'.

qua in re quanta fuerit uterque vestrum perfidia in Dolabellam quis ignorat?: *qua* is a connecting relative (= *ea*). The phrase *qua in re* belongs inside the indirect question introduced by *quanta*, which is an interrogative adjective modifying *perfidia*. The phrase is an ablative of description ('of how much treachery'). The main clause comes at the end (*quis ignorat?*): 'Who does not know (*quis ignorat*) of how much treachery (*quanta... perfidia*) in this matter (*qua in re*) each one of you (*uterque vestrum*) was towards Dolabella (*fuerit in Dolabellam*)?' — or, more elegantly: 'Who does not know how treacherously each of you behaved towards Dolabella in this matter?'

uterque vestrum: *vestrum* is the (partitive) genitive plural of the second person personal pronoun, dependent on *uterque*.

ille induxit ut peteret, promissum et receptum intervertit ad seque transtulit: *ille* is Caesar, who is the subject of three main verbs: *induxit*, *intervertit*, and *transtulit*. The first and the second clash in asyndeton,

---

28   See most recently Martelli (2016).

the second and third are linked by the -*que* after *se*. The design is thematically appropriate, enacting the break of Caesar's promise: *induxit* clashes with *intervertit* and *transtulit*. The implied accusative object of *peteret*, *intervertit*, and *transtulit* is *consulatum*, which also governs the two perfect passive participles *promissum* and *receptum*, which are adversative in sense ('he revoked the consulship even though it had been promised and accepted').

ut peteret: sc. *consulatum*. The implied subject of the *ut*-clause is Dolabella. The common verb *peto* can have the technical sense of 'to be a candidate for, seek a magistracy' (with accusative object of the office sought, at times — as here — implied) or, generally, 'to be a candidate for office, stand for election': see *OLD* s.v. 9.

tu eius perfidiae voluntatem tuam ascripsisti: the meaning of *ascribo* here is 'to attribute, assign' an accusative object [here: *voluntatem tuam*] 'to a cause or origin' in the dative [here: *eius perfidiae*]: see *OLD* s.v. 5. Cicero 'is accusing Antony of trying to shift the blame to Caesar for what was, in fact, Antony's own desire (to block Dolabella's advancement): "you attributed … your wish to Caesar's perfidy" (and yet you were the one who caused Caesar to change his mind about giving the consulship to Dolabella)' (Ramsey 2003: 276). If in the previous sentence, Cicero attributes treachery (*perfidia*) to both Caesar and Antony, here he singles out Antony's alone — indeed suggests that Caesar's 'treachery' is one in appearance only, an impression generated by Antony.

eius: refers to Caesar.

veniunt Kalendae Ianuariae: the Romans called the first day of every month 'calends' (related to *kalendarium* = accounting-book for debts due at the beginning of each month; whence our 'calendar'). On 'the calends of January', i.e. the beginning of the year, elected magistrates entered their offices.

cogimur in senatum: phrases such as *senatum cogere* ('to summon the senate') or *senatum in curiam cogere* ('to summon the senate into the Curia') are standard; the phrasing that Cicero uses here — *aliquem in senatum cogere* ('to summon someone into the senate') — is not. In its passive variant, this formulation hints at an element of coercion (it's a round up — 'we were herded') and hence a disjunction or non-identification between the recipients of a dictatorial order (individual senators, among whom Cicero counts himself: 'we') and 'Caesar's senate'. The chosen idiom thus articulates a sense of Cicero's republican resistance to Caesar's manipulation of this institution (including enforced attendance).

invectus est copiosius multo in istum et paratius Dolabella quam nunc ego: in the passive, *inveho* means 'to attack verbally'. The word order (or rather 'dis-order') enacts the blast of Dolabella's verbal onslaught: Cicero puts the verb (*invectus est*) up front, places *multo*, an ablative of the measure of difference, which usually stands before the comparative, behind it, and disjoins the two comparative adverbs *copiosius* and *paratius*, which, in this order, also constitute a *husteron proteron* (see below), through the insertion of *in istum*. Put differently, the sentence climaxes in the middle (with *in istum*), before petering out from *et* onwards.

copiosius multo... et paratius: 'with much greater fullness of expression and much better preparation'. Both *copiosius* and *paratius* are technical terms in Roman rhetorical discourse. *copiose* refers to the ability to speak eloquently and at length (*copia* = fullness of expression), *parate* to being well-prepared. (See e.g. *de Oratore* 1.150, *Brutus* 241, *Divinatio in Caecilium* 47.) The placement of *copiosius* ahead of *paratius* constitutes a *husteron proteron* ('an inversion of the natural / logical sequence') since the latter is a precondition of the former.

in istum: a contemptuous reference to Antony, now that Cicero has switched to a third-person perspective.

quam nunc ego: however much Cicero waxes rhetorically, he is usually keen to come across as exercising self-restraint, at least comparatively speaking. At the same time, he is clearly writing tongue-in-cheek here: there is no way that Dolabella's speech was fuller and better prepared than *Philippic* 2.

§ 80: Antony Augur,
Addled and Addling

In the run-up to the election of Dolabella as suffect consul, Antony seems to have announced that he would try to prevent the election of Dolabella to the consulship by making use of a religious veto that he could issue in his capacity as augur. In the event, he made good on his threat. Over the next few paragraphs, Cicero rakes him over the coals for this. To understand his lines of attack, we need to come to terms with some technicalities of Rome's civic religion. This dimension of Roman culture is not easy to get one's head around: its 'cultural logic' is in many ways quite alien to our own religious intuitions.[29]

For our concerns, it is important to distinguish between Roman religion *tout court* (in the sense of *any* religious thought and practice in republican Rome) and 'Rome's civic religion', i.e. the religious dimension of Roman *politics*.[30] Religious and political practices and procedures were therefore mutually implicated: changes in the field of power could not help but have repercussions for Rome's civic religion and, conversely, reconfigurations or innovations in the handling of religious material were bound to be politically sensitive. The enmeshing of religious and political concerns that we capture in our late-republican sources and that has often been taken as evidence for a decline in

---

29 The following paragraph draws on Gildenhard (2011: 246–54).
30 This distinction is best worked out in Bendlin (2000). It is also implied in Feeney's (1998) critique of religion or culture as a 'monolithic' meaning system. Further bibliography includes Beard, North, and Price (1998), Rosenberger (1998), Rüpke (2007), Santangelo (2013), and Scheid (1998/2003).

religion was in fact co-extensive with the Roman commonwealth. Much of the communication that Rome's civic community entertained with the divine sphere revolved around apparent signs from the gods, which manifested themselves in atmospheric phenomena (thunder and lightening, esp. when the sky was otherwise clear), the entrails of sacrificial victims, or monstrous occurrences that violated the natural order of things (such as the birth of a double-headed calf). Elaborate protocols regulated how such signs were to be identified and processed: who was entitled to report or look for them, what they meant and who was charged with interpreting them. Since Rome's civic religion co-evolved with the political culture of the republican commonwealth and formed an integral part of it, it should not surprise that its peculiar outlook suited the needs of a society whose gravitational center was the senatorial oligarchy. The religious communication that formed part of Rome's public sphere was designed to promote, not least, a politics rooted in consensus: the possibility of a religiously motivated veto by a magistrate or priest against any course of action constituted a strong incentive to ensure widespread acceptance and collaboration ahead of any major decision. This set-up helped to keep the willful politics of maverick power brokers in check — but it of course also opened the possibility that an individual with the right to communicate with the gods could (ab-)use his religious veto to obstruct political proceedings or decisions he disliked for purely personal reasons.

In 44, Antony held two positions that gave him the right to interact with the divine sphere — though in two slightly different ways:

(i) As consul he had the right of *spectio*: he could actively look for divine signs (of disapproval) before an event and even announce that he would do so. Since the assumption was that anyone seeking an unfavourable divine sign would also find it, events were cancelled or postponed as soon as a magistrate announced that he would exercise his right of *spectio*.

(ii) As augur — a priesthood he held since 50 BCE — he was able to report adverse signs that materialized during the course of the actual event (= *nuntiatio*), such as thunder or lightening.[31]

---

31   See Broughton (1991: 51) for the election of Antony (and Cicero) to the augurate, in, respectively, 50 and 53 BCE.

During the election of Dolabella to the suffect consulship Antony seems to have conflated consular *spectio* and augural *nuntiatio*: he announced he would make use of his religious veto ahead of the election; the election went ahead nevertheless; but towards the end he pronounced the augural formula that rendered the proceedings invalid from a religious point of view. Or, in the words of Linderski (1986: 2198):

> In his description of Antonius' *obnuntiatio* against the election of Dolabella as consul in 44, Cicero contrasts the *spectio* of the magistrates and the *nuntiatio* of the augurs (*Phil.* 2.81): *Nos enim nuntiationem solum habemus, consules et reliqui magistratus etiam spectionem.* The augurs could report only oblative signs, and oblative signs had to be observed entirely by chance. It was not possible to predict that one would see them. And according to the rule of *vinculum temporis* ... governing the observation and interpretation of oblative signs, the augurs could announce only such oblative signs that occurred after the beginning of the *comitia*. The magistrates had on the other hand both *spectio* and *nuntiatio*: the right to take impetrative auspices and to announce adverse omens. They could proclaim in advance that they would watch the skies; however, as the magisterial *nuntiatio* was exclusively based on impetrative auspices, the magistrate had to make the announcement of an adverse omen before the beginning of the *comitia*. Antonius, who was consul and augur, had proclaimed in advance *se Dolabellae comitia ... prohibiturum auspiciis*, thus implying that he would block Dolabella's election by means of the announcement of adverse auspices based upon his right to *spectio*. However, when he actually reported an adverse omen, he did it in his capacity as augur, for he uttered the ritual formula *alio die* after the beginning of the comitia or, more exactly, shortly before the conclusion of the gathering. He obnuntiated on the basis of an oblative sign, the occurrence of which it was impossible to predict, and hence Cicero was justified in contending that it must have been a fake.[32]

According to Cicero, Antony was plain stupid (end of § 80: *stupiditas*) for reasons specified in § 81: he would have been much smarter to object on religious grounds in his office of consul (rather than as augur); and also shameless (§ 81: *impudentia*).

Hic autem iratus quae dixit, di boni!: the deictic *hic* refers to Antony, who, incensed by Dolabella's diligently prepared, if hard-hitting, show

---

32   See also Santangelo (2013: 273) and Berthelet (2016), both with further bibliography.

of eloquence, responded with some frightful verbiage of his own. The word order of the exclamation again creates a vivid image of the situation: pulled up front we get 'angry Antony' (*hic ... iratus*) — here objectified, in the third person, put on show, like a distasteful (yet fascinating) insect, for a case study in emotional incontinence and rhetorical idiocy. The laconic *quae dixit* teases the imagination. And with *di boni*, Cicero turns to the gods in mock-fear at recalling Antony's outburst: 'This exclamation clearly originated as a cry for help: a person suddenly faced with some horrible sight or anything threatening him invokes instinctively the help and protection of the gods. A Roman Catholic will cry out "Jesus Maria", ...' (Fraenkel 1957: 441) — and an atheist 'Jeez-us!'. The effect is therefore different from the moments of import, pathos, and, more generally, high emotions, that Cicero underscores by invocations such as *per deos immortales* or *o/pro di immortales*, which belong to a higher stylistic register.

primum cum Caesar ostendisset se, priusquam proficisceretur, Dolabellam consulem esse iussurum — quem negant regem, qui et faceret semper eius modi aliquid et diceret — sed cum Caesar ita dixisset, tum hic bonus augur eo se sacerdotio praeditum esse dixit ut comitia auspiciis vel impedire vel vitiare posset, idque se facturum esse asseveravit: the opening adverb *primum* sets up the expectation that Cicero here launches into a catalogue of all the outrageous things Antony spluttered at the meeting; but after 'first' (*primum*), we never get a 'second' (*deinde*) — rather, we get another *primum* at the end of the paragraph! What follows is a complex period, best taken bit by bit:

- **cum Caesar ostendisset se, priusquam proficisceretur, Dolabellam consulem esse iussurum**: the verb of the *cum*-clause (*ostendisset*) introduces an indirect statement with *se* as subject accusative (referring back to Caesar) and *iussurum* (*esse*) as infinitive, which in turn governs a further indirect statement with *Dolabellam* as subject accusative, *esse* as verb and *consulem* as predicative complement. (Note that the *esse* in the text is the infinitive of the indirect statement dependent on *iussurum*, which in its turn is the periphrastic future active infinitive (with *esse* elided) of the indirect statement dependent on *ostendisset*: '... when Caesar made it known that he (*se*) would issue an order (*iussurum*) that Dolabella be (*esse*) consul...')

Embedded within the *cum*-clause is a further temporal subordinate clause with Caesar as subject (*priusquam proficisceretur*: the reference is to his planned departure for Parthia — *proficisci* here has the sense of 'to set out on campaign').

- **quem negant regem, qui et faceret semper eius modi aliquid et diceret**: at this point, Cicero steps outside his period for a parenthetical gloss on Caesar's highhanded conduct. The main verb is *negant*, which introduces an indirect statement with *quem* (a connecting relative = *et eum*) as subject accusative, an (implied) *fuisse* as verb, and *regem* as predicative complement, followed by a relative clause. (The imperfect subjunctives *faceret* and *diceret* are concessive: people deny that Caesar was a despot *even though* his words and deeds provide ample proof that he was.)

- **sed cum Caesar ita dixisset**: the parenthesis necessitates a brief recapitulation: *sed cum ita dixisset* essentially repeats, summarily, *cum Caesar ostendisset … iussurum*, as Cicero finds his feet again in his period after the parenthetical gloss.

- **tum hic bonus augur eo se sacerdotio praeditum esse dixit ut comitia auspiciis vel impedire vel vitiare posset, idque se facturum esse asseveravit**: the bipartite main clause follows, with *dixit* and *asseveravit* as verbs (linked by the *-que* after *id*). Each of them governs an indirect statement: *se… praeditum esse*; *se facturum esse*. The *ut*-clause is consecutive.

regem: Rome was founded by kings and even though the last king, Tarquinius Superbus, abused his power and was driven from the city, the term *rex* retained (at least some) positive connotations in early and mid-republican sources — though it became increasingly tarnished, not least through its assimilation to the Greek *tyrannus* ('tyrant'), which the Romans imported as a loanword. While some authors adopted a neutral position towards 'kingship' as a form of government and preferred to work with the distinction between a 'good king' v. a 'bad king', others — among them Cicero — came to see any kind of autocratic regime as irreconcilably at variance with republican principles such as (oligarchic) *libertas*. Meanwhile, power-brokers, and especially Caesar, tested the waters on how far they could go in assuming the trappings of monarchy (recognizing the significant amount of goodwill and symbolic capital to be acquired from refusing royal honours). This cluster of issues underwrites Cicero's account of the Lupercalia (coming up in § 84).[33]

semper eius modi aliquid: Cicero is rather fond of the 'characterizing *semper*', used to pin down the essence of a person. Compare *On Duties* (*de Officiis*) 3.82, again with reference to Caesar: *ipse autem socer in ore semper Graecos versus de Phoenissis habebat...*: 'The father-in-law [= Caesar] always had Greek verses from Euripides' *Phoenissae* on his lips...' that proved him to be a tyrant at heart. The point is that Caesar's conduct after his victory in the civil wars was invariably and systematically — rather than just occasionally — that of an autocrat, with no regards for traditional republican institutions or procedures in either deeds or words.

tum hic bonus augur eo se sacerdotio praeditum esse dixit: *bonus* is cutting and condescending; *dixit* introduces an indirect statement with *se* as subject accusative, *esse* as verb, and *praeditum* as predicative complement, which governs the instrumental ablative *eo sacerdotio*: 'this excellent augur here said that he was endowed with this priestly office...' *sacerdotium* refers to Antony's augurship, which he assumed in 50 BCE.

ut comitia auspiciis vel impedire vel vitiare posset: *comitia* refers to the electoral assembly that would vote Dolabella into his consulship. Antony announced that he would use his powers of religious objection either to prevent them from taking place (*impedire*) or, if they proceeded, to cast religious doubt over — or invalidate altogether — the outcome (*vitiare*). The basic meaning of *vitiare* is 'to cause faults or defects in', 'to impair', but it also had the technical sense of 'to invalidate political proceedings or public business because of some technical fault that violated religious protocols'. In our case, the *vitium* marring the *comitia* would be Antony's augural pronouncement that he spotted signs of divine displeasure with the proceedings.

---

33   A classic passage is Livy 27.9.4 (Scipio speaking): *regium nomen, alibi magnum, Romae intolerabile esse.* See further Berry (1996: 177).

idque se facturum esse asseveravit: *asseveravit* introduces an indirect statement with *se* as subject accusative and *facturum esse* as infinitive. *id* refers back to Antony's reminder in the *ut*-clause that he could obstruct and/or invalidate the consular elections. It is the accusative object of *facturum esse*. Antony does not simply remind his audience that as augur he has the power to obstruct the elections; he feels obliged to assert emphatically (*asseveravit*) that he would actually do so.

in quo primum incredibilem stupiditatem hominis cognoscite: *in quo* is another connecting relative (= *et in eo*), picking up the entirety of Antony's statement in the previous sentence. *primum* is again adverbial ('first of all').

§ 81: Compounding Ignorance through Impudence

Cicero hammers away at Antony's seemingly incomplete understanding of the nuances of Rome's augural law and the different remits it offered to augurs and consuls (as well as other magistrates) — before shifting his focus halfway through from Antony's ignorance to his impudence. When a magistrate intended to obstruct public proceedings by observing the sky, political etiquette demanded that he announced his intentions ahead of time: since he would invariably find a sign of divine displeasure, the proceedings could be postponed before they had even started, thus keeping the inconvenience for everyone else to a minimum. By contrast, Antony announced way in advance what he planned to do; nevertheless got the voting procedure underway (over which he presided as consul); and then after proceedings drew to a close pronounced his religious objection — a stupid, shamefully inconsiderate, and reckless abuse of religious prerogatives, at least according to Cicero's spin. However, Cicero too would have known that Antony behaved with extraordinary shrewdness. By letting the election happen but casting a religious doubt over the (inevitable) outcome, he gained an important bargaining chip in interactions with his future colleague in office. As Santangelo (2013: 3) points out: 'The events that unfolded a few weeks later, after the Ides of March, confirmed the value of Antony's use of his augural prerogatives. When Dolabella and Antony decided to mend fences and co-operate in the aftermath of Caesar's assassination, Antony's willingness to accept Dolabella's election and set aside his opposition was a central part of the deal. The tactical advantage that he had earned with his handling of

Dolabella's election was rooted in his expert knowledge of the complex rules that governed the interaction between politics and religion in the late Republic'.[34]

Quid enim?: the elliptical question introduces a confirmatory statement (*OLD* s.v. *quis, quid* 14c): Cicero uses it as a transitional phrase to link his invitation to observe Antony's unbelievable stupidity with an explication thereof: 'Why?' or 'If that is not the case, what is?'

istud quod te sacerdoti iure facere posse dixisti, si augur non esses et consul esses, minus facere potuisses?: translate in the following sequence: *si augur non esses et consul esses, potuisses minus facere istud, quod dixisti te sacerdoti iure facere posse?* Put differently, *istud* up front is the accusative object of the supplementary infinitive *facere* and in turn serves as antecedent of the relative clause introduced by *quod*. Cicero invites Antony to consider whether he could not have done what he did had he only been consul at the time (rather than both consul *and* augur). The question is entirely rhetorical: of course he could have, given that the powers of a consul to impede electoral proceedings exceeded those of an augur. Overall, the sentence is a past counterfactual condition (though Cicero uses imperfect, rather than pluperfect subjunctives in the protasis, perhaps because Antony not just was an augur and consul back then but still is at the time of writing).

et consul esses: the past counterfactual condition enables Cicero to include a sly dig at Antony's status as consul: 'if you had not been an augur (but you were) and had been a consul (which Antony was — but Cicero implies that he was one in name only)...'

vide ne etiam facilius [facere potuisses]: 'See if you could not have / You'll find that you could have done it even more easily!'

nos enim nuntiationem solum habemus, consules et reliqui magistratus etiam spectionem: Cicero here uses the first person plural (*nos... habemus*) since he is speaking as a member of the augural college. Augurs only had the right of *nuntiatio* — the observation and

---

34 See Santangelo (2013: 273–78) for an extended discussion of 'Mark Antony the augur and the election of Dolabella'.

announcement of an (unanticipated) unfavourable divine sign, which would cast a religious doubt over ongoing proceedings or subsequent decisions; consuls and other magistrate could actively seek out such signs by observation (*spectio*) of the sky. And it was generally understood that anyone intent on seeking would indeed find what he was looking for. Therefore the mere announcement of a magistrate that he intended to engage in *spectio* (or watch the sky: *se servare de caelo*) with respect to an upcoming event would entail its cancellation or postponement. Put differently, *spectio* by magistrates tended to happen before, *nuntiatio* by augurs had to happen during, an event. Indeed, *considerate* use of *spectio* required the magistrate to signal his intentions to make use of his privilege well in advance (rather than waiting until the proceedings had started) so as not to unduly inconvenience all concerned. This is precisely what Antony fell short of doing, as Cicero goes on to point out below, ascribing it to his impudence.

esto: hoc imperite [dixit / factum est]: *esto* is the third person singular future imperative of *sum*, with a concessive sense (see *OLD* s.v. *sum* 8b): 'so be it!' *hoc imperite* is elliptical, with the verb, modified by the adverb *imperite* [*in* + *peritus* + *e*], needing to be supplied. Possibilities include *dixit* or *fecit*, which would turn *hoc* into an accusative object ('this he pronounced / did ignorantly') or *factum est*, with *hoc* as subject ('this was done out of ignorance'). The theme of Antony's ignorance, firmly established by the phrase *incredibilem stupiditatem* at the end of § 80, recurs at the end of the paragraph, where it gets married to his impudence.

nec enim est ab homine numquam sobrio postulanda prudentia: with mock affability, Cicero quickly dismisses Antony's failure to grasp a key aspect of Rome's augural lore: it wouldn't do to dwell too pedantically on such technicalities given Antony's state of permanent intoxication: that those under the influence do not tend to have the sharpest of minds is a well-known fact — 'From a Drunk-only, discriminating insight is not to be expected'. The advanced placement of *est* in the periphrastic gerundive enables a humorously alliterated ending to the sentence, with the subject — the climactic *prudentia* — coming last. Antony's heroic application to the bottle is a recurrent theme throughout the speech, receiving its most extensive coverage at *Phil.* 2.63:

Tu istis faucibus, istis lateribus, ista gladiatoria totius corporis firmitate tantum vini in Hippiae nuptiis exhauseras, ut tibi necesse esset in populi Romani conspectu vomere postridie. o rem non modo visu foedam, sed etiam auditu! si inter cenam in ipsis tuis immanibus illis poculis hoc tibi accidisset, quis non turpe duceret? in coetu vero populi Romani negotium publicum gerens magister equitum, cui ructare turpe esset, is vomens frustis esculentis vinum redolentibus gremium suum et totum tribunal implevit!

[You with that gullet of yours, with those lungs, with that gladiatorial strength of your whole body, had gulped down so much wine at Hippias' wedding that you were forced to vomit the following day right in front of the Roman people. How disgusting it must have been to watch — just to hear of it makes one gag! If during the banquet, in the very midst of those enormous potations of yours, this had happened to you, who would not think it disgraceful? But at an assembly of the Roman people, while in the conduct of public business, a master of the horse, for whom it would be disgraceful to belch, vomited and filled his own lap and the whole tribunal with bits and pieces of food reeking of wine.]

The portrayal of Antony as a permanently intoxicated alcoholic is a leitmotif throughout the speech — and beyond. As Hall (2002: 288–89) observes 'Antony's notorious drinking habits provide rich material for such a caricature. Through judicious hyperbole Cicero turns a drunken indiscretion into a scene of striking repugnance... It is typical of the speech's technique, however, that this hit at Antony's drunkenness is not a casual or isolated one. Elsewhere Cicero evokes the smell of stale wine on Antony's breath (*Phil.* 2.30 and 2.42), slyly suggests that his inconsistent pronouncements as augur were a result of the drink (*Phil.* 2.81; 84), and that his attempts to found a colony at Capua were affected by *furiosam vinolentiam* (*Phil.* 2.101). This accumulation of detail gives the depiction a persuasive consistency and depth'. The theme recurs in later *Philippics*, such as 3.20 and 6.4, and culminates at *Phil.* 13.4, where he turns the entire family-clan of the Antonii into a bunch of tipplers permanently reeking of wine. Antony thus falls woefully short of even the baseline requirements for a public speaker and statesman, i.e. being careful, thoughtful, and sober. (See *On the Ideal Orator / de Oratore* 2.140: ... *omnes diligentes et memores et sobrii oratores*...).

sed videte impudentiam: Cicero's tone now switches from the avuncular (used to comment on Antony's alleged ignorance) to the aggressive (deployed to attack his putative impudence).

multis ante mensibus in senatu dixit se Dolabellae comitia aut prohibiturum auspiciis aut id facturum esse quod fecit: the main verb is *dixit*, which is preceded by specifications of time (*multis ante mensibus*) and place (*in senatu*). It introduces an indirect statement with *se* as subjective accusative and *prohibiturum* (*esse*) (taking *comitia* as accusative object) and *facturum esse* (taking *id* as accusative object) as infinitives. *Dolabellae* is genitive depending on *comitia*: 'Dolabella's election'. Regarding the first part of what Antony purportedly said, i.e. that he would prevent the election from going forward, it is not entirely clear whether Cicero blames him for ignorance or for impudence:

- Option 1: on the basis of his position as augur he had no right to interfere with the meeting before it had started (= ignorance).

- Option 2a: as consul who had just entered office (if the senate-meeting in question is the one on 1 January 44), announcing his intent to use religious obstruction so far in advance of the actual event amounts to impudence.

- Option 2b: Perhaps Cicero vague temporal indicator *multis ante mensibus* (see below) is meant to suggest that Antony insisted on his right of *spectio* already in 45, as consul-elect (= impudence[2]).

Options 2a and 2b are of course difficult to reconcile with Cicero's earlier claim that Antony preferred to position himself as augur rather than consul. Matters get even more confusing if we factor in the second part of the indirect statement: Cicero claims that Antony announced months beforehand that he would exercise his right of *spectio*, but only after the proceedings had already run their course! All of this amounts to a great muddle in which elements of ignorance and elements of impudence are difficult to disentangle — precisely the impression Cicero arguably wishes to generate.

multis ante mensibus: with reference to the senate meeting that took place on 1 January 44, the phrase seems an exaggeration, but perhaps not by much; indeed, in the context of invective oratory, calling two and a half months 'many' would seem only mildly hyperbolic, if at all. But Cicero may of course allude to an even earlier pronouncement in late 45, which, if it is not entirely invented, perhaps even triggered Dolabella's seemingly well-prepared invective outburst during the meeting on 1 January 44, which Cicero mentioned in § 79. As § 83 shows (*id igitur* *obvenit vitium quod tu iam Kalendis Ianuariis futurum esse provideras et tanto ante praedixeras*), Antony certainly was not silent during this particular meeting either. But it remains unclear whether he *stated* or *restated* his intent to block Dolabella's election to suffect consul. (*et tanto ante praedixeras* could either refer to the meeting on the calends of January or an earlier one — in which case it would presumably be the same as the one Cicero has in mind here.)

quisquamne divinare potest quid viti in auspiciis futurum sit, nisi qui de caelo servare constituit?: 'Can anyone foresee what is going to be flawed in the auspices unless he has decided to observe the sky'? The point of the question seems to be that Antony, who seems to have acted in his role as augur by practicing *nuntiatio*, announced that he would do something that is only compatible with his role as consul (*spectio*), according to the (accepted) rule that magistrates who had the prerogative of *spectio* and announced that they would exercise it, as a matter of course found the negative signs they were looking for. Hence they could be said 'to foresee' (*divinare*) them. Augurs did not have this privilege.

quisquamne: the indefinite pronoun *quisquam* + the enclitic -*ne*, used to introduce a question.

quid viti in auspiciis futurum sit: an indirect question (hence the subjunctive). *viti* is a partitive genitive (from *vitium*) dependent on *quid*, literally 'what of religious flaw there will be in the auspices'.

quod neque licet comitiis per leges et si qui servavit, non comitiis habitis sed priusquam habeantur, debet nuntiare: *quod* is a connecting relative (= *et id*). The two parts of the main clause specify legal restrictions (*licet, per leges*) and normative expectations (*debet*) that governed (or ought to govern) the exercise of consular *spectio* (though, importantly, not augural *nuntiatio*): Cicero first refers to legislation that seems to have been introduced by his nemesis Publius Clodius Pulcher in 58 BCE (hence, perhaps, his use of the generic phrase *per leges* rather than a specific reference to the *lex Clodia*) which stipulated that a magistrate exercising his right of *spectio* with a mind to obstructing public business (*obnuntiatio*) had to do so (*a*) in person; and (*b*) before official proceedings started. This piece of legislation seems to have come as a direct response to the practice of Bibulus, who was Caesar's consular colleague in 59 BCE, to issue a religious objection to anything Caesar did from his own house (because otherwise Caesar's charges would rough him up). It also seems to have repealed at least some of the stipulations of the earlier *lex Aelia et Fufia* of c. 150 BCE. As far as we can reconstruct, this earlier law extended the right of *obnuntiatio* (= the reporting of unfavourable omens during a legislative or voting assembly, with the result that any public business had to be suspended until the next lawful day) from the College of Augurs to all of the magistrates.[35]

The second part of the sentence (*et si qui … debet nuntiare*: note that the *et* links *licet* and *debet*) refers to the expectation that any magistrate who practised *spectio* ought to announce the outcome of his observation before, rather than during the assembly. Commentators disagree on what precisely Cicero is saying here. Mayor (1861: 124) thinks that the legal prohibition covers both parts of the sentence, with Cicero acknowledging that the law was routinely breached: 'Thus Cicero says: it is illegal *de caelo servare* at the *comitia*, but if it is done, it should be done before they begin, and not when business is actually in progress'. This is not quite right: the law did not rule out *de caelo servare* on the part of a magistrate with the right to take auspices before the *comitia*. What Cicero says is that whoever engaged in *spectio* in the run-up to an assembly (note that *servavit* is perfect) ought to announce the outcome beforehand as well, and not wait until it is underway or, even worse, until it is finished. Some commentators suggest that in the phrase *comitiis habitis* the perfect passive participle is used instead of the non-existent present one, with the sense being 'while the voting assembly is in process'. This is possible grammatically, but I recommend a more literal reading: those who announced their intent to exercise their right of *spectio* before a voting assembly ought not to wait to announce their findings until after the event had finished (*comitiis habitis*) AS ANTONY (all but) DID (see § 83: *confecto negotio* etc.), but before it got underway (*priusquam habeantur*).

comitiis: ablative of time. As Mayor (1861: 124) points out, the use is idiomatic with a range of nouns that refer to public events: *ludis* ('during the festival'); *gladiatoribus* ('during the gladiatorial games').

---

35   See *pro Sestio* 33 with Kaster (2006: 197–98), further Tatum (1999: 125–33).

comitiis habitis: an ablative absolute. *comitia habere* = to hold or conduct an assembly. See *OLD* s.v. *habeo* 20.

verum implicata inscientia impudentia est: nec scit quod augurem [*scire decet*] **nec facit quod pudentem** [*facere*] **decet**: it is impossible to decide whether *inscientia* is the subject of *implicata est* and *impudentia* an instrumental ablative with *implico* or vice versa — and this might just be part of the point Cicero is trying to make: with Antony, 'ignorance and impudence are all of a piece' (Lacey 1986: 119). The elliptical follow-up sentence equally reinforces on the formal level the impression of Antony Cicero is trying to convey: there are significant gaps in his knowledge and his sense of decency: 'He neither knows what befits an augur to know nor does he do what it befits a decent man to do'.

§ 82: Antony Galloping after Caesar Only to Hold his Horses

This transitional paragraph begins by portraying Antony as Caesar's lackey who is unable to do anything during his consulship without first asking his colleague for guidance — even if this involves running after Caesar's litter. This utter lack of independence serves as foil for his conduct during the election of Dolabella to the suffect consulship over which Caesar presided, though initially it appeared that Antony would hold his peace: Cicero gives a quick blow-by-blow of the different stages of a late-republican voting assembly, while noting that Antony missed every single opportunity during the proceedings to voice his pre-announced religious objections.

To make sense of the second half of the paragraph, we need to establish how one specific voting assembly worked, the so-called *comitia centuriata*, which was used to elect the higher magistrates (here a suffect consul).[36] Rome's population of citizens was distributed into so-called *classes* on the basis of an assessment of the wealth of each individual (with an eye to the ability to arm himself for military service), called *census*.[37] For voting purposes, people within each class were grouped into 'centuries'. The wealthier the class, the higher the number of

---

36   Roman voting practice is a minefield. For a first accessible orientation, try Valentina Arena's article 'Elections in the Late Roman Republic: How Did They Work?', in *Historyextra*, https://www.historyextra.com/period/roman/elections-in-the-late-roman-republic-how-did-they-work/

37   Classics comes from *classis*: it is the study of those texts or authors — designated 'classical' — who are deemed to belong to the 'first class' of literary production because of their allegedly timeless quality and relevance.

centuries it received. Thus of the 193 centuries in the *comitia centuriata*, 83 belonged to the first class and 104 to the second to the fifth class taken together, with 6 centuries formed from the ancient clan tribes Tities, Ramnes, and Luceres making up the rest. Voting took place by these units. Simple majority determined which way a specific century voted. The overall outcome was determined by a simple majority of centuries, which meant that the first candidate who got the votes of 97 centuries would win the election. The system was clearly skewed in favour of the wealthy, though recent scholarship has argued against the consensus of earlier literature that the lower classes were not entirely disenfranchised: see Yakobson (1999).

On the day of the election of consuls and praetors (those magistracies endowed with *imperium*, i.e. the right to command an army), the order of voting included a complex procedure as follows (Taylor 1966: 84):

(i)   Lots were drawn to determine which of the centuriate units (*centuriae*) from the first class (*prima classis*) would cast their votes first. This *centuria* was labeled *centuria praerogativa*. (*praerogativus* literally means 'that is asked before others for their opinion' or, specifically, 'that votes first'; our 'prerogative' comes from it.)

(ii) The members of the designated *centuria praerogativa* would cast their votes and the outcome would be announced.

(iii) The remaining *centuriae* of the first class (*prima classis*) cast their votes.

(iv) The so-called *six suffragia* (the six centuries formed from the clan tribes Tities, Ramnes, and Luceres) cast their votes.

(v)   The lower classes cast their votes, in order.

In the case of Dolabella's election, there was no rival candidate, hence, on the basis of simple majority, the election would be over well before any of the lower classes got to cast their votes. He would have received the vote of the *centuria praerogativa* (1), the rest of the *prima classis* (1 + 82), the *six suffragia* (1 + 82 + 6), and would have reached the magic number of 97 after eight centuries from the *secunda classis* had cast their vote (1 + 82 + 6 + 8).

Itaque ex illo die recordamini eius usque ad Idus Martias consulatum: *recordamini* is the second person plural imperative (identical with the indicative) of the deponent *recordor*. Cicero exhorts his audience to recall Antony's conduct in the period stretching from the calends of January (*ex illo die*) right up to (*usque ad*) the Ides of March 44 BCE.

eius... consulatum: Cicero delays *consulatum*, the key noun and accusative object of *recordamini* on which *eius*, the genitive of the demonstrative pronoun *is*, (= Antony) depends, until the very end, perhaps for ironic effect. Along the lines of his earlier suggestion that Antony is not a 'real' consul, here the design of the sentence drives a wedge between Antony (*eius*) and the consulship (*consulatum*).

usque ad Idus Martias: *Idus, -uum* ('Ides') is a feminine plural noun of the fourth declension, here in the accusative plural following the preposition *ad*. In the Roman calendar, the Ides fell on the 15th day of March, May, July, and October and the 13th day of the other months. It was the day when payment of interest was due. *Martius* (here in the feminine accusative plural, modifying *Idus*) is the adjective to the god Mars, but also came to signify the month over which the god presides, i.e. March. In light of what happened on the Ides of March 44 BCE, the phrase has an ominous ring.

quis umquam apparitor tam humilis, tam abiectus?: Cicero suppresses the verb (*erat*). An *apparitor* was a (free) public functionary (such as a lictor) who attended on a Roman magistrate. Put differently, Antony's conduct was more subservient than that of those whose role it was to *be* subservient. In a status-conscious society such as Rome, his obsequious incompetence debased both himself and the office of the consulship.

nihil ipse poterat; omnia rogabat; caput in aversam lecticam inserens, beneficia quae venderet a collega petebat: Cicero claims that Antony's incompetence had no limits: he proved himself capable of — nothing. (*nihil* is an internal accusative with *poterat*: see *OLD* s.v. *possum* 8.) He therefore has to ask Caesar's approval for everything — which entails running after the litter of the fast-moving dictator (the adjective *aversam* implies that he is behind). And once he manages to get an audience of sorts (head in, butt out: the resulting image is entirely undignified), the outcome is — corruption. He seeks favours from Caesar — here referred to mockingly if technically correct as his 'colleague' (*collega*) in the consulship — in order to sell them: *quae venderet* is a relative clause of purpose (hence the subjunctive). Use of market language (buying and selling) in the context of distributing *beneficia* is crass: it deliberately ignores euphemistic protocols centred on ideas of goodwill, friendship and generosity that were commonly employed to obfuscate the economic realities of the nepotistic exchange of services at the heart of Rome's patronage system.

caput in aversam lecticam inserens: it might initially be tempting to take this as a Latin gloss on the phenomenon of 'brown-nosing' (what with Antony sticking his head in via the backside of the litter) and thus also a sly gesture to Caesar's rumored pathic tendencies ('queen of Bithynia' and all that), but the *OLD* entry on *insero* contains no encouragement along those lines.

ecce Dolabellae comitiorum dies: in classical Latin the particle *ecce* is construed with the nominative (*dies*). 'Insofar as it [sc. *ecce*] has a definable meaning, it is that of expressing immediacy and engagement, in relation to happenings, people or thoughts, whether visible or not' (Dionisotti 2007: 83). Here *ecce* is used for dramatic effect to encourage the audience to visualize the day (*dies*) of the voting assemblies (*comitia*) organized to elect Dolabella to the consulship. The effect is enhanced by the absence of a verb.

(i) **sortitio praerogativae** [*centuriae fit*]; **quiescit.** (ii) **renuntiatur: tacet.** (iii) **prima classis vocatur,** (iv) **renuntiatur.** (v) **deinde, ita ut assolet** [fieri], **suffragia** [fiunt]; (vi) **tum secunda classis** [vocatur]: Cicero details the stages of the election process, each of which ran its course without Antony saying anything:

(i) **sortitio praerogativae** [*centuriae fit*]: 'The drawing of lots (*sortitio*) to establish the *centuria* with the right to vote first (*praerogativae*) happened'. Cicero uses extremely condensed language, though the moment in the process he refers to will have been understood by anyone familiar with Roman voting procedure. In the *comitia centuriata*, the Roman people were divided into units (*centuriae*) for the purpose of voting, which were in turn grouped and ranked according to wealth. The lot was used to establish which *centuria* from the 'first class' (*prima classis*) had the right to cast the first vote. This is what the noun *sortitio* refers to. *praerogativae* is an adjective in the feminine genitive singular modifying an implied *centuriae* ('the drawing of lots of the *centuria* who had the right to vote first'). Cicero suppresses the verb (*fit*).

(ii) **renuntiatur**: 'the result of how that *centuria* voted is announced'

(iii) **prima classis vocatur**: 'the rest of the first class is called to the vote'

(iv) **renuntiatur**: 'the result of how the rest of the first class voted is announced'

(v) **deinde, ita ut assolet** [fieri], **suffragia** [fiunt]: 'the voting of six special equestrian *centuriae* (= *suffragia*) happened as is customary' (for the ellipsis of *facere* and *fieri* with *possum* and *assolet* (less frequently with *solet*) see Kühner-Stegmann 2.554)

(vi) **tum secunda classis** [vocatur]: 'the second class is called to the vote'

Cicero continues with terse, paratactic, highly elliptical prose, to give an impression of how smoothly the election unfolded, in reaching its foregone conclusion. The clockwork nature of the proceedings even squeezes out the refrain 'and he remained silent' — though we of course need to imagine a *quiescit* or a *tacet* also after stages (iii), (iv), (v), and (vi). The Latin here is trying to reproduce what Cicero verbalizes in the following sentence, i.e. that the various stages of the voting process happened more quickly than he was able to put them into words.

quae omnia sunt citius facta quam dixi: *quae* is a connecting relative (= *et ea*). *citius* is the comparative adverb of *citus*, 'quick, fast' (cf. the Olympic motto: *citius, altius, fortius*).

§ 83: Antony's Fake Auspices

In this and the following paragraph Cicero dwells on the moment Antony decided to invalidate or at least vitiate the election of Dolabella, which had just run its course, by announcing that he had become aware of a natural disturbance that signaled divine displeasure. He used the ritual phrase that calls for postponement: *alio die* means 'Sorry, just got a communiqué from above: let's reconvene to repeat the proceedings *on another day*'. This reiteration never happened; and hence Dolabella's suffect consulship was technically speaking marred by a religious flaw in the electoral proceedings that would need to be referred to the augural college for discussion. A passage in Cicero's dialogue *On the Laws* (*de Legibus*) gives a sense of the importance of augural approval (or disapproval) in the political decision-making processes of the Roman republic (2.31):[38]

> Maximum autem et praestantissimum in re publica ius est augurum cum auctoritate coniunctum, neque vero hoc quia sum ipse augur ita sentio, sed quia sic existimari nos est necesse. quid enim maius est, si de iure quaerimus, quam posse a summis imperiis et summis potestatibus comitiatus et concilia vel instituta dimittere vel habita rescindere? quid gravius quam rem susceptam dirimi, si unus augur 'alio <die>' dixerit? quid magnificentius quam posse decernere, ut magistratu se abdicent consules? quid religiosius quam cum populo, cum plebe agendi ius aut dare aut non dare? quid, legem si non iure rogata est tollere...? nihil domi, nihil militiae per magistratus gestum sine eorum auctoritate posse cuiquam probari?

---

38 See also Cicero, *de Divinatione* 1.29.

[But the highest and most important legal instance in the commonwealth is that of the augurs, to whom is accorded great authority. I hold this opinion not because I am an augur myself, but because it is necessary for us the augurs to be esteemed thus. For if we consider their legal rights, what power is greater than to be able to adjourn assemblies and meetings convened by the most powerful magistrates endowed with the highest imperium, or to declare null and void the acts of assemblies presided over by such officials? What is of graver import than to abandon any business already begun, if a single augur says, 'On another day'? What power is more impressive than that of forcing the consuls to resign their offices? What right is more sacred than that of giving or refusing permission to hold an assembly of the people or of the plebs, or that of abrogating laws illegally passed? ... Indeed, no act of any magistrate at home or in the field can have any validity for any person without their authority.]

The religious flaw could be summoned as an argument in political discussion about the validity of Dolabella's actions as consul. Indeed, it was made to backfire on Antony once he accepted Dolabella's election to the consulship as valid: his own religious objection now also came to vitiate any action he jointly undertook with his colleague. Cicero does not fail to point this out. See *Phil.* 3.9, where Antony is blasted as being a worse tyrant than the kings of old (at least those respected the auspices): *servabant auspicia reges; quae hic consul augurque neglexit, neque solum legibus contra auspicia ferendis, sed etiam conlega una ferente eo quem ipse ementitis auspiciis vitiosum fecerat* ('The kings observed the auspices, which this consul and augur has neglected, not only by putting through laws in defiance of the auspices, but by doing so jointly with the very colleague whose election he had flawed by falsifying the auspices') and *Phil.* 5.9.

Confecto negotio bonus augur — C. Laelium diceres — 'alio die' inquit: The sentence begins with an ablative absolute (*confecto negotio*) that sums up the previous sentence. Cicero places the participle first to stress the aspect of completion. The verb of the main clause is *inquit*, which sets up the bit of direct speech that Cicero quotes (*alio die*). *C. Laelium diceres* is a parenthetical gloss on *bonus augur*.

bonus augur: sarcastic.

[eum esse] C[aium] **Laelium diceres**: *diceres* is an indefinite second person singular (equivalent to the English 'one') imperfect subjunctive active, signifying potential. It introduces an indirect statement, though Cicero suppresses the subject accusative (*eum*) and the verb (*esse*), leaving only the predicative complement (*C. Laelium*): 'one could have said that he was a Gaius Laelius'. C. Laelius (c. 188–129 BCE; consul in 140), who stars in Cicero's treatise *Laelius On Friendship* (*Laelius de Amicitia*), written about the same time as *Philippic* 2, boasted the sobriquet *Sapiens* ('the Wise') and was a famous augur: put differently, he was everything Antony was not.

alio die: the augural formula that magistrates observing the sky uttered when they became aware of an unfavourable omen (such as thunder or lightening — taken to articulate Jupiter's displeasure) to adjourn proceedings: 'Let proceedings continue *some other time*!'

o impudentiam singularem!: an accusative of exclamation. As Gibbs (2009: 59) puts it: 'In Latin [as opposed to English where it is limited to some standard frozen phrases such as "Dear me!"], the accusative of exclamation is a productive form of speech; you can just put whatever noun phrase you want into the accusative case, and exclaim!'

quid videras, quid senseras, quid audieras?: a snappy rhetorical question cast as an asyndetic tricolon reinforced by anaphora of *quid* and homoioteleuton (*-eras*) to bring out the fact that Antony's sensory input was precisely nothing. The three pluperfect verbs refer to three different types of signs: lightening (*videras*); haziness in the atmosphere (*senseras*); and thunder (*audieras*). Compare *Phil.* 5.8 where Cicero lashes out against Antony for having passed a law with all the heavens in turmoil: *quam legem igitur se augur dicit tulisse non modo tonante Iove, sed prope caelesti clamore prohibente, hanc dubitabit contra auspicia latam confiteri?* ('Will he therefore hesitate to admit that a law which he, an augur, says he carried not only while Jupiter was thundering but almost against the veto of a heavenly clamour, was carried in violation of the auspices?').

neque enim te de caelo servasse dixisti nec hodie dicis: the connecting logic of *neque enim* is as follows: 'for you must have made some such observation, as you certainly did not declare *te de caelo servasse*' (Mayor

1861: 127). This harks back to the distinction between consular *spectio* (which involves prior announcement of intent) and augural *nuntiatio* (observation during the proceedings). Antony did not do the former, so he must have performed the latter. *dixisti*, the first of the two main verbs, refers to the time of the elections; it introduces an indirect statement with *te* as subject accusative and *servasse* (the syncopated perfect active infinitive = *serva│vi│sse*). *hodie dicis* feeds into the fiction that *Philippic* 2 is part of a live confrontation between Cicero and Antony on the senate floor on 19 September 44.

id igitur obvenit vitium quod tu iam Kalendis Ianuariis futurum esse provideras et tanto ante praedixeras: the front position of *id* ('that very'), a demonstrative adjective modifying *vitium*, enhances Cicero's piercing sarcasm and has a correlate in *tu* at the beginning of the relative clause. In the relative clause, the relative pronoun *quod* is both the accusative object of *provideras* and *praedixeras* and the subject accusative of the indirect statement introduced by *provideras* (with *futurum esse* as infinitive). The construction goes into English reasonably well: '… which already on the Calends of January you had foreseen would happen…'.

tanto ante: *tanto* is an ablative of the measure of difference modifying the adverb *ante*: '(by) so long beforehand'. It could refer either to the Calends of January or an even earlier moment in time: see above on § 81 *multis ante mensibus*.

ergo hercule magna, ut spero, tua potius quam rei publicae calamitate ementitus es auspicia: (implied) subject, verb, and accusative object cluster at the end of the sentence: *ementitus es auspicia*: 'you fabricated the auspices'. *auspicium mentiri* is 'a standard augural expression'.[39] What leads up to them is, after the connective *ergo* and the interjection *hercule*, a long phrase in the ablative that specifies the result of Antony's blasphemy: 'resulting, as I hope, in *your* grand destruction rather than the destruction of the commonwealth'.[40] *magna* and *tua* both modify an implied *calamitate*.

---

39 Linderski (1995: 615), with reference to Cic. *Div.* 2.72–73 and Servius *ad Aen.* 6.198.
40 See Kühner-Stegmann II.1, 410–12: this 'resultative ablative' tends to take the preposition *cum*, but can also occur without any preposition.

In Roman political culture, it was a key (yet open) question whether (and if so to what extent) the commonwealth was liable for the religious misdeeds of one of its functionaries. A story in Livy illustrates the issues at the stake — as well as the legalistic logic that informs Rome's civic religion. Before a battle against the Samnites in 293 BCE, the consul L. Papirius asks his chicken-keepers to take the auspices. (The Romans used the way chicken fed as a way to ascertain the will of the gods: greedy eating was considered a good omen; it thus helped to have put the chicken on a temporary diet just before offering them auspicious food…) In this particular instance, the chicken refused to eat, but one of the chicken-keepers nevertheless reported to the consul that they had eaten greedily, thus 'falsifying the auspices'. Consul Papirius, who was left in the dark of how the chicken actually fed, was of course delighted and got his army ready for battle, only to be told by his nephew that the auspices might have been meddled with. Papirius' reply is telling:

> … ceterum qui auspicio adest, si quid falsi nuntiat, in semet ipsum religionem recipit; mihi quidem tripudium nuntiatum, populo Romano exercituique egregium auspicium est.

> [He who assists at the auspices (*auspicio adest*) if he reports anything that is false, draws down the *religio* (ritual pollution) upon himself; as for me I received a report of *tripudium* [i.e. a very positive omen], and I take it as an excellent *auspicium* for the Roman People and the army (trans. Linderski 1995: 615).]

Linderski (1995: 615) draws attention to the remarkable fact that Papirius assumes that 'Jupiter is bound by the false announcement of a favorable *auspicium*'. Put differently, according to the logic of Rome's augural law, 'an augur who announced a prohibitive sign, even one that he had made up, was felt to bring it into existence by his very act of proclaiming it' (Ramsey 2003: 281, with reference to Linderski 1986: 2214). Papirius proved to be right, though as an extra precaution he positioned the chicken-keepers in the front-line. Sure enough, the *pullularius* who had falsified the auspices got hid by an errant spear even before the battle started, which the Romans went on to win handily. In short, we have a falsified report that paradoxically establishes both (*a*) a legally binding contract between Jupiter and the Roman magistrate (acting on behalf of the *res publica*); and (*b*) a state of religious pollution that requires expiation. The question of interest to us is who carries the religious stigma and will become the target of divine wrath: the individual person who committed the religious transgression or the commonwealth of which he is a part? Both Livy (consider the safety-measures of Papirius who deliberately placed the *pullularius* in harm's way) and Cicero (see the hedge *ut spero*) suggests that this was not entirely clear and may change from case to case, depending on various variables. Either the individual or his community could be punished, and Cicero of course hopes that in this particular instance divinely inflicted catastrophe would redound on the individual (Antony) rather than the *res publica*.

obstrinxisti religione populum Romanum; augur auguri, consul consuli obnuntiasti: the two alliterated verbs *obstrinxisti* and *obnuntiasti* form a weighty frame for the two clauses. Both are technical terms, which might be glossed as follows: *obstringere religione* = to taint with pollution through a breach in religious protocol; *obnuntiare* = to oppose a public act or decision with reference to an adverse sign from the gods. Together, they generate a vivid image of the chaos Antony caused, which is reflected in the inverted word-order of the first clause, the clashing polyptoton of the second clause, and the *husteron proteron* (*obstringere* is the outcome of performing an *obnuntiatio* on the basis of fake auspices).

augur auguri, consul consuli obnuntiasti: *augur* and *consul* stand in apposition to the subject of the sentence: 'you, an augur, objected to an augur, you, a consul, objected to a consul'. The datives *auguri* and *consuli* refer to Caesar, who, like Antony, was both augur and consul at the time. (He had himself been elected to the priestly college of augurs in 47 BCE; see Crawford 1974: 494). The utter lack of solidarity between holders of the same position or office displayed by Antony is reminiscent of civil war, which pitched citizen against citizen.

nolo plura [dicere], **ne acta Dolabellae videar convellere, quae necesse est aliquando ad nostrum collegium deferantur**: *nolo* governs an (elided) supplementary infinitive, which takes *plura* as accusative object. The *ne*-clause is one of purpose: 'lest I seem…'. Cicero concedes that he is walking on a tight rope — the more he lays into Antony's conduct at the election of Dolabella, the more he undermines the legitimacy of Dolabella's actions in office, which for present purposes he deems inopportune.

quae necesse est aliquando ad nostrum collegium deferantur: Cicero continues with a relative clause with *acta* as antecedent of *quae*, built into which is a substantive consecutive clause dependent on *necesse est* (with the *ut* — as often — omitted), hence the subjunctive *deferantur*: '… which must at some future time (*aliquando*) be referred to our college [= the college of augurs, of which Cicero was a member, hence *nostrum*]', sc. to make a decision about their validity. As Denniston (1926: 149) explains: 'It rested with the college of augurs to decide whether or not a magistrate's action had been "vitiated" by neglect of the auspices. … Cicero speaks of Dolabella's acts being referred to the augural college, because the validity of his acts rested on the invalidity of Antony's *obnuntiatio* to his election, and the question of the validity of the *obnuntiatio* would be referred to the college'.

§ 84: On to the Lupercalia...

Cicero is winding down the discussion of Antony's augural objections to the consulship of Dolabella. The next topic on the agenda is the festival of the Lupercalia on 15 February 44 BCE. At *Phil.* 13.41 Cicero suggests that Antony as good as murdered Caesar on that day by trying to crown him with a diadem. What exactly happened — and why — is difficult to establish with certainty — not least since it is tied up with the significance of a rather strange religious rite, the Lupercalia, which has been the subject of much scholarly controversy. Here is North's summary of what this festival entailed (2008: 147–48):

> before February 44 B.C.E., there were two teams (*sodalitates*) of Luperci — one the team of Romulus, the other the team of Remus. Each was apparently called after an ancient Roman *gens* — the Fabii and the Quinctii or Quintilii, though the exact names of the *sodalitates* are variously reported. Romulus' team was the Quinctii, Remus' the Fabii. How these groups, named after particular ancient *gentes*, came to be associated with one each of the twin founders is not recorded. The traditional ritual programme had two stages. In the first stage, at the Lupercal itself (i.e. the scene of the discovery of the twins suckled by the wolf), the Luperci sacrificed a goat and a dog. They then smeared the forehead of the young Luperci (perhaps the initiates) with blood and milk. The new bloods then gave a laugh. The hide of the sacrificed goat (or goats?) was cut up to provide loin-cloths for the runners and strips of hide to be used as whips, also by the runners. There was then feasting, with much wine. The second stage consisted of running around in the Palatine / *forum* / *sacra via* area of Rome, striking all the people they met with their strips of hide and joking, laughing, larking about and exchanging obscenities with those who attended the ritual. It was believed that women who had been struck with the goatskin whip would

become pregnant. Gerhard Binder has pointed out, rightly in my view, how these practices imply that the ritual was of the Carnival type. In my view this is a fundamental point, which needs to be borne in mind later on in this argument. At least our sources, not least Valerius Maximus, are emphatic about the joking, jeering, obscenity and play that accompanied the progress of the run.

North encourages us to distinguish between at least three layers of meaning during the celebration of the festival in 44 BCE:

(i) The traditional ritual and its functions: purification, fertility, protection: he locates the themes of 'purification', 'fertility', and 'protection' at the centre of the 'ritual programme' (2008: 154–55), all carried out in a spirit of Carnival and the celebration of the annual renewal of the life-cycle at the beginning of spring. The legend associates the origins of the ritual with the founders of the city, Romulus and Remus, recalling also in its name their suckling by a she-wolf. North's analysis of the basic elements of this programme is as follows (2008: 148):

- the invocation of the first creation of the community (the respective *sodales* of Remus and of Romulus, the founders);
- the confrontation of primitive to civilized (i.e. the naked Luperci in contrast with the onlookers from the contemporary city);
- the annual ritual purification of the community (the sacrifice and the running and the actions of the runners);
- the ritual fertilization of the human community (the ritual of whipping).

(ii) The inscription of Caesar in the ritual programme: becoming a founder: in some accounts, the twins headed the initial two group of naked runners (called *sodalitates*): Remus the Fabii, Romulus the Quintilii. In 44 BCE, in honour of Caesar, a third group of runners representing the *gens Iulia* was added. The head of this *sodalitas* was Antony: 'We know again from Dio [45.30], though also from Plutarch [*Ant.* 12.2] and, if a bit confusedly, from Nicolaus of Damascus [*Life of Augustus* 71], that Antony was running specifically for the new group of Luperci, the Iuliani, and that he was in fact their leader' (North 2008: 147). Put differently, even without the incident with the diadem, Caesar had coopted the ritual for purposes of self-promotion, elevating himself to the status of a founding figure. That Antony was chosen to run as representative of the *gens Iulia*

must have been a great honour for him – and signals his proximity to the dictator at the time.

(iii) The incident of the diadem: one honour too far?: despite the royal associations of the golden chair and the magnificent rope, Caesar's status at the time of the festival was not yet that of a king — it seems to have been the crowning with the diadem that put the nail in this particular coffin. As North (2008: 146) points out: 'Note that Cicero is not implying here that Caesar was already enthroned as King: it is clear that the robe (even if it was kingly, as Stefan Weinstock argued) and the golden throne (clearly not a consul's proper seat) are both honours he can use, but evidently are not to be seen as making him the *rex* of Rome'.

This raises the question of why the crowning incident happened. Pelling (1988: 144) outlines the different options:

> (1) Perhaps A. acted on his own initiative. If so, he may (*a*) genuinely have wished C. to take the title of king, or to force his hand; or (*b*) have hoped to gratify C. with a welcome gesture; or (*c*) have wished to discredit or embarrass him. (2) But it is more reasonable to assume that A. would not have risked this gesture without C.'s prior encouragement. If so, C. may (*a*) have aimed for kingship, and intended to accept the diadem if the people reacted favourably; or (*b*) have wished to make a public gesture of his *refusal* to become king; or (*c*) have intended this as a test of public opinion, if he was himself unsure.

To fully appreciate the historical dynamics that shaped this event (as well as later interpretations of it, both ancient and modern), we need to look into the economy of honours that defined the relationship between Caesar as de-facto ruler of Rome and the disempowered, but by no means powerless members of the traditional ruling elite. In his *Life of Julius Caesar*, Suetonius offers an interesting take on the social and psychological 'dynamics of honouring' (76):

> Praegravant tamen cetera facta dictaque eius, ut et abusus dominatione et iure caesus existimetur. non enim honores modo nimios recepit: continuum consulatum, perpetuam dictaturam praefecturamque morum, insuper praenomen Imperatoris, cognomen Patris patriae, statuam inter reges, suggestum in orchestra; sed et ampliora etiam humano fastigio decerni sibi passus est: sedem auream in curia et pro tribunali, tensam et ferculum circensi pompa, templa, aras, simulacra

iuxta deos, pulvinar, flaminem, lupercos, appellationem mensis e suo nomine; ac nullos non honores ad libidinem cepit et dedit.

[At the same time, certain other actions and words so turn the scale, that it is thought that he abused his power and was justly slain. For not only did he accept excessive honours, such as an uninterrupted consulship, the dictatorship for life, and the censorship of public morals, as well as the forename Imperator, the surname of Father of his Country, a statue among those of the kings, and a raised couch in the orchestra; he also allowed honours to be bestowed on him which exceeded mortal measure: a golden throne in the senate house and in court; a chariot and litter in the procession at the circus; temples, altars, and statues beside those of the gods; a special priest, an additional college of the Luperci, and the calling of one of the months by his name. In fact, there were no honours which he did not receive or confer at will.]

John Henderson encourages us to read this as Suetonius' final verdict on Julius Caesar, that, yes, on balance, he was a tyrant, so fair game. The historiographer Cassius Dio (c. 155–235 CE, so writing centuries after the events) also embeds the incident at the Lupercalia within a double-edged dynamics of honouring Caesar (44.3):

It happened as follows, and his death was due to the cause now to be given. He had aroused dislike that was not altogether unjustified, except in so far as it was the senators themselves who had by their novel and excessive honours encouraged him and puffed him up, only to find fault with him on this very account and to spread slanderous reports how glad he was to accept them and how he behaved more haughtily as a result of them. It is true that Caesar did now and then err by accepting some of the honours voted him and believing that he really deserved them; yet those were most blameworthy who, after beginning to honour him as he deserved, led him on and brought blame upon him for the measures they had passed. He neither dared, of course, to thrust them all aside, for fear of being thought contemptuous, nor, again, could he be safe in accepting them; for excessive honour and praise render even the most modest men conceited, especially if they seem to be bestowed with sincerity.

Dio goes on to enumerate the 'number and nature' of the privileges that were granted to Caesar, including (for our purposes) the use of a gilded chair and attire once worn by the kings, and the creation of a third priestly college (called 'Julian') in his role as overseer of the Lupercalia. This festival later on comes in for a closer look (44.11):

Another thing that happened not long after these events proved still more clearly that, although he pretended to shun the title [sc. of king], in reality he desired to assume it. For when he had entered the Forum at the festival of the Lupercalia and was sitting on the rostra in his gilded chair, adorned with the royal apparel and resplendent in his crown overlaid with gold, Antony with his fellow-priests saluted him as king and binding a diadem upon his head, said: 'The people offer this to you through me'. And Caesar answered: 'Jupiter alone is king of the Romans', and sent the diadem to Jupiter on the Capitol; yet he was not angry, but caused it to be inscribed in the records that he had refused to accept the kingship when offered to him by the people through the consul. It was accordingly suspected that this thing had been deliberately arranged and that he was anxious for the name, but wished to be somehow compelled to take it; consequently the hatred against him was intense.

Sed arrogantiam hominis insolentiamque cognoscite: the -*que* links *arrogantiam* and *insolentiam*, the two accusative objects of *cognoscite* (second person plural present imperative active). *hominis* goes with both nouns, which are virtual synonyms of each other.

quamdiu tu voles, vitiosus consul Dolabella [erit]**; rursus, cum voles, salvis auspiciis creatus** [est]: Cicero foregrounds the whim of Antony by using the personal pronoun *tu* (to be pronounced with contempt and outrage in equal measure), which, from a syntactical point of view is strictly speaking unnecessary. Cicero here seems to be objecting to Antony's inconsistent behaviour in the aftermath of the election. In a senate meeting on 17 March, i.e. shortly after the assassination of Caesar, he accepted Dolabella as his colleague in the consulship despite his *obnuntiatio* during the election. This shift towards a more accommodating stance will likely have come as a reaction to Dolabella's strategic schmoozing with the liberators, motivated no doubt by his desire to have his consulship officially recognized: see Ramsey (2003: 143–44). Cicero ignores these pragmatic considerations, preferring to portray Antony's oscillations as an index of his arrogance — the action of a high and mighty individual who does not play by the republican rule book and enjoys jerking his peers around.

quamdiu tu voles: *quamdiu* is a temporal conjunction used to express contemporaneous action ('as long as'); *voles* is the second person singular future active of *volo, velle*: Antony's control over the status of

Dolabella's election to the consulship depends on his whim and will and extends indefinitely into the future (at least until the college of augurs considered the case and produced a definitive ruling: but Cicero isn't interested in such nuances).

vitiosus consul Dolabella: a very condensed way of saying 'Dolabella will be a consul, whose election to office is tainted by a religious flaw'. *vitiosus* is short for *vitio creatus*: see Mayor (1861: 127).

rursus: introduces the second of two contrasting terms (*OLD* s.v. 6), here *vitiosus* and *salvis auspiciis creatus*.

cum voles: a case of 'conditional *cum*'. See Gildersleeve & Lodge 373: '*cum* with the Future, Future Perfect, or Universal Present, is often almost equivalent to *si*, if, with which it is sometimes interchanged'. Cicero drives home the point that Antony, whenever it suits him, considers Dolabella's election unflawed, ignoring his own religious objection.

salvis auspiciis: a nominal ablative absolute (consisting of an adjective and a noun) and technical phrase meaning 'with the auspices in order'.

si nihil est cum augur eis verbis nuntiat quibus tu nuntiasti, confitere te, cum 'alio die' dixeris, sobrium non fuisse; sin est aliqua vis in istis verbis, ea quae sit augur a collega requiro: we are here dealing with two simple conditions in the present:

  (i)   protasis: *si nihil est* (followed by a temporal *cum*-clause in the indicative and a relative clause) — apodosis: the present imperative *confitere* (of the deponent *confiteor*), which introduces an indirect statement with *te* as subject accusative, *sobrium* as predicative complement, and *non fuisse* as verb.)

  (ii) protasis: *sin est aliqua vis* — apodosis: *requiro*.

They map out two different ways to explain Antony's inconsistent attitude towards his own augural objection to scupper his attempt to have it both ways: (i) one may assume that an augur using the phrase *alio die* makes a meaningless utterance — in which case Antony was drunk when he made it. The drift of Cicero's thought here is not entirely obvious given that the premise specified in the *si*-clause is false (augural utterances *are* meaningful), and the inference (Antony must have been drunk when he said it) hence seemingly arbitrary. Arguably, what Cicero wishes to say is that if Antony considers his own utterance of no moment, it is because he was not qualified at the time to make it owing to his intoxication. As Lacey (1986: 219) explains: 'The madman (*furiosus*) and the man who had had a seizure (*mente captus*) were debarred from legal acts... Cicero suggests that this could be true of the drunk too'.

(ii) or perhaps Antony operates on the basis of a special force of the formula so far only known to himself, which renders one and the same pronouncement valid at one moment and invalid the next, depending on the whim of the augur in question: Cicero, as a fellow augur, asks Antony with mock politeness whether he is able to explain this novel usage of the ritual idiom.

si nihil est: 'if it means nothing'

cum augur eis verbis nuntiat quibus tu nuntiasti: *eis verbis* refers to the formula *alio die*. Cicero uses *nuntiat* and *nuntiasti* (the syncopated second person singular perfect indicative active of *nuntio* = *nuntia⏐vi⏐sti*) in an absolute sense, without an accusative object or object sentence: 'to make an announcement'.

sin est aliqua vis in istis verbis, ea quae sit augur a collega requiro: *ea* picks up *vis* and belongs into the indirect question *quae sit* (hence the subjunctive); the nominative *augur* stands either in apposition or in predicative position to the subject of the sentence, with Cicero self-identifying: 'I, an augur / as augur, ask from his colleague what that (sc. force) is'.

sed ne forte ex multis rebus gestis M. Antoni rem unam pulcherrimam transiliat oratio, ad Lupercalia veniamus: At this point, Cicero breaks off his discussion of Antony's manipulation of augural law to ensure coverage of the anecdote he labels the most disgraceful (*pulcherrimam* = *turpissimam*) on Antony's record, his attempt to crown Caesar king at the Lupercalia, which took place on 15 February 44.

ex multis rebus gestis M. Antoni: a partitive use of the preposition *ex*. Cicero here harks back to his earlier point that the number of Antony's misdeeds calls for abbreviated and selective treatment. *res gestae* usually refers to (glorious) deeds done in the service of the state; Antony has been accumulating the debauched counterfeit of the real thing.

veniamus: first person plural present subjunctive active (exhortative): 'Let us…'

non dissimulat, patres conscripti: apparet [eum] **esse commotum; sudat, pallet**: upon his mention of the Lupercalia, Cicero imagines Antony showing physical signs of distress. He is unable to suppress (*non dissimulat*) his inner turmoil (*apparet esse commotum*), breaks out in cold sweat (*sudat*) and turns pale (*pallet*).

apparet: the accusative *commotum* indicates that *apparet* is an impersonal verb ('it appears') that governs an indirect statement. The subject accusative (*eum*) needs to be supplied. (Alternatively, Cicero could have written *apparet esse commotus*: 'he appears to be agitated'.)

quidlibet [faciat]**, modo ne faciat quod in porticu Minucia fecit**: i.e. puking all over the place. The signs of physical distress that Cicero attributes to Antony are so powerful that he begins to wonder whether Antony is going to be sick — not least since he has a track record of letting it all out. The reference in the *quod*-clause is to Antony doing the technicolour yawn after over-indulging the night before while conducting public business — an anecdote Cicero dwells on at length at 2.63 (cited above 227–28).

modo ne faciat: *modo ne* (= *dummodo ne*) here means 'provided that' and introduces a conditional wish (hence the present subjunctive *faciat*).

in porticu Minucia: the porticus Minucia, located in the Campus Martius, was built by M. Minucius Rufus (consul in 110 BCE), with the spoils of a military campaign in Thrace. See Velleius Paterculus 2.8.3: *per eadem tempora clarus eius Minuci qui porticus, quae hodieque celebres sunt, molitus est, ex Scordiscis triumphus fuit* ('about the same time took place the famous triumph over the Scordisci of Minucius, the builder of the porticoes which are famous even in our own day').

quae potest esse turpitudinis tantae defensio?: *quae* is an interrogative adjective modifying *defensio*: 'what defence can there be of shamefulness so profound?'

cupio audire, ut videam ubi campus Leontinus appareat: Cicero continues by saying 'let's hear it!' — after all, Antony has gifted his teacher in rhetoric with such riches that we can expect an outstanding performance. After *Phil.* 2.8–9 and 42–43, he thus has yet another dig at Sextus Clodius, whom Antony enriched with money and a chunk of what had been public land (*ager publicus*) in a particularly fertile region in Sicily around the town of Leontini, which Antony distributed among his followers as part of his settlement projects earlier in the year. Sextus Clodius had a hand in drafting Antony's response to Cicero's first *Philippic*, delivered in the senate on 19 September 44 BCE, so he is an obvious proxy target in the second. His entry in Suetonius' *On Teachers of Grammar and Rhetoric* (*De Grammaticis et Rhetoribus*), which is partly based on evidence from Cicero's *Philippic* 2, reads as follows (29):[41]

> Sextus Clodius e Sicilia, Latinae simul Graecaeque eloquentiae professor, male oculatus et dicax par oculorum in amicitia M. Antoni triumviri extrisse se aiebat; eiusdem uxorem Fulviam, cui altera bucca inflatior erat, acumen stili temptare dixit, nec eo minus — immo vel magis — ob hoc Antonio gratus. a quo mox consule ingens etiam congiarium accepit, ut ei in Philippicis Cicero obicit (2.42–43).

> [Sextus Clodius, from Sicily, taught both Greek and Latin rhetoric. Having poor sight but a ready tongue, he used to say that he had worn out both his eyes in the friendship of Marcus Antonius the triumvir. He also once said that Antonius' wife Fulvia — one of whose cheeks was rather puffy — was 'testing the point of his pen'; and yet Antonius found him no less agreeable — or rather, all the more agreeable — on this account. Soon, when Antonius was consul, he also gave Clodius a huge gift, as Cicero charges in the *Philippics*.]

More generally, Cicero likes to show up his adversaries not just in substance but also in style. (For example: in the *Divinatio in Caecilium* and the *pro Caelio*, Cicero delights in demonstrating to a younger orator how things are done.) See also *Phil.* 2.84, 2.101; 3.22; 5.19.

---

41   Text and translation from Kaster (1995).

§ 85: *Vive le roi! Le roi est mort*

Cicero now moves on to a vivid account of what happened on 15 February 44 BCE. He starts with Caesar sitting on the speakers' platform (which is were the run of the Luperci came to an end), decked out in quasi-royal regalia (a purple toga, a golden chair, a crown) but not yet unequivocally a 'king'. The runners arrive, in the nude as is ritual practice, but somehow Antony has a diadem on him: where does it come from? Cicero ponders various possibilities he rejects (for instance: Antony just found one abandoned on the roadside…) and argues for premeditation and prior arrangements as the only plausible explanation. Antony tries repeatedly to put the diadem on Caesar, who keeps rejecting it, as the people alternately groan and cheer. According to Cicero, the charade outs Antony unambiguously as a proponent of autocracy at Rome — and thereby hastened and sealed Caesar's assassination.[42] (Here and again at the funeral we should recognize that when claims to say what 'the people' thought and felt feature, these are, as always, bound to be hooked to partisan interpretations passed off as accounts; their counterpart is the denunciation of rent-a-crowd or mobster seizure of public space and the citizenry displaced.)

Sedebat in rostris collega tuus amictus toga purpurea, in sella aurea, coronatus: the subject of the sentence is *collega tuus* (= Caesar). In part through front position of the verb (in the imperfect: a durative, establishing the background scene for an action about to happen), postposition of *tuus,* and the descending asyndetic tricolon *amictus toga purpurea, in sella aurea, coronatus* the sentence paints a stately tableau of

---

42   See *Phil.* 13.41.

Caesar, displaying three of the honours that had recently been voted for him: the right to dress up in a purple garment, the use of a golden chair, and the wearing of a certain kind of crown. By ending with *coronatus*, Cicero also hints at the incident about to happen, though it is important to note that these *insignia* in and of themselves did not seem to have turned Caesar (fully) into a 'king' — it took Antony's proffering of the diadem (and Caesar's acceptance of it) that would have resulted in him truly crossing this particular line.

in rostris: *rostra* is a standard metonym for the platform from which speakers addressed the people. The *rostra* were the Latin ship-beaks that the Roman naval forces under C. Maenius captured at the battle of Antium (on the river Astura) in 338 BCE, which were subsequently attached to the platform (Livy 8.14.12; Pliny, *Natural History* 34.20). Antony decided it was the appropriate location to display Cicero's head and hands the following year (Plutarch, *Life of Antony* 20–21).

amictus toga purpurea: *amictus* is the perfect passive participle of the fourth-conjugation verb *amicio*, 'to throw round', 'to wrap about'. It is used exclusively of loose outer garments, in contrast to *induere* (of clothes that are put or drawn on) or *vestire* (of items put on for protection or ornament): 'wrapped in a purple toga'. The magnificent purple toga amounted to a quasi-royal robe: 'in 45 Caesar was granted the triumphal dress for all games and for the sacrifices' and the purple gown that Cicero refers to here seems to have evolved out of this 'perpetuation of the triumphal privileges':

> Examining the relevant decree of 44 we notice a certain change in the terminology. The dress was still occasionally, as in 45, 'triumphal dress', but more often just 'purple' and twice even 'regal dress'. The distinction is important. The regal dress was always purple and so was the early triumphal dress until the third century B.C. when it was replaced by the embroidered dress, the toga picta. If the archaic dress was adopted in 44, it may have appeared as another triumphal dress but was in fact the regal dress.[43]

Caesar's attire thus stood in particularly stark contrast to the stripped-down appearance of the Lupercus Antony, generating another instance

---

43   Quotations are from Weinstock (1971: 270 and 271).

of sartorial satire. As Dyck (2001: 122) puts it: 'Cicero reacts with consternation to the bare-chested Antony who, *nudus* after running in the Lupercalia, appeared as consul in the theater to offer a crown to Caesar. Caesar himself was dressed in the purple toga Romans associated with kingship: a sartorial deficiency on the one side, excess on the other'.[44]

in sella aurea: the golden chair is one of the extravagant honours enumerated by Suetonius and Dio (both cited above): 'while an ivory *sella curulis* served as a marker of the higher magistracies of the Roman Republic, the gilded version could not avoid regal associations: golden thrones were regularly used by kings throughout the Mediterranean and thus seem to have been previously avoided by the Romans both in honoring their own and in presenting gifts to foreign kings' (Pasco-Pranger 2006: 232). Together with the purple robe it also features in a lurid incident that happened just before Caesar's death, reported by Cicero in his dialogue *de Divinatione* 1.119: *qui* (sc. *Caesar*) *cum immolaret illo die quo primum in sella aurea sedit et cum purpurea veste processit, in extis bovis opimi cor non fuit* ('While Caesar was offering sacrifices on the day when he sat for the first time on a golden throne and first appeared in public in a purple robe, no heart was found in the vitals of the votive ox').[45]

coronatus: Caesar embraced the (tactfully granted) honour to wear a crown made of laurel leaves on all occasions in order, what else?, to hide receding hairline: it trumped a toupée, bigly. See Suetonius, *Life of Julius Caesar* 45:

> Circa corporis curam morosior, ut non solum tonderetur diligenter ac raderetur, sed velleretur etiam, ut quidam exprobraverunt, calvitii vero deformitatem iniquissime ferret, saepe obtrectatorum iocis obnoxiam expertus. Ideoque et deficientem capillum revocare a vertice adsueverat et ex omnibus decretis sibi a senatu populoque honoribus non aliud aut recepit aut usurpavit libentius quam ius laureae coronae perpetuo gestandae.

---

44   Instances in which the Romans bared their chests to reveal scars from wounds suffered in warfare — a highly emotive gesture of persuasion, which proved that the individual had put his body on the line in battle: see e.g. Liv. *per.* 70, Cic. *de Orat.* 2.124, 194, further Dyck (2001: 120–21) — follow a different cultural logic.

45   Cf. Rasmussen (2003: 119–20).

[He was rather fastidious in the care of his body, being not only carefully trimmed and shaved, but even having superfluous hair plucked out, as some have charged. His baldness was a disfigurement which troubled him greatly, since he found that it was often the subject of gibes of his detractors. Because of it he used to comb forward his scanty hair from the crown of his head, and of all the honours voted him by the senate and people there was none which he received or made use of more gladly than the privilege of wearing a laurel wreath at all times.]

At the Lupercalia, though, his choice of head-gear seems to have been a crown made of gold (Dio 44.11.2, cited above). Scholars disagree on what the crown signified: on the basis of numismatic evidence, Pelling (1988: 145–46) thinks the crown at issue is 'the jewelled *corona aurea* of the triumphator', whereas others see it as evoking the insignia of the ancient kings of Rome (e.g. Weinstock 1971: 272).

escendis [rostra], **accedis ad sellam** {Lupercus} — **ita eras Lupercus, ut te consulem esse meminisse deberes** — **diadema ostendis**: Cicero uses another asyndetic tricolon, consisting of the three vivid historical presents *escendis*, *accedis*, and *ostendis*. The third colon (*diadema ostendis*), which contains a transitive verb after two intransitive ones, forms a powerful climax, set off and emphasized by the parenthetical inset *ita... deberes*.

accedis ad sellam {Lupercus}: Shackleton Bailey suggests that the word *Lupercus* has dropped out after *ad sellam*; its presence in the text certainly would help to set up the parenthesis, improve the flow of the sentence, and reinforce the tension between Antony's two identities as consul (all but forgotten — appropriately, *consulem* is in an oblique case hidden away in an indirect statement embedded within a subordinate clause) and Lupercus (preponderant — appropriately, the noun occurs twice in the nominative, both times in a main clause).

ita eras Lupercus, ut te consulem esse meminisse deberes: literally, 'you were in such a way Lupercus that you ought to have remembered that you were consul': the *ita* is concessive ('even if you were a Lupercus...') and is followed by a consecutive-restrictive *ut*-clause (hence the subjunctive) '... yet you still ought to have remembered that you were consul'). *deberes* takes *meminisse* as object infinitive, which in turn governs an indirect statement with *te* as subject accusative, *esse* as verb, and *consulem* as predicative complement. Two free translations are: 'your office of Lupercus could not dispense you from the duty of remembering that you were consul' (Mayor) or 'you *were* a Lupercus, but you should have remembered that you were a consul' (Shackleton Bailey).

diadema: re-popularized by *Harry Potter and the Deathly Hallows* (the diadem of Ravenclaw turned into a horcrux by Voldemort), the diadem became a popular symbol of royal power in the Graeco-Roman world from Alexander the Great onwards. But this is the first time the word and the thing appear at Rome (except in women's hairdo's) — and was never fully naturalized in Latin. (See for instance Horace, *Odes* 2.2, where it is associated with the Parthian king.) *Philippic* 2 makes sure *diadema* ties — pins — Julius Caesar to tyranni… cide. For further details (and images) see http://www.livius.org/articles/objects/diadem/

gemitus toto foro [oriuntur]. **unde diadema** [venit / accepisti]?: Cicero keeps his prose snappy, suppressing the verbs, here supplied exempli gratia, but perhaps best left out in the translation as well: 'Groans all over the Forum! Whence the diadem?' As Toher (2016: 310) points out, the rhetorical question is odd, but sets up Cicero subsequent rejection of a different version that was clearly in circulation at the time, namely that Antony had picked the diadem up along the way, on the spur of the moment: 'It is possible that Cicero here engages in a rhetorical ploy: his question suggests an alternative explanation whose plausibility is then rejected in order to highlight the presentation of the diadem as a premeditated act by Antonius. But Cicero's statement might also be explained by the fact that he thought it necessary to refute the idea that Antonius' action was spontaneous, which would only have been necessary if Cicero thought his audience knew of another version … of how Antonius came to have the diadem' (with reference to the Caesar-friendly historiographer Nicolaus of Damascus 20.69; see also Suetonius, *Life of Julius Caesar*, 79.1 and Dio 44.9, cited above: they recount or allude to an incident that supposedly happened a few weeks before the Lupercalia and involved the two tribunes Flavus and Marullus lifting a diadem from a statue of Caesar and discarding it in the streets).

non enim abiectum [diadema] **sustuleras, sed attuleras domo, meditatum et cogitatum scelus**: Cicero presents his audience with a false dilemma: each of the two options he outlines is rather implausible on its own, but the absurdity of the first is designed to endow the second with credibility. That Antony came across a diadem abandoned in the streets is a rather unlikely scenario — despite the earlier incident mentioned in the previous note; but it is also rather unlikely that he had the diadem on him from the moment he left his house (*domo*): how (and where) would he have carried it while running his naked mile as Lupercus? By far the likeliest scenario seems to be that someone handed Antony the diadem as he was nearing the end of his route — but Cicero does not even consider this option since it does not fit into his agenda of turning Antony into the sole culprit who cooked up and executed the nefarious scheme all by himself. Built into the question of how Antony got hold of the diadem is another question: was his act of crowning Caesar spontaneous (implied and dismissed in *non... abiectum sustuleras*) or premeditated (tautologically endorsed by *meditatum et cogitatum scelus*). (Note that Cicero does not go into the question whether Antony came up with the scheme himself or followed Caesar's instructions.)

meditatum et cogitatum scelus: the accusative phrase stands in apposition to (and explains) the whole preceding sentence: see Gildersleeve & Lodge 204: 'you had brought the diadem with you from home — (we are dealing with) a well-rehearsed and premeditated crime!' For the meaning and grammar of *meditatum* see Mayor (1861: 129): '*meditari*... is used of speakers rehearsing, conning over their speeches, of actors "getting up" their parts. ... *meditatum* is here passive, though *meditor* is a deponent'.

tu diadema imponebas cum plangore populi; ille cum plausu reiciebat: the imperfect in Latin is principally used to express duration (durative) or repetition (iterative) of an action in the past. But it can also signify (failed) attempt (conative — from *conor, conari*, 'to try, attempt'): Antony *repeatedly*, but unsuccessfully, *tried* to put the diadem on Caesar (*imponebas*: iterative + conative); Caesar *kept* refusing it / refused it again and again (*reiciebat*: durative or iterative). The imperfects suggest a rather long-drawn out process, a drama of refutation, unfolding in dialogue with reactions (approving / disapproving) from the crowd.

cum plangore populi: *plangor* is the noun to *plango, -gere, -xi, -ctum*, which means 'to beat, to strike' and specifically 'to beat one's breast in a sign of mourning', hence 'to mourn, to lament'. Cicero makes it out that the entire people who were watching the scene broke out in collective lamentation, a much stronger reaction than the groans of horrified premonition (*gemitus*) that went up when Antony first flashed the diadem.

cum plausu [populi]: *plausus* is the noun to *plaudo, -dere, -si, -sum*, which means 'to strike with a flat or concave surface, to clap', specifically 'to clap the hands in applause'. It thus correlates antithetically with *plangor* — the people (responsible for both soundtracks) change beating their breasts in mourning at the prospect of a king to clapping their hands in delight at Caesar's gesture of refusal.

tu ergo unus, scelerate, inventus es qui, cum auctor regni esses eumque quem collegam habebas dominum habere velles, idem temptares quid populus Romanus ferre et pati posset: the sentence explores the motivations behind Antony's action, which, according to Cicero, were twofold: (i) he wanted to enslave himself — and, more generally, the entire Roman people — to Caesar by turning Caesar unequivocally into a kingly figure; (ii) he wanted to test the waters whether (or to what extent) the Roman people would follow suit. The syntax is rather intricate:

> Main clause: *tu... inventus es*
> > relative clause: *qui... temptares*
> > > *cum*-clause: *cum... esses eumque... velles*
> > > > relative clause: *quem... habebas*
> > > indirect question: *quid... posset*

Cicero starts by singling Antony out in the main clause *tu ergo unus, scelerate, inventus es*. Note the emphatic front position of *tu*, the cacophonic hiatus *ergo | unus*, and the jingle *u-nus ~ inven-tus*. *tu* is the antecedent of the subsequent relative clause of characteristic (hence the subjunctive *temptares*). Embedded within the relative clause is a circumstantial *cum*-clause: *cum auctor... velles*, with the *-que* after *eum* linking *esses* and *velles*. *habere*, an object infinitive with *velles*, governs the double accusative *eum* and *dominum*: '… to have *him* as *master*…'. Within the *cum*-clause we get another relative clause (*quem collegam habebas*). We conclude with an indirect question (*quid… posset*). The intricate syntax is the result of Cicero trying to combine an assessment of Antony's personal motivation (the wish to be king-maker and enslave himself) with a strategic experiment in crowd-psychology (how will the people react to seeing Caesar crowned king?). The word that coordinates the two prongs is the pronoun *idem* (in the masculine nominative singular), 'the very same', which coordinates the content of the *cum*-clause with the content of the relative clause and the indirect question. This is difficult to render elegantly into English; it is perhaps best to turn the *cum*-clause into a self-standing main clause: 'It was you who was the mastermind of establishing kingship and you who wanted Caesar as master rather than as colleague — and so you were the only person who could be found to try out what the Roman people could bear and suffer'.

The key thing to note is that Cicero assumes throughout that Antony acted on his own initiative, which is perhaps not the most likely scenario — and utterly implausible with respect to reason (ii): if the incident unfolded at least in part in order to test the public reaction to the possibility of Caesar assuming the kingship, then Caesar surely must have been involved in the planning and the stage-management.

scelerate: the vocative of the adjective *sceleratus*, here used as a noun. It picks up on (by etymological indication of the source of) *meditatum et cogitatum scelus*.

quem collegam habebas: the relative clause picks up on the earlier parenthesis *ita eras Lupercus, ut te consulem esse meminisse deberes*: Cicero keeps emphasizing that Antony was a consul at the time.

§ 86: Antony as Willing Slave and Would-Be King-Maker

Cicero continues to dwell on Antony's attempt to crown Caesar king — acting on his perverse desire to enslave himself, together with everyone else. His associations with tyranny are such that Cicero considers the task of the conspirators only half done with the murder of Caesar — in fact, he suggests that Antony, who volunteered Caesar for the position of monarch and willingly embraced a condition of servitude, deserved even more to be killed than the dictator.

At etiam misericordiam captabas: supplex te ad pedes abiciebas: apparently, after Caesar's initial refusal, Antony persisted to try to win him over by pathos-fraught rhetoric and the performance of a so-called *proskunesis* (= throwing oneself at the feet of the ruler, perhaps even kissing the hem of his robe) — a royal Persian custom, later also adopted by the (Greek) Hellenistic kings, which the Romans associated with extreme subservience or indeed enslavement. *captabas* is another conative use of the imperfect ('you even *tried* to go in for pathos'); *abiciebas* is durative, underscoring how long Antony abased himself by being prostrate at the feet of Caesar. Denniston (1926: 153) offers the interesting suggestion that Cicero here deliberately misrepresents a detail of the scene: 'Our other authorities say nothing of this. If Antony stooped to pick up the crown from the ground, his attitude might have been mistaken for prostration. If he really did prostrate himself, in oriental fashion, he can hardly have done so except with the intention of making Caesar odious'.[46]

---

46   *Proskunesis* tended not to go down well even in imperial Rome, as Tacitus, *Annals* 1.13 shows: Haterius almost gets himself killed by performing a clumsy one on the

supplex te ad pedes abiciebas: technically speaking, *supplex*, modifying the subject of the sentence (embedded in *abiciebas*), is unnecessary. Its use brings out the utter self-abasement of Antony, who was consul at the time. The highest Roman magistrate going weak-kneed at the feet of a would-be king is the stuff of political nightmares for any member of the senatorial elite. The reflexive pronoun *te* (= yourself) is the accusative object of *abiciebas*.

quid petens? ut servires?: Cicero follows up the tableau of Antony at Caesar's feet with two sentence fragments: an interrogative particle + participle (*quid petens*) and a subsequent purpose clause cast as a question (*ut servires?*): 'Asking for what? So that you may be a slave?' The loss of coherent syntax might be expressive of his indignation at the conjured scene.

tibi uni peteres, qui ita a puero vixeras ut omnia paterere, ut facile servires: *peteres* is in the imperfect subjunctive to express a command with reference to a past state of affairs: it refers to an action that Antony, according to Cicero, *should* have undertaken (but did not). So the order implied by the iussive can no longer be carried out. See Pinkster (2015: 503–04). The following relative clause, which segues into two consecutive *ut*-clauses, refers back to § 44, *a puero...*, where Cicero claimed that Antony began his public career as a common whore (*primo vulgare scortum*), implying a willingness to be sexually penetrated: his sexual submissiveness serves as analogue (and premonition) of his political subservience.

tibi uni: 'for yourself alone'. *uni* is here in the dative singular modifying *tibi* as a predicative apposition (literally: 'for yourself as the only one'), but English prefers an adverbial expression: see Gildersleeve & Lodge 206.

paterere: alternative form of the second person singular imperfect subjunctive passive of the deponent *patior, pati* (= *patereris*). The verb hints at Antony's status as a *pathicus* — the passive partner in a homosexual relationship.

(walking) Tiberius, causing the emperor to fall flat on his face and thereby alarming the bodyguards who thought their charge under attack.

a nobis populoque Romano mandatum id certe non habebas: *a nobis*
here refers to the senate, and Cicero thereby invokes the traditional
formula by which the Romans of the republic self-identified as a
political community: SPQR, *senatus populusque Romanus*: 'You certainly
did not have this ordered by...' = 'You certainly did not receive any
such mandate from...'. By closely aligning the senate and the people,
Cicero undoes the endeavour of Antony and Caesar to drive a wedge
between these two constituencies, with Caesar and the people forming
a united front against the old but outdated senatorial elite — a rhetorical
maneuver that informed Caesar's propaganda from the day he crossed
the Rubicon (in partial defence of the tribunes of the people). Here it
specifically preempts Cicero's reference in the following paragraph to
the entry of the incident in Rome's official calendar, which recorded that
Antony acted 'at the behest of the people' (*populi iussu*).

o praeclaram illam eloquentiam tuam cum es nudus contionatus!:
a long, sarcastic accusative of exclamation (*o... tuam*), followed by a
temporal *cum*-clause (in the indicative). The periphrastic embrace of
nudus by the verb for public speaking (*es... contionatus*) is delicious:
only magistrates had the right to address an assembly of the Roman
people (*contio*), so Antony acts here in his role as consul, but does so
with his toga down (as it were), turning the hallowed occasion into a
revolting strip-show. In contrast to the Greeks with their gymnasia,
Romans didn't have much time for public nudity, and certainly not for
a magistrate doing the full Monty — though Antony would presumably
have worn the traditional loincloth of the Lupercus.

quid hoc turpius, quid foedius, quid suppliciis omnibus dignius?: *hoc*
is an ablative of comparison with the ascending tricolon of comparatives
turpius, foedius, dignius. The verb (*est*) is implied. *suppliciis* picks up
supplex at the beginning of the paragraph — the lexical relation suggests
the idea of retribution.

num exspectas dum te stimulis fodiamus?: the interrogative particle
num here introduces a rhetorical question that calls for a negative
answer: 'Are you waiting till we pierce you with ox-goads [sc. to feel the
requisite punishment for your misdeeds]?' As Lacey (1986: 221) points
out, the reference to ox-goads turns Antony either into a notional farm

animal (picking up on § 30: *sed stuporem hominis vel dicam pecudis attendite*: 'observe the thickness of the man or I should rather say brute') or a slave (who were pierced with ox-goads as punishment, no doubt to remind them of their dehumanized status).

dum: the subjunctive *fodiamus* indicates an expected / possible event: see *OLD* s.v. *dum* 5b.

haec te, si ullam partem habes sensus, lacerat, haec cruentat oratio: Cicero uses a simple condition with present indicative in both protasis (*habes*) and apodosis (*lacerat, cruentat*), which implies nothing as to its fulfillment. It might just be the case that Antony has *nullus sensus* — and is therefore unable to appreciate the (unconventional) punishment that Cicero's oration is inflicting on him. Unorthodox forms of punishment are a staple of Cicero's oratory: he likes to insist that his adversaries suffer from various non-obvious modes of retribution for their misdeeds, such as divinely inspired madness (in the case of such characters as Verres, Clodius, or Piso) or, as here, oratorical torture. Cicero sets up the — long delayed — subject of the sentence with the anaphora of the demonstrative adjective *haec*: the *oratio* at the end turns the verbs *lacerat* and *cruentat*, which evoke gruesome images of (literal) carnage, into graphic metaphors designed to bring out the cutting nature of Cicero's invective.[47]

ullam partem... sensus: *sensus* is a partitive genitive (fourth declension) dependent on *partem*.

vereor ne imminuam summorum virorum gloriam; dicam tamen dolore commotus: Cicero here sets up the following sentence, in which he claims that given that Caesar has justly been killed for harbouring royal ambitions (though he rejected the diadem), Antony, who tried to crown him king, should have been killed twice over. Such a claim, however, — so Cicero fears — potentially diminishes the glory that the conspirators (here referred to as *summi viri*: absolutely outstanding men, the best in the commonwealth) won by killing Caesar. Still, the powerful emotion of *dolor*, the basic meaning of which is 'pain' but here refers to the strong resentment he feels towards Antony, pushes him over the edge.

---

47 Cf. *pro Sulla* 47.3 with Berry (1996: 226), where Cicero speaks of the 'barbs' of his oratory.

dicam: future indicative.

quid [est] **indignius quam vivere eum, qui imposuerit diadema, cum omnes fateantur iure interfectum esse qui abiecerit?**: Cicero suppresses the main verb (*est*): 'what is more shameful than for the sort of person to live [literally: that the sort of person lives], who...' The subjunctive *imposuerit* is generic. The following *cum*-clause is concessive ('even though all admit that...'). *fateantur* introduces an indirect statement with an implied *eum* (sc. *Caesarem*) as subject accusative (and antecedent of the second *qui*) and *interfectum esse* as verb.

omnes: Cicero massively exaggerates: in fact, public opinion was desperately divided as to whether the killing of Caesar was a glorious act of tyrannicide or the despicable murder of a friend and benefactor. Elsewhere, Cicero deplores that the assassins only did half the job by not getting rid of Antony as well, killing the tyrant, but leaving (the prospect of future) tyranny alive insofar as the next despot was already waiting in the wings.

§ 87: Historical Precedent Demands Antony's Instant Execution

Cicero follows up on his claim in the previous paragraph that Antony ought to have been killed a long time ago. After a reference to the official entry in Rome's calendar (the so-called *fasti*) on what had happened on 15 February, Cicero adds some generic abuse about Antony's debauchery (drinking through the day with his depraved mates) before returning to his impact on the political culture of the republic: his subversion of peace (Cicero uses both *otium* and *pax*) and his destruction of the legal order (the laws and the law courts) qualify Antony for being included among the ranks of those who were expelled or killed in the past because of their tyrannical conduct or royal ambitions. In his appeal to historical *exempla* that call for drastic action, Cicero reworks the shtick he already used in the opening part of his first speech against Catiline.

At etiam ascribi iussit in fastis ad Lupercalia C. Caesari dictatori perpetuo M. Antonium consulem populi iussu regnum detulisse, Caesarem uti noluisse: it is unclear who the implied subject of *iussit* is: Antony or Caesar? Scholars, too, are undecided. Perhaps the most likely scenario is that it was Caesar, and Cicero opts for a text that suggests Antony (without explicitly falsifying history), to keep his target under invective fire. *iussit* governs the impersonal passive infinitive *ascribi* ('he ordered it to be inscribed...'), which in turn governs the bipartite indirect statement *C.* [= *Gaio*] *Caesari… noluisse* (which covers the text of the inscription), with *M. Antonium* and *Caesarem* as subject accusatives and *detulisse* and *noluisse* as infinitives.

Here we capture the 'Caesarian' version of the events, though it remains unclear whether it was planned as such from the start or the product of retrospective spin. In this version, the *auctor* of the affair was the *populus Romanus* as a sovereign body of citizens giving an order (*populi iussu*) to its highest elected magistrate M. Antonius to offer the dictator for life (*dictatori perpetuo*) C. Caesar the kingship — an offer which Caesar declined. The point of the episode seems to have been to draw a fine, but important distinction between the title *dictator perpetuo*, awarded to Caesar by the senate, which conformed at least in name to the political culture of the Roman republic (see below on *C. Caesari dictatori perpetuo*) and kingship, which does not. The offer and its refusal, at least in Rome, sent a double message to Caesar's senatorial peers, who must have thought that the title *dictator perpetuo* was already beyond the pale: far from being a power grab, the title of dictator for life is an exercise in self-restraint — the people wouldn't hesitate to crown him king.

in fastis: the masculine plural noun *fasti* is formed from the adjective *fastus, -a, -um*, 'lawful for the transaction of business' (not to be confused with the fourth-declension noun *fastus, -ûs*, m. = arrogance, pride), which in turn is formed from the indeclinable neuter noun *fas* = 'that which is right and permissible by divine law' (the opposite is *nefas* = sacrilege) + *tus*. It has three related but distinct meanings:

(i)   days on which business may be transacted: in the field of civil law, the Romans distinguished between *dies fasti*, on which the praetor could preside over court proceedings, and *dies nefasti*, when no such proceedings could take place;

(ii)   the list of annually recurring festivals = the calendar;

(iii) the list of consuls who gave their name to the year (i.e. a chronological *sequence* year by year, as opposed to the *cyclical* nature of the calendar).

The term was therefore absolutely central to how the Romans situated themselves in time and history and, across the range of meanings it accrued over time (the combination of the calendar with the consular list dates to the first half of the second century BCE), incorporates important religious and political elements. No one was more attuned to the politics of time than Caesar — indeed, one of his most long-lasting legacies consisted in the reform of the Roman calendar: see Feeney (2007). Caesar or Antony decided to put the diadem-incident permanently on record by adding an annotation to the calendar under 15 February (*ad Lupercalia*: 'under the date of the Lupercalia'). Some fragments of inscribed Roman calendars survive, and none of them contains this particular text, which may owe itself either to an accident of transmission (our surviving calendars feature significant variation in outlook, especially in terms of historical annotations) or the fact that Caesar was killed soon thereafter and this particular entry never found proper dissemination.

C. Caesari dictatori perpetuo: the office of dictator was a recognized magistracy in republican Rome (and does not inherently carry the connotations of illegitimacy and abuse of power as our English equivalent). Dictators were appointed in times or crises and emergencies, but — until Caesar — for a strictly limited period of time. Even Sulla, who was appointed *dictator legibus faciundis et reipublicae constituendae causa* ('dictator for making laws and settling the constitution'), which did not carry a specified time limit, abdicated after he felt he had completed the specified task. Sulla was the most powerful strongman before Caesar; and having himself called dictator for life, Caesar thus outdoes all of his predecessors and enters unknown territory. The dative renders it ambiguous as to whether *perpetuo* is the adjective or the adverb, but the latter is the case. Caesar's official title, which he assumed in late January / early February 44, was *dictator perpetuo* ('dictator in perpetuity') rather than *dictator perpetuus* ('perpetual dictator').

populi iussu: the forth-declension noun *iussus, -ûs*, m. (as opposed to the second-declension noun *iussum, -i*, n.) only occurs in the ablative singular, usually with either a possessive adjective or (as here) a genitive; the expression has an official, formulaic feel.

iam iam minime miror te otium perturbare, non modo urbem odisse sed etiam lucem; cum perditissimis latronibus non solum de die sed etiam in diem bibere: *miror* introduces a tripartite indirect statement, with *te* as subject accusative throughout and *perturbare, odisse,* and *bibere* as infinitives.

otium: the opposite of *negotium* (business), *otium,* in its basic sense, means 'freedom from business', i.e. 'leisure time', 'ease', 'relaxation' (or, in a negative sense, 'idleness', 'inactivity'). More generally, it came to signify a condition of 'peaceful relations', 'tranquillity in civic life' — an equivalent to *pax,* with *otium* primarily (but not exclusively) referring to the domestic sphere and *pax* primarily (but not exclusively) referring to Rome's relation with external peoples as well as the gods on some kind of contractual basis (see further below on *in pace*). This is the meaning of the term here. (Cicero captures his ideal state of affairs with the expression *'otium cum dignitate',* which might be glossed as 'a state of peaceful relations in civic affairs with due respect accorded to the rightful rank and standing of each individual'.)

non modo urbem odisse sed etiam lucem: *urbs* (the city of Rome) and *lux* (the light of day) form a climactic pairing, as Cicero ups the ante by moving from the (cosmic) city to the cosmos itself, or from a socio-political to an existential perspective. The transition is easy, especially if the identification of the city of Rome with the entire universe (*urbs = orbis*; cf. the papal blessing *urbi et orbi*) registers. Compare Cicero, *in Catilinam* 4.11: *haec urbs lux orbis terrarum* — 'this city is the light of the entire world'.

cum perditissimis latronibus non solum de die sed etiam in diem bibere: *perditus* is the past participle of *perdo* ('to cause ruin or destruction') and, in the positive and, especially, (as here) the superlative one of Cicero's favourite words of abuse. It signifies a state of moral and financial bankruptcy in which the individual concerned has lost any kind of bearing that would enable some kind of positive contribution to society. *latro* ('bandit') too is a standard term in Cicero's invective lexicon, which he used to inveigh against Catiline and his followers: it refers to outlaws who do not abide by the socio-political protocols that govern life in a peaceful civic community.[48] *bibere* is a conjecture for the *vivere* of the manuscripts, first mooted by Badham.[49] It is not entirely

---

48   See further Habinek (1998: 69–87)
49   See Housman (1896/1972: 379).

clear what *de die* and *in diem* mean in this context: what Cicero seems to be imagining is a scenario in which Antony and his drinking buddies booze through the night into the dawn, till sun-up (*de die*) and then keep going into the day (*in diem*).

ubi enim tu in pace consistes?: the phrasing Cicero here uses is ominous: *consistes* is in the future tense, which implies that at present, Rome does not have (internal) peace. He therefore applies a term designed to capture Rome's relations with (subdued) external people to domestic politics — a development of civil war (*bellum* initially also referred only to Rome's external wars until internal developments made it necessary to endow it with the attribute *civile*). At the same time, *pax* retains its wider geographical remit, implying that in a world at peace Antony has no place. Given this fluidity, it is unsurprising that what precisely *pax* signified — and to what state of affairs it is possible to apply the label *pax* — became controversial in late-republican times. See in particular *Phil.* 14.19–20, where Cicero, looking back, asserts that the people recall that he had, from January 43 onwards, always called Antony an enemy, always the current condition a war, had always been an adviser of genuine peace (*verae pacis auctor*), but hostile to the name of any 'pestilent peace' (*nomini pestiferae pacis inimicus*). See further Cornwell (2017).

qui locus tibi in legibus et in iudiciis esse potest, quae tu, quantum in te fuit, dominatu regio sustulisti?: *qui* is an interrogative adjective modifying *locus* ('what place can there be for you…'); the relative pronoun *quae* (accusative neuter plural) refers back to both *legibus* and *iudiciis* but agrees in number and gender with the closer of the two nouns.

in legibus et in iudiciis: in a situation of domestic peace that includes respect for republican traditions and values, the basis of civic life is the rule of law, which Cicero captures with reference to laws (*in legibus*) and law courts (*in iudiciis*). Put differently, there is no place for someone like Antony in civic society.

quantum in te fuit: *quantum* introduces an adverbial clause: 'so far as it was in your power'.

dominatu regio: the first thing to disappear under an autocratic regime is the rule of law — since the despot is above it: his whim and will *become* law. Cicero dwells extensively on the unpredictability of a world in which a tyrant reigns supreme. See e.g. a passage from a letter to his friend Paetus, from mid-July 46 about life under Caesar (*ad Familiares* 9.16.3 = 190 SB):

> De illo autem quem penes est omnis potestas, nihil video quod timeam, nisi quod omnia sunt incerta cum a iure discessum est nec praestari quicquam potest quale futurum sit quod positum est in alterius voluntate, ne dicam libidine.

> [As for the All-Powerful, I see no reason why I should be apprehensive, unless it be that all becomes uncertain when the path of legality has been forsaken, and that there is no guaranteeing the future of what depends on someone else's wishes, not to say whims.]

Essentially, Cicero here reduces the world of Rome to the will of Caesar: the future depends on the *voluntas* ('will') or, indeed, libido ('whim') of the dictator. Caesar's ascendancy entails chaos for those living within the remit of his reign: *omnia sunt incerta*. Caesar's ability to exercise power unrestrained by institutional or normative checks results in comprehensive uncertainty for everyone else.

ideone L. Tarquinius exactus [est], **Sp. Cassius, Sp. Maelius, M. Manlius necati** [sunt] **ut multis post saeculis a M. Antonio, quod fas non est, rex Romae constitueretur?**: Cicero's outraged rhetorical question (marked as such by the enclitic *-ne* attached to *ideo*: 'was it for this that...?') is an incitement to murder. Lucius Tarquinius Superbus was the last legendary king of Rome, driven out in 509 BCE for his rape of Lucretia, after which the Romans adopted a republican form of government. Spurius Cassius, who was executed in 485 BCE, Spurius Maelius, who suffered the same fate in 435 BCE, and Marcus Manlius Capitolinus, who was put to death in 385 BCE, were three early-republican powerbrokers suspected of aiming for kingship. They became *exempla* of how (aspiring) tyrants were dealt with in Rome.[50] Cicero returns to the *exempla* in § 114.

---

50   See further Chassignet (2001), Smith (2006), Flower (2006: 44–51), Kaplow (2012), who discusses the three figures as a trio of *popularis* politicians whose enemies tried to discredit their political agenda by accusing them of aiming at tyranny, and Roller (2018: 238–51).

multis post saeculis: an ablative of time. *post* is adverbial: 'many centuries thereafter'.

a M. Antonio: an ablative of agency with *constitueretur*.

quod fas non est: Cicero asserts that, in Rome, kingship is a form of government that violates religious taboos (*fas* specifies what is — and what isn't — permissible according to divine law).

rex Romae: *Romae* is in the locative. The brutal juxtaposition of the antithetical *rex* and *Roma* strikes a deliberately jarring note, underscored by the alliteration.

§ 88: Antony on the Ides of March

Cicero now returns to the issue of the (fake) auspices that Antony produced to challenge the validity of Dolabella's election to the (suffect) consulship. Caesar planned to have the matter discussed at the senate meeting scheduled for the Ides of March, but his murder upset the agenda and Cicero follows the lead opened up by the assassination to dwell on Antony's reaction: fear for his life and a panicky flight from the senate house. His apprehension was justified: no-one knew at the time whether Caesar was the only target of the conspirators. As it turned out, it was — and there seems to have been nothing for Antony to fear; but Cicero uses his escape as foil for reiterating, in § 89, a point he already made in § 86, namely that the liberators ought to have done away with Antony as well.

Sed ad auspicia redeamus; de quibus Idibus Martiis fuit in senatu Caesar acturus: *redeamus* is a present exhortative subjunctive in the first person plural: 'but let us return…'. *quibus* is a connecting relative, picking up *auspicia* (= *de eis*). Apparently, Caesar had Antony's *obnuntiatio* at the elections that made Dolabella a suffect consul for 44 BCE on the agenda for the senate meeting scheduled for 15 March during which he was killed.

Idibus Martiis: an ablative of time ('during the senate meeting scheduled for the Ides of March').

quaero: tum tu quid egisses?: the question doubles as the apodosis of an (implied) past counterfactual condition: 'I ask you: *if Caesar had had the chance to make it a matter for business*, what would you have done then?'

tum and *tu*, nicely alliterated, are placed up front to give the personal challenge further emphasis.

audiebam equidem te paratum venisse, quod me de ementitis auspiciis, quibus tamen parere necesse erat, putares esse dicturum: the main verb *audiebam* (imperfect with iterative sense: 'I was told more than once') introduces an indirect statement with *te* as subject accusative and *venisse* as infinitive; *paratum* is a predicative complement to *te*. *quod* introduces a causal clause with *putares* as verb (in the subjunctive to underscore the fact that this is what Antony supposed, without any necessary basis in the facts), which introduces another indirect statement with *me* as subject accusative and *esse dicturum* as infinitive. So: 'I was told more than once that you had come prepared because you believed that I intended to speak on the falsification of the auspices, which it was nevertheless (i.e. despite the fact that they had been falsified) necessary to obey', sc. until the college of augurs had assessed the matter. Cicero interrelates himself and Antony syntactically here: in the main clause he is the subject of the main verb (*audiebam*) and Antony (*te*) the subject accusative of an indirect statement; in the *quod*-clause, Antony is the subject of the main verb (*putares*) and Cicero the subject accusative of an indirect statement (*me*).

equidem: with an expressed or implied first person singular, the particle *equidem* serves to emphasize the *ego*: *OLD* s.v. 1.

de ementitis auspiciis: 'on the falsification of the auspices': Latin frequently uses the perfect passive participle (and *ementior* is used in a passive sense here, despite being a deponent) to modify a (concrete) noun where English would traditionally use an abstract noun and the preposition 'of'. Compare, for instance, *ab urbe condita* = 'from the foundation of the city' (or, increasingly, 'from the city foundation').

quibus tamen parere necesse erat: the relative pronoun *quibus* is in the dative governed by *parere*. The negative auspices remained in force until the college of augurs (or the senate) had passed a verdict, either upholding Antony's *obnuntiatio* or invalidating it.

sustulit illum diem Fortuna rei publicae: some editors capitalize Fortuna, turning her into the goddess that watches over the Roman commonwealth. Otherwise, *fortuna* here simply means 'good luck'. *diem tollere*, which literally means 'to lift up = remove the day' (Shackleton Bailey translates: 'The Fortune of the Commonwealth struck that day out of time') is standard idiom for 'to prevent the senate from conducting business on the day': *OLD* s.v. *tollo* 12b.

num etiam tuum de auspiciis iudicium interitus Caesaris sustulit?: the subject of the sentence is *interitus*. Cicero's repetition of *sustulit* puns on the technical use of *tollere* in the previous sentence, here applied to Antony's judgment about the auspices. As Lacey (1986: 222) notes, '*num* (expecting the answer "no") is sarcastic, since A did abandon his objection at the meeting of the Senate on March 17' — and the only significant event that occurred between his endorsement and subsequent dismissal of the auspices was the murder of Caesar.

sed incidi in id tempus quod eis rebus in quas ingressa erat oratio praevertendum est: the main verb is *incidi* (first person singular perfect indicative active; not to be confused with, but in form indistinguishable from, the present passive infinitive). The verb of the relative clause is the gerundive of obligation *praevertendum est*, which governs the dative *eis rebus*, with *quod* as subject: 'I have fallen on that time period (i.e. the time after Caesar's assassination), which (now) must be given precedence over those matters (*eis rebus*, i.e. Antony's manipulation of the auspices), on which my speech (initially) embarked'. Cicero makes it out as if he cannot help but be sidetracked; in fact, he never comes back to the topic of the auspices in the remainder of *Philippic* 2.

quae tua fuga, quae formido praeclaro illo die, quae propter conscientiam scelerum desperatio vitae, cum ex illa fuga beneficio eorum qui te, si sanus esses, salvum esse voluerunt, clam te domum recepisti!: the main clause consists of a gleeful ascending tricolon *fuga – formido – desperatio*, reinforced by the triple anaphora of *quae*, designed to capture the actions, the emotions, and the general outlook of Antony in the moment right after the murder of Caesar: he takes flight (*fuga*) in panic (*formido*) and mortal fear for his life (*desperatio vitae*). The main verb (*erat*) is implied; *tua* serves as predicative complement to all three subjects. What follows is a so-called 'inverse *cum*-clause', which takes the indicative (usually in the perfect) and is used to introduce a new development that dramatically changes or 'inverts' the action of the main clause. We arrive at the verb of the *cum*-clause (*te… recepisti*) by way of a circuitous route: the prepositional phrase *ex illa fuga* picks up the beginning of the sentence; it is followed by the ablative of means *beneficio eorum*, which segues into a relative clause (*qui… voluerunt*) that comprises an indirect statement with *te* as subject accusative and *esse* as infinitive and functions as the apodosis of a conditional sequence with *si sanus esses* as protasis. After the bloody death of Caesar, Antony had every reason to suppose that he was next in line — there were about 60 senators in on the plot, and more than twenty lined up to share in the bloodshed: Caesar received a public ritual-sacrificial 'send off'.[51] On the day, the numbers must have sparked pandemonium, and nowhere safe to turn. But by getting rid of Caesar without wiping out his principal supporters as well, the conspirators hoped to minimize bloodshed and thereby facilitate a smooth return to a republican form of government: Antony's life seems not to have been in danger, though he couldn't have known it. Cicero of course started to deplore not long afterwards that the assassins stopped too soon: *vivit tyrannis, tyrannus occidit!* (*Att.* 14.9.2 = 363 SB; 17 April 44: 'the tyranny lives on, the tyrant is dead').

praeclaro illo die: 15 March 44 BCE — the day the dictator died and freedom was reborn! In this instance, *praeclarus* truly means 'glorious', without a shred of irony.

quae propter conscientiam scelerum desperatio vitae: *conscientia* is a favourite notion of Cicero's. In the sense of 'conscience' it plays a key role in his conception of the human being as a creature naturally endowed with an instance that enables him to judge right from wrong. In such instances, *conscientia* becomes an internal court of law and agent of punishment, inflicting mental torture (pangs of conscience) on the miscreant. Here the meaning of *conscientia* is more akin to 'consciousness' (without necessarily excluding the sense of 'conscience'): Antony was a leading figure in Caesar's (criminal, from Cicero's point of view) regime and now fears for his life because he is fully aware that his track record

---

51 Contrast the rather more confined personal-political action taken by the Attic lover-boys Harmodius and Aristogeiton when they killed the tyrant Hipparchus — even though the pair then mutated into the archtypal tyrannicides.

turns him into a likely target on the (in the end, non-existent) hit list of the senatorial assassins.

beneficio eorum: Cicero leaves it unclear who these people are and what they did to help Antony escape. (Some other sources spin a flimsy yarn on how Antony fled disguised as a slave.) Cicero's reticence here suggests that these are later novelistic elaborations.

si sanus esses: a gratuitous piece of spite — Cicero intimates, without any supporting evidence, that even Antony's friends harboured qualms about his mental health. The imperfect subjunctive implies that Antony's sanity was part of what they wished for and considered a requisite condition for helping him escape — but that was misjudged!

domum: an accusative of direction: 'you in secret withdrew to your house'.

§ 89: No Compromise with a Public Enemy!

Cicero here revisits the tense period right after Caesar's assassination, 15–17 March. Here is a brief blow-by-blow account of the most important developments over these action-packed few days:[52]

15 March: c. 11 a.m.

murder of Caesar; Antony and other Caesarians flee from the senate house; the conspirators march to the Capitoline Hill; when they test public opinion later in the day, they are greeted with a significant level of hostility; start of negotiations with Antony (as consul) and Lepidus (Caesar's Master of the Horse).

Night of 15/16 March

Antony, acting either on his own or together with Lepidus, summons some of Caesar's troops into the city; Caesar's widow Calpurnia hands over Caesar's state papers to him, as well as funds (4000 talents according to Plutarch, *Life of Antony* 15). Antony also secures the war chest Caesar had deposited in the temple of Ops for his campaign against the Parthians (see also *Phil.* 2.35 and 93).

16 March

tense negotiations between Antony and the conspirators, who fear for their safety; as surety, Antony and Lepidus hand over their sons as hostages (see *Phil.* 2.90 below; also *Phil.* 1.31).

---

52   Pelling (1988: 150–51).

17 March

senate meeting in the Temple of Tellus; Caesar's veterans surround the
building; the outcome is a compromise: amnesty for the assassins (still holed
up on the Capitoline Hill) on a motion by Cicero in return for the *en-bloc*
ratification of Caesar's *already published* acts and arrangements. (According to
Suetonius, *Life of Julius Caesar* 82.4, the conspirators would have preferred to
chuck Caesar's corpse into the Tiber, confiscate his property, and declare all
his political arrangements null and void (= *acta rescindere*)).

This bare-bones version of the main events does nothing to capture
the striking degree of uncertainty that must have prevailed at the time.
Everything was up in the air: further moves by the liberators and key
Caesarians, the mood of the populace (and Caesar's veterans), the cred
of the assassins (criminal killers or heroes?), the postmortem image
of Caesar (public enemy or murdered benefactor?), the status of his
appointments and decrees, the future of those of his policies that were
in the works but not yet finalized and officially disseminated, access to
his unpublished papers. It soon transpired that the liberators wished for
no further bloodshed and wanted to reach out to Antony (as consul) to
negotiate some sort of compromise, which then actually came to pass
during the senate meeting of 17 March.

When Cicero revisits this period here in invective mode, the
uncertainty and volatility of the situation all but disappears. He
reduces politics to personality. His assessment of Antony's character —
rotten — is all he needs as guide for political action. Cicero claims that
already at the time he warned against any course of compromise and
conciliation with someone he considered the public enemy number
one — but his premonition and recommendations were left unheeded.

O mea frustra semper verissima auguria rerum futurarum!: Cicero
starts the paragraph with an exclamatory sentence consisting for the
main part of a noun phrase in the nominative (*o mea… verissima auguria…
!*), a device he also elsewhere uses in contexts of desperate pathos (cf. *pro
Milone* 94: *o frustra, inquit, mei suscepti labores, o spes fallaces, o cogitationes
inanes meae!*, where Cicero reports Milo deploring the loss of prospects
for his political career; see Pinkster (2015: 367). The adverb *semper*,
placed deftly in-between the adverb *frustra* and the adjective *verissima*,
goes with both (*apo-koinou*): Cicero claims that his predictions were

always absolutely (note the superlative) spot-on — and always in vain. He casts himself as a Cassandra-figure, i.e. someone who has a clear sense of a dismal future, but is unable to get his voice heard so as to affect the course of events for the better. The posture of the prophet who has special insight into the future appealed to Cicero — and he adopts it in several of his speeches and letters. The first speech against Catiline for instance ends with a powerful prediction about divine action taken on behalf of the commonwealth and the fourth speech against Catiline concludes with the affirmation that his care and insight will secure the Roman people a prosperous future (*providebo*). Closer to home (and the passage here), in a letter to Atticus (10.8.6 = 199 SB) Cicero claims to have foreseen the full trajectory of the civil war — though his prediction in 49 BCE that Caesar's reign would not last longer than six months, owing to the self-destructive tendencies he believed to be inherent in tyranny (following Plato), was off by several years. And in two letters to Atticus, he recalls his own take on the aftermath of the Ides of March, when the conspirators were holed up on the Capitoline Hill protected by a bodyguard of gladiators and he dispensed advice that was not followed (*Att.* 14.10.1 = 364 SB; 19 April 44; cf. *Att.* 14.14.2 = 368 SB; 28 or 29 April).

dicebam illis in Capitolio liberatoribus nostris, cum me ad te ire vellent ut ad defendendam rem publicam te adhortarer, quoad metueres, omnia te promissurum; simul ac timere desisses, similem te futurum tui: the sentence consists of two main elements, with further constructions attached:

- a main clause (*dicebam... nostris*) followed by a bipartite indirect statement dependent on *dicebam*; each of the two parts involves a temporal subordinate clause (a) *quoad metueres, omnia te promissurum (esse)*; (b) *simul ac timere desisses, similem te futurum (esse) tui*.

- a circumstantial *cum*-clause with *vellent* as verb and the (implied) liberators as subject. *vellent* governs an indirect statement with *me* as subject accusative and *ire* as verb, followed by the purpose clause *ut... adhortarer*.

In his interactions with the liberators holed up on the Capitoline Hill, Cicero is predicting two things about Antony: that he would promise anything at all while he was afraid for his life; and that he would revert to being his old self as soon as he was no longer afraid.

dicebam: Latin can use the imperfect with verbs of saying to narrate a past action that the speaker remembers (Kühner-Stegmann 1.124, listing our passage as an example). But there may be a bit more edge to *dicebam* if we take it to refer to a *repeated* action in the past: Cicero kept reiterating his convictions, sticking to his guns (cf. *in sententia mansi* below), but the liberators would not listen: the tense thus picks up on the preceding exclamation.

liberatoribus nostris: as noted above, the assassination of Caesar met with a bipolar reception, which registers in the labels that the assassins attracted. As Leber (2018: 1) puts it:

> The enormity of Caesar's assassination provided an opportunity to use a plethora of terms for the conspirators, most conspicuously seen in Cicero's treatment of Cassius and Brutus following the death of Caesar. The act itself had a polarizing effect. On one side were the invective terms for assassins, murderers and parricides (*sicarii, homicidae, interfectores, parricidae*). On the other side were the favourable terms, such as liberators (*liberatores*), heroes (*heroes*) and tyrannicides (*tyrannoctoni*). Cicero also included in his correspondence Greek words, as well as their transliterations into Latin. Each word would seem to have its own subtle characteristics, focussing on different aspects and interpretations of the conspirators and their act of tyrannicide or political murder.

The uneasy truce that emerged right after the event did little to resolve the status of the assassins: their political identity has remained a matter of controversial debate even after the battle of Philippi in 42 BCE, when the Caesarian triumvirate of Antony, Octavian, and Lepidus triumphed over the republicans Cassius and Brutus. Already by the time Cicero penned the *Philippics* they had been put on the defensive, forced to leave Rome since their personal safety could no longer be guaranteed, and Cicero uses the speeches as a means to assert his view of history as the right one. Early on in *Philippic* 1, he laments the fact that the liberators of Rome had been driven from the city they had set free (1.6: *patriae liberatores urbe carebant ea, cuius a ceruicibus iugum seruile deiecerant…*: 'the liberators of their country were exiles from the city from whose neck they had struck off the yoke of slavery…'). And at *Phil.* 2.30–31, he exposes Antony to the dilemma that the killers of Caesar are either heroic freedom fighters to be held in the highest esteem or the lowest scum on earth, as basis for arguing that Antony's own behaviour proves that he endorses the former position.

ad defendendam rem publicam: after the assassination of Caesar, various parties tried to claim to represent the commonwealth. The fact that Antony as consul was technically speaking the official representative of the *res publica* made the situation tricky for the conspirators. For the notion of *res publica* in the political discourse of republican Rome see further Hodgson (2017).

simul ac timere desisses: *desisses* is 2nd person singular pluperfect subjunctive active in indirect speech, representing a future perfect: 'as soon as you will have ceased from fear, you will be your old self again'.

similem te futurum [esse] **tui**: *te* is subject accusative, *similem* the predicative complement; the genitive of the personal pronoun *tui*, delayed for point and punch, depends on *similem*: 'you will be like yourself'. See Gildersleeve & Lodge 229: '*similis* is said to be used with the Genitive when the likeness is general and comprehensive; with the Dative when it is conditional or partial'. The absence of fear, an emotion that for some time caused uncharacteristically sound comportment on Antony's part, entails a re-centering of his self in the old criminal mold. Antony is a coward and a criminal.

itaque cum ceteri consulares irent redirent, in sententia mansi: at this time in Roman history, not too many former consuls who could act as go-betweens were still alive: much of the traditional ruling elite had been wiped out in the civil war. And — so Cicero's message here — only one among this illustrious group had sufficient foresight and backbone to remain unmoved by the alluring delusion of a possible compromise with Antony. ‖ *ire redire* means 'to go to and fro'. As Mayor (1861: 132) notes, 'asyndeton is very common in the case of words of opposite signification'.

neque te illo die neque postero [die] **vidi neque ullam societatem optimis civibus cum importunissimo hoste foedere ullo confirmari posse credidi**: two main clauses linked by the third *neque* (… *vidi neque ullam…*), with *vidi* and *credidi* as verbs. The latter introduces an indirect statement with *ullam societatem* as subject accusative and *posse* as verb:

'I did not see you on either that day or the next nor did I believe that…' *confirmari* is supplementary present passive infinitive with *posse*.

Cicero here digs deep into the charged lexicon of Rome's political culture to ostracize Antony from the civic community. The phrases are extremely weighty: *ullam societatem* ‖ *optimis civibus* ‖ *cum importunissimo hoste* ‖ *foedere ullo*: the first and the last form a chiastic frame (*ullam societatem* :: *foedere ullo*), the central two constitute a powerful antithesis reinforced by the superlatives *optimis* and *importunissimo*. In what amounts to a rhetorical enactment of civil war, he strips a Roman citizen and magistrate (Antony is *civis* and *consul*) of his legal status and his (Roman) identity and transforms him into the exact opposite, an enemy (*hostis*) of the Roman people, with whom any association or relationship (*societas*), any formal bond or agreement (*foedus*) is impossible and the only conceivable condition of co-existence is terminal warfare.

illo die … postero [die]: 15 and 16 March on the Julian calendar instituted on 1 Jan 45…

ullam societatem: *societas* and related terms (*socius, sociare*), which refer to social relationships grounded in trust, respect for law, and mutual advantage and extending from a partnership to all of civic society, play a key role in Cicero's political thought. See, for instance, *On the Commonwealth* (*de Republica*) 1.49:

> ex utilitatis varietatibus, cum aliis aliud expediat, nasci discordias; itaque cum patres rerum potirentur, numquam constitisse civitatis statum; multo iam id in regnis minus, quorum, ut ait Ennius, 'nulla [regni] sancta societas nec fides est'. quare cum lex sit civilis societatis vinculum, ius autem legis aequale, quo iure societas civium teneri potest, cum par non sit condicio civium?… quid est enim civitas nisi iuris societas civium?

> [discord arises from conflicting interests, where different measures are advantageous to different citizens. Therefore they maintain that when aristocrats were in power, the condition of the citizenry has never been stable, and that such stability is less attainable by far in kingdoms, in which, as Ennius says, 'No sacred partnership or honour exists'. Therefore, since law is the bond of civic association, and the justice enforced by law is the same for all, by what justice can an association of citizens be held together when there is no equality among the citizens?… For what is a citizenry if not an association of citizens committed to justice?]

Cicero penned *On the Commonwealth* in the late fifties. As the quoted passage shows, even before Caesar's rise to the dictatorship he insisted on the mutual incompatibility of civil society and autocracy. In *On Duties* (*de Officiis*), written after the death of Caesar at the same time as the *Philippics*, he reiterates and radicalizes this principle with specific reference to recent and contemporaneous events, elevating tyrannicide into an ethical duty (3.32):

> Nulla est enim societas nobis cum tyrannis et potius summa distractio est, neque est contra naturam spoliare eum, si possis, quem est honestum necare, atque hoc omne genus pestiferum atque impium ex hominum communitate exterminandum est. etenim, ut membra quaedam amputantur, si et ipsa sanguine et tamquam spiritu carere coeperunt et nocent reliquis partibus corporis, sic ista in figura hominis feritas et immanitas beluae a communi tamquam humanitatis corpore segreganda est.

> [we have no ties of association with a tyrant, but rather the sharpest separation; and it is not against Nature to rob, if one can, a man whom it is morally right to kill: all that pestilent and abominable race should be exterminated from human society. As certain limbs are amputated if they show signs of being bloodless and virtually lifeless and thus jeopardize the health of the other parts of the body, so those fierce and savage monsters in human form should be cut off from what may be called the common body of humanity.]

foedere ullo: an ablative of means. Like *societas*, the term *foedus* carries weighty ideological connotations. It refers to any kind of formalized socio-political bond or alliance grounded in ritual and hence invoking a sense of cosmic order. See further Gladhill (2016).

post diem tertium veni in aedem Telluris et quidem invitus, cum omnis aditus armati obsiderent: the force of the particle (*et*) *quidem* here is adversative, expressing a partial concession 'to confirm the preceding statement and at the same time to offer another which in part undermines the first' (Solodow 1978: 82): 'after the third day I did come to the temple of Tellus — *and yet* against my will because…'. The subject of the causal *cum*-clause are the *armati*; *omnis* (= *omnes*) *aditûs* is the accusative object of *obsiderent*. Cicero refers to the veterans of Caesar, whom Antony and/ or Lepidus had summoned to the city to exert pressure on the senate and the assassins.

post diem tertium: 'on the third day after' (sc. the assassination of Caesar), i.e. 17 March since the Romans counted both the start-day and the end-day in a sequence. With the adverbs *ante* ('before') and *post* ('after') one might expect an ablative of measure of difference (*paucis diebus post* = a few days after), but the accusative can also be employed (as here): see Gildersleeve & Lodge 260. Ironically, the 17 March was the day of the Liberalia, a festival in honour of Liber Pater (literally: 'The Free Father'), an ancient god of fertility and wine, who came to be identified with the Greek god Bacchus / Dionysus.

in aedem Telluris: the temple of Tellus (built in 268 BCE) was situated on the Esquiline Hill.

§ 90: Antony's Finest Hour

Cicero spends most of this paragraph speculating on what might have been had Antony been willing to sustain the conciliatory outlook he adopted right after Caesar's assassination, and especially during the senate meeting of 17 March. Cicero claims it was Antony's finest hour — and if he had continued to act in the spirit in which negotiations were conducted, a lasting peace and much fame would have ensued. But from the point of view of *Philippic* 2, these musings are past counterfactuals. As Cicero had predicted (see the previous paragraph), as soon as Antony's fear evaporated, his *audacia* kicked back in. It manifested itself not least in the way he conducted Caesar's funeral, which took place a couple of days later (c. 20 March) — the subject of the following paragraph.

Qui tibi dies ille, M. Antoni, fuit!: The interrogative adjective *qui*, which modifies *dies*, here introduces an exclamation (see *OLD* s.v. *qui* 3), with *ille* in predicative position: 'What a day that was for you, Marcus Antonius!' Cicero uses the same construction in *qui… vir* below.

quamquam mihi inimicus subito exstitisti, tamen me tui miseret quod tibi invideris: *inimicus* ('personal enemy' as opposed to *hostis*, 'external enemy') stands in predicative position to the subject of the *quamquam*-clause, an implied *tu*, and governs the dative *mihi*: 'even though you have suddenly become my personal enemy'. With *subito*, Cicero refers to the events that unfolded in September, more specifically the first *Philippic*, delivered in the senate on 2 September. The speech provoked Antony's anger — and an official declaration of *inimicitia*: see *Phil.* 5.19: *at ille homo vehemens et violentus… inimicitias mihi denuntiavit* ('then that

rash and violent man declared himself my enemy'). Despite this state of
enmity, Cicero professes to feel pity for Antony nevertheless (*tamen me
tui miseret*) — because he did harm to himself (*quod tibi invideris*) instead
of becoming a hero of the republic (elaborated on in the subsequent
sentences).

me tui miseret: *miseret* is an impersonal present indicative active, with
the person who feels the pity in the accusative (*me*) and the person pitied
in the genitive (*tui*): 'pity of you affects me' = 'I pity you'.

quod tibi invideris: *invideris* is the 2nd person singular perfect
subjunctive active of *invideo*, which takes the dative (*tibi*): literally,
'because you regarded yourself with envy'. *quod* here follows a verb
of emotion (*miseret*) and is used to indicate the reason for Cicero's pity:
Gildersleeve & Lodge 341. The oblique relation to the main clause
accounts for the subjunctive. The thought here is convoluted: during
the senate meeting of 17 March, Antony showed himself willing to
co-operate with the senate and thereby acquired goodwill and credit
in senatorial circles; but by the time of *Philippic* 2, he had changed his
political outlook. Cicero here mockingly imputes that he did so because
he had become envious of the stellar reputation he had managed to gain.
He thus continues to presuppose that Antony suffers from awkward
personality splits.

**qui tu vir, di immortales, et quantus fuisses, si illius diei mentem
servare potuisses!**: a past counterfactual condition with both the
(up-front) apodosis (*qui... fuisses*) and protasis (*si... potuisses*) in the
pluperfect subjunctive: 'What a man and how great you would have
been, if you had been able to...'

illius diei mentem servare: *mens* here refers to the mental disposition
(anxious, hence conciliatory, and willing to cooperate with the
conspirators) Antony had on 17 March.

**pacem haberemus, quae erat facta per obsidem puerum nobilem,
M. Bambalionis nepotem**: the imperfect subjunctive *haberemus* can be
understood as forming another apodosis to the *si*-clause in the previous
sentence: '[if you had been able to retain the mental disposition you
had on that day,] we would (still) have the peace (now), which was (at

the time) brokered through…' Both *puerum nobilem* and *M. Bambalionis nepotem* stand in apposition to *obsidem*.

M. Bambalionis nepotem: Antony's child with Fulvia was the grandson of M. Fulvius Bambalio, Fulvia's father. Cicero disses father and daughter at *Phil.* 3.16: *tuae coniugis, bonae feminae, locupletis quidem certe, Bambalio quidam pater, homo nullo numero. nihil illo contemptius qui propter haesitantiam linguae stuporemque cordis cognomen ex contumelia traxerit* ('the father of your wife, the good woman — and at any rate rich —, is a certain Bambalio, a complete nobody. Nothing is more contemptible than he who got his humiliating nickname from his stammer and dimwittedness'). Bambalio comes from the Greek verb βαμβάλειν = to stammer. It is unlikely that Bambalio was a *nobilis*, so the phrase *puerum nobilem* is designed to highlight the low social rank of Fulvia's family (as opposed to Antony's): see Shackleton Bailey (1992: 51). And even if he was, the juxtaposition of *nobilem* with Bam*balionis* (which contains within itself, but also soundly jumbles up, *nobilis*) gives the impression that any claim of Antony's offspring to nobility laughably dissolves in a preposterous stammer. Arguably, it was this piece of spiteful mischief that encouraged Cicero to use the otherwise rather cumbersome periphrasis *puerum nobilem, M. Bambalionis nepotem* (a phrase that in itself produces an onomatopoeic stammer: *-um, -lem, Bam-, tem-*) in the first place: there are many more obvious ways to refer to Antony and Fulvia's child. See e.g. Cicero, *Philippic* 1.2 (in a conciliatory moment): *pax denique per eum et per liberos eius cum praestantissimis civibus confirmata est* ('Finally, through him and his son [the plural *liberos* refers to a single child], peace with our most outstanding fellow-citizens was established').

quamquam bonum te timor faciebat, [timor] **non** [est] **diuturnus magister offici;** [te] **improbum fecit ea quae, dum timor abest, a te non discedit, audacia**: Cicero here considers how the countervailing forces of (momentary) fear (*timor*) and natural insolence (*audacia*) shape Antony's conduct. Even though fear made Antony a politically sound (*bonum*) person (*facio* here means 'to cause to be / become', 'make', 'render', with *te* as accusative object and *bonum* as predicate) for a little while (note the imperfect *faciebat*, expressing duration in the past), it is not an emotion that will ensure a permanent change in outlook — as Cicero states in the gnomic main clause, in which both the subject (*timor*) and the verb (*est*) is implied: 'fear is not a long-term teacher of duty'. In the end, insolence, which is Antony's default condition unless it is temporarily suspended because of fear, reasserted itself and has made Antony villainous (*improbus*) again. The perfect *fecit* refers to a moment in the past when Antony's *audacia* reasserted itself, and the relative clause *quae... discedit* makes it apparent that this state is continuing at the time of speaking.

ea... audacia: the hyperbaton of the demonstrative adjective *ea* and the noun it modifies (effectively placed at the very end of the sentence) reinforces the sense that insolence is Antony's default condition.

etsi tum, cum optimum te [esse] **multi putabant me quidem dissentiente, funeri tyranni, si illud funus fuit, sceleratissime praefuisti**: *etsi* here introduces a main clause with *praefuisti* as verb and an implied *tu* as subject: 'and yet, at the time when (*cum*)..., you presided over the funeral (*praesum* takes the dative) of the tyrant... in the most criminal fashion'. *cum* introduces a temporal clause with *multi* as subject and *putabant* as verb, which governs an indirect statement with *te* as subject accusative, an implied *esse* as verb, and *optimum* as predicative complement. *me quidem dissentiente* is a (concessive) ablative absolute.

tyranni: this is the first of several instances in *Philippic* 2 where Cicero refers to Caesar with the Greek loanword *tyrannus*. See also §§ 96 and 117.

si illud funus fuit: 'if that was a funeral'. Cicero expresses his doubts that what happened around 20 March can be classified as a (proper) funeral, underscoring his contempt with a disagreeable *f*-alliteration in *funus fuit*. (At *Orator* 49, he calls 'f' the most unpleasant of letters — *insuavissima littera*.)

§ 91: Antony as
Dr Jekyll and Mr Hyde

The paragraph falls into two parts: in the first, devoted to Caesar's funeral, Antony plays Mr Hyde — a subversive monster out to destroy the city and murder its best citizens; in the second, which revisits senatorial business in late March / early April conducted in the spirit of the compromise reached between Caesarians and liberators on 17 March, Antony has a moment as Dr Jekyll — a high magistrate who conducts affairs of state with sense and sensibility. Cicero singles out for appreciation two aspects from Antony's early collaboration with the senate: his initial restraint in the use of Caesar's unpublished state papers; and his apparent aversion to any future form of autocracy at Rome. All three topics (Caesar's funeral; Caesar's unpublished state papers; anti-autocratic politics) can benefit from some context.

(i) Caesar's Funeral (c. 20 March)

In ancient Rome, the funeral of a former magistrate was a key political occasion. Ordinarily, the family of the deceased would be in charge of the ritual. It would hire a troupe of actors who would put on the wax-masks (the so-called *imagines*) awarded to those members of the clan who had reached public office in the past and don the appropriate official garb and then march the corpse to the forum (= *pompa funebris*), where the son or another close relative would deliver a eulogy, praising in turn each of the ancestors (impersonated by the actors) who had helped shape public affairs, down to the recently deceased (= *laudatio funebris*). Beyond this (ephemeral) ritual, the families that made up Rome's ruling elite would display records of former office holders in the atria of their houses, in the form of *tituli* (short inscriptions detailing the most significant achievements, such as offices, military victories, or triumphs) and *stemmata*, below little shrines containing the corresponding wax-mask (*imago*). This constant advertisement of past success helped to ensure that current and future generations of the same family enjoyed a significant advantage in terms of name recognition during elections. Overwhelmingly, elected officials in Rome hailed from families who had a track record of public service — so-called 'new men' (*homines novi* = men without any ancestral consular wax-mask in the family) were far and few between.

Given the central role of the aristocratic funeral in the political culture of republican Rome and the charged nature of the occasion, Caesar's funeral was of momentous importance as it afforded an ideal opportunity to influence public opinion — not least concerning the perception of the deceased (tyrant or benefactor?) and his killers (criminals or liberators)? As Lacey (1986: 223–24) observes, 'Atticus, one of the shrewdest political observers of the day, warned Cicero against the senate agreeing to a public funeral…, and predicted the result — which Antony probably also desired — which was to show the assassins that the people regarded their act as unforgivable'. The passage from the letter to Atticus to which Lacey refers is worth citing in full (*Att.* 14.10.1 = 364 SB; 19 April 44):

> meministine te clamare causam perisse si funere elatus esset? at ille etiam in foro combustus laudatusque miserabiliter serviique et egentes in tecta nostra cum facibus immissi.

> [Do you remember how you cried out that the cause was lost if he had a public funeral? Well, he was actually cremated in the Forum with a pathetic eulogy, and slaves and beggars were sent with firebrands to attack our homes.]

What actually happened on the day is difficult to ascertain since our main sources differ in significant details, not least with respect to the role that Antony played. Here is Suetonius (*Life of Julius Caesar* 84):

> Funere indicto rogus extructus est in Martio campo iuxta Iuliae tumulum et pro rostris aurata aedes ad simulacrum templi Veneris Genetricis collocata; intraque lectus eburneus auro ac purpura stratus et ad caput

tropaeum cum veste, in qua fuerat occisus. Praeferentibus munera, quia suffecturus dies non videbatur, praeceptum, ut omisso ordine, quibus quisque vellet itineribus urbis, portaret in Campum. Inter ludos cantata sunt quaedam ad miserationem et invidiam caedis eius accommodata, ex Pacuvi Armorum iudicio: 'men servasse, ut essent qui me perderent?' et ex Electra Acili ad similem sententiam. Laudationis loco consul Antonius per praeconem pronuntiavit senatus consultum, quo omnia simul ei divina atque humana decreverat, item ius iurandum, quo se cuncti pro salute unius astrinxerant; quibus perpauca a se verba addidit. Lectum pro rostris in forum magistratus et honoribus functi detulerunt. Quem cum pars in Capitolini Iovis cella cremare pars in curia Pompei destinaret, repente duo quidam gladiis succincti ac bina iacula gestantes ardentibus cereis succenderunt confestimque circumstantium turba virgulta arida et cum subselliis tribunalia, quicquid praeterea ad donum aderat, congessit. Deinde tibicines et scaenici artifices vestem, quam ex triumphorum instrumento ad praesentem usum induerant, detractam sibi atque discissam iniecere flammae et veteranorum militum legionarii arma sua, quibus exculti funus celebrabant; matronae etiam pleraeque ornamenta sua, quae gerebant, et liberorum bullas atque praetextas.

[When the funeral was announced, a pyre was erected in the Campus Martius near the tomb of Julia, and on the rostra a gilded shrine was placed, made after the model of the temple of Venus Genetrix; within was a couch of ivory with coverlets of purple and gold, and at its head a pillar hung with the robe in which he was slain. Since it was clear that the day would not be long enough for those who offered gifts, they were directed to bring them to the Campus by whatever streets of the city they wished, regardless of any order of precedence. At the funeral games, to rouse pity and indignation at his death, these words from the *Contest for the Arms* of Pacuvius were sung: 'Saved I these men that they might murder me?' and words of similar purport from the *Electra* of Atilius. Instead of a eulogy the consul Antonius caused a herald to recite the decree of the Senate in which it had voted Caesar all divine and human honours at once, and likewise the oath with which they had all pledged themselves to watch over his personal safety; to which he added a very few words of his own. The bier on the rostra was carried down into the Forum by magistrates and ex-magistrates; and while some were urging that it be burned in the temple of Jupiter of the Capitol, and others in the Hall of Pompey, suddenly two persons with swords by their sides and brandishing a pair of darts set fire to it with blazing torches, and at once the throng of bystanders heaped upon it dry branches, the judgment seats with the benches, and whatever else could serve as an offering. Then the musicians and actors tore off their robes, which they had taken from the equipment of his triumphs and put on for the occasion, rent them to bits

and threw them into the flames, and the veterans of the legions the arms
with which they had adorned themselves for the funeral; many of the
women too, offered up the jewels which they wore and the amulets and
robes of their children.]

In Suetonius, then, Antony's role is minimal: as consul he presides over
the event and adds a very few words (*perpauca verba*) himself, but the
major part of the eulogy for Caesar is delivered by a herald. By contrast,
Plutarch's account in his *Life of Antony* grants Antony a much larger part
in the proceedings (14.3–4):

> Now, it happened that when Caesar's body was carried forth for burial,
> Antony pronounced the customary eulogy over it in the forum. And
> when he saw that the people were mightily swayed and charmed by
> his words, he mingled with his praises sorrow and indignation over the
> dreadful deed, and at the close of his speech shook on high the garments
> of the dead, all bloody and tattered by the swords as they were, called
> those who had wrought such work villains and murderers, and inspired
> his hearers with such rage that they heaped together benches and tables
> and burned Caesar's body in the forum, and then, snatching the blazing
> faggots from the pyre, ran to the houses of the assassins and assaulted
> them.

Thirdly, there is the elaborate account of Appian, *The Civil Wars* 2.143–47,
which perhaps derives from the historical narrative of Asinius Pollio (a
contemporary and supporter of Caesar), though no doubt interspersing
facts with fiction. It is worth citing in full, despite its length since it
contains a suggestive re-imagining of Antony's incendiary rhetoric:

> When Piso brought Caesar's body into the forum a countless multitude
> ran together with arms to guard it, and with acclamations and
> magnificent pageantry placed it on the rostra. Wailing and lamentation
> were renewed for a long time, the armed men clashed their shields, and
> gradually they began to repent themselves of the amnesty [granted to
> the assassins]. Antony, seeing how things were going, did not abandon
> his purpose, but, having been chosen to deliver the funeral oration, as a
> consul for a consul, a friend for a friend, a relative for a relative (for he
> was related to Caesar on his mother's side), resumed his artful design,
> and spoke as follows:
>   'It is not fitting, citizens, that the funeral oration of so great a man
> should be pronounced by me alone, but rather by his whole country.
> The decrees which all of us, in equal admiration of his merit, voted to
> him while he was alive — the Senate and the people acting together — I

will read, so that I may voice your sentiments rather than my own.' Then he began to read with a severe and gloomy countenance, pronouncing each sentence distinctly and dwelling especially on those decrees which declared Caesar to be superhuman, sacred, and inviolable, and which named him the father, or the benefactor, or the peerless protector of his country. With each decree Antony turned his face and his hand toward Caesar's corpse, illustrating his discourse by his action, and at each appellation he added some brief remark full of grief and indignation; as, for example, where the decree spoke of Caesar as 'the father of his country' he added 'this was a testimonial of his clemency'; and again, where he was made 'sacred and inviolable' and 'everybody else was to be held unharmed who should find refuge with him' — 'Nobody,' said Antony, 'who found refuge with him was harmed, but he, whom you declared sacred and inviolable, was killed, although he did not extort these honours from you as a tyrant, and did not even ask for them. Most lacking the spirit of free men are we if we give such honours to the unworthy who do not ask for them. But you, faithful citizens, vindicate us from this charge of lacking the spirit of free men by paying such honours as you now pay to the dead.'

Antony resumed his reading and recited the oaths by which all were pledged to guard Caesar and Caesar's body with all their strength, and all were devoted to perdition who should not avenge him against any conspiracy. Here, lifting up his voice and extending his hand toward the Capitol, he exclaimed, 'Jupiter, guardian of this city, and you other gods, I stand ready to avenge him as I have sworn and vowed, but since those who are of equal rank with me have considered the decree of amnesty beneficial, I pray that it may prove so.' A commotion arose among the senators in consequence of this exclamation, which seemed to have special reference to them. So Antony soothed them again and recanted, saying, 'It seems to me, fellow-citizens, that this deed is not the work of human beings, but of some evil spirit. It becomes us to consider the present rather than the past, since the greatest danger approaches, if it is not already here, lest we be drawn into our former civil commotions and lose whatever remains of noble birth in the city. Let us then conduct this sacred one to the abode of the blest, chanting over him our accustomed hymn and lamentation.'

Having spoken thus, he gathered up his garments like one inspired, girded himself so that he might have the free use of his hands, took his position in front of the bier as in a play, bending down to it and rising again, and first hymned him as a celestial deity, raising his hands to heaven in order to testify to Caesar's divine birth. At the same time with rapid speech he recited his wars, his battles, his victories, the nations he had brought under his country's sway, and the spoils he had sent home, extolling each exploit as miraculous, and all the time exclaiming,

'You alone have come forth unvanquished from all the battles you have
fought. You alone have avenged your country of the outrage put upon it
300 years ago, bringing to their knees those savage tribes, the only ones
that ever broke into and burned the city of Rome.' Many other things
Antony said in a kind of divine frenzy, and then lowered his voice from
its high pitch to a sorrowful tone, and mourned and wept as for a friend
who had suffered unjustly, and solemnly vowed that he was willing to
give his own life in exchange for Caesar's.

Carried away by an easy transition to extreme passion he uncovered
the body of Caesar, lifted his robe on the point of a spear and shook
it aloft, pierced with dagger-thrusts and red with the dictator's blood.
Whereupon the people, like a chorus in a play, mourned with him in
the most sorrowful manner, and from sorrow became filled again with
anger. After the discourse other lamentations were chanted with funeral
music according to the national custom, by the people in chorus, to the
dead; and his deeds and his sad fate were again recited. Somewhere from
the midst of these lamentations Caesar himself was supposed to speak,
recounting by name his enemies on whom he had conferred benefits,
and of the murderers themselves exclaiming, as it were in amazement,
'Oh that I should have spared these men to slay me!' The people could
endure it no longer. It seemed to them monstrous that all the murderers
who, with the single exception of Decimus Brutus, had been made
prisoners while belonging to the faction of Pompey, and who, instead
of being punished, had been advanced by Caesar to the magistracies
of Rome and to the command of provinces and armies, should have
conspired against him; and that Decimus should have been deemed by
him worthy of adoption as his son.

While they were in this temper and were already near to violence,
somebody raised above the bier an image of Caesar himself made of wax.
The body itself, as it lay on its back on the couch, could not be seen. The
image was turned round and round by a mechanical device, showing the
twenty-three wounds in all parts of the body and on the face, that had
been dealt to him so brutally. The people could no longer bear the pitiful
sight presented to them. They groaned, and, girding up their loins, they
burned the senate-chamber where Caesar was slain, and ran hither and
thither searching for the murderers, who had fled some time previously.

It is impossible to reconstruct which version captures what happened
most faithfully.[53] Pelling (1988: 153–54) argues that 'perceptive
scholars follow Suetonius and believe that Antony's speech was
restrained' — though makes allowance for the possibility that Plutarch

---

53   Other sources include Cassius Dio 44.35.4–50.4 (with Kierdorf 1980: 150–58).

and Appian may have based their accounts on a very good source (Pollio). In addition, we ought to consider that Antony's disappearance act in Suetonius is part of a conspiracy of silence in Augustan and imperial literature that systematically diminishes Antony's status and significance in the historical events after the death of Caesar: see Gotter (1996: 267). And it was indeed an easy task to rile up popular outrage against the conspirators. As Koortbojian (2013: 26) notes: 'Caesar, like Clodius, had received the *tribunicia sacrosanctitas*, and so the assault on each of them was not only a violation of religious law, but one that called for the perpetrators to suffer the penalty of death. Thus, Antony's calculated display of Caesar's wounds (or merely of his bloody toga) was meant to rouse the people against the conspirators despite the amnesty voted by the Senate, in a time-honored call for vengeance'.

(ii) Dealing with Caesar's Unpublished State Papers

Soon after this emotional occasion, the senatorial elite and the presiding magistrates, republicans and Caesarians alike, returned to the tricky business of governance on the basis of the compromise reached on 17 March (amnesty for the assassins; validation of Caesar's already established arrangements, appointments, and policies). One of the most urgent and potentially explosive issues concerned the question of what to do with Caesar's *unpublished* state papers and policies that were still work in progress. Caesar's sudden demise had resulted in a messy situation: as the person who ultimately had pulled all the strings in Roman politics, he left behind a full slate of unfinished business, including oral promises and guarantees, draft papers, incomplete negotiations etc., which had all orbited around him as the reigning dictator and depended on his whim and will. Antony had managed to get hold of Caesar's unpublished state papers (see above 279), which put him in the driver's seat, but in the spirit of collaboration he agreed to subject them to an orderly review. Soon after 20 March and before 7 April (Ramsey 1994: 133, n. 12), Servius Sulpicius was tasked to draft a senatorial decree 'to arrange for the orderly review and selective publication of Caesar's *commentarii*' (Ramsay 1994: 144). Ramsey's reconstruction, based not least on the two references to this decree in the *Philippics* (1.3 and 2.91), is as follows (1994: 138):

(senatus decreuit) *ne qua tabula post Idus Martias ullius decreti Caesaris aut benefici figeretur* <prius quam consules> de Caesaris actis <cum consilio> cognossent, statuissent, iudicassent.

[The Senate decreed that no tablet containing any decree of Caesar after the Ides of March, or any grant, was to be posted before the consuls, with their *consilium*, had reviewed, decided and passed judgment on Caesar's *acta*.]

It seems that all parties involved supported this motion — including Antony and Cicero. As Ramsey (1994: 139–40) explains: 'Antony had in his possession the archives in which many genuine, unpublished *decreta Caesaris* were to be found; Atticus and other important Romans will have desired some of these documents to be registered. On the other hand, the Senate could take comfort in the expectation that Antony's colleague Dolabella and the *consilium* would serve as a watchdog on Antony's activities'. In the event, the constitution of such a *consilium* and the formal and systematic vetting of Caesar's state papers, however, were delayed until June — though the consuls submitted select documents to the senate for ratification in the meantime. This arrangement left plenty of room for manipulation and forgery. And Cicero soon grew deeply suspicious of Antony. In a letter to Cassius, written on 3 May 44, he complained specifically of the fast and loose way in which Antony had started to handle state documents (*ad Familiares* 12.1.1 = 327 SB):

nam ut adhuc quidem actum est, non regno sed rege liberati videmur. interfecto enim rege regios omnis nutus tuemur, neque vero id solum, sed etiam quae ipse ille, si viveret, non faceret, ea nos quasi cogitata ab illo probamus. nec eius quidem rei finem video. *tabulae figuntur, immunitates dantur, pecuniae maximae discribuntur, exsules reducuntur, senatus consulta falsa referuntur*, ut tantum modo odium illud hominis impuri et servitutis dolor depulsus esse videatur, res publica iaceat in iis perturbationibus in quas eam ille coniecit.

[As things have gone so far, it appears that we are free of the despot, but not of the despotism. Our king has been killed, but we are upholding the validity of his every regal nod. And not only that, but we sanction measures which he himself would not be taking if he were alive on the pretext that he had them in mind. I see no end to the business. Laws are posted up, exemptions granted, large sums of money assigned, exiles brought home, decrees of the Senate forged — it seems we are merely rid of the disgust we felt for an abominable individual and of the mortification of slavery, while the state still lies in the chaotic condition into which he flung it.]

In *Philippic* 2.92–100 Cicero also makes a big deal of Antony's forgeries. But in § 91, which is designed to set up this prolonged treatment, he recalls the moment of conciliatory honesty he already lauded at the opening of *Philippic* 1 (§2–3):

> Praeclara tum oratio M. Antoni, egregia etiam voluntas; pax denique per eum et per liberos eius cum praestantissimis civibus confirmata est. atque his principiis reliqua consentiebant. ad deliberationes eas quas habebat domi de re publica principes civitatis adhibebat; ad hunc ordinem res optimas deferebat; nihil tum nisi quod erat notum omnibus in C. Caesaris commentariis reperiebatur; summa constantia ad ea quae quaesita erant respondebat. num qui exsules restituti? unum aiebat, praeterea neminem. num immunitates datae? 'Nullae,' respondebat. Adsentiri etiam nos Ser. Sulpicio, clarissimo viro, voluit, ne qua tabula post Idus Martias ullius decreti Caesaris aut benefici figeretur.

> [Marcus Antonius made a fine speech on that occasion and also showed outstanding goodwill. Finally, through him and his son, peace with our most distinguished fellow citizens was established. And the rest tallied with these beginnings. Antonius regularly brought the leaders of our community into the deliberations on the commonwealth that he was in the habit of holding at his home. He laid admirable proposals before this body. Nothing at that time was discovered in Gaius Caesar's memoranda except what was common knowledge. He replied to questions with perfect consistency. Had any exiles been restored? He mentioned just one, nobody else. Had any exemptions from taxes been granted? 'None,' he replied. He even wanted us to vote for a motion by Servius Sulpicius, a most distinguished man, the terms of which were that no tablet inscribed with any order or grant of Caesar's should be posted after the fifteenth of March.]

(iii) Anti-Autocratic Politics

In the immediate aftermath of the initial compromise between Caesarians and conspirators, Antony proposed a law that eliminated the dictatorship from Roman politics.[54] It was an act of symbolic politics, no doubt designed to underscore his republican credentials and

---

54   Sources include: App. *Civ.* 3.25, 94; Cass. Dio 44.51.2, Liv. per. 116.

commitment to collaboration with the senate. Cicero acclaims the act at the beginning of the first *Philippic* right after praising Antony for his sensible handling of Caesar's papers (*Phil.* 1.3–4):

> dictaturam, quae iam vim regiae potestatis obsederat, funditus ex re publica sustulit; de qua ne sententias quidem diximus. scriptum senatus consultum quod fieri vellet attulit, quo recitato auctoritatem eius summo studio secuti sumus eique amplissimis verbis per senatus consultum gratias egimus. lux quaedam videbatur oblata non modo regno, quod pertuleramus, sed etiam regni timore sublato, magnumque pignus ab eo rei publicae datum, se liberam civitatem esse velle, cum dictatoris nomen, quod saepe iustum fuisset, propter perpetuae dictaturae recentem memoriam funditus ex re publica sustulisset.

> [The dictatorship, which had already usurped the might of royal power, he removed completely from the commonwealth. We did not even debate the subject. Antonius brought the draft of a decree that he said he wished the senate to pass. As soon as it had been read aloud, we followed his authority with the utmost enthusiasm and by a decree voted him our utmost thanks. It seemed as though a light of sorts had dawned, with the removal not only of the monarchy which we had endured, but even of the fear of its recurrence; it seemed as though Antonius had given the commonwealth a mighty pledge of his desire for a free community when, because of the memory of the recent 'Dictatorship for Life', he completely removed from our commonwealth the office of dictator, even thought it had often been legitimate.]

And he returns to it towards the end (*Phil.* 1.32):

> Proximo, altero, tertio, denique reliquis consecutis diebus, non intermittebas quasi donum aliquod cotidie afferre rei publicae, maximum autem illud, quod dictaturae nomen sustulisti. haec inusta est a te, a te, inquam, mortuo Caesari nota ad ignominiam sempiternam. ut enim propter unius M. Manli scelus decreto gentis Manliae neminem patricium Manlium Marcum vocari licet, sic tu propter unius dictatoris odium nomen dictatoris funditus sustulisti.

> [The next day and the next and the following and onwards, one day after another you brought the commonwealth a daily gift, so to speak; the greatest of all, when you abolished the name of dictatorship. Thereby you — yes, *you* — branded Caesar in his grave with everlasting infamy. Because of a crime committed by one of its members, Marcus Manlius, no patrician belonging to the Manlian clan may be called Marcus; so the clan decreed. Just so you totally abolished the name of dictator because of the hatred felt for one particular dictator.]

The dictatorship was a traditional magistracy that the Romans resorted to in moments of crisis that called for extraordinary measures. The *imperium* of the dictator, who was always appointed for a strictly limited period of time only, outranked even that of a consul. But in the wake of Sulla (who had himself appointed dictator to restore the commonwealth) and Caesar (who was killed shortly after assuming the dictatorship for life), the office had become tainted with autocratic associations. Cicero's appreciation of the move, both in *Philippics* 1, 2.91, and elsewhere (see 2.115 below), suggests the shrewdness of Antony's symbolic politics: the motion gained him credit with the republican contingent in the senate, while it also managed to imply that those senators who voted in favour of Caesar's perpetual dictatorship were accountable for his murder and the subsequent malaise.[55]

* * *

Tua illa pulchra laudatio [Caesaris], **tua miseratio, tua cohortatio** [erat]: an asyndetic tricolon, reinforced by the triple anaphora of *tua*, rendered even punchier by the suppression of the verb (*erat*): 'That "beautiful" funeral oration, the pathos, the exhortations — they were yours' (alternatively, one could take *laudatio, miseratio,* and *cohortatio,* together with *tu, tu,* as subjects of *incendisti*). The first colon gives the generic reference to the type of speech (a funeral oration, *laudatio funebris*, consisting in a eulogy of the deceased); the second (*miseratio*) specifies the emotional register of Antony's speech (it was fraught with pathos designed to generate sympathy for the deceased), the third (*cohortatio*) pinpoints its intended impact on the audience, i.e. incitement of anger to be unleashed in violent action against the killers.

Caesar's funeral is an awkward moment for Cicero not least since Antony here truly proved his worth as orator. As consul, he was in charge of delivering the funeral oration in praise of the deceased, and he managed to use this opportunity to sway public opinion in favour of Caesar and the Caesarians, including himself, while stirring up ill-will towards the conspirators. Cicero was present at the occasion and also acquired a written version of it afterwards (*Att.* 15.20.2 = 397 SB).

---

55   In response, Cicero argued that Antony was to blame for trying to crown Caesar king at the Lupercalia: see *Phil.* 13.41.

tu, tu, inquam, illas faces incendisti, et eas quibus semustilatus ille est et eas quibus incensa L. Bellieni domus deflagravit: Cicero continues in anaphoric mode as he pivots from Antony's inflammatory rhetoric to real flames. *et eas… et eas…* stands in apposition to *illas faces*: 'both those… and those…'. *incensa* is perfect passive participle in the nominative feminine singular, modifying *domus*. Lucius Bellienus is not otherwise known, but presumably supported the conspirators.

semustilatus ille est: the reference is to Caesar (*ille*), or rather his corpse. *semi-ustilo* means 'to half-burn' and suggests the undignified nature of the proceedings: whipped into a frenzy by Antony's speech, the crowd lost any sense of ritual decorum and turned the funeral into a riot. One of the victims was Caesar's corpse: instead of receiving a proper cremation, Cicero suggests, it only got scorched in the context of a city-wide conflagration. The — decidedly rare — verb is not coincidentally the same that Cicero used at *pro Milone* 33 to refer to the half-burnt corpse of Clodius, whose death caused a similarly violent aftermath.

tu illos impetus perditorum et ex maxima parte servorum quos nos vi manuque reppulimus in nostras domos immisisti: the third sentence in a row that begins with a second person pronoun or pronominal adjective. Here Cicero casts Antony as a general who directs the attacks of villains and slaves against the houses of senators with republican convictions. If Suetonius (*Life of Julius Caesar* 85) is right that the houses which suffered a mob attack were those of the two leading conspirators Cassius and Brutus, Cicero — by using the first person plural *nos… reppulimus* — generates the hyperbolic impression of a much more widespread attack, while also declaring his solidarity with the republican ringleaders.

idem tamen quasi fuligine abstersa reliquis diebus in Capitolio praeclara senatus consulta fecisti, ne qua post Idus Martias immunitatis tabula [figeretur] **neve** [tabula] **cuius benefici figeretur**: the *ne* introduces a (bipartite) noun-clause. The two parts are linked by the *-ve* attached to the second *ne* that specifies the contents of two decrees that Cicero endorsed. *qua* is in the nominative feminine singular (= *aliqua*; after *si, nisi, ne* and *num, ali-* goes 'bum!') modifying *tabula*, the subject of the clause, which also has to be supplied in the second part as the noun on which the genitive *cuius* [= *alicuius*] *benefici* depends. Public regulations, such as laws and decrees, were inscribed on bronze tablets (*tabulae*) and put on display on the Capitoline Hill:[56] '... you saw to the passing of outstanding decrees of the Senate, providing that after the Ides of March no record of exemption or of any special favour be posted'. Cf. *Phil.* 1.3: *assentiri etiam nos Ser. Sulpicio, clarissimo viro, voluit, ne qua tabula post Idus Martias ullius decreti Caesaris aut benefici figeretur* ('He even wished us to assent to the motion of Servius Sulpicius, a man of great distinction, that from the Ides of March no notice of any decree or grant of Caesar's should be posted'). As Ramsey (1994: 131–32) shows, Cicero here tries 'to convey the false impression that there was such a ban because Cicero deliberately chose to quote a single clause from this decree in order to suggest that Antony agreed to surrender more power than he in fact did under the terms of the decree'. (For a reconstruction of the decree, see above 297–98: there was most likely never a complete ban — the decree rather called for a systematic review of the archive by the consuls, under the general supervision of an advisory board (*consilium*).)

quasi fuligine abstersa: an ablative absolute. The *quasi* indicates that Cicero is speaking figuratively.

meministi ipse de exsulibus [quid dixeris], **scis de immunitate quid dixeris**: the two ablative phrases *de exsulibus* and *de immunitate* belong into the indirect questions (the first very elliptical). At *Philippic* 1.2–3 (cited above), Cicero reproduces the cross-examination of Antony in the senate before the passing of Sulpicius' motion, giving reassurances that Caesar's state papers did not contain unwelcome surprises.

de immunitate: *munus, -eris*, n. denotes a 'task', 'duty' or 'obligation', and *im-muni-tas* 'was the exemption of a community or an individual from obligations [*munera*, such as the payment of taxes] to the Roman state or of an individual from obligations to a local community' (Burton 2012).

---

56   See further Meyer (2004).

optimum vero [erat] **quod dictaturae nomen in perpetuum de re publica sustulisti**: the main verb (*erat*) needs to be supplied. *quod* (+ indicative) introduces a substantive clause, i.e. a clause that functions like a noun. Here it is the predicative complement to *optimum*: 'But the best thing was that…'. The subject of the *quod*-clause is an implied *tu*, the verb is *sustulisti*.

dictaturae nomen in perpetuum … sustulisti: *dictaturae* is an appositional genitive dependent on *nomen*: 'the term dictatorship'. *in perpetuum* is an adverbial phrase with *sustulisti*. Cicero could have used other words to express the idea of 'forever' (*sempiterno, aeterno*; at *Phil.* 1.4 (cited above) he used *funditus* 'entirely' in this context), but *in perpetuum* generates a nice antithesis with — and ironically recalls — Caesar's last title *dictator perpetuo* ('dictator in perpetuity').

quo quidem facto tantum te cepisse odium regni videbatur ut eius omnem propter proximum dictatorem metum tolleres: *quo* is a connecting relative (= *et eo*) and part of the ablative of cause *quo quidem facto*: 'because of this deed at least'. The subject is *tantum … odium* (the degree of hatred is underscored by the hyperbaton), which sets up the consecutive *ut*-clause. The objective genitive *regni* depends on *odium*: '… such hatred of kingship seemed to have taken hold of you that…'

eius omnem … metum: *eius*, which refers back to *regni*, is an objective genitive dependent on *metum*. *omnem … metum* (note the hyperbaton) correlates thematically and stylistically with *tantum … odium* in the main clause: hatred and fear are two powerful and complementary emotions.

propter proximum dictatorem: a reference to Caesar's recent dictatorship and a condensed rephrasing of *propter perpetuae dictaturae recentem memoriam* at *Phil.* 1.4 (cited above).

§ 92: Selling the Empire

Cicero continues to insist on his clairvoyant pessimism, by which he sets himself apart from peers more susceptible to the allure of a short-term reconciliation. While others at the time hailed the compromise reached between Caesarians and conspirators back in March as a re-establishment of the *res publica*, he remained highly skeptical of the prospects for a lasting settlement while Antony remained at the helm. Subsequent events, he argues, proved him right. It did not take Antony long to abuse his privileged access to the state papers of Caesar, which afforded him the opportunity to 'discover' (a.k.a. invent) new edicts as it suited him. In this paragraph, Cicero lambasts Antony for selling off rights and privileges (such as grants of citizenship and immunity from taxation) to non-Romans for personal gain, under the cover of executing Caesar's will but using forged documents for the purpose.

Constituta res publica videbatur aliis, mihi vero nullo modo, qui omnia te gubernante naufragia metuebam: *constituta* stands in predicative position to *res publica* ('to some the commonwealth seemed established...'). Its placement up front conveys a sense of finality and relief — an upbeat, optimistic start to a sentence that then progressively loses its lustre: *videbatur* moves us from the realm of facts to that of appearance, *aliis* introduces a further qualification (the commonwealth did not seem safe and sound to everyone), further reinforced by *mihi*, which clashes in antithesis with *aliis* and receives instant backup from the discourse particle *vero*, which has its origins in a case form of *verus* = 'true', 'real' (Kroon 1995: 285), thereby helping to suggest that Cicero's understanding of constitutional realities, profoundly bleak as it may be (cf. *nullo modo*) is unfortunately also much more realistic. With Antony in charge, any catastrophe may happen.

omnia te gubernante naufragia: the ablative absolute *te gubernante* breaks up the accusative object *omnia naufragia*. Both phrases comprise the common metaphor of the 'ship of state', with the consul or other leading politician as helmsman (*gubernator*) steering the commonwealth safely through troubled waters — or, alternatively, causing wreckage. (The adjective *omnia* lessens the metaphorical force since it goes better with a generalized meaning of *naufragia* in the sense of *calamitas*: 'every kind of disaster'; the implication may be that Antony is not a true *gubernator* anyway.)

The 'ship-of-state' metaphor has a long pedigree in Greek and Roman thought (going back to the lyric poet Alcaeus, it was also used by Theognis, Solon, Aeschylus, Sophocles, and Plato, *Republic* 6.488a–489d, among others). It was a favourite of Cicero's.[57] Related ideas are the figure of the *gubernator rei publicae* and (when things go wrong) the notion of political shipwreck (*naufragium*). The metaphor is still alive today: during World War II, for instance, Franklin Roosevelt is said to have quoted the following bit from Henry Wadsworth Longfellow's poem 'The Ship' in a letter to Winston Churchill: '… Sail on, O Ship of State! | Sail on, O Union, strong and great! | Humanity with all its fears, | With all the hopes of future years, | Is hanging breathless on thy fate!'. As a 'dead metaphor', the group of words around *gubernare* ('to steer') inform contemporary political discourse in English, on the back of the following linguistic evolution: Greek *kubernan* > Latin *gubernare* > Middle English (from Old French) *governer* > Modern English *to govern* (hence government etc.).

num igitur me fefellit, aut num diutius sui potuit esse dissimilis?: Cicero changes focus, shifting from a direct address to Antony to talking about him in the third person to the rest of the audience. The anaphoric *num … num* introduces two rhetorical questions that both demand a negative answer.

diutius: the comparative form of the adverb *diu*.

---

57   See e.g. *Cluent.* 94, 153; *Verr.* 2.1.46, 2.3.98; *Cat.* 1.22, 2.15; *Pis.* 21; *Rep.* 1.7; and *de Orat.* 1.1–3 with Fantham (1972), May (1980), and Zarecki (2014).

sui ... dissimilis: cf. above § 89: *dicebam... similem te futurum tui*, with a note on the grammar of the genitive of the personal pronoun (*tui / sui*) dependent on *similem / dissimilis*. Cicero bases his expectations on the principle that the leopard does not change his spots.

inspectantibus vobis toto Capitolio tabulae figebantur, neque solum singulis venibant immunitates sed etiam populis universis: civitas non iam singillatim, sed provinciis totis dabatur: Cicero follows up the ablative absolute *inspectantibus vobis* ('under your very eyes', 'with you looking on') with three main clauses (*tabulae figebantur* – *venibant immunitates* – *civitas ... dabatur*) that capture Antony's illegal activity to enrich himself at the expense of the Roman people: *tabulae* are notices that publicize (forged) decrees supposedly found in Caesar's papers; they were put up (*figebantur*) 'all over the Capitol'. Cicero proceeds to specify two kinds of transactions: the selling of exemption from taxation (*immunitates*); and the granting of citizenship (*civitas*), in return for a handsome bribe. In each case, he is keen to stress the utterly unrestrained way Antony went about his business. In line with the hyperbole that the entire Capitol Hill was plastered in announcements (*toto Capitolio*), the following two clauses operate with universalizing attributes (*populis universis, provinciis totis*) that stand in antithesis to individual instances (*singulis; singillatim*).

venibant: the third person plural imperfect of *veneo*, which is active in form, but passive in meaning: 'exemptions were sold...'

provinciis totis: a hyperbole; only one province (Sicily) acquired citizenship-status at the time. Cicero complains about this grant in a letter to Atticus (*Att.* 14.12.1 = 366 SB; 22 April 44):

> scis quam diligam Siculos et quam illam clientelam honestam iudicem. multa illis Caesar, neque me invito (etsi Latinitas erat non ferenda. verum tamen). ecce autem Antonius accepta grandi pecunia fixit legem 'a dictatore comitiis latam' qua Siculi cives Romani; cuius rei vivo illo mentio nulla.

> [You know how warm a feeling I have for the Sicilians and what an honour I consider it to have them as my clients. Caesar was generous to them and I was not sorry that he should be — though the Latin franchise was intolerable, but let that pass. Well, here is Antony posting up (in return for a massive bribe) a law allegedly 'carried by the Dictator in

the Assembly' under which the Sicilians become Roman citizens, a thing never mentioned in his lifetime!]

Caesar seems to have granted a lower form of citizenship called *Latinitas* ('Latin franchise') to (some part of) Sicily, which Antony upgraded to full citizenship status in return for a hefty bribe, while claiming that Caesar himself had wanted to pass a law to this effect. The difference between the letter and the speech is telling: invective hyperbole transforms one instance of forgery and corruption into a wholesale crisis of empire.

itaque si haec manent, quae stante re publica manere non possunt, provincias universas, patres conscripti, perdidistis, neque vectigalia solum sed etiam imperium populi Romani huius domesticis nundinis deminutum est: the two main clauses — (a) *provincias universas ... perdidistis*; (b) *vectigalia... + imperium ... deminutum est* — linked by *neque* constitute the apodosis of a conditional sequence. The protasis is *si haec manent*, with *haec* referring back to the decrees of Caesar that Antony forged.

stante re publica: an ablative absolute, which functions as the protasis of a conditional sequence: '... which, if the republic is to survive, cannot remain in place...' Cicero insists on the incompatibility of Antony's approach to imperial riches (turning them into a private source of income) and the survival of the commonwealth.

vectigalia ... imperium: the two subjects of *deminutum est* (which agrees with the nearest one). *vectigalia* here denotes sources of revenue accruing to the Roman commonwealth from the non-citizen territories (*provinciae*) over which the Romans exercised control. The transformation of the populace of these regions into Roman citizens drastically reduced the ability of Rome to extract wealth and resources from the imperial periphery. Cicero here clearly wears a different hat from the one he wore in his prosecution of Verres, where he struck a blow against provincial exploitation. (Tacitus, at *Annals* 1.2, grudgingly concedes that the provinces welcomed the principate since it put a limit on the abusive practices widespread in republican times.) *imperium*, which originally meant 'the right to issue commands', in time acquired the secondary meaning 'the territory over which one has the right to issue commands', i.e. empire. This is the meaning here: Cicero argues that Antony's unlawful activities diminish not only Rome's income, but its very empire.

huius domesticis nundinis: *huius* refers to Antony. The *nundinae* were the market-days in the Roman calendar, which recurred at regular intervals of eight days. The use of this civic term here with the ill-fitting attribute *domesticis* ('Antony's private market-days') is perversely appropriate: Antony is selling off public resources for personal enrichment. The right to hold a market was an important asset for local economies and, as Ker (2010: 377) points out, 'Cicero was able to exploit anxieties about the privatization of *nundinae* in his orations: in the *Philippics* he portrays Antony as having squandered whole Roman provinces through his own "domestic markets" (*domesticis nundinis*), thereby diminishing Rome's tax-base and territory (*Phil.* 2.92)'. See already 2.35; Cicero returns to the topic in 2.115, 3.10 and 5.11: *calebant in interiore aedium parte totius rei publicae nundinae* ('there was a lively traffic in every interest of the commonwealth in the inner part of the house'). The appropriation of public resources and institutions for personal gain and the relocation of civic events in private spaces are hallmarks of tyrannical conduct.

§ 100: Further Forgeries and a Veteran Foundation

In §§ 92–97, Cicero blasts Antony for the forged decrees of Caesar that he used to enrich himself or to recall exiles, following up with two paragraphs (§§ 98–99) devoted to Antony's alleged mistreatment of his uncle C. Antonius Hybrida (Cicero's colleague as consul in 63), who had otherwise a rather checkered record: in 70, he was temporarily expelled from the senate because of bankruptcy and in 59 he was exiled because of provincial mismanagement. At the beginning of § 100, Cicero returns to Antony's mishandling of Caesar's state papers (*ad chirographa redeamus*), a topic which he here brings to a close with reference to the timeframe initially established for a review of Caesar's archive. The relevant senatorial decree was passed at the end of March / beginning of April. The official review was supposed to begin in June. In the intervening period, Antony was largely absent from Rome on a trip to Southern Italy: he tried to shore up personal support among Caesar's veterans, who were also being wooed by Caesar's heir Caesar Octavianus (the future Augustus), by securing land for their settlement. This trip and Antony's return to Rome is Cicero's main focus in §§ 100b–108.

In the course of imperial expansion, the Romans evolved a set of procedures involving politics, law and religion which regulated the use of public lands acquired through conquest, including the establishment of colonies, which was one way of helping former soldiers and needy citizens.[58] At the same time, land distribution to veterans was a highly

---

58   See Gargola (1995) and below 323–24.

controversial issue in late-republican Rome and helped to precipitate the civil war. When generals returned from campaigns abroad, they wanted to settle their long-serving soldiers, to reward them for their services and to establish a powerful base of clients. This transformation of ephemeral military glory into a long-standing source of social capital grated with the senatorial elite, especially when the settlements were large-scale — as when Pompey returned after his defeat of Mithridates. At every turn, the senate blocked his attempts to have his arrangements in the East ratified and his soldiers settled — and thus drove Pompey into the arms of Caesar, who, as consul of 59 BCE, pushed through the necessary legislation even against massive senatorial resistance. Caesar himself arranged for the settlement of his soldiers in 45 BCE; and in June 44 BCE, Antony and Dolabella passed a law that set up a commission of seven charged with dividing up land among veterans and the urban poor.[59]

Sed ad chirographa redeamus: *chirographum* is a loanword from the Greek (*cheirographon*), consisting of the Greek term for 'hand' (*cheir*) + the word for writing (*graphein*). Here it refers to those acts of Caesar that only existed in draft form — and had not yet been inscribed on bronze and displayed in public. One could imagine Cicero investing *ad chirographa* with a knowing touch of sarcasm. *redeamus* is an exhortative subjunctive ('let us return...').

quae tua fuit cognitio?: *cognitio* here has the technical sense of 'formal review' undertaken by the magistrate in charge. See Kunkel (1995: 145–46), who discusses *cognoscere* and *cognitio* of magistrates in the context of civil law. Among other things, Kunkel notes that the *cognitio* of magistrates was undertaken as a quasi-legal exercise, i.e. following certain procedural principles. One of these principles was the constitution and participation of a *consilium*, at least in those circumstances when the case at issue was of significance. Conversely, *cognitio sine consilio* ('a formal examination of the facts of the matter without involvement of a board of advisors') was considered reprehensible. This fact endows the emphatic separation of *tua* from *cognitio* with a particular punch. The attribute suggests that Antony conducted the formal review according

---

59   See Cic. *Att.* 15.19.2 = 396 SB, *Phil.* 5.7, 5.21, 8.26, 12.23; Dio 45.9.

to his own whim and will, without subjecting his findings to the oversight of others. It is hence hardly surprising that Antony's so-called 'review' somehow managed to unearth hitherto unknown (= forged) acts of Caesar — a fraudulent abuse of magisterial authority.

acta enim Caesaris pacis causa confirmata sunt a senatu; [ea] quae quidem Caesar egisset, non ea quae egisse Caesarem dixisset Antonius: Cicero inserts a meta-comment into his string of questions, recapitulating the compromise reached between Antony and the senate in the meeting on 17 March — i.e. to approve Caesar's acts, but of course only those that actually were Caesar's. The comment is set up by the dialogic discourse particle *enim*, by which a speaker appeals to interpersonal consensus (Kroon 1995); the sense here is akin to: 'let's briefly rehearse some obvious facts'. The second part of the sentence (*quae ... Antonius*) stands in apposition to *acta*, as Cicero sees an obvious need to define the notion of 'Caesar's *acta*' further with two relative clauses of characteristic (hence the subjunctive, here expressing restriction and proviso: Allen and Greenough 535d). The 'particularizing-limiting' sense of the particle *quidem* here, which often occurs in restrictive relative clauses (*OLD* s.v. 1d), reinforces the distinction between *acta* that are genuine and *acta* forged by Antony. The second *quae* doubles as accusative object of both *dixisset* and *egisse*; *dixisset* introduces an indirect statement with *Caesarem* as subject accusative and *egisse* as infinitive.

pacis causâ ... a senatu: the ablative of *causa* can function as a preposition + genitive: 'for the sake of peace'. Here the phrase stresses that Cicero is unwilling to invest Caesar's acts with any inherent authority — the only reason they were confirmed was to broker peace between the liberators and the Caesarians. The postponed ablative of agency *a senatu* has the same purpose — it emphatically re-establishes the senate as the centre of political decision-making.

quae ... Caesar egisset, non ea quae egisse Caesarem dixisset Antonius: the chiasmus *Caesar : egisset :: egisse : Caesarem* and the emphatic postponement of *Antonius* (as far away from *Caesar* in the nominative as possible) reinforce the contrast between genuine and forged *acta*. Cicero implies, tendentiously, that all the acts that Antony claims to have found in Caesar's archive are forgeries.

unde ista erumpunt, quo auctore [ista] **proferuntur? si sunt falsa, cur probantur? si** [sunt] **vera, cur veneunt?**: Cicero uses four questions grouped in two pairs (*unde – quo auctore; cur – cur*) to present a dilemma designed to shore up the point that Antony is abusing his privileged access to Caesar's state papers: either his archival 'discoveries' are forged inventions — then they should not be approved; or they are authentic manifestations of Caesar's will — then they should not command a bribe for being put into practice. Cicero's use of the present tense throughout (*erumpunt, proferuntur, probantur, veneunt*) is ominous: he is not talking of a past transgression, but an ongoing scandal. The (scornful) deictic pronoun *ista* refers back only and specifically to those acts that Antony pretends to be Caesar's — *ea quae egisse Caesarem dixisset Antonius* — and not Caesar's actual acts (*quae ... Caesar egisset*).

quo auctore proferuntur?: the interrogative pronoun *quo* is here part of a nominal ablative absolute ('nominal' since it consists of a pronoun and a noun, rather than the usual noun + participle combination); to translate, turn the pronoun into a genitive: 'on *whose* authority are they produced?'

at sic placuerat ut ex Kalendis Iuniis de Caesaris actis cum consilio cognosceretis: *placet* in the past tenses (perfect *placuit* or, as here, pluperfect *placuerat*) is used to refer to decisions made by the senate or some other authority (*OLD* s.v. 5b): 'it had been resolved that...' Cicero's prose leaves it entirely ambiguous who was responsible for postponing the formal examination of Caesar's archive until June. As Ramsey (1994: 134, n. 13) points out, 'the decree itself did not contain the provision for the postponement until 1 June, nor did the Senate pass a separate decree providing for the postponement, although quite a few scholars have jumped to this false conclusion'.

ex Kalendis Iuniis: *ex* here specifies the moment in time when the review was supposed to begin ('commencing on the calends of June').

de Caesaris actis ... cognosceretis: *cognoscere de* here has again the technical, quasi-legal sense of 'to investigate formally to ascertain the facts about...'

cum consilio: the *consilium* is a typically Roman institution: it was in effect a group of esteemed and experienced persons who acted in an advisory capacity; any Roman in a position of power, whether in his role as *paterfamilias* or as a (pro-)magistrate of the Roman people, was expected to consult his *consilium* before making an important or difficult decision. See Kunkel (1995: 135–41). Here, the advisory group was designed to ensure that Antony played by the rules in his handling of Caesar's state papers.

quod fuit consilium, quem umquam advocasti, quas Kalendas Iunias expectasti? an eas [Kalendas] **ad quas te peragratis veteranorum coloniis stipatum armis rettulisti?**: Cicero here blasts Antony for failing to put the senatorial decree drafted by Sulpicius (above 297–98) into practice: he did not summon any advisory council and let the specified deadline at which the review of Caesar's *acta* was supposed to begin (the Calends of June) pass. *an eas* picks up *Kalendas*: 'those perhaps, by which…?' The verb is the reflexive *te … rettulisti* (lit. 'returned yourself'); *stipatum* is a perfect passive participle in the accusative masculine singular, agreeing with the reflexive pronoun *te* and governing the ablative *armis*: 'you returned, loaded with weapons'.

peragratis veteranorum coloniis: an ablative absolute, even though the one who is doing the traversing is Antonius, the subject of the relative clause.

o praeclaram illam percursationem tuam mense Aprili atque Maio, tum cum etiam Capuam coloniam deducere conatus es!: *o … tuam* is an accusative of exclamation, followed by an ablative of time ('in April and May').

Capuam coloniam deducere: *Capuam* is a so-called 'accusative of place to which', which normally takes a preposition such as *ad*, except when the destination is a city (as here), town, a small islands, 'home' (*domus*) or the countryside (*rus*). (Cf. English: I am going home — *domum eo*; 'I am going *to* Capua' — *Capuam eo*.) *coloniam deducere* means 'to found a colony'. See Gargola (1995: 217): 'Forms of two verbs usually denoted the act of establishing a colony. The more frequently encountered expression, preferred by writers affecting the annalistic style, was some form of the words, *coloniam deducere,* while another, less frequently used phrase was *coloniam condere'*.

quem ad modum illinc abieris vel potius paene non abieris scimus: *quem ad modum ... non abieris* is an indirect question (hence the subjunctive) governed by *scimus*. Apparently, Antony 'was roughly handled in Capua, as the old settlers looked with an evil eye on his new colonists, as intruders on their rights' (Mayor 1861: 141). Cicero suggests that he 'barely' (*paene*) escaped with his life — surely an exaggeration.

abieris: second person singular perfect subjunctive active.

§ 101: Revels and Remunerations

Cicero continues to blast Antony for his conduct in Southern Italy. His attack is three-pronged: a brief reference back to the close shave he had at Capua with disgruntled locals treated at the end of the previous paragraph; dissolute living to the point of self-harm; and dissolute squandering of public patrimony on undeserving mates, thus inflicting harm on everyone else and the commonwealth as such. Already in the transitional § 43, Cicero lashed out at Antony's absurd remuneration of his teacher in rhetoric, one Sextus Clodius, who supposedly had been gifted with 2000 *iugera* in the plain of Leontini, some of the finest arable land in Sicily. At that moment he deferred more detailed treatment of this and similar matters to some later point in the speech: *sed dicam alio loco et de Leontino agro et de Campano, quos iste agros ereptos rei publicae turpissimis possessoribus inquinavit* ('But I shall be speaking elsewhere both of the Leontine and the Campanian lands, the lands Antonius snatched from the Republic and befouled with disgraceful tenants'). The reference is to §§ 101–02.

Cui tu urbi minitaris: *cui* is a connecting relative, agreeing with *urbi* (= *et eae*); the dative goes with the deponent *minitaris* (in form the second person singular present indicative passive). *minitari* can be used either intransitively ('to threaten') with the person or thing threatened in the dative or transitively (with an accusative object, an accusative + infinitive, or an infinitive), again with the person threatened in the dative. The sense here seems intransitive, though a more specific threat, i.e. to retry to found a colony in the city's territory, hangs in the air.

utinam conere [coloniam deducere Capuam?], **ut aliquando illud 'paene' tollatur!**: *conêre* is the alternative form of the second person singular present subjunctive of the deponent *conor* (= *conêris*) — 'If only you would try' — followed by a consecutive *ut*-clause, in which Cicero quotes the *paene* from the end of the previous paragraph: next time Antony seeks trouble with Capua, he may well fail to make another lucky escape. Cicero does not specify what Antony should try, and the vagueness may be deliberate, but given the end of the previous paragraph (... *tum cum etiam Capuam coloniam deducere conatus es*), what Cicero may have in mind is a second attempt to found a colony at Capua.

utinam: the particle *utinam* introduces a wish clause.

at quam nobilis est tua illa peregrinatio!: *quam nobilis*, exposed by its front position, is highly derisive. Cicero mocks Antony, shockingly untroubled as he is by any instinct for propriety, for his failure to live up to his family pedigree (and his *nobilitas*) during his 'peregrinations'. In fact, the phrase *nobilis peregrinatio* amounts to something of an oxymoron. A *peregrinus* is a foreigner or alien, someone who has come from abroad, and if a Roman engages in *peregrinatio*, foreign travel, he turns himself into one as well — both abroad and, more to the point, back in Rome: 'For Cicero *peregrinatio* may turn the traveller into a *peregrinus* in his own country', writes Catharine Edwards (1996: 116), with an apposite reference to Cicero's letter to Caelius Rufus (*Fam.* 2.12.2 = 95 SB): *urbem, urbem, mi Rufe, cole et in ista luce vive. omnis peregrinatio ... obscura et sordida est iis, quorum industria Romae potest illustris esse* ('Rome! Stick to Rome, my fear fellow, and live in the limelight! Sojourn abroad of any kind ... is squalid obscurity for those whose efforts can win lustre in the capital'). Put differently, one cannot possibly be *nobilis* or *illustris* in foreign parts — rather, *peregrinatio* destroys *nobilitas*.

quid prandiorum apparatus [proferam], **quid furiosam vinulentiam tuam proferam?**: *quid* here means 'why?', 'For what reason?' (see *OLD* s.v. *quis* 16). *proferam* is in what grammars call the 'deliberative subjunctive'. See e.g. Allen and Greenough 443: 'The subjunctive was used in sentences of interrogative form, at first when the speaker wished information in regard to the will or desire of the person addressed.

The mood was therefore *hortatory* in origin. But such questions when addressed by the speaker to himself, as if asking his own advice, become *deliberative* or, not infrequently, merely *exclamatory*. In such cases the mood often approaches the meaning of the Potential.... In these uses the subjunctive is often called *Deliberative* or *Dubitative'*.[60] Rhetorically, we are here dealing with a *praeteritio* — the nifty move of mentioning something in passing, to implant it firmly in the imagination of the audience, without dwelling on details. See further above 166–68.

prandiorum apparatus: sumptuous lunches. *apparatus* (a fourth-declension noun) is here in the accusative plural. *prandium* was the Roman midday meal, not as substantial as the evening repast (*cena*) and not a meal to which guests were usually invited: Balsdon (1969: 25). The phrase therefore amounts to something like an oxymoron. (I owe this point to Emily Gowers: for the ideology of eating at Rome, see her *The Loaded Table: Representations of Food in Roman Literature*, Oxford 1993).

furiosam vinulentiam tuam: one of the main vices that Cicero ascribes to Antony is over-indulgence, in particular when it comes to booze. His compulsive desire for intoxication is symbolic of his lack of self-control and moderation throughout the *Philippics*. See *Phil.* 2.68 (*vinulentus*), 6.4 and 12.26 (*vinulentia*), 13.31 (*obrutus vino*), 5.24 (*semper ebrium*) with Evans (2008: 69). See further above 227–28. The *furiosus* (as noun) is a legal category in Rome, dating back to the 12 Tables: as opposed to the phrase *mente captus*, which referred to someone in a permanent state of mental insanity, *furiosus* was the label for a lunatic who experienced periods of lucidity.

tua ista detrimenta sunt, illa [detrimenta sunt] **nostra**: Cicero again uses chiasmus (*tua : ista :: illa : nostra*, with *tua* and *nostra* in predicative position) around the central term *detrimenta* to differentiate (and keep firmly apart) the harm caused by Antony to himself and the harm he causes to the rest of Rome's civic community (evoked by means of the self-identifying *nostra*). *ista* refers back to Antony's over-indulgence in food and drink; *illa* refers forward to his embezzlement of public funds.

---

60   Cf. Batstone's critique of what he considers a fallacious grammatical category at https://classics.osu.edu/Undergraduate-Studies/Latin-Program/Grammar/mood/subjunctive/independent-subjunctive

agrum Campanum, qui cum de vectigalibus [agris] **eximebatur ut militibus daretur, tamen infligi magnum rei publicae vulnus putabamus, hunc tu compransoribus tuis et collusoribus dividebas**: *agrum Campanum*, picked up again by the demonstrative pronoun *hunc* after the intervening *qui*-clause, is the accusative object of *dividebas*. It is also the antecedent of *qui*. The relative clause does not present problems initially ('... which, when it was taken out of the public revenues to be given to soldiers...'), but its syntax goes awry from *tamen* onwards, when Cicero suddenly abandons his construction (= anacoluthon). What he wants to say is: 'Even when part of the *ager Campanus* was taken out of the revenue-generating lands to be given over to veterans (Pompey's in 59 BCE; Caesar's in 45 BCE), we nevertheless believed that a grave wound was being inflicted on the commonwealth (though we can concede that settling veterans is a worthy cause); but Antony was parcelling out this public land to his table mates and gambling buddies!'

agrum Campanum... hunc tu compransoribus tuis et collusoribus dividebas: the *ager Campanus* ('domain of Capua' — as Mayor (1861: 142) points out '*Campanus* (not *Capuanus*) is the adjective for "Capuan"') is the Capuan territory that the Romans had sequestered as public land after the Second Punic War (a conflict in which Capua had sided with Hannibal). The tax levied on its usage provided a steady source of public revenue until Caesar turned the land into allotments for Pompey's veterans in 59 and his own in 45 BCE.

qui cum de vectigalibus [agris] **eximebatur**: a temporal *cum*-clause referring to the gradual distribution of the public land around Capua to veterans over the past fifteen years. *vectigalis ager* = land in the possession of the Roman people (as opposed to private patrimony) that yielded public income.

ut militibus daretur: technically speaking, the land was given to ex-soldiers or veterans at the end of their service as a retirement settlement.

mimos dico et mimas, patres conscripti, in agro Campano collocatos: *dico* introduces an indirect statement with *mimos* and *mimas* as subject accusatives and *collocatos* (*esse*) as infinitive. The jarring juxtaposition of *mimas* ('mime-actresses') and the vocative *patres conscripti* ('senators') rams home the social perversions perpetrated by Antony. Mimes were as popular as they were disreputable: actors in general carried a stigma (*infamia*) in Roman society. Cicero expresses his outrage at Antony's consorting with a star of the mime-stage as early as 49. In the early stages of the civil war he writes to Atticus from Cumae about Antony's peculiar entourage of girlfriends and toy-boys (*Att.* 10.10.4 = 201 SB; 3 May 49):

> hic [sc. Antonius] tamen Cytherida secum lectica aperta portat, alteram uxorem. septem praeterea coniunctae lecticae amicarum; et sunt amicorum.

> [But Antony is carrying Cytheris around with him in an open litter, a second wife. Seven other litters are attached, containing mistresses; and there are some containing friends.]

Earlier on in *Philippic* 2, he claims that Antony had mimes and pimps in train already as tribune of the people (§ 58):

> Vehebatur in essedo tribunus plebis; lictores laureati antecedebant, inter quos aperta lectica mima portabatur, quam ex oppidis municipales homines honesti, obviam necessario prodeuntes, non noto illo et mimico nomine, sed Volumniam consalutabant. Sequebatur raeda cum lenonibus, comites nequissimi; reiecta mater amicam impuri fili tamquam nurum sequebatur.

> [As tribune of the plebs, he used to ride about in a two-wheeled carriage; lictors decked with laurel led the way, and in their midst a mime actress was carried in an open litter. Respectable folk from the country towns, who were obliged to come out and meet the cortege, greeted her not by her well-known stage name but as 'Volumnia'. Then followed a carriage full of pimps, Antonius' utterly worthless entourage. His mother, relegated to the rear, followed her worthless son's mistress as if a daughter-in-law.]

Antony's alleged provision of financial welfare for the dregs of society at the expense of the commonwealth's coffers remains a source of invective also in later *Philippics*. See e.g. *Phil.* 8.26: *cavet mimis, aleatoribus, lenonibus, Cafoni etiam et Saxae cavet, quos centuriones pugnaces et lacertosos inter mimorum et mimarum greges conlocavit* ('he provides for mimes, gamblers, and pimps; he provides even for Cafo and Saxa, pugnacious and brawny centurions whom he has posted amid his herd of male and female mimes').

quid iam querar de agro Leontino? quoniam quidem hae quondam arationes Campana et Leontina in populi Romani patrimonio grandiferae et fructuosae ferebantur: Cicero moves on to another region that Antony used for land distributions, the *ager Leontinus* in Sicily, which he already mentioned in § 43. Unlike the earlier question, which functions as *praeteritio*, Cicero here answers his own question: 'Why should I at this point grumble about the *ager Leontinus*? Because — needless to say (*quidem*) — (both of) these arable regions of Campania and Leontini used to be contained within the inheritance of the Roman people, as (particularly) fertile and profitable'. Cicero underscores the outrageous misappropriation of public lands by means of a querulous *qu*-alliteration (*quoniam quidem... quondam*, picking up on *querar*) and lexical grand-standing (reinforced by etymological and alliterative play) in *grandi-ferae et fructuosae ferebantur*. The sense of *ferebantur* is '... used to be contained within...': *OLD* s.v. *fero* 12b. The compound adjective *grandiferae* (consisting of the adjective *grandis* 'great in volume', and the adjectival suffix *-fer, -fera, -ferum*, from *fero*, denoting 'carrying, bearing, bringing') refers to the large volume of produce that the land yielded, whereas *fructuosae* designates the correspondingly large tithes for Rome's coffers.

quoniam: a causal conjunction construed with the indicative in direct discourse.

hae ... arationes Campana et Leontina: 'these arable lands of Campania and Leontini'. Note that the two attributes *Campana* and *Leontina* are both in the singular, though *arationes*, the noun each modifies (the subject of *ferebantur*) is in the plural: 'those arable lands, i.e. that of Campania and that of Leontini'.

arationes... grandiferae et fructuosae: *aratio* is initially the action of ploughing and sowing the field and then came to refer also to 'arable land' (as opposed to lands used for pasture and forests).

in populi Romani patrimonio: 'in the possession of the Roman people'

quondam: the adverb specifies a point in time in contrast to the present, which may be located in the past (as here) or in the future.

medico tria milia iugerum [dedisti]**: quid** [dedisses] **si te sanasset? rhetori duo** [milia iugerum dedisti]**: quid** [dedisses] **si te disertum facere potuisset?**: Cicero moves on to professionals in Antony's entourage (an anonymous doctor and his teacher in rhetoric, Sextus Clodius), to whom he gave lavish handouts for no services rendered, asking rhetorically in two past counterfactual conditions how much they would have received if they had actually done their job, i.e. healing Antony of his manifest insanity and teaching him how to speak properly. The amount of land Antony parcelled out to his associates is huge, given that veterans received allotments in the range of 10–12 *iugera*.

sanasset: the syncopated form of the third person singular pluperfect subjunctive active (*sana|vi|sset*).

sed ad iter Italiamque redeamus: for some moments Cicero's discourse had jumped to the land distributions around the Sicilian town of Leontini. He now exhorts himself (*redeamus* is exhortative subjunctive: 'let us…') to return to Antony's journey through Italy (*ad iter Italiamque* is perhaps best understood as a hendiadys).

§ 102: Antony Colonized a Colony!

In republican Rome, founding a new colony was a complex political act that followed a detailed political and religious script.[61] In Rome itself, this included a senatorial decree, the passing of a law by a legislative assembly, the election of colonial commissioners, the enlistment of the colonists, and the official departure to the settlement location (*deductio*). On site, the officials would take the auspices, demarcate the urban core of the new settlement with a special plow with a bronze plowshare by plowing the so-called *sulcus primigenius* ('primeval furrow') around the site of the new city, and purify the colonists in a ritual called *lustrum*, thereby also constituting them as a new civic community grounded in the new urban settlement.

Respect for ritual protocols and political procedures was deeply engrained in Rome's cultural imaginary, and every magistrate was well advised to abide as far as possible and/or convenient by the system of rules that governed public affairs, simply to avoid trouble down the road. And thus, when Antony had the idea of re-establishing a colony at Capua to settle veterans, a territory that Caesar had used for the same purpose, he seems to have checked with Cicero, as an expert in augural law and a consular, whether the plan would run into religious objections. Cicero's reply was that, from the point of view of religious law, it was not permitted to found another colony in the territory of an already existing one; what *was* feasible was to add new settlers to the colony already in place. This was probably not quite the response

---

61   For the following see Gargola (1995: 75–76).

Antony was hoping for, but he seems to have accepted Cicero's ruling — for Capua. But when his mind turned to another location in the vicinity — Casilinum — , which had also been used for a colonial settlement by Caesar, he decided to dispense with consultation and simply went ahead, founding (it seems) an entirely new colony in the territory of the old one, essentially ignoring Cicero's ruling on Capua (which, so Cicero argues, of course applied to Casilinum, as to any other location, as well).

Deduxisti coloniam Casilinum, quo Caesar ante [coloniam] **deduxerat**: Cicero uses verbal spacing and an implied chiasmus to reinforce the contrast between Antony and Caesar — (a) *deduxisti* (b) *coloniam* (c) *Casilinum* :: (c) *quo* (b) [*coloniam*] (a) *deduxerat*. The up-front placement of the verb *deduxisti* inverts the natural word order, which is on display in the relative clause, and thus enacts Antony's seemingly perverse upending of Caesar's settlement.

Casilinum: an accusative of direction. Casilinum is a town in Campania, located about 3 miles to the North-West of Capua on the river Volturnus at the crossroads of the Via Appia and the Via Latina. In 59 BCE, Caesar established a colony of Pompey's veterans there, which Antony 're-founded' during his trip to Southern Italy in April / May 44 BCE.

ante: adverbial.

consuluisti me per litteras de Capua tu quidem, sed idem de Casilino respondissem: possesne, ubi colonia esset, eo coloniam novam iure deducere: Cicero here deviates from reporting events in strict chronological order: (i) *consuluisti … tu quidem*: he concedes that Antony consulted him about establishing a colony at Capua (though not with regard to Casilinum); (ii) *sed idem … respondissem* is a truncated past counterfactual condition: 'if you *had* consulted me about Casilinum (*si me consuluisses*), I would have given you the same response as I did with regard to Capua'; (iii) *possesne … deducere*: now Cicero specifies what precisely Antony consulted him about. The following sentence (*negavi … rescripsi*) contains his answer.

quidem: concessive ('you, it is true, did consult me…')

idem ... respondissem: *idem* is neuter accusative — the object of *respondissem* (in the pluperfect subjunctive as the apodosis of the (implied) past counterfactual condition).

possesne ... deducere: a question (flagged by the enclitic *-ne*) in indirect discourse (hence the subjunctive) introduced by *consuluisti*. The second person singular is generic: 'can one...'

per litteras: still used as a pretentious Latin tag in contemporary English ('by means of letters', 'through written correspondence'). The correspondence — if it existed — has not survived. (It's fishy that Antony, who was an augur himself, felt the need to turn to Cicero for advice given that he could have anticipated an uncooperative response. It's bound to make you think... — not for the first time, the invective stance is wearing all too thin?)

negavi in eam coloniam quae esset auspicato deducta, dum esset incolumis, coloniam novam iure deduci: colonos novos ascribi posse rescripsi: Cicero's finicky reply drew a distinction between founding a whole new colony (*colonia*) within the territory of a previously establish colony (not to be done) and enrolling new settlers (*coloni novi*) in the existing colony (quite possible). Instead of subsuming his negative ruling on the new colony within his response, Cicero presents it upfront as a self-standing main clause (*negavi* thus correlates with *deduxisti* and *consuluisti*), governing an indirect statement with *coloniam novam* as subject accusative and *deduci* as (passive) infinitive (hence the subjunctives in the *quae*- and *dum*-clauses). A second main clause follows, with *rescripsi* as verb governing the indirect statement with *colonos novos* as subject accusative and *posse* as infinitive.

quae esset auspicato deducta: as Ramsey (2003: 311) points out, the adverb *auspicato* 'is in origin an ablative absolute comprising the perfect participle of *auspicor*'. Its meaning here is 'with due regard to the auspices', i.e. after due consultation of the will of the gods, which manifested their approval.

dum esset incolumis: *incolumis* here has a technical, legal-constitutional sense: while an already established colony is 'fully functional' / 'in good condition' *as* a colony, its territory is unavailable for a new foundation. (Cicero's phrasing implies that the territory of a foundation that has collapsed could be re-colonized.)

ascribi: present passive infinitive: 'to be added to — and hence enrolled in — the already existing list of settlers'. The point is that these colonists could join the established community, but were not permitted to found one of their own.

rescripsi: *rescribere* ('to reply') here has a technical sense: '"Rescripts" were issued by authorities in reply to questions raised with them, giving advice or rulings' (Lacey 1986: 231).

tu autem insolentia elatus omni auspiciorum iure turbato Casilinum coloniam deduxisti, quo [colonia] **erat paucis annis ante deducta, ut vexillum tolleres, ut aratrum circumduceres**: in forceful antithesis (cf. the contemptuous opening *tu autem*), Cicero now presents Antony as disregarding Cicero's expert advice on the technicalities of colonial settlements. To add insult to injury, Antony (so Cicero claims) took an active hand in the ritual procedures of the new foundation.

insolentia elatus: *elatus* (the perfect passive participle of *effero*) modifies *tu*: the sense seems to be: 'raised above consideration for augural law because of your arrogance'.

omni auspiciorum iure turbato: an ablative absolute, even though the person who does the confounding of the augural law is Antony, the subject of the main clause.

Casilinum coloniam deduxisti: *Casilinum* is another accusative of direction (without preposition).

paucis annis ante: ablative of time followed by temporal adverb: 'a few years previously'. The reference is to Caesar's foundation during his consulship in 59 BCE.

ut vexillum tolleres: *vexillum tollere* is formed on the analogy *signa tollere*, which, in the sense of 'to raise up [sc. by planting them into the ground]' means 'to strike camp'. See Haynes (2013: 218): 'The standards are … the symbols par excellence of the Roman military community.

In times of peace, they lie at the heart of the camp; in times of war, at the heart of the battle force. ... The actions of the standard-bearers marked the pitching or striking of camp; so much so, in fact, that the term *signa tollere* came to represent striking camp in Latin speech'. But it could also mean 'to raise them up [sc. by removing them from the ground]' in order to march on. The ambiguity may be deliberate insofar as Antony does both: he moves the old Caesarian standards and plants the new ones. Perhaps the reference is specifically to the censorial rites performed during the new foundation at Casilinum, which included (i) taking of the auspices, (ii) summoning of the people according to centuries for purification, (iii) the leading of three sacrificial victims (a bull, a boar, and a ram: *suovetaurilia*) around the assembled citizen body, (iv) the actual sacrifice complete with vow for its repetition the following year if public welfare continued, and, finally, (v) the return of the citizen body into the city led by the censor with a standard or *vexillum*. See Gargola (1995: 77) with reference to Varro, *de Lingua Latina* 6.93: ... *censor exercitum centuriato constituit quinquennalem, cum lustrare et in urbem ad vexillum ducere debet* ('... the censor arranges in centuries the citizen-army for a period of five years, when he must ceremonially purify it and lead it to the city under its standards').

cuius quidem vomere portam Capuae paene perstrinxisti, ut florentis coloniae territorium minueretur: *cuius* is a connecting relative (= *et eius*), referring back to *aratrum*: 'And indeed [emphatic *quidem* after connecting relative: *OLD* s.v. 2b], with its share [i.e. the share of the plough] you all but (*paene*) grazed the gate of Capua...' Antony seems to have used this opportunity to get his own back for the hostile treatment he received from the city: see above § 100. But whether 'Mark Antony personally directed the *lustrum* and plowed the furrow for the colony at Casilinum in 44' (Gargola (1995: 180), following Cicero) remains a matter of speculation.

§ 103: Antony's Enrichment Activities

Rome's civil-war years saw a drastic redistribution of wealth, as the victorious warlords oversaw the confiscation of property and land owned by those who ended up on the losing side of history. It was one of the ways by which the winners were able to reward the loyalty of their supporters, many of whom (according to Cicero) joined Caesar's cause precisely in the expectation that it would prove financially beneficial. As he says in *Philippic* 4.9 about Antony and his followers:

> sed spes rapiendi atque praedandi obcaecat animos eorum, quos non bonorum donatio, non agrorum adsignatio, non illa infinita hasta satiavit; qui sibi urbem, qui bona et fortunas civium ad praedam proposuerunt.
>
> [But hope of pillage and plunder blind the minds of men whom no gift of property, no assignment of lands, nor that never-ending auction [sc. of property confiscated from Pompey and his supporters] has sated; men that have set before themselves for plunder the city and the goods and fortunes of its citizens.]

In this paragraph and the following two, Cicero focuses on the property of Marcus Terentius Varro, in part because Varro, in terms of literary standing in late republican Rome second only to Cicero and the acknowledged 'polymath of the Roman World', was a particularly illustrious Pompeian, whose live(lihood) and property came under threat in the civil war period.[62] Here are some brief biographical details:

---

62 For Varro see Dahlmann (1935), Rawson (1985), Dix and Houston (2006: 673–75) (on his library), Drummond (2013), and, most recently, Butterfield (2015).

- c. 116: born into an established senatorial family
- Education: wide-ranging, including in Greek culture (L. Aelius, the Academic philosopher Antiochus)
- 67: commander in Pompey's campaign against the pirates
- 49: declares for Pompey and commands the republican forces in Spain
- 48: surrenders to Caesar near Corduba, gets pardoned and released; he joins the Pompeian forces again at Dyrrhachium; after Pompey's defeat at Pharsalus, Varro (just like Cicero) gives up active resistance and withdraws from public life
- 47: while Caesar is in Egypt, Antony tries to get his hands on Varro's villa near Casinum, but Caesar objects
- 45: reconciliation with Caesar upon Caesar's return to Rome; gets put in charge of establishing and stocking what would have been Rome's first public libraries with Greek and Roman books, a project that never came to fruition.[63] See Suetonius, *Life of Julius Caesar* 44:

  Nam de ornanda instruendaque urbe, item de tuendo ampliandoque imperio plura ac maiora in dies destinabat: ... bibliothecas Graecas Latinasque quas maximas posset publicare data Marco Varroni cura comparandarum ac digerendarum.

  [In particular, for the adornment and convenience of the city, also for the protection and extension of the Empire, he formed more projects and more extensive ones every day: ... to open to the public the greatest possible libraries of Greek and Latin books, assigning to Marcus Varro the charge of procuring and classifying them.]

- 43: Antony has him put on the list of the proscribed — he gets spared Cicero's fate through the intervention of Fufius Calenus who manages to hide Varro from the henchmen (Appian, *Bellum Civile* 4.203); his library, though, gets plundered[64]
- 27: dies, 90 years of age

Varro was one of the most learned men of Rome, the antiquarian par excellence, who produced a massive literary *oeuvre*. One of his writings,

---

63   Credit for setting up the first public library in Rome goes to Asinius Pollio.
64   Aulus Gellius, *Noctes Atticae* 3.10.17, with Hemelrijk (1999: 257, n. 168) and Houston (2014: 31–32).

the *De Re Rustica* (3.5) contains a detailed description of his property at Casinum (the dialogue was written in the 30s, so Caesar must have ensured that he got it back). §§ 103–05 revolve around this estate, with Cicero, for invective purposes, deliberately and confusingly skipping back and forth between two occasions several years apart:

(i) Sometime in 47 BCE, Antony attempted to confiscate Varro's property. The attempt failed because Caesar, who was fighting in Alexandria at the time and whom Antony consulted by letter, withheld his approval.

(ii) During his sojourn in Southern Italy in April / May 44 BCE, Antony and his entourage visited Varro's villa and enjoyed some (enforced?) hospitality.

What does Cicero make of this?

- § 103a: *Ab hac perturbatione … liberavisti*: reference to the visit of 44 BCE, but with the (false) insinuation that Antony came to confiscate the property (as he had tried to do in 47 BCE)

- § 103b: *Varronis quidem … praeconis audivit*: rejection of the notion (held by nobody) that any part of Varro's property was ever confiscated and sold at auction

- § 103c: *misisse … magnum fuit*: reference to Antony's unsuccessful attempt to confiscate Varro's property back in 47 BCE

- § 104a: *quis vero audivit … detractam*: renewed rejection of the notion (held by nobody) that any part of Varro's property was ever confiscated and sold at auction

- § 104b: *quid? si etiam scripsit ad te Caesar … temeritatis tuae*: renewed reference to Antony's unsuccessful attempt to confiscate Varro's property back in 47 BCE

- § 104c–105a: *At quam multos dies … scorta inter matres familias versabantur*: description of the disgraceful conduct of Antony and his mates during their visit at Varro's villa in 44 BCE

Put differently, Cicero uses an initial reference to Antony's visit at Varro's villa in 44 BCE to slip back in time and rehearse the tussle over ownership that happened in 47 BCE. This enables him (*a*) to draw, yet again, a sharp contrast between Caesar and Antony; (*b*) to recall a failure by Antony; (*c*) to insinuate that during his recent visit Antony behaved *as if* he owned the property.

Ab hac perturbatione religionum advolas in M. Varronis, sanctissimi atque integerrimi viri, fundum Casinatem: Cicero already relied on *advolare* for the purpose of negative characterization in § 50. *ad* + *volare* — literally 'to fly towards', but also used in military contexts to signify 'to rush to the attack', 'to swoop down on' — generates the dehumanizing image of Antony rapaciously 'swooping in on and snatching up' Varro's estate in his greedy claws, with the significant hyperbaton *in … fundum* highlighting both the distance and the speed of the descent. Positioned neatly in-between the two prepositional phrases *ab…* and *in …*, *advolas* further suggests restless agitation of the compulsive kind: Antony seems beset by the obsession to perpetrate one outrage after another in quick succession. When Roman aristocrats travelled in foreign parts, they would routinely rely on the hospitality extended by senatorial peers, even those with whom relations were fraught. So it is not at all unusual that Antony and his entourage, while in the area, stayed a while at Varro's villa. Cicero himself records a similar visit paid to him by Caesar in December 45 in a letter to Atticus (*Att.* 13.52 = 353 SB), noting that Caesar is not the kind of guest one is keen to host twice.

M. Varronis, sanctissimi atque integerrimi viri: embedded within *in … fundum Casinatem* is the name and a longish appreciation in apposition of the victim. Cicero hails the moral integrity and unblemished record of Marcus Terentius Varro in superlatives. The use of *vir* (especially in the context of the metaphorical assimilation of Antony to a monstrous bird of prey) is not accidental either: 'Cicero's speeches make it evident that *vir* is a term of utmost respect which he applies to Rome's foremost senators and magistrates. That the word is not to be thrown about at random is evident from a letter to Atticus about the late dictator in which Cicero bristles that he heard "that tyrant" called *clarissimum virum* in a public meeting (*Att.* 15.20.2). To Cicero, a man who has misused his power is unworthy of the time-honoured epithet' (Santoro L'Hoir 1992: 13).

quo iure, quo ore [advolas]**? 'Eodem** [iure / ore]**', inquies, 'quo in heredum L. Rubri** [praedia advolavi / invasi]**, quo in heredum L. Turseli praedia** [advolavi / invasi]**, quo in reliquas innumerabiles possessiones** [advolavi / invasi]**'**: By suspending with further verbs after the *advolas* of the previous sentence, but continuing the syntax of '[elided verb] + *in* + accusative' in Antony's imagined response, Cicero has Antony buy into the idiom of his attack and thus agree with the accusation of greedy land-grabbing. (Mayor (1861: 144) suggests that a 'more general notion' such as *invasi* ought to be supplied from *advolas*.) Cicero here sets up an analogy between Antony's insolence in sequestering the property of Varro and the unrestrained greed that informed his desire to benefit from legacies, to the point of short-changing their next of kin. Lucius Rubrius and Lucius Turselius, it seems, composed testaments that left their landed property (*praedia*: neuter accusative plural after the preposition *in*) to Antony, instead of their natural heirs: both *heredum* (genitive plural of *heres*) depend on *praedia* (the first implied), *L. Rubri* depends on the first *heredum*, *L. Turseli* on the second: '… I snatched up the properties of the heirs of L. Rubrius and the heirs of L. Turselius'.

quo iure, quo ore?: the two questions pull in opposite direction: *quo iure* ('by what right?') requires a negative answer ('you had no right at all!'), whereas *quo ore* ('with what face?') issues a protest against the expression on Antony's face (a mixture of greed and cheek?) he wore during the confiscation. Nisbet (1960: 103) notes that *quo ore?* 'does not combine well with *quo iure?*, and the difficulty is increased by the following sentence'. He suggests reading *quo more?*.

inquies: second person singular future indicative active ('you will say').

L. Rubri … L. Turseli: we know from §§ 40–41 that Lucius Rubrius was an inhabitant of Casinum; perhaps the same applies to Lucius Turselius as well, though the two individuals are otherwise unknown.

et si ab hasta [in eas possessiones invasisti / advolavisti ‖ eas possessiones emisti]**, valeat hasta, valeant tabulae modo** [ut sint tabulae] **Caesaris, non tuae,** [eae] **quibus debuisti, non** [eae] **quibus tu te liberavisti**: 'If you took possession of them at a public auction, let the auction stand / be valid, let the sale-books stand — only provided they are Caesar's, not your own, those through which you were in debt, not those through which you freed yourself of debt'. The sentence is difficult, not least because of frequent ellipsis, and best tackled bit by bit:

- *et si ... valeat hasta*: the opening conditional sequence is mixed, with an (implied) perfect indicative in the protasis (positing a past fact), followed in the apodosis by a third-person present hortatory subjunctive (*valeat*) to express a concession that Cicero is making *now*. The verb and related accusatives in the *si*-clause are again elided and need to be provided from context. Mayor (1861: 144) supplies *invasisti*, Ramsey (2003: 313) *emisti*.

- *valeant ... tuae*: a second third-person present hortatory subjunctive (*valeant*) segues in asyndeton, followed by a highly elliptical qualification introduced by *modo*. For *modo ut...* = 'only provided that...', also with ellipsis of verb, see *OLD* s.v. *modo* 4.

- *quibus debuisti ... liberavisti*: at the end of the sentence, the (implied) antecedents (*eae*) of the two relative pronouns *quibus* stand in apposition to *tabulae*, with *quibus debuisti* picking up *tabulae Caesaris*, which registered Antony in deep debt, and *quibus tu te liberavisti* picking up *tabulae tuae*, showing Antony debt-free owing to his illegal enrichments.

ab hasta: 'from the public auction of confiscated property'. At a public auction a spear was stuck in the ground — the *hasta* thus 'is the characteristic sign of auctions and hence functions as a metonymy for the allotment of possessions by auction' (Manuwald 2007: 515).

valeant tabulae: on the meaning of *tabulae*, see Denniston (1926: 164): '*Tabulae* means here the bills of sale at an auction; but the mention of the word suggests one of its other meanings, "accounts", and Cicero goes off at a tangent: "When I uphold the validity of 'tabulae', I mean Caesar's accounts, in which you are entered as owing money for the property of Pompey which you bought and never paid for; not the accounts which you falsified at the temple of Ops, in order to get money to free yourself from debt"'.

Varronis quidem Casinatem fundum quis venisse dicit, quis hastam istius venditionis vidit, quis vocem praeconis audivit?: a tricolon, reinforced by the triple anaphora of *quis*, of three pugnacious rhetorical questions. *dicit* governs an indirect statement with *fundum* as subject accusative and *venisse* as verb. The placement of *Varronis quidem Casinatem fundum* before the interrogative pronoun *quis* brings out the full contrastive force of *quidem*: 'As far as the estate of Varro at Casinum is concerned, who says that it was ever up for sale…?'

venisse: perfect infinitive of *veneo*, active in form but passive in meaning ('to be for sale'), NOT of *venio* ('to come') even though the forms are indistinguishable. *veneo* functions as the passive to *vendo* ('to sell').

misisse te dicis Alexandriam [aliquem] **qui emeret a Caesare; ipsum enim expectare magnum fuit**: *dicis* introduces an indirect statement with *te* as subject accusative and *misisse* as verb. The accusative object (and antecedent of the relative pronoun *qui*) is implied. *Alexandriam* is an accusative of direction (without preposition since Alexandria is a city). The subjunctive in the relative clause (*emeret*) expresses purpose. Cicero follows up this imagined interjection and explanation by Antony with a highly sarcastic meta-comment set up by *enim* (Kroon 1995: 180) that mockingly 'explains' the apparent motivation for Antony's dispatch of an agent to Alexandria: 'it would of course (*enim*) have been difficult to wait for Caesar['s return]!'

ipsum: referring to Caesar.

magnum fuit: for the indicative (where the English calls for a subjunctive) see Gildersleeve & Lodge 167–68: 'The Latin language expresses *possibility* and *power*, *obligation* and *necessity*, and abstract relations generally, as *facts*; whereas, our translation often *implies the failure to realise*'. One of their examples, Cicero, *de Natura Deorum* 2.159, offers a good parallel to our passage: *longum est persequi utilitate asinorum* — 'it would be tedious to rehearse the useful qualities of asses (I will not do it)'.

§ 104: *Animal House*

Cicero continues to insinuate, wrongly, that Antony, during his recent sojourn in Southern Italy, tried to stage another hostile take-over of Varro's villa at Casinum. During his visit, it appeared as if the property had changed ownership, from the learned Varro to the loathsome Antony, who turned a house of erudition into a cesspool of vice. In § 104, Cicero focuses on boozing and gambling, including the emetic consequences of over-indulgence. In § 105, he adds sexual debauchery to the portfolio of sins.

Quis vero audivit umquam — nullius autem salus curae pluribus fuit — de fortunis Varronis rem ullam esse detractam?: *audivit* introduces an indirect statement with *rem ullam* as subject accusative and *esse detractam (de…)* as infinitive. The particle *vero* ('in fact') suggests that Cicero's rhetorical question (*quis … audivit?*) operates on the level of commonly acknowledged facts.

nullius autem salus curae pluribus fuit: a double dative construction with *esse*: lit. 'the well-being (*salus*) of no-one (*nullius*: genitive singular of *nullus*) was of concern (*curae*: dative of end / purpose) to more people (*pluribus*: dative of person affected)'; more elegantly: 'no man has a larger number of concerned well-wishers' (Shackleton Bailey). The particle *autem* here has an adversative sense ('no-one has heard, *even though* virtually everyone cared…') and marks the parenthetical status of the sentence as a discrete textual unit in its own right (see Kroon (1995: 270), who defines the discourse function of *autem* as 'indication of the discrete status of a text segment in relation to its preceding verbal or non-verbal context').

de fortunis Varronis: the basic meaning of *fortuna* is 'fortune', but in the plural (as here) it often refers to 'fortunate material circumstances', i.e. 'wealth', 'property'.

quid? si etiam scripsit ad te Caesar ut redderes, quid satis potest dici de tanta impudentia?: *quid?* ('Well then') is often used as a transitional device. *si etiam* (followed by the perfect indicative *scripsit*, which indicates that Cicero is reporting a fact) is best translated with 'as' or 'since'. The reference to Caesar's intervention on Varro's behalf sets up the rhetorical question *quid ... impudentia?*, which consists of a well-known topos, i.e. the impossibility to do a real-life phenomenon (here Antony's insolence) justice in discourse.

ut redderes: *scripsit* implies that Caesar's letter contained a directive to Antony to return the estate: the *ut*-clause is one of indirect command. Cicero here gives us Caesar's (negative) response to Antony's enquiry mentioned at the end of the previous paragraph whether he could take possession of Varro's villa.

quid satis potest dici de tanta impudentia?: lit. 'what that is sufficient (*satis*) can be said about such impudence?' ~ 'what discourse can do such impudence justice?' *satis* here functions as a noun and is the predicative complement to the subject of the sentence (*quid*).

remove gladios parumper illos quos videmus: iam intelleges aliam causam esse hastae Caesaris, aliam [causam] **confidentiae et temeritatis tuae**: Cicero's imaginary interactivity (*remove* is an imperative addressed to Antony) here includes the setting: *gladios ... illos* stands metonymically for Antony's armed henchmen that Cicero imagines can be glimpsed (*videmus*) as they crowd threateningly around the senate house while he delivers his speech. In Cicero an imperative [*remove*] in (asyndetic) parataxis with a future [*intelleges*] often stands in for a conditional sequence ('Remove / If you remove those swords..., at that moment (*iam*) you will realize...'): see Mayor (1861: 145) citing Madvig, and Ramsey (2003: 121). *causam* here has the technical sense of 'legal situation / position' (*OLD* s.v. *causa* 14b): Cicero contrasts the procedural legality of Caesar's auctions (*hastae Caesaris*) with the arbitrary insolence of Antony's illegal wealth-grab, pursued by violent means. But the distinction is of Cicero's own making: it was, for instance, Caesar who sold the confiscated property of Pompey — to Antony.

confidentiae et temeritatis tuae: the company of *temeritas*, which is unambiguously negative, clarifies the meaning of *confidentia*, which can have a positive ('self-confidence') or — as here — a negative ('audacity') sense.

non enim te dominus modo illis sedibus sed quivis amicus, vicinus, hospes, procurator arcebit: translate as follows: *non modo dominus sed etiam quivis amicus ... procurator te illis sedibus arcebit*. In addition to the owner (*dominus*), any lesser stakeholders will (now) also ward off Antony from Varro's property. (Cicero lists four categories in asyndetic sequence, designed to suggest comprehensive hostility towards Antony in the area: friend – neighbour – guest – manager.) In line with his deliberate blurring of the confiscation attempt in 47 BCE and his more recent visit in the spring of 44 BCE, Cicero leaves it ambiguous what precisely 'warding off Antony' implies: protection against wrongful repossession or refusal to extend hospitality.

illis sedibus: an ablative of separation with *arcebit*.

procurator: 'the agent of an absent owner, who had full power to act in his behalf' (Mayor 1861: 145).

at quam multos dies in ea villa turpissime es perbacchatus! ab hora tertia bibebatur, ludebatur, vomebatur: Cicero identifies Antony as the lead-reveller (*es perbacchatus*: the prefix *per-* intensifies the activity) before continuing with an asyndetic tricolon of impersonal passives to capture the carousing Antony and his cronies engaged in, from 9 o'clock in the morning onwards: drinking, gambling, vomiting. Cicero leaves it open whether the frequent regurgitation breaks he posits were spontaneous (the result of binge-drinking) or deliberately induced, as part of excessive banqueting, or both.

multos dies: accusative of duration of time.

o tecta ipsa misera, 'quam dispari domino' — quamquam quo modo iste dominus? — sed tamen quam ab dispari tenebantur!: Cicero personifies the house by addressing it directly and metonymically: *tecta*, the roof, stands in for the whole. He ratchets up the pathos by citing the beginning of a tragic verse that laments a mismatch (cf. *dispari*) between a house (*domus*) and its owner (*dominus*). Given that labeling Antony 'the owner' (*dominus*) of Varro's estate is incorrect, he feels the need to follow up with a parenthetical gloss (*quamquam … dominus?*), which recalls Antony's unsuccessful attempts at confiscating Varro's property a few years back, before reiterating the opening words of the tragic citation, now adjusted to the situation and integrated into the syntax of his sentence: *dispari* [*homine*], endowed with the preposition *ab*, becomes an ablative of agency with *tenebantur*; the subject are the *tecta* (nominative neuter plural).

The theme of mismatches between houses and their occupants had a personal and a political relevance for Cicero. In 62 BCE he bought a house of illustrious pedigree located on the Palatine Hill for 3.5 million sesterces, which many thought was too grandiose for a *homo novus*. And in the civil wars many striking estates changed owners through confiscation and enforced auctions. In the eyes of many, many a new owner did not match the quality of his new property. For Cicero, the most blatant mismatch concerned Antony's residency in the house of Pompey the Great, which he laments at length at *Philippic* 2.65–69, to the point of pitying the very walls of the house because of the desecrations and debaucheries they were forced to witness (69: *me quidem miseret parietum ipsorum atque tectorum* — 'For my part, I pity the very walls and roof'). Here he treats Antony's presence in Varro's house in a similar spirit.

In his contemporary treatise *On Duties* (*de Officiis*), Cicero includes a little disquisition on what *domus* is fitting for a leading statesman (1.138: *dicendum est etiam, qualem hominis honorati et principis domum placeat esse*). As a basic principle he maintains that the inhabitants ought to endow the house with dignity — and despite the hopes of many, it does not work the other way around: 1.139: *ornanda enim est dignitas domo, non ex domo tota quaerenda, nec domo dominus, sed domino domus honestanda est*. He then goes on to quote from the same tragedy as in *Philippic* 2:[65]

Odiosum est enim, cum a praetereuntibus dicitur:
    O domus antiqua et quam dispari
    dominare domino
quod quidem his temporibus in multis licet dicere.

---

65   For the 'diachronic inventory of owners' as a widespread practice in late republican Rome, with specific reference to *Phil.* 2.67–68, 104, and *Off.* 139 see Harnett (2017: 121–22).

[For it is unpleasant, when passers-by remark: 'O good old house, alas! how different the owner who now owns you!' And in these times that may be said of many a house!]

his temporibus refers to the recent period of civil warfare, confiscations, and repossessions — though Cicero must have been quite aware of the fact that others may well have applied the verses to his own residency on the Palatine Hill.

studiorum enim suorum receptaculum M. Varro [esse] **voluit illud, non libidinum deversorium**: M. Varro is the subject of the sentence, *voluit* the verb. The supplementary infinitive *esse* is implied. The deictic pronoun *illud* refers to his estate at Casinum, which Antony defiled by turning it from its original purpose as inspirational retreat for Varro's literary activities (*studia*) into a cesspool of vice. See McGinn (2004: 18): 'Other terms for lower-class lodging, such as *deversorium* and *meritorium*, were sometimes explicitly associated with the practice of prostitution, that is, as words for brothels … See Cic. *Phil*. 2.104–05, where the former villa of Varro becomes a *libidinum deversorium*, and thus the haunt of both male and female prostitutes, as well as more respectable debauchees'. For the meaning of *deversorium* = 'lodging house that provided a place where travellers could have a meal, a drink, and a bed for the night', see Holleran (2012: 140–41).

§ 105: *Animal House*: The Sequel

Cicero continues to lambast Antony for defiling Varro's domicile of learning, contrasting Varro's intellectual achievements across all areas of culture with Antony's obscene indulgence in orgies of booze and sex. Towards the end of the paragraph, he moves on to rake Antony over the coals for his asocial behaviour towards representatives of local communities who came to greet him (as was expected of them when a Roman consul happened to stay in the vicinity).

Quae in illa villa antea dicebantur, quae cogitabantur, quae litteris mandabantur! iura populi Romani, monumenta maiorum, omnis sapientiae ratio omnisque doctrinae: Cicero hails Varro's intellectual achievements in two tricola. First, we get a tricolon of generic verbs (reinforced by the triple anaphora of *quae*), referring to speech (*dicebantur*), thought (*cogitabantur*), and writing (*litteris mandabantur*). Then comes a tricolon of noun phrases in apposition, referring more specifically to a cross-section of Varro's extensive literary *oeuvre*: fifteen books on law the *de Iure Civili* (*iura populi Romani*); a range of antiquarian writings, including his *Antiquitates Rerum Humanarum et Divinarum* in 41 books (*monumenta maiorum*); and the recently completed three books *de Forma Philosophiae* (though *omnis sapientiae ratio omnisque doctrina* may be a generalizing appreciation of Varro's comprehensive learning).

omnis sapientiae ratio omnisque doctrinae: 'systematic comprehension (*ratio*) of every kind of wisdom (*omnis sapientiae*) and every kind of learning (*omnis doctrinae*)'; the *-que* after *omnis* links the two genitive phrases dependent on *ratio*.

at vero te inquilino — non enim domino — personabant omnia vocibus ebriorum, natabant pavimenta vino, madebant parietes [vino], **ingenui pueri cum meritoriis, scorta inter matres familias versabantur**: by contrast to the lofty intellectual pursuits of Varro, with Antony as lodger the house has become a den of iniquity. Note the strongly adversative particle *at*, followed by the consensus-asserting particle *vero*. We first get an asyndetic tricolon of clauses with the verbs in front position (*personabant, natabant, madebant*) that sketch out the impact of Antony's inebriated entourage on the domestic spaces and the architecture — the visitors make an infernal din and slop wine everywhere — before Cicero goes on to provide details of the debaucheries that allegedly took place: in an appalling eradication of social distinctions, free-born boys (*ingenui pueri*) consort with toy-boys for hire (*cum meritoriis*), whores from street-corners (*scorta*) with matrons (*matres familias*). We're hardly going to take Cicero's fanciful description at face value, but cf. Edwards (1993: 188): 'The after-dinner entertainers and the beautiful slave boys who serve the food and wine are often represented as providers of sexual gratification. This was … a costly pleasure'.

te inquilino: a nominal ablative absolute consisting of a personal pronoun (*te*) and a noun (*inquilino*) with no verb. Cicero keeps rubbing it in that Antony, who would have very much liked to be the *dominus* of the house, failed in his attempt at confiscation.

non enim domino [dicam]: Cicero adds a brief gloss on his use of *inquilino* ('lodger'): 'because (*enim*: the particle is explanatory) I won't say "domino"' ('master').

Casino salutatum veniebant, Aquino, Interamna: admissus est nemo: *Casino, Aquino,* and *Interamna* are ablatives of origin: 'people came from…'. Aquinum was located seven miles west, Interamna six miles south of Casinum.

salutatum: a supine expressing purpose: 'to pay their respects'.

iure id quidem [factum est]**; in homine enim turpissimo obsolefiebant dignitatis insignia**: Cicero mockingly approves: 'this (*id*), at any rate (*quidem*), was done with good reason (*iure*)' — and then gives the reason (another explanatory *enim*): 'the marks of rank and distinction were disappearing in this utterly disgraceful human being'. *dignitas* refers to the (official) socio-political rank and standing of Antony, owed to his achievements and his office (he was, after all, consul at the time). Cicero argues that Antony's moral turpitude has rendered any claim to special homage and respect obsolete — and that Antony acts accordingly.

§ 106: Antony Cocooned

After the drunken debaucheries at Varro's villa, Antony made his way back to Rome, shut off from the world in his litter. For a high magistrate of Rome, whom everyone wants to meet and greet, travelling behind closed curtains was in principle a violation of socio-political etiquette, not least since it humiliated the inhabitants of the townships located en route who were keen to see (and curry favour with) the representative of Roman power. There may of course have been perfectly good reasons for an official not to interact with the local population, such as the need for speed or ill health, but a closed litter also reminded people of a funeral procession with the corpse shielded from sight — and this is the association Cicero activates for invective purposes here. Commentators refer to a story attributed to Gaius Gracchus found in Aulus Gellius, *Noctes Atticae* 10.3.5, to illustrate the point about travel habits and the expectations and dynamics that informed face-to-face encounters between Roman magistrates and locals:[66]

> Item Gracchus alio in loco ita dicit: 'Quanta libido quantaque intemperantia sit hominum adulescentium, unum exemplum vobis ostendam. his annis paucis ex Asia missus est qui per id tempus magistratum non ceperat, homo adulescens pro legato. is in lectica ferebatur. ei obviam bubulcus de plebe Venusina advenit et per iocum, cum ignoraret qui ferretur, rogavit num mortuum ferrent. ubi id audivit, lecticam iussit deponi, struppis, quibus lectica deligata erat, usque adeo verberari iussit, dum animam efflavit.'

---

66   The incident occurred between 129 and 125 BCE and is one example of the 'extremely harsh and arbitrary treatment being meted out by Roman magistrates in Italian communities' (Dart 2014: 57) that would fuel the Social War (91–88 BCE).

[Gracchus also in another place speaks as follows: 'I will give you a single example of the lawlessness of our young men, and of their entire lack of self-control. Within the last few years a young man who had not yet held a magisterial office was sent as an envoy from Asia. He was carried in a litter. A herdsman, one of the peasants of Venusia, met him, and not knowing whom they were bearing, asked in jest if they were carrying a corpse. Upon hearing this, the young man ordered that the litter be set down and that the peasant be beaten to death with the thongs by which it was fastened.']

Cum inde Romam proficiscens ad Aquinum accederet, obviam ei processit, ut est frequens municipium, magna sane multitudo: Cicero now traces Antony's return journey back to Rome up the via Latina — and how he treated the representatives of the townships (*municipia*: see below) that he encountered on the way. *obviam* is here construed with the dative: a large number of the inhabitants of Aquinum (*magna sane multitudo* — placed last not least to sharpen the adversative *at iste* at the start of the following sentence) came forth (*processit*) 'to meet him' (*obviam ei*).

Romam proficiscens: *proficiscor* with the straight accusative (as here) means 'to depart for a place, with the intent of entering it', in contrast to *profisciscor* + *ad* + accusative, which means 'to depart for a place, without the intent of entering it'.

municipium: in republican times, the status of *municipium* was given to 'a [pre-existing] self-governing community in Italy (originally, one that accepted *ciuitas sine suffragio* [= citizenship without voting rights] in return for the performance of certain duties, *munia*)' (*OLD* s.v.). After the Social War (91–89 BCE), the inhabitants of all Italian *municipia* become full Roman citizens, with equal voting rights. See further Adkins and Adkins (2014: 142): '*Coloniae* … were new settlements of colonies established by the state to form a self-administering community, often with a strategic defensive function. Most colonies were founded on state-owned land, but sometimes they were established on land belonging to a *municipium* — an existing town incorporated into the Roman state, whose inhabitants might or might not be Roman citizens. … During the republic the title *municipium* (pl. *municipia*) was given to existing Italian towns, the inhabitants of which had been granted Roman citizenship without voting rights. These towns had a certain amount of independence, but foreign affairs came under the control of Roman magistrates. ... After voting rights were conferred on all Italian communities in the early 1st century BC, citizens of *municipia* became full Roman citizens'. Also Rosenstein (2012: 82–93).

at iste operta lectica latus per oppidum est ut mortuus: the verb of the sentence is *latus ... est* (third person singular perfect indicative passive from *fero, ferre, tuli, latum* — 'to carry'). *operta lectica* is ablative: 'in a closed litter'.

ut mortuus: corpses were carried to the funeral in closed litters — Antony, Cicero suggests, behaved as if he were dead.

stulte Aquinates [fecerunt]: **sed tamen in via** [Latina] **habitabant**: The Aquinates behaved foolishly, says Cicero — as they should have known what to expect; but at least there is a ready explanation for their futile efforts to greet Antony with the respect ordinarily owed to a Roman magistrate: their town is located right on the road (*in via*). The same excuse does not apply to the inhabitants of Anagna. See the following sentence.

quid Anagnini [fecerunt]**? qui cum essent devii, descenderunt ut istum, tamquam si esset consul, salutarent**: *qui* is a connecting relative (= *ei*), the subject of the adversative *cum*-clause ('Even though they live in remote parts...')

ut istum ... salutarent: a purpose clause.

tamquam si esset consul: the *tamquam-si*-clause indicates the reason why the inhabitants of Anagna behaved the way they did. And of course Antony *was* a consul. But Cicero implies that, far from being an obvious fact, Antony being a consul is a mistaken assumption. He thus launches another attack on Rome's constitutional realities. In his world, political identities get redefined according to his personal understanding of civic ethics: in his world, Antony does not fulfill the requisite criteria for being a consul; he is therefore a consul in name only, an impostor to be disregarded or even killed, rather than a 'genuine' magistrate of the Roman people. The searching examination of what key terms of Roman political culture such as 'consul' mean and what responsibilities and obligations they confer on the office-holder and to redefine them in terms of a civic ethics is a hallmark of Cicero's speeches and philosophical writings: it is a Greek-inspired, philosophical approach to political discourse — and has the power to challenge fundamental certainties built into the Roman sense of reality.

See also *ad Atticum* 14.6.2 = 360 SB, where Cicero complained about the incongruity that the tyrannicides are praised to the skies, while the tyrant's actions are defended: *sed vides consules, vides reliquos magistratus, si isti magistratus, vides languorem bonorum* ('But you see our Consuls and the rest of our magistrates, if these people are magistrates, and the apathy of the honest men'). This captures the dilemma and stalemate that Cicero struggled with: all the magistrates held their offices because of Caesar and would therefore saw off the branches on which they were sitting if they undid Caesar's arrangements, whereas the liberators (the *boni*) believed that killing Caesar would in and of itself suffice to restore the senatorial commonwealth.

incredibile dictu + sed cum vinus + inter omnis constabat neminem esse resalutatum, praesertim cum duos secum Anagninos haberet, Mustelam et Laconem, quorum alter gladiorum est princeps, alter [princeps] poculorum: *incredibile dictu* is a self-contained parenthetical phrase, consisting of adjective + ablative supine of *dico*: 'incredible as it is to say so'; the main verb is the impersonal *constabat*, which governs an indirect statement with *neminem* as subject accusative and *esse resalutatum* as verb. The force of *praesertim cum* is adversative: despite the fact that / even though.

+ sed cum vinus +: this part of the manuscript tradition is so corrupt that modern editors have struggled to come up with a truly compelling restitution and many leave the words between so-called *cruces* (= corrupt beyond plausible restoration). The most recent proposal comes from Dyck (2017: 313): 'I suspect that *cum* is intrusive from the preceding or following line and that *uinus* conceals *ad unum*: "incredible to say, but all to a man agreed that no one returned their greeting...". *ad* may have dropped out following *sed*'. If that does not convince you, just ignore the muddle between the *cruces*.

Mustelam et Laconem: we know from a letter to Atticus (16.11.3 = 420 SB) that Cicero, in the draft of *Philippic* 2 he sent to Atticus, stopped the sentence after *haberet*. Atticus enquired about the identity of the two chaps from Anagnia, to which Cicero responded by supplying their names and identity tags: *'Anagnini' sunt Mustela taxiarchês et Laco qui plurimum bibit* ('The "men of Anagnia" are Mustela, the *taxiarch*, and Laco, the champion toper'). The revised version of the speech contains this material, suitably adjusted: while Cicero litters his letters to Atticus ('Mr. Greek') with Greek words (like *taxiarchês*), he keeps foreign terms out of his speeches. *princeps gladiorum* is a humorous and humiliating translation of *taxiarches*, especially when paired with *princeps poculorum*. Mustela also appears elsewhere as one of Antony's henchmen: see *Phil.* 5.18, 8.26, and 12.14. Mustela is also the Latin term for 'weasel', an animal associated in Latin folklore with brides (indeed Mustela could also be a woman's name): see Bettini (2000). Perhaps, then, the two chaps are designed to recall the two principal sins of Antony from the previous paragraph, i.e. lechery and boozing (in his company even someone called Laco, 'Spartan', gets addicted to the bottle).

§ 107: Symbolic Strutting after Caesar

The paragraph falls into two halves: in the first (*Quid ego … cliens esse*), Cicero continues to belabour the theme of Antony's maltreatment of local communities in Italy that happened to pique his anger, though the *praeteritio*-mode he now adopts suggests that he is starting to run out of steam. Halfway through, his focus turns back to Rome (*interea dum tu abes … ut dissimilis esset sui*), and he homes in on an event that happened in the capital during Antony's absence: Dolabella's destruction of the altar to Caesar erected by Amatius. The thematic link between the two halves consists in the invocation of the persons and policies that support Cicero's republican politics.

Roman aristocrats functioned as patrons of local communities both in Italy and beyond. The patronage system tied patrons and clients together in a reciprocal, if hierarchical economy: 'Patrons were expected to provide a range of services: To mediate when dissension broke out, to defend the interests of the town before Senate and magistrates, to provide significant material benefactions. Some were involved in the foundation of the community; others were coopted because they owned significant estates in the territory of the client. In return, patrons expected their clients to support them at elections, to enhance their prestige, to serve as a base for recruiting soldiers and to provide bodyguard in emergencies' (Nicols 2014: 70). These arrangements became a highly sensitive issue in the wake of Caesar's assassination. Some evidence suggests that one of the honours proposed to Caesar before his death was the title of patron (*prostates*) of the City and of the whole Empire (Cassius Dio 44.48.1–2 with Nicols 2014: 65–66), which would have highlighted his autocratic monopolization of oligarchic structures of power. After the Ides of March, others vied for similar innovative nomenclature to validate their position and prestige (see e.g. *Phil.* 6.12). Conversely, local communities faced the tough political choice whether to side with the liberators or leading Caesarians, in the full knowledge that request for support and patronage extended to one party would alienate others, with potentially dire repercussions. Still, many Italian townships seem to have greeted the assassination of Caesar with delight — or so Cicero suggests, in a letter to Atticus (*Att.* 14.6.2 = 360 SB; 12 April 44):

> exsultant laetitia in municipiis. dici enim non potest quanto opere gaudeant, ut ad me concurrant, ut audire cupiant mea verba de re <publica>.

> [In the country towns they are jumping for joy. I cannot tell you how delighted they are, how they flock to me, how eager they are to hear what I have to say on the state of the country.]

Cicero's report should obviously be taken with a grain of salt: it is not surprising that those local notables who interacted with him expressed unalloyed enthusiasm. Still, the dominant factions among the Sidicini and the inhabitants of Puteoli clearly sympathized with the liberators and sought out Cassius and the two Bruti as patrons, thereby coming into the (verbal) firing line of Antony.

Meanwhile, in Rome, the jostling for position in a post-Caesarian world manifested itself not least in tussles over his post-mortem status. The person who took the lead in pushing the envelope here is the curious figure of Amatius, a.k.a. as Pseudo-Marius, Herophilus (a Greek speaking name), or Chamates.[67] He claimed descent from C. Marius, Sulla's opponent and kinsman of Caesar, and took the lead in fomenting religious worship of the dead (but, he argued, deified) dictator, around a column and an altar erected on the site of Caesar's funeral pyre (Koortbojian 2013: 26–27). We can glean the considerable degree of popularity he and his cultic veneration of *divus Iulius* started to command from the fact that Antony had him executed shortly before

---

67   For Amatius see Cic. *Att.* 12.49 = 292 SB (20 May 45), then *Att.* 14.6 = 360 SB (12 April 44), *Att.* 14.7 = 361 SB and 14.8 = 362 SB (15 April 44) and, for his names, Deniaux (2003).

his departure for Southern Italy. This pleased the republicans and Cicero just as much as it was designed to shore up Antony's position among the Caesarians through the elimination of a rival to the prestige and affection of the people of Rome and Caesar's veterans. Yet he left the altar and the column — as a monument to Caesar's memory — intact, and during his sojourn away from Rome Dolabella deemed their destruction a useful symbolic gesture to enhance his own standing with the republicans (and thereby also to increase his leverage with his fellow consul Antony). Cicero already recalled this sequence of events at *Philippic* 1.5. Elsewhere in the speech he condemns any attempt to conceive of Caesar as a deified human to be honoured with cultic worship in the strongest possible terms — and lambasts Antony for a change of tack, triggered by the significant appeal (exploited to the utmost by Caesar Octavianus) the notion of divine Caesar commanded among the populace and the veterans. If in April Antony had pseudo-Marius executed, in early September he himself pushed through a decree that added an extra day to every *supplicatio* ('thanksgiving for public successes') dedicated to offerings to the deified Caesar.

Cicero's strictures against the idea that Caesar had become a god presuppose the strict divide between the human and the divine within Rome's civic religion. Attempts at crossing the boundary, in whatever form, while feasible in theory (there existed, in principle, no *religious* objections to humans becoming gods — in literary texts, it happened all the time), were *politically* incorrect moves in the field of power, a potential threat to the republican tradition of senatorial government:[68] elevating one individual, albeit *post mortem*, to the status of a god violated fundamental principles of oligarchic equality. Still, already long before Caesar outstanding aristocrats found it tempting to explore the boundary between human and divine (for instance by claiming a special relationship with a supernatural being) for reasons of self-promotion. Inspiration came from the Greek East, in both theory and practice. Poets and other litterateurs domesticated a variety of literary genres that explored different forms of divinity and deification; in Ennius'

---

68   Feeney (1998: 108–10), further Gildenhard (2011: 255–57), on which the following
     pages are based.

oeuvre, for instance, apotheosis (of Romulus in the *Annals*), Pythagorean metempsychosis (the reincarnation of Homer in Ennius himself), and Euhemerism all find an airing — as well as (in the *Scipio*) the idea of a living (or recently deceased) Roman noble ascending to the stars.

In the context of imperial expansion, the Romans also encountered cults that bestowed religious honours upon living rulers — a practice that had started to proliferate in the wake of Alexander the Great.[69] The perceived divinity of (royal) power had little to do with the proclivity of eastern subjects to emote irrationally about their kings, as some ancient sources, including Cicero, imply. Rather the Hellenistic ruler cult constituted an ideological form and social practice by which kings justified their reign and cities negotiated their existence within the domineering presence of 'a supra-poliadic power'.[70] Given that the award of cultic honours to (potential) benefactors was part and parcel of city diplomacy, it is hardly surprising that Romans, too, received religious adulation.

The civil conflicts of the late republic accelerated the development of novel forms of religious self-promotion. The Gracchi claimed religious prerogatives and special divine favours for their careers and policies, and they received posthumous honours—as did Marius and Gratidianus.[71] Matters came to a head with Sulla. His claim to permanent *felicitas* was incompatible with fundamental tenets of Rome's civic religion since it signalled a privileged and personal relationship with the gods.[72] In his autobiography, Sulla suggested that he could sidestep the protocols of Roman *religio*, such as collective negotiation of the meaning of divine signs; statements such as that he liked to converse in private with a *daimon* by night made a mockery of this principle.[73] His rise to the dictatorship

---

69 Habicht (1956/2017), Price (1984), Badian (1996), Mikalson (1998) (esp. ch. 3: 'Twenty years of the divine Demetrios Poliorcetes'), and Chaniotis (2003). Flower (2006: 31–34) offers a useful reminder that the transition from deified human to disgraced dead could be a quick one.

70 Ma (2003: 179), with reference to Price (1984); further Stevenson (1996) on the social ideals that informed the elevation of human beings to divine status, Ma (1999/2002) and Chaniotis (2003).

71 Santangelo (2005) and Flower (2006: 302, n. 41; 305, n. 7, and 306, n. 23).

72 Classen (1963: 330).

73 For Sulla's (religious) self-promotion see frs. 9, 17, 20, 23 Chassignet, further Ramage (1991) and Lewis (1991) (1993: 665–69).

demonstrated beyond any reasonable doubt that a darling of the gods did not fit into the political culture of the republic. At the same time, his maverick self-promotion as the recipient of special supernatural support raised the stakes in the game of competitive emulation: any aristocrat who did not lay claim to similar privileges would implicitly concede that he was only second best. Others followed in pushing the boundaries of the acceptable, not least Caesar, who, in the funeral oration for his aunt, proclaimed descent from gods and kings.[74] Pompey, too, promoted himself as enjoying special divine favours, deploying what had long been part of strategic diplomacy in the East as a political argument at Rome.[75] And Cicero, in particular in his speeches against Catiline and the epic poem he wrote about his consulship (the *de Consulatu Suo*) also asserted privileged relations with the supernatural sphere.

Quid ego illas istius minas contumeliasque commemorem quibus invectus est in Sidicinos, vexavit Puteolanos, quod C. Cassium et Brutos patronos adoptassent?: Cicero launches into another *praeteritio* cast in the form of a rhetorical question. The main verb is *commemorem* (in the 'deliberative' subjunctive), followed by a bipartite relative clause (*invectus est, vexavit*), in asyndetic sequence introduced by *quibus*. The sentence finishes with a causal *quod*-clause, with a syncopated third person plural pluperfect subjunctive active (*adopta|vi|ssent*) as verb. Causal sentences with *quod* (*quia, quoniam, quando*) take the indicative in direct discourse, but the subjunctive in indirect discourse, whether explicit or — as here — implied: 'because [so Antony said] they had adopted...': see Gildersleeve and Lodge 349–50.

illas istius minas contumeliasque: the two accusative objects (linked by *-que*), the demonstrative adjective *illas* and the demonstrative pronoun *istius* form a phonetically well-balanced unit, with touches of alliteration (*il-, is-*), homoioteleuton (*-las, -nas, -lias*), and sound-play (*minas ~ -melias*). The disdain built into *istius* stands out more prominently against a background of three words ending in *-as*.

Sidicinos: the Sidicini inhabited territory along the Liri River around their capital Teanum Sidicinum (modern day Teano).

---

74   Suet. *Jul.* 5–6, Plu. *Caes.* 5.
75   Santangelo (2007: 230).

Puteolanos: the Puteolani were located at the northern end of the bay of Naples. Their capital was Puteoli (modern day Pozzuoli).

C. Cassium et Brutos: Gaius Cassius and Marcus and Decimus Brutus (note that *Brutos* is in the plural) were the three leading figures among the assassins of Caesar.

magno quidem studio, iudicio, benevolentia, caritate [C. Cassium et Brutos patronos adoptaverunt], **non, ut te et Basilum, vi et armis, et alios vestri similis quos clientis nemo habere velit, non modo illorum cliens esse**: to understand the syntax here, it is necessary to import the verb and the accusative object from the previous sentence. Cicero compares and contrasts the reasons why the Sidicini and the people of Puteoli adopted Cassius and the Bruti as their patrons (detailed in four causal ablatives in asyndetic sequence at the beginning of the sentence) with the reason why other, unnamed communities 'preferred' Antony and Basilus: *vi et armis* — as a result of force of arms. He concludes the sentence by turning Antony and Basilus into representatives of a larger ilk (*et alios vestri similis*), which no one wishes to have as clients, let alone as patrons.

magno quidem studio, iudicio, benevolentia, caritate: 'out of great devotion, esteem (for this sense of *iudicium*, see *OLD* s.v. 10), goodwill, and affection': the reason for this outpour of positive emotion is the fact that Cassius and the two Bruti freed the commonwealth from tyranny. *iudicium*, which emphasizes considered judgement and free decision-making, offers a sharp contrast to the use of physical force by Antony and his ilk.

Basilum: the reference is to M. Satrius, who acquired the cognomen Basilus when he was adopted by his maternal uncle L. Minucius Basilus; according to Cicero, *On Duties* (*de Officiis*) 3.74, he became a patron of the Picenian and Sabine territory (*patronum agri Piceni et Sabini*), which Cicero considered a disgrace (*o turpem notam temporum illorum*), apparently by employing the same means as Antony to get what he wanted — the threat of physical violence.

alios vestri similis: *similis* is accusative plural agreeing with *alios* (= *similes*). The genitive *vestri*, which depends on *similis*, refers back to Antony and Basilus: 'others similar to you (pl.).

quos clientis nemo habere velit, non modo illorum cliens esse: 'whom no-one wishes to have as clients (*clientis* is accusative plural = *clientes*), let alone be a client of theirs'. With *non modo* ('not to speak of, let alone': *OLD* s.v. 2b; here 'curiously used for *nedum*': Denniston (1926: 165), Cicero partly falls out of the syntax of the relative clause introduced by *quos*, continuing with the demonstrative pronoun *illorum* (rather than a second relative pronoun), but carrying over subject (*nemo*) and verb (*velit*): *quos clientis nemo habere velit [et quorum] cliens (nemo) esse (velit)*. He lands a double punch, not just disqualifying Antony as a desirable *patronus*, but also hitting below the belt by haughtily assessing (and dismissing) him as a potential *cliens*.

interea dum tu abes, qui dies ille collegae tuo fuit, cum illud quod venerari solebas bustum in foro evertit!: *dum* + present indicative (here *abes*) captures an on-going situation in the course of which a single event occurs, quite irrespective of the tense of the main verb (here the perfect *fuit*): *OLD* s.v. *dum* 3b: 'during the time that', 'while'. Retaining the present tense in English would sound weird, but a noun phrase could do the trick: 'Meanwhile, during your absence, what a day that was for your colleague, when…'

illud … bustum: *illud* agrees with *bustum*, which is the antecedent of the relative pronoun *quod* and the accusative object of *evertit*. The monument that Amatius and his followers erected seems to have consisted of a column made of Numidian marble inscribed with PARENTI PATRIAE ('To the Father of the Country') (see Suetonius, *Life of Julius Caesar* 85) and an altar (*ara*) for sacrifices (Cic. *Fam.* 11.2.2 = 329 SB). Cicero's consistent reference to the monument as a *bustum* (which means 'funeral pyre' or 'tomb') in his *Philippics* (see already *Phil.* 1.30) is therefore polemical: it was designed to bring to mind the botched funeral and the half-burnt corpse (see §§ 90–91) and emphasize Caesar's mortality: the dictator is dead and done, rather than dead and deified.

qua re tibi nuntiata, ut constabat inter eos qui una fuerunt, concidisti: Cicero lines up his unanimous eyewitnesses first (*ut constabat … fuerunt*) before specifying what they saw: that Antony collapsed upon hearing the news. Why he should do so is a puzzle: with his execution of pseudo-Marius, he had done his bit to suppress the cultic worship of Caesar. The news that Dolabella had taken a further step will have been unwelcome, but not sufficiently so to justify a collapse on the spot. Perhaps Cicero simply hams up Antony's mental instability — or he wishes to suggest that Antony is emotionally invested in the veneration of a dead person. *Philippic* 2, after all, postdates Antony's endorsement of Caesar's deification on 1 September, and Cicero wouldn't have thought twice of falsely superimposing the implications of recent developments onto the events in spring if this served his invective purpose.

qua re tibi nuntiata: *qua* is a connecting relative (= *et ea*) modifying *re*; the whole phrase is an ablative absolute.

quid evenerit postea nescio — metum credo valuisse et arma; collegam quidem de caelo detraxisti effecistique non tu quidem etiam nunc ut similis tui [esset], sed certe [effecisti] ut dissimilis esset sui: the previous sentence suggests radical differences between Antony and Dolabella, even though Cicero knew all too well that they were very much in cahoots during the period in question. He now feigns ignorance, before speculating about the reason why Dolabella, after trying to increase his republican credentials with the destruction of the place of Caesar's worship, continued to collaborate closely with Antony. As a result, Dolabella, shortly after elevating himself to the stars (or being praised to the sky by people like Cicero: see *Fam.* 9.14 = 326 SB and *Att.* 14.15–16 = 369–370 SB), comes back down to earth in terms of republican esteem, and while he is not quite as bad as Antony, his close association with Antony means that he is no longer his old self.

quid evenerit postea nescio: *nescio* governs an indirect question (*quid … postea*), hence the (perfect) subjunctive *evenerit*.

metum credo valuisse et arma: *credo* governs an indirect statement with *metum* and *arma* — in *husteron proteron*: the threat of physical violence (*arma*) induces fear (*metum*) — as subject accusatives and *valuisse* as infinitive. As his correspondence shows, Cicero knows that the reasons he gives here are false: Antony won Dolabella over by paying off his debts with public money. See *Att.* 14.18 = 373 SB and 16.15.1 = 426 SB.

effecistique non tu quidem etiam nunc ut similis tui [esset], sed certe [effecisti] ut dissimilis esset sui: and (while) you indeed (*tu quidem*) did not achieve even now (*etiam nunc*) that he became like you (*tui* is the genitive of the personal pronoun in the second person singular depending on *similis*), you certainly (*certe*) did manage that he became unlike himself (*sui* is the genitive of the personal pronoun in the third person singular depending on *dissimilis*). Cicero is trying to grade political villainy, suggesting that Antony has a corrupting influence on someone of sound moral and political fibre. He perverts Dolabella's true identity — though falls short of turning him into a spitting image of himself.

§ 108: Swords Galore, or: Antony's Return to Rome

Around 20 May 44 BCE, Antony returned to Rome — together with several thousand veterans settled at Casilinum and Calatia (Appian, *Bellum Civile* 3.5 mentions 6,000), whom he had recruited by means of *evocatio* ('recall into active service') in the course of his journey through Southern Italy. From then on, he used this army as a bodyguard and to intimidate senate and people. At *Philippic* 5.17–20, Cicero gives an extensive account of how the presence of Antony's troops shaped events in September 44 (the imaginary context of *Philippic* 2). The sections of greatest relevance to our passage are 17–18:

> An illa non gravissimis ignominiis monumentisque huius ordinis ad posteritatis memoriam sunt notanda, quod unus M. Antonius in hac urbe post conditam urbem palam secum habuerit armatos? quod neque reges nostri fecerunt neque ii, qui regibus exactis regnum occupare voluerunt. Cinnam memini, vidi Sullam, modo Caesarem; hi enim tres post civitatem a L. Bruto liberatam plus potuerunt quam universa res publica. non possum adfirmare nullis telis eos stipatos fuisse, hoc dico: nec multis et occultis. at hanc pestem agmen armatorum sequebatur; Cassius, Mustela, Tiro, gladios ostentantes sui similes greges ducebant per forum; certum agminis locum tenebant barbari sagittarii. cum autem erat ventum ad aedem Concordiae, gradus conplebantur, lecticae conlocabantur, non quo ille scuta occulta esse vellet, sed ne familiares, si scuta ipsi ferrent, laborarent. illud vero taeterrimum non modo aspectu, sed etiam auditu, in cella Concordiae conlocari armatos, latrones, sicarios, de templo carcerem fieri, opertis valvis Concordiae, cum inter subsellia senatus versarentur latrones, patres conscriptos sententias dicere.

[As a record for posterity, must we not brand with a memorial of the most severe censure by this order that in this city, since its foundation, only Mark Antony has openly kept an armed guard at his side! Neither our kings nor those who after the expulsion of the kings tried to seize the kingship ever did this. I remember Cinna, I saw Sulla, recently Caesar. These three possessed more power than the entire commonwealth since Lucius Brutus liberated the community. I cannot affirm that they were surrounded by no weapons, but this I do affirm: not by many, and they were concealed. By contrast, an armed column attended this pest. Cassius, Mustela, Tiro, brandishing their swords, led gangs like themselves through the forum. Barbarian archers had their assigned place in the column. When they reached the Temple of Concord, the steps were packed, the litters were set down — not that he wanted the shields to be hidden, but to save his friends the effort of carrying them. The most loathsome thing of all, not only to see, but even to hear of is that armed men, bandits, cutthroats were stationed in the shrine of Concord. The temple became a prison. The doors of Concord were closed, and members of the senate expressed their views while bandits were moving about amid the benches.]

Cicero luxuriates in the chaos Antony allegedly caused — and his oratory has had a powerful impact on how later ages (including ours) have viewed his actions. It is therefore salutary to try to recover Antony's own view, as attempted by Sumi (2005: 132):

Antonius himself no doubt would have advertised his return differently. He easily could have called himself Rome's savior and enumerated all the reasons to justify such an appellation. We know that he did so on two other occasions. ... after the senate meeting in the Temple of Tellus, Antonius appeared before a *contio*, wearing an armored breastplate beneath his tunic, which he showed to the crowd as an indication of the peril he faced on behalf of the Republic (App. *BC* 2.130.543). At a later *contio*, he called himself guardian of the city (*custos urbis*) and described his efforts to protect Rome [*Phil.* 3.27; 5.21]. He could have explained his recruitment of soldiers and subsequent march on Rome in the same way: he was returning to defend the Roman people, not enslave them. D. Brutus was in Gaul mustering forces; C. Trebonius was on his way to Asia where he soon would have access to enormous resources and manpower; M. Brutus and Cassius had fled from Rome but were still in Italy — and who could say whether they would attempt to regain their *dignitas* through force of arms? It appeared that everyone had an army except the consul who was obligated to defend the state.

Qui vero inde reditus Romam [erat]**, quae perturbatio** [erat] **totius urbis!:** After his brief glance at Dolabella, Cicero returns to his account of Antony's actions in May 44, focusing on his return to Rome with two exclamations. *qui* and *quae* are pronominal interrogative adjectives, modifying, respectively, *reditus* and *perturbatio*; the discourse particle *vero* asserts the supposedly acknowledged factual basis of Cicero's report; and *inde* has a temporal sense ('next', 'then'): 'What a return was there then to Rome! What upheaval of the entire city!' Essentially, Cicero 'describes Antonius' return with highly charged and colorful language that all but declares the consul an enemy of the state (*hostis*)' (Sumi 2005: 132).

Romam: an accusative of place to which (without *ad* because Rome is a city). The verb of movement is implied in the noun *reditus*: Pinkster (2015: 1043).

memineramus Cinnam nimis potentem, Sullam postea dominantem, modo Caesarem regnantem videramus: Cinna, Sulla, and Caesar are a notorious trio of late-republican strongmen who resorted to violent means in the pursuit of (excessive — or, in Caesar's case, absolute) power. Cicero uses them elsewhere in the *Philippic* corpus as foils for Antony: see e.g. *Phil.* 5.17 (cited above), 8.7 (cited below), 11.1, 13.1–2, 14.23. The sentence sports an apparent symmetry, with the two verbs *memineramus* and *videramus* emphatically placed at the beginning and the end and three accusative objects (*Cinnam, Sullam, Caesarem*). Each potentate comes with an attribute, which together constitute a climactic sequence: we move from an adjective (*potentem*) to two participles (*dominantem, regnantem*) that express two highly objectionable modes of wielding power, with *regnare* topping *dominari* by a tick in loathsomeness since it implies a greater degree of permanence. Once we reach *modo*, however, it becomes apparent that the symmetry breaks down and thereby further sharpens the climax: whereas *nimis* and *postea* go with *potentem* and *dominantem*, *modo* goes with *videramus* — and what in some ways looks like (and is) a tricolon breaks apart into two unequal halves: Cinna and Sulla are distant memories (and comparatively harmless forerunners) when set against the much more recent visual impact of Caesar's obnoxious reign.

The *potentia* of Cinna, the *dominatio* of Sulla, and the *regnum* of Caesar
are three illegitimate forms of power, which Cicero adduces throughout
the corpus of *Philippics* for his scaremongering about Antony. In his
endeavour to push a reluctant senate into an armed confrontation with
Antony, he casts the conflict as a new chapter in the sequence of civil
wars that defined late-republican politics. Always, Antony emerges as
worse than his predecessors — including Caesar. Apart from 5.17 (cited
above), see in particular *Philippic* 8.7–8, delivered on 4 February 43,
when the dice had been cast and Cicero constructs the following history
of civil conflict during his lifetime:

> Utrum hoc bellum non est, an etiam tantum bellum quantum numquam
> fuit? ceteris enim bellis maximeque civilibus contentionem rei publicae
> causa faciebat: Sulla cum Sulpicio de iure legum, quas per vim latas esse
> dicebat; Cinna cum Octavio de novorum civium suffragiis; rursus cum
> Mario et Carbone Sulla, ne dominarentur indigni et ut clarissimorum
> hominum crudelissimam puniretur necem. horum omnium bellorum
> causae ex rei publicae contentione natae sunt. de proximo bello civili non
> libet dicere: ignoro causam, detestor exitum. hoc bellum quintum civile
> geritur — atque omnia in nostram aetatem inciderunt — , primum non
> modo non in dissensione et discordia civium, sed in maxima consensione
> incredibilique concordia.

> [Is this not a war, or rather a war such as has never been before? In other
> wars, and especially in civil wars, some political question gave rise to the
> quarrel. Sulla clashed with Sulpicius on the validity of the laws which
> Sulla asserted had been carried by violence; Cinna with Octavius on the
> votes of the new citizens; Sulla again with Marius and Carbo over the
> tyranny of the unworthy, and to punish the most savage slaughter of
> eminent men. The causes of all these wars originated from a political
> quarrel. Of the last civil war I do not care to speak: I do not know
> its cause; I detest its outcome. This is the fifth civil war that is being
> waged — and all have fallen on our own times — the first that has arisen,
> not amid civic variance and discord, but amid the utmost unison and
> marvellous concord.]

Cicero thus lists the following five clashes: (i) Sulla v. Sulpicius; (ii) Cinna
v. Octavius; (iii) Sulla v. Marius and Carbo; (iv) Caesar v. Pompey; (v)
Everyone v. Antony. He characterizes the first three as understandable,
if deplorable outbreaks of violence over legitimate political differences.
He passes over the fourth civil war, unleashed by Caesar, in silence
because he is unable to identify a valid cause and loathes the outcome.

The fifth of the civil wars is special in a different sense: there is no dividing line to speak of — it is Antony against everyone else.

memineramus: first person plural pluperfect indicative active. *memini* (like *coepi, odi*, and *novi*) is a verb used only in the perfect system. The perfect tense has a present sense (*memini*: I remember) and the pluperfect a perfect sense (*memineram*: I remembered).

Cinnam nimis potentem: Cinna, an ally of Marius, bossed Rome from 87–84 BCE after Marius' death.

Sullam postea dominantem: Sulla returned from the war against Mithridates in 83 BCE and took charge of Rome until 79 BCE, when he resigned his dictatorship.

erant fortasse gladii, sed absconditi nec ita multi: ista vero quae et quanta barbaria est!: the sentence contrasts the behaviour of earlier strongmen with that of Antony, trying to bring out — also at the level of style — by how much matters deteriorated with the latter. The verbs (the imperfect *erant* and the present *est*) are strategically placed at the beginning and end to underscore the historical trajectory from bad to worse. Cicero further downplays past outrage with the adverbial hedge *fortasse* and instantly qualifies *gladii* with two provisos, trailing in predicative position (*sed absconditi nec ita multi*). Contrast the sharp demonstrative pronoun *ista*, which modifies *barbaria* (note the emphatic hyperbaton) and gets reinforced by the two interrogative adjectives *quae* and *quanta*, which, respectively, underscore quality and quantity in an exclamation that, thematically and grammatically, recalls the opening sentence of the paragraph: 'What and how great a barbarity this is!' *barbaria* is an abstract concept that carries associations to do with geography and ethnicity as well as political ethics: it brings to mind foreign, uncivilized tribes that inhabit the wilderness at the periphery of Greco-Roman culture, are inherently savage and cruel, and (with particular reference to the East) practise despicable forms of political organization (such as autocracy). Antony had archers from Ituraea (the Greek name of a region in the Levant) in his entourage, who made him look 'like an oriental king' (Lacey (1986: 236); cf. Mayor (1861: 149): 'But what an Asiatic despotism is this of yours!'). Put differently, Cicero here cast the previous tyrants in a tolerable light as far as the presence of armed bodyguards in the city of Rome was concerned. All three tried to keep the number of weapons under control and their presence out of sight. By contrast, he makes Antony's return resemble a barbarian invasion, both in the kind and the quantity of armed troops flooding into the city. This is in line with insults found elsewhere in the *Philippic* corpus, where Antony routinely outdoes all other political monsters: at *Phil.* 3.9–11, for instance, he is more tyrannical than Tarquinius Superbus and at *Phil.* 14.9 he is worse than Hannibal.

agmine quadrato cum gladiis sequuntur, scutorum lecticas portari videmus: two main clauses in asyndetic sequence; the subject of the first is implied in *sequuntur*: 'Antony's men followed with their swords drawn, in battle-order; we saw litters filled with shields being carried along'. The phrase *agmine quadrato* (an ablative absolute) designates a marching formation in which the army has taken the baggage into the middle for protection against attacks from all sides and is ready for battle at any moment. Cicero uses the same phrase with reference to the meeting of the senate on 19 September, at which Antony delivered the speech to which Cicero's *Philippic* 2 is a response (5.20): *agmine quadrato in aedem Concordiae venit atque in me absentem orationem ex ore impurissimo evomuit. quod die, si per amicos mihi cupienti in senatum venire licuisset, caedis initium fecisset a me* ('he entered the Temple of Concord with his bodyguard in battle formation and vomited from that foulest of mouths a speech against me in my absence. If my friends had allowed me to come to the senate on that day as I wished, he would have started his slaughter with me').[76]

scutorum lecticas: litters *full of* shields: 'The genitive is akin to that after verbs of filling, cf. *cadus vini*, "a cask (full of) wine"' (Allcroft 1901: 117). The reference to shields complements the mention of swords: Antony's troops are on the move, ready to attack or to defend themselves.

atque his quidem iam inveteratis, patres conscripti, consuetudine obduruimus: *atque* here has a slight adversative sense (OLD s.v. 9): 'and

---

76   On the notion of *os impurum*, see Worman (2008: 322): 'Although…Cicero seems largely to reserve imputations of oral turpitude for his less powerful targets, the implications of the *os impurum* (i.e., the mouth when used especially for sex and/or excessive drinking) clearly underlies his characterization of Antony'.

yet': yes, Antony outdoes anyone, but he is still part of a tradition. *his ... inveteratis* is an ablative absolute: 'with these things having become the norm now', with the idea of repetition expressed by *inveteratis* continued with *consuetudine*: 'we have become hardened by repeated experience'. With bitter resignation, Cicero diagnoses in himself and his senatorial peers (addressed directly) the weary acceptance of the abnormal (i.e. individual statesmen surrounding themselves with a private army, a military presence in the city of Rome, and the threat of violence as a factor in domestic politics) as the new normal.

Cicero invoked the idea that repeated exposure to brutality results in a loss of sensitivity (or even humanity) already in the peroration of his speech for Sextus Roscius, delivered at the very beginning of his oratorical career (*Sext. Rosc.* 154: *nam cum omnibus horis aliquid atrociter fieri videmus aut audimus, etiam qui natura mitissimi sumus adsiduitate molestiarum sensum omnem humanitatis ex animis amittimus*: 'For when, every hour, we see or hear of an act of cruelty, even those of us who are by nature most merciful lose from our hearts, in this constant presence of trouble, all feeling of humanity', perhaps reworking Lysias 6.50, but broadening the idea 'from paradox to a universal and devastating vision': Hutchinson (2005: 190–91).) See also *Att.* 13.2.1 = 297 SB: *iam ad ista obduruimus et humanitatem omnem exuimus* ('But I am hardened now to such treatment and have cast off all sensibility').

Kalendis Iuniis cum in senatum, ut erat constitutum, venire vellemus, metu perterriti repente diffugimus: this sentence follows on somewhat incongruously from the previous one. The contrast between the *cum*-clause, which presents constitutional business as usual, and the abnormal reaction of Cicero and other senators in the main clause is stark. Given that dealing with armed forces and the threat of violence has become a routine occurrence, one would have thought that the senators just shrug their shoulders and get on with their daily routine. In fact, the exact opposite is the case: panic-stricken, they know how to disperse on the spot. An *emergency routine* kicks in, which Cicero underscores stylistically. The *cum*-clause comes along in a boring plod of homoioteleuta (*-is, -iis*; *cum, -tum, -tutum*) and alliteration (*ve-, ve-*) capturing business as usual ('another senate-meeting') according to Rome's constitutional arrangements; then a subtle shift in stylistic register occurs: the four words that constitute the main clause and conclude the sentence, each on its own and in combination, paint a dark picture of constitutional chaos.

Kalendis Iuniis: ablative of time ('on the calends of June').

metu perterriti: seemingly tautological, but *metus* is a quasi-legal term (see *de Officiis* 1.32 with Dyck 1996: 131) that serves to justify certain courses of action also in the eyes of the law: 'alarmed by justified fear' — though *perterreo* often carries nuances of comedy, melodrama, and hyperbole: the sense is one of sheer panic, with people frightened out of their wits.

diffugimus: the verb ('we dispersed' — a.k.a. 'ran for our lives') is, quite deliberately, as undignified as the participial phrase *metu perterriti*.

§ 109: Playing Fast and Loose with Caesar's Legislation

Scholarly opinion on Caesar's stature as a 'statesman' is divided (as opposed to his unanimously acknowledged genius as a military strategist and commander). Many feel that he did not have a (or any) viable vision for the Roman commonwealth beyond installing himself as quasi-omnipotent dictator. Be that as it may, he did initiate a significant programme of innovations and reforms across various cultural spheres (not least the calendar), including a slate of legislative measures. In the years 49–44 BCE a large number of laws were passed (proposed by different magistrates who of course did so with the dictator's approval and encouragement) that ranged from the taxation of provinces to the award of citizenship to non-Roman communities to legislation dealing with Pompeian exiles to social and economic measures, such as land distributions.[77] After the Ides of March, the continuing validity of Caesar's legislative legacy was part of the compromise struck between Caesarians and the self-styled liberators — a by and large uncontroversial item of business given the chaos that would have ensued if the realities put in place under Caesar's watch over the last half decade had suddenly lost their legal foundation. More problematic was the question of what to do with those of Caesar's plans and policies that had remained

---

77 For a full list of the legislation see Yavetz (1983: 59–160), including extensive discussion along the following three guiding questions: '1 *Cui bono*? Who reaped advantages from this legislative activity with its many ramifications? 2 Is it really true that Caesar operated without a plan, or is a well-considered line of action detectable behind his activities? 3 Is it possible to pin down Caesar's image as reflected by Roman public opinion, even if we cannot plumb the depths of his personality?'

work-in-progress. Earlier in the speech, Cicero berated Antony for his nefarious handling of Caesar's archive that contained his unpublished *acta*, claiming that Antony feigned Caesarian authorship for any kind of measure that served his interests. In the light of this track record of insisting that Caesar's word (oral, written, drafted, or invented) was — or had to become — law, Antony's disrespect for certain aspects of Caesar's legislative record emerges as hypocritical. This is the invective angle Cicero explores in the present paragraph, lambasting his adversary for his 'optional' commitment to Caesar's legacy and testament: Antony, Cicero claims, gives overriding importance to Caesar's acts when it suits him, but thinks nothing of doing away with those of his measures he deems inconvenient. But, as Matijević (2006) convincingly shows, the issue here is not so much (or just as much) Antony falsifying Caesar's *acta* as Cicero falsifying Antony's handling of Caesar's *acta*.[78]

At iste, qui senatu non egeret, neque desideravit quemquam et potius discessu nostro laetatus est statimque illa mirabilia facinora effecit: after his picture of frightened senators at the end of § 108, Cicero now refocuses on Antony (with evident distaste, expressed by the adversative particle *at* and the contemptuous demonstrative pronoun *iste*): far from being upset by a depleted senate, Antony exulted in the opportunity to push through his nefarious agenda — and did so at once (*statim*): 'But this man here, since he had no need of a senate, did not miss anyone (of us), and rather rejoiced at our departure, and immediately proceeded to those stunning exploits of his'. The connectives here take some sorting: Cicero, unusually, correlates *neque* with *-que* (after *statim*) rather than *et*. (The *et potius discessu nostro laetatus est* continues, and glosses, *neque desideravit quemquam*.)

qui senatu non egeret: *senatu* is an ablative of separation with *egeret* (the imperfect subjunctive in a relative clause with causal force).

discessu nostro laetatus est: *laetor* here governs the ablative *discessu nostro* ('he took delight in our departure').

---

78   Caesar's legislative activities (both completed and in draft form) — and the status of his documents after the Ides of March — were already important topics in *Philippic* 1 (§§ 18–19, 21, 23–24). Here it is important to bear in mind that the *leges* that Caesar passed during his lifetime formed a subsection of his (published and unpublished) *acta*, which Cicero believed ought to be upheld.

illa mirabilia facinora effecit: the noun *facinus*, which is etymologically related to the verb *facio* (hence *facinora effecit* forms a so-called *figura etymologica*), can have the neutral meaning of 'deed' or 'act' ('something that has been done'); here, though, the sense is 'misdeed', 'crime', or 'outrage'. *mirabilis* [from the deponent *miror, -ari, -atus*: 'to be surprised, amazed, or bewildered + *bilis*] has the value-neutral meaning of 'causing wonder', 'extraordinary'.

qui chirographa Caesaris defendisset lucri sui causa, is leges Caesaris easque praeclaras, ut rem publicam concutere posset, evertit: *qui* might look like a connecting relative, but it is not: it introduces a — concessive: hence the pluperfect subjunctive *defendisset* — relative clause with *is* as antecedent: 'this man, who / even though he had defended Caesar's holographs for his personal profit...' Cicero here targets Antony's contradictory approach towards the legacy of Caesar: handwritten drafts are treated like Scripture cast in stone when they bring Antony financial benefits (for instance through bribes by those you would like to see them published), whereas any piece of legislation he finds inconvenient is unceremoniously binned, even if it has already been put on permanent record.

leges Caesaris easque praeclaras: the *-que* after *eas* introduces a gloss on *leges*; the sense is: 'even though they were excellent'. Cicero uses the same adjective with reference to Caesar's legislation at *Phil.* 1.18 (cited above): *leges multas ... et praeclaras* (focalized through Caesar).

ut rem publicam concutere posset: the purpose-clause strikes an odd and aggressive chord: Cicero makes it out as if causing upheaval of the commonwealth for its own sake is Antony's overriding motivation.

numerum annorum provinciis prorogavit: Cicero here singles out a law that regulated the length of provincial governorships. *prorogo* is a technical term here with the sense of 'to extend a term of office'. The need to create so-called 'pro-magistrates', i.e. magistrates that had completed their term in office but then moved on to administrative positions 'on behalf of' (*pro*) a magistrate emerged in the context of Rome's imperial expansion when two consuls ceased to suffice to cover the needs for military leadership. But prolonged pro-magistracies, as attractive as they were for those holding them, also constituted a huge problem for the senatorial oligarchy — as (not least) the case of Caesar showed, who used his terms as pro-consul (initially five years, then extended, in 55 BCE, for another five-year period) to build up an invincible army loyal to him above all. It is somewhat ironic that in 46 BCE Caesar passed a law, the *Lex Iulia de provinciis*, which restricted the tenure of such position to one year for ex-praetors and two years for ex-consuls — no doubt in part to keep potential rivals in check. Yet Antony, looking ahead to his own pro-consulship, passed a law in the summer of 44 BCE, the *Lex (Antonia?) de provinciis consularibus*, that extended his (and Dolabella's) period as pro-consuls to five years, thus overriding Caesar's legislation. Since he was unable to get the law approved in the senate, he had the tribunes of the plebs (one of whom was his brother Lucius) pass the law in the *comitia tributa* by plebiscite. For a slightly fuller account see *Phil.* 5.7 (*tribuni plebis tulerunt de provinciis contra acta C. Caesaris: ille biennium, hic sexennium* — 'The tribunes of the plebs proposed a law concerning the provinces which ran counter to the acts of Gaius Caesar: he had fixed a two-year tenure, Antony a six-year') with Manuwald (2007: 577–78).

idemque, cum actorum Caesaris defensor esse deberet, et in publicis et in privatis rebus acta Caesaris rescidit: the main verb — *rescidit* — here has the technical sense of 'rescinding something officially decreed', such as a law. The *cum*-clause is concessive ('even though...'). Cicero now proceeds to identify the various areas in which Antony was busy undoing Caesar's arrangements. Here he differentiates between *res publicae* and *res privatae*; in the following sentence, he identifies laws (*leges*) as the most important element of *res publicae* and a testament (*testamentum*) as the most important element of *res privatae*, before proceeding to give examples of how Antony attacked Caesar's *leges* and arrangements set down in his testament.

actorum Caesaris defensor: 'Verbal agent nouns in -*tor* [here: *defensor*], socalled nomina agentis, can take objective genitives [here: *actorum*]', where 'the genitive denotes the entity defended, more rarely the danger defended against' Devine and Stephens (2006: 343, 346).

in publicis [rebus] **nihil est lege gravius; in privatis** [rebus] **firmissimum est testamentum**: Cicero here draws an analogy between the status of law in the public sphere and the status of a testament in personal affairs, moving on from a comparative (*gravius*; *lege* is an ablative of comparison) to a superlative (*firmissimum*).

leges alias sine promulgatione sustulit, alias ut tolleret [novas leges] **promulgavit**: the sentence picks up *in publicis nihil est lege gravius*: 'as for [Caesar's] laws, some he annulled without prior public notice (*promulgatio*), to annul others, he gave public notice [of new legislation]'.

promulgare (noun: *promulgatio*) is a technical term from Roman law. See Kaster (2006: 425): 'The public reading and posting of any proposed piece of legislation: the proposal had to receive this publicity on at least three successive market days (*nundinae*) before an assembly could be convened for a vote' that would turn the bill into law. In terms of syntax, we get two sentences in asyndetic sequence, but the elliptical and unbalanced nature of Cicero's prose conjures the chaos that Antony (so Cicero suggests) is causing in Rome's legal sphere. Note in particular the antithesis of *sine promulgatione* and *promulgavit*, which underscores that whatever Antony does in terms of legislation undoes Caesar's legal arrangements; and the slippage from *leges alias*, the accusative object of the main verb *sustulit*, to *alias* [*leges*], which is the accusative object of the subordinate clause introduced by *ut*. The facts are much less sensational: it is true that the plebiscite that extended the pro-consulships of Antony and Dolabella violated the restrictions imposed by Caesar's *Lex Iulia de provinciis*; but that does not mean that it rendered Caesar's legislation void. The new laws that Antony proposed also did not constitute an assault on Caesar's legal order, but formed the kind of adjustments to existing legislation that a consul might be expected to make. As Ramsey (2003: 124) explains with reference to a piece of Caesarian legislation that regulated jury service: 'Caesar's *lex iudiciaria* of 46 eliminated the lowest of the three classes from which juries were drawn (*tribuni aerarii*) and limited jury service to senators and *equites* (Suet. *Iul.* 41.2; Dio 43.25.1). Antony's law establishing a third panel may have been designed to address a resulting shortage of jurors'.

testamentum irritum fecit, quod etiam infimis civibus semper obtentum est: the sentence picks up *in privatis firmissimum est testamentum*. Cicero here refers overdramatically to the tussle that followed the unsealing and reading of Caesar's will after the Ides of March (for which see the report in Suetonius, *Life of Julius Caesar*, 82–83):

> Fuerat animus coniuratis corpus occisi in Tiberim trahere, bona publicare, acta rescindere, sed metu Marci Antoni consulis et magistri equitum Lepidi destiterunt. postulante ergo Lucio Pisone socero testamentum

eius aperitur recitaturque in Antoni domo, quod Idibus Septembribus proximis in Lavicano suo fecerat demandaveratque virgini Vestali maximae.

[The conspirators had intended after slaying him to drag his body to the Tiber, confiscate his property, and revoke his decrees; but they desisted through fear of the consul Marcus Antonius and Lepidus, the master of the horse. Then at the request of his father-in-law Lucius Piso, the will was unsealed and read in Antony's house, which Caesar had made on the preceding Ides of September (= 13 September 45) at his place near Lavicum, and put in the care of the chief of the Vestal Virgins.]

While Antony did his best to obstruct execution of those provisions that he disliked, he never claimed the will as such to be 'invalid': *irritum* is Ciceronian hyperbole. One particular grievance for Antony was Caesar's nomination of Octavian as his heir and executor. See Plutarch, *Life of Antony*, 16:

While matters went thus in Rome, the young Caesar, Caesar's niece's son, and by testament left his heir, arrived at Rome from Apollonia, where he was when his uncle was killed. The first thing he did was to visit Antony, as his father's friend. He spoke to him concerning the money that was in his hands, and reminded him of the legacy Caesar had made of seventy-five drachmas of every Roman citizen. Antony, at first, laughing at such discourse from so young a man, told him he wished he were in his health, and that he wanted good counsel and good friends to tell him the burden of being executor to Caesar would sit very uneasy upon his young shoulders. This was no answer to him; and, when he persisted in demanding the property, Antony went on treating him injuriously both in word and deed, opposed him when he stood for the tribune's office, and, when he was taking steps for the dedication of his father's golden chair, as had been enacted, he threatened to send him to prison if he did not give over soliciting the people. This made the young Caesar apply himself to Cicero, and all those that hated Antony...

quod etiam infimis civibus semper obtentum est: the antecedent of *quod* is *testamentum*; *etiam* here means 'even': 'Caesar's will he annulled — a thing, which has always been upheld even for citizens of the lowest social rank'. *infimus* is the superlative of *inferus*, and *infimis civibus* is in the dative of advantage.

signa, tabulas, quas populo Caesar una cum hortis legavit, eas hic partim in hortos Pompei deportavit, partim in villam Scipionis: In his will, Caesar bequeathed (*legavit*) the so-called *Horti Caesaris trans Tiberim* ('The Gardens of Caesar across the Tiber') to the Roman People. Already before his death, he used this estate to stage public entertainments, such as feasts for the entire populace: the garden parties in his *Horti* consciously rivaled the enjoyments on offer in the *Horti Pompeiani*, which were most likely part of the plot of land on the Campus Martius that also included Pompey's house and his theater: see Russell (2016: 162) with references to further literature. In the wake of Pompey's death, this complex passed into the possession of Antony, and Cicero claims that Antony, after Caesar too lost his life, plundered the *Horti Caesaris trans Tiberim* to prettify two places he had acquired when properties of Pompey and his followers were auctioned off, the *Horti Pompeiani* and the villa of Scipio, thereby essentially despoiling the Roman people. See further Wood (2010: 78):

> The *Horti Caesaris trans Tiberim* should be seen as a direct challenge to the *Horti Pompeiani*. Positioned on the river's right bank along with a series of other aristocratic holdings, it was essentially a private estate and the venue where Caesar hosted Cleopatra in 45 B.C. (Cic. *Att.* 15.15.2). However, in attempting to outmanoeuvre Pompey, Caesar is known to have hosted a grand public banquet in his *horti trans Tiberim* also in 45 B.C. (Val. Max. 9.15.1), where according to Dio (43.42.1) he feasted the entire populace. The true extent of Dio's assertion may be questionable, but it certainly exemplified Caesar's exploitation of the communal meal as a popular measure (Plut. *Caes.* 5.5, 55.2, 57.5; Suet. *Iul.* 26.2). Additionally, it underlines the extent of Caesar's *horti* in that it was capable of hosting such a grand, large scale spectacle. As with Pompey's *horti*, Caesar's expansive gardens would have afforded Rome's poorest citizens a visual treat, surrounded by numerous statues, paintings and other works of art within verdant grounds on the banks of the Tiber, allowing them to bask in the ambience of their surroundings away from the chaos of Rome beyond. It is significant that while Pompey's *horti* passed on to Mark Antony and in turn Agrippa, Caesar chose to will his estate and all its enclosed artworks to the Roman people on his death (Cic. *Phil.* 2.109; Dio Cass. 44.35.3; Suet. *Iul.* 83.2). This would have been a conscious ploy, intended to counter the daily access offered by the *Horti Pompeiani* in Caesar's lifetime.

§ 110: Caesar: Dead Duck or Deified Dictator?

One of the most hotly contested issues after the Ides of March was Caesar's 'ontological status': was he a dead mortal or had he become divine? Caesar's religious identity was above all a political matter: whereas the senatorial oligarchy resisted any attempt to elevate Caesar to the level of a god, followers of Caesar had good reasons to push him skywards, not least once it became apparent that such a move was very much in tune with popular feelings. Earlier on in the speech, Cicero touched upon this issue when he discussed the so-called 'false Marius' and the altar and column spontaneously erected at the site of Caesar's funeral, but then torn down by Dolabella and Antony: see above on § 107. After these events in March and April of 44 BCE, several developments revitalized Caesar's claim to divine status. Octavian in particular found resonance among the people and the veterans when insisting that Caesar had become a god — and was helped by a comet that became visible in the second part of July 44 during his celebrations of games in honour of Caesar.[79] The aggressive promotion of a deified Caesar by his adopted son put Antony in a double bind: to maintain his position as the leading Caesarian he could hardly boycott endeavours to honour Caesar; yet turning Caesar into a god would inevitably endow his main rival Octavian with powerful divine ancestry.

The *Philippics* bear witness to earlier tussles around this matter. In the senate meeting on 1 September 44, which Cicero did not attend,

---

79   Bechtold (2011: 171).

Antony pushed through legislative measures which stipulated honours for Caesar that came close to turning him into a god. Specifically, Cicero offers a scathing commentary on Antony's motion to add an extra day in honour of Caesar to all festivals of thanksgiving (*supplicationes*) (*Phil.* 1.13):

> An me censetis, patres conscripti, quod vos inviti secuti estis, decreturum fuisse, ut parentalia cum supplicationibus miscerentur, ut inexpiabiles religiones in rem publicam inducerentur, ut decernerentur supplicationes mortuo? nihil dico cui. fuerit ille L. Brutus qui et ipse dominatu regio rem publicam liberavit et ad similem virtutem et simile factum stirpem iam prope in quingentesimum annum propagavit: adduci tamen non possem ut quemquam mortuum coniungerem cum deorum immortalium religione; ut, cuius sepulcrum usquam exstet ubi parentetur, ei publice supplicetur.

> [Or do you think, Members of the Senate, that I would have supported the decree you passed against your will, that a sacrifice in honour of the dead should be mixed up with public thanksgivings, that sacrilege incapable of expiation should be introduced into the commonwealth, that public thanksgivings be decreed to a dead man? I don't say for whom. Let that man be the Brutus who freed the commonwealth from regal despotism and who after almost five hundred years has left descendants to show similar courage and to achieve a similar deed. Even so, I could not have been induced to associate any dead man with the worship of the immortal gods so that a public thanksgiving should be made for him while somewhere a tomb exists at which offerings can be made.]

Cicero accuses Antony of conflating two religious spheres that ought to be kept strictly apart: thanksgivings to the gods (*supplicationes*) and the *parentalia*, i.e. rites performed in honour of dead relatives (*parentes*). The results of this confusion, he stipulates, are religious pollution and divine wrath — for Cicero an absolute boundary between the divine and the human sphere exists that is not to be crossed by anybody, let alone Caesar. Caesar is D-E-A-D! Throughout *Philippic* 1 and 2 he never misses an opportunity to emphasize this point, most strikingly at *Phil.* 1.24, where he mocks Antony's postmortem publication of Caesar's acts: *de exsilio reducti multi **a mortuo**, civitas data non solum singulis, sed nationibus et provinciis universis **a mortuo**, immunitatibus infinitis sublata vectigalia **a mortuo*** ('Men have been brought back from exile **by a dead**

man; citizenship has been given, not only to individuals, but to whole tribes and provinces **by a dead man**; by boundless exemptions revenues have been done away with **by a dead man**').

Our passage revisits the religious politics revolving around Caesar, with a specific focus on the Catch-22 that Antony found himself in: as a leading Caesarian, he was expected to promote divine honours for the dead dictator; yet to do so could not help but have the — for Antony undesirable — consequence of empowering his main rival among the Caesarians for the leading role he coveted for himself: given Caesar's adoption of Octavian, his deification would render Octavian the son of a god: '[Antony] surely had grasped that the confirmation of Caesar's divine status would — and indeed, did — deliver to Octavian something far grander than the name of *Caesar*: the appellation *divi filius*' (Koortbojian 2013: 39). It is indeed telling that when in January 42 BCE the senate finally recognized Caesar's deification and thereby turned Octavian officially into *Divi Filius*, the son of *Divus Iulius* ('the deified Julius'), Antony, who had been *flamen* designate of Caesar already in 44 BCE, continued to delay his *inauguratio* until October 40 BCE.

Paradoxically, just as Antony had a vested interested in down-playing Caesar's divinity, so Cicero, because of his belief that he could instrumentalize Octavian for his variant of senatorial politics, abandoned his categorical refusal to accept Caesar's claim to divine status as anything but blasphemy in subsequent orations, so as not to alienate Octavian — which meant that he needed to entertain, at least notionally, Caesar's divinity. See the discussion by Cole (2014: 174): 'Cicero's representation of Antony's role as *flamen* in the subsequent, publicly delivered *Philippics* provides additional evidence for consideration along with 2.110 in an assessment of Cicero's approach to cult for Caesar. The strategy of shaming Antony for his neglect of Caesar's cult becomes a way to alienate Antony from Octavian and a public already embracing Caesar's divinity. Cicero's handling of Caesar's honors in the *First Philippic* could hardly have pleased the young Octavian, who was actively promoting *Divus Iulius* and his singular tie to him. But Octavian would have been encouraged by the new tack in following *Philippics* wherein Cicero promotes the legitimacy of Octavian's yet-unratified adoption and also insistently connects Caesar's heir with divinity'.

Et tu in Caesaris memoria diligens [es], tu illum amas mortuum?: the sarcastic rhetorical question leads on from the end of the previous paragraph, where Cicero blamed Antony for plundering artistic treasures from the park that Caesar left to the Roman people. Cf. § 51, where Cicero also uses *et tu* (here reinforced by the repetition of *tu* at the beginning of the second clause) to kick-start a question brimming with sarcasm and outrage. *Caesaris* is an objective genitive dependent on *memoria*. *diligens* can be construed with various prepositions (*OLD* s.v. 2), here it is *in* + ablative. The verb of the first clause (*es*) is elided: 'And are you attentive to Caesar's memory, do you love him — dead as he is?' *mortuum* is an (exposed and programmatic) expansion of *illum* (note the homoioteleuton), picking up *me-mor-ia* in the first clause in paronomasia. The figure here carries an ideological punch: *memoria*, in the sense of (collective) remembrance through various means and media of commemoration, is the way Rome's community has traditionally kept the dead (*mortui*) present — *not* deification. At the beginning of a paragraph devoted to a discussion of religious honours for Caesar, Cicero emphatically and programmatically calls the dictator dead (rather than deified), preparing for the ironic use of the formulation *divus Iulius* two sentences later (see below).

quem is honorem maiorem consecutus erat quam ut haberet pulvinar, simulacrum, fastigium, flaminem?: *quem* is an interrogative adjective agreeing with *honorem*: 'what greater honour...'. *is*, the subject of the sentence (and rather squashed between *quem* and *honorem*) refers to Caesar: 'what greater honour had this man attained than...'. *ut* introduces a consecutive clause after the comparative *maiorem* + *quam*. Scholars debate when the four honours Cicero here lists were actually awarded to Caesar — and whether they amount to his full-scale deification in official religious practice. According to Koortbojian, the standard here has to be the practice of a cult dedicated to the worship of Caesar deified (2013: 32): 'which — if any — of these honors can be linked directly with the *publica sacra* of state cult — "those performed at public expense on behalf of the *populus*" — and which connote the ritual offerings (*sacrificia* or *supplicationes*) by which such cult was defined'. He explores each of the four honours in turn and reaches the conclusion that none implies Caesar's actual godhood, even though all are *symbols of* divinity: they may have been designed to signal that Caesar had begun to approximate, rather than (as of yet) fully transformed into, a divine being. These fine distinctions are important, but they are fine: and while Caesar may not have officially entered Roman state cult by the time Cicero composed *Philippic* 2, the passage here clearly shows that some of his supporters deemed his transformation into a god successfully completed: his divinity was very much in the eyes of the beholder.

pulvinar, simulacrum, fastigium, flaminem: an asyndetic, climactic sequence, with the last two items related by alliteration. We move from sacred, ceremonial cushion (*pulvinar*), to a statue of a (quasi-)divinity (*simulacrum*), which on certain ritual occasions rested on a *pulvinar*, to a piece of temple architecture (*fastigium* – pediment) that would house statues of gods, to a priest responsible for the cult of a specific divinity (*flamen*). All of these constituted senatorial honours for Caesar, shortly before (or, in the case of the *flamen*, perhaps soon after) his assassination.

pulvinar: deriving from *pulvinus, -i*, m. ('cushion' or 'pillow'), *pulvinar* (n.) has a range of meanings: '1) divine couch, 2) sacred marriage-bed, 3) sacred edifice or space (similar to *aedes*, *fanum*, or *templum*), including the *Pulvinar* in the *Circus Maximus*, and 4) *lectisternium* (a sacrificial meal for a god)': van den Berg (2008: 240). Cicero here uses the term in sense 1), i.e. a cushioned, ceremonial couch on which the image of a deity — or of a person honoured like a deity — was placed for ceremonial purposes or worship. At the end of the paragraph, he uses the term again (*pulvinaria*), but in sense 4). Sometime in January or February 44 (?), Caesar seems to have been accorded the privilege, hitherto restricted to gods, to have a statue or image of his placed on a sacred, ceremonial couch during public festivals and processions.

simulacrum: the context makes it clear that *simulacrum* here refers to a kind of statue that implies Caesar's divinity (or special association with the divine) (cf. *OLD* s.v. 3a). However, it remains unclear which statue of Caesar Cicero has in mind. Possibilities include the statue with the inscription *Deo Invicto* ('To the Unconquered God') that the senate voted to set up in the temple of Quirinus in 45 BCE; or the statue that appeared next to Victory during a circus procession that inaugurated games in honour of Caesar's victory in the civil war, also in 45 BCE (to the displeasure, as Cicero notes with glee, of a significant portion of the audience: *Att.* 13.44.1). See Koortbojian (2013: 36) for discussion.

fastigium: *fastigium* here as the technical meaning of 'pediment', i.e. the triangular upper part of the front of a building, typically a temple. Caesar — again following a vote by the senate — added such a pediment to his house in the Forum, which gave it the appearance — but *only* the appearance, as Koortbojian is keen to stress — of a temple: 'a house with a pediment was not a temple and, without an altar, no place for cult. Like all the *insignia* bestowed upon Caesar, this too acknowledged his new status, but that new status cannot yet be understood institutionally. Just as the *ornamenta triumphalia* signaled a victor's status by likening him, visibly, to Jupiter, so too Caesar's house might now *look* like a shrine, and thus liken its inhabitants to a god. But temple, altar, and cult were yet to come, and with them, *only* with them, the advent of cult and the institutionalization of Caesar's divine status. No *veneratio* here' (2013: 32). At the same time, Suetonius implies that for some Romans (arguably including himself) this piece of architecture (as well as the term for it) carried particularly noxious connotations of self-aggrandizement and all but turned Caesar into a tyrant — and hence fair game (*Life of Julius Caesar* 76.1, cited above 247–48). As Jenkyns (2013: 23) notes: 'The word [sc. *fastigium*] is interesting here, for the Senate did indeed vote a *fastigium* for the dictator's house; the acme — *fastigium* — of achievement is embodied literally at the tip of the gable. Cicero indignantly lists this ornament among the other quasi-divine honours that Julius received; the city's profile expresses both the ups and downs of the political rat race and a kind of continuum extending from gods to men. As a *fastigium* crowns the pediment of a temple, so it adorns a dynast's home. Calpurnia, Julius Caesar's wife, was said to have dreamt before his murder that the *fastigium* on his house toppled down [Plut. *Caes.* 63.5; Suet. *Jul.* 81.3]. This is a symbolism close to reality'.

flaminem: a *flamen* was a special priest appointed to carry out the rites of a specific divinity. Traditionally, there were 15 *flamines* in all — three so-called higher ones (*flamines maiores*) filled by patricians for Jupiter (*Flamen Dialis*), Mars (*Flamen Martialis*), and Quirinus (*Flamen Quirinalis*); and twelve minor ones (*flamines minores*) filled by plebeians and dedicated to less important — not to say: obscure — divinities, many of whom associated with the sphere of agriculture. Only ten of them are known by name: *Flamen Carmentalis* (the *flamen* for Carmentis), *Flamen Cerialis* (for Ceres), *Flamen Falacer* (for Falacer), *Flamen Floralis* (for Flora), *Flamen Furrinalis* (for Furrina), *Flamen Palatualis* (for Palatua), *Flamen Pomonalis* (for Pomona), *Flamen Portunalis* (for Portunus), *Flamen Volcanalis* (for Vulcan), and *Flamen Volturnalis* (for Volturnus). Unlike the first three honours, i.e. *pulvinar*, *simulacrum*, and *fastigium*: the list is clearly climactic, having a *flamen* unequivocally means that one is a divinity.

A scholarly debate rages over the question whether Caesar was awarded the honour of a *flamen* during his lifetime or after his death, with our passage figuring prominently. Here are Beard, North, Price (1998: 2.222): 'This passage is one of the main pieces of evidence to suggest that Caesar was aiming at deification during his lifetime. ... Cicero is teasing Antony by asking him why, if he was as devoted to Caesar's memory as he said he was, he had not yet gone through the formal ceremony of inauguration as *flamen*, that is special priest of Caesar's new cult. In doing this, Cicero claims detailed knowledge of the cult — the god's title, the priest's title, even the new priest's identity. In fact, the formal recognition of Caesar as a god (*divus* Julius) did not occur till after Cicero's death and Antony only became *flamen divi Iulii* in 40 B.C. (Plutarch, *Life of Antony* 33.1). The only explanation for Cicero's apparent knowledge is that he knew of detailed plans for deification drafted in Caesar's lifetime, but only implemented in the years after his death'. Cole (2014: 173) is somewhat more circumspect: 'The tenses in this passage ... make it clear that Cicero is speaking of honors granted in Caesar's lifetime — honors not mentioned by Cicero until after Caesar's death'. But does our passage really offer decisive evidence 'for a cult of the living Caesar'? Cole rightly asks: 'Why are there no comments on this development in letters to Atticus? Can this passage in the *Second Philippic* be isolated as Cicero's principled, categorical objection to cult for Caesar?' And Koortbojian (2013: 35) argues that 'in contrast to the *fastigium* and the *pulvinar*, the *flaminate* — like the *simulacrum*... — must have been among the *posthumous* honors that figured in the accommodations that the Senate enacted with the rival parties in the wake of Caesar's assassination'.

est ergo flamen, ut Iovi, ut Marti, ut Quirino, sic divo Iulio M. Antonius. quid igitur cessas? cur non inauguraris? sume diem, vide qui te inauguret: collegae sumus; nemo negabit: whether the honour of a *flamen* was voted to Caesar while he was still alive or as a posthumous award, what primarily matters for our passage is the fact that the designated *flamen* Antony had not yet undergone inauguration: it is Antony's delay in bringing the honour to fruition that Cicero singles out for sarcastic commentary. The chiastic design and the *ut ... sic* structure of (a) *flamen* : (b) *Iovi, Marti, Quirino* :: (b) *divo Iulio* : (a) *M. Antonius* gives the (wrong) impression of a basic equivalence between the priesthoods of the *flamines maiores* (see previous note) and the new priesthood of divine Julius — an impression deliberately reinforced by the opening *est ergo*, which forcefully suggests the statement of a fact. But as the subsequent series of questions, exhortations, and encouragements makes apparent, Antony has so far fallen woefully short of putting this greatest of all honours into (cultic) practice. Cicero mockingly offers to help him out: like Antony, he was an augur (*collegae sumus*) and could have assisted in Antony's inauguration as *flamen*.

o detestabilem hominem, sive quod tyranni sacerdos es sive quod mortui sacerdos es]!: Cicero shouts out an accusative of exclamation — the Latin equivalent of WRITING AN EMAIL IN CAPS. *o detestabilem hominem* then segues into two alternative *quod*-clauses (coordinated by *sive ... sive ...*: 'be it that ..., be it that...') that conjure Antony as priest (Cicero slips from the technical *flamen* to the generic *sacerdos*) of Caesar, whether when still alive as tyrant (*tyranni sacerdos*) or dead (*mortui sacerdos*). Being the priest of either a tyrant or a dead man is of course abominable.

tyranni: the text is disputed: some manuscripts have *Caesaris* instead. One will have been a marginal gloss for the other. For the dilemma to bite, *tyranni* is clearly the superior option.

quaero deinceps num hodiernus dies qui sit ignores: *quaero* governs the indirect question *num ... ignores*: 'I next ask whether by any chance you do not know...' *ignores* governs the further indirect question *hodiernus dies qui sit*, with the emphatic prolepsis of *hodiernus dies*: 'which day today is'.

nescis heri quartum in circo diem ludorum Romanorum fuisse, te autem ipsum ad populum tulisse ut quintus praeterea dies Caesari tribueretur?: the main verb of the rhetorical question, *nescis*, introduces a twofold indirect statement linked by the adversative particle *autem*: *quartum ... diem ... fuisse*; *te ... ipsum ... tulisse*. 'Don't you know that...?' The *ut*-clause specifies what Antony proposed to the people. Cicero cast *Philippic* 2 as a speech delivered on 19 September 44, so *heri* ('yesterday') refers to 18 September, which was the fourth day of the period of games (15–18 September) that, after a brief interval, followed on the festival of the *ludi Romani* ('Roman Games', 4–12 September). Antony, at some unspecified point in time, seems to have proposed to add a fifth day of games to the *Ludi Romani*, but then abandoned the plan

Alternatively, Cicero here picks up on the motion Antony carried in the senate meeting of 1 September, namely that an extra day should be added to all festivals of thanksgiving to the gods (so-called *supplicationes*) in honour of Caesar: see *Phil.* 1.13, cited above; further Weinstock (1971: 62–64). As Lacey (1986: 238) points out, 'It was an open question whether the Roman Games were, or were not, thanksgivings. In origin they were, but as they were held annually, and on the same date whether there were or were not any victories to celebrate, it could be thought that they were not, and "thanksgivings" meant only those voted to honour commanders for their successes, when appropriate'. Clearly, Antony did not believe that the *Ludi Romani* were affected by his motion on *supplicationes* — whereas Cicero posits that they were, and that a fifth day of games should have been added — gleefully interpreting Antony's 'failure' to institute an extra day in Caesar's honour (which would have been the 19 September) as a sign of disrespect for the dead dictator. On this reading, Cicero 'invents' his evidence here, on the basis of divergent interpretations of Antony's own motion (and differing definitions of the *Ludi Romani* and the applicability of the label *supplicatio*).

cur non sumus praetextati? cur honorem Caesaris tua lege datum deseri patimur?: Cicero continues with two further rhetorical questions, addressed to himself and the rest of the senators or augurs (*sumus*, *patimur*), which are grounded in the claim that Antony failed to follow through on his own legislation and add an extra day of games to the *Ludi Romani*. If that extra day had been added, Cicero, as augur, and perhaps also other high-ranking Romans who had held curule office, would have been dressed in the *toga praetexta*.

an supplicationes addendo diem contaminari passus es, pulvinaria contaminari noluisti?: *an* here introduces an irritable direct question (*OLD* s.v. 1). The passage is obscure. Cicero seems to be saying that Antony was happy to profane *supplicationes*, but somehow became squeamish when it came to the *pulvinaria*. But given that *supplicationes* were carried out in front of the *pulvinaria*, the question arises: 'How could Antony defile the *supplicationes* without also defiling the *pulvinaria*?' (Denniston 1926: 170). The sentence clearly presupposes that *supplicationes* and *pulvinaria* have a distinct religious identity and significance — but precise details of the scenario he has in mind elude us.

aut undique religionem tolle aut usque quaque conserva: Cicero concludes with two imperatives (*tolle, conserva*) coordinated by *aut ... aut*. His either — or ('all or nothing') is a false alternative.

§ 111: A Final Look at Antony's Illoquence

Cicero concludes his examination of Antony's inconsistency in handling Caesar and his legacy by lambasting him a final time for his alleged lack of eloquence: put on the spot to defend his policies Antony (so Cicero insinuates) will have nothing to say. His abject failure to articulate himself in supple and muscular speech stands in dismal contrast to the heights of eloquence achieved by his grandfather — Antony is the sad offspring of a once great family. The paragraph thus also brings to a close the competition in eloquence that runs throughout *Philippic* 2 from § 2 onwards.

Quaeris placeatne mihi pulvinar esse, fastigium, flaminem: Cicero imagines Antony asking whether he approves of the divine honours awarded to Caesar — given his curious insistence that they are properly observed. The inverted word order, with the verb *placeat* up front, conveys a sense of challenge and surprise in Antony's imagined interjection. The alliterations *placeat – pulvinar* and *fastigium – flaminem* underscore the mocking tone.

mihi vero nihil istorum placet: sed tu, qui acta Caesaris defendis, quid potes dicere cur alia defendas, alia non cures?: the particle *vero* here emphasizes the personal pronoun *mihi* and reinforces the way in which Cicero continues on from the previous sentence chiastically: ... *placeatne mihi :: mihi ... placet*. His response to Antony's imagined query amounts to a sarcastic rejection ('As should be obvious, *I* approve of none of these!'), which serves him as base to revisit Antony's inconsistent approach to Caesar's religious-political patrimony.

nihil istorum: strongly contemptuous, referring back to *pulvinar*, *fastigium*, and *flaminem*.

sed tu: in sharp antithesis to *mihi vero*, reinforced by chiasmus and prolepsis (the *tu* is the subject of the *quid-potes* clause).

quid potes dicere cur alia defendas, alia non cures: the adverb *cur* can be either interrogative or (as here) relative, when it is usually followed by the subjunctive (cf. *defendas, cures*), especially in the idiom *quid est cur?* (*OLD* s.v. *cur* 3): 'what can you say on account of which…', 'what can you say that justifies that…'

alia … alia…: 'some … others', picking up *acta Caesaris*.

[potes dicere nihil] **nisi forte vis fateri te omnia quaestu tuo, non illius dignitate metiri**: Cicero suppresses the implied answer to his rhetorical question (i.e. 'you can say nothing') before adding 'the truth' in a conditional proviso (*nisi forte…*). *vis* is the second person singular present indicative active of *volo, velle*, 'to want'. It takes the supplementary infinitive *fateri* (a deponent), which governs an indirect statement with *te* as subject accusative and *metiri* as infinitive: '… unless perhaps you want to confess that you measure all things by your own profit, not by Caesar's honour'.

forte: the adverb drips irony: 'on the off-chance' (you wish to tell the truth).

quaestu tuo, non illius dignitate metiri: the basic meaning of *metiri* is 'to measure', and Latin expresses *the standard by which* something is measured — here Antony's personal profit (*quaestu*) rather than the honour (*dignitate*) of Caesar — in the so-called 'ablative of measurement'. *quaestu tuo* :: *illius dignitate* forms a contrastive chiasmus with *non* as pivot.

quid ad haec tandem [respondebis]?: the adverb *tandem* is 'used to emphasize an asseveration, expressing a strong sense of protest or (as here) impatience' (*OLD* s.v. 1): 'so, what will you reply to this?' The verb has to be supplied: cf. below *respondebisne ad haec…?*

exspecto enim eloquentiam: disertissimum cognovi avum tuum, at te etiam apertiorem in dicendo: *enim* gives the assertion *exspecto …*

eloquentiam a deeply ironic appeal to interpersonal consensus (Kroon (1995: 202). Cicero then explains why he has such high expectations of Antony's rhetorical ability: his grandfather Marcus Antonius was supremely eloquent — and Antony has a track record of being even 'more outgoing' in public speech, so he should be well poised to answer back eloquently now. However, a double entendre in *apertiorem* turns the apparent praise into an insult: in the sense of 'open-hearted', 'frank', *apertus* is an attribute of high praise in Cicero. See e.g. *On the Commonwealth* (*de Republica*) 3.26: *de viro bono quaeritur, quem apertum et simplicem volumus esse* ('the search is for a good man, whom we want to be open and frank') or *On Duties* (*de Officiis*) 1.109: *sunt his alii multum dispares, simplices et aperti, qui nihil ex occulto, nihil de insidiis agendum putant, veritatis cultores, fraudis inimici*... ('Then there are others, quite different from these, straightforward and open, who think that nothing should be done by underhand means or treachery. They are lovers of truth, haters of fraud...'). The implication is that the speaker bares his mind (*ad Familiares* 1.9.22: *animum ... cum magnum et excelsum tum etiam apertum et simplicem* — 'a high-minded, unselfish, frank, and straightforward disposition') or heart (*de Amicitia* 97: *apertum pectus*). But as the following sentence makes clear, with reference to Antony, Cicero understands the 'baring' literally, not metaphorically (*apertus = nudus*): unlike his grandfather, Antony once spoke buck naked — a reference to his shocking state of dishabille when addressing the people at the Lupercalia in his jockstrap.

cognovi: the verb coordinates a pair of accusative objects (*avum tuum, te*) each with an attribute in predicative position. The arrangement is chiastic: *disertissimum : avum tuum :: te : apertiorem* (*in dicendo*), which reinforces the contrast between Antony and his grandfather, just as the adversative particle *at* placed at the centre of the design.

disertissimum... avum tuum: Cicero already held up Antony's grandfather Marcus Antonius (143–87 BCE) as a model of excellence towards the end of *Philippic* 1.34:

> Utinam, M. Antoni, avum tuum meminisses! de quo tamen audisti multa
> ex me eaque saepissime. putasne illum immortalitatem mereri voluisse,
> ut propter armorum habendorum licentiam metueretur? illa erat vita,
> illa secunda fortuna, libertate esse parem ceteris, principem dignitate.

[Marcus Antonius, I wish you remembered your grandfather! Though of him you have heard much from me and very often. Do you think that he would have wished to earn immortality by being feared for his ability to keep an armed guard? To him life, to him prosperous fortune, was to be equal to all others in freedom and the first in distinction.]

And in *Philippic* 2.42, Cicero draws a sharp contrast between Antony's and his grandfather's way with words: *vide autem quid intersit inter te et avum tuum. ille sensim dicebat quod causae prodesset; tu cursim dicis aliena* ('observe, however, the contrast between you and your grandfather: he spoke cautiously using words that helped his case; you produce irrelevant drivel'). As van der Blom (2010: 95) elaborates: 'Cicero often refers to the importance of choosing an *exemplum* within the family, especially if the family formed part of the nobility. Cicero's appeal for the imitation of family *exempla* and his praise or blame of a specific choice formed part of his (alleged) efforts to steer his subject in a specific direction and, in particular, to pass a public judgement on his subject'. She discusses this strategy with specific reference to the *Philippics*, where Cicero more than once brings Antony's grandfather into play — whom he had already memorialized as a paragon of eloquence in his dialogue *On the Ideal Orator* (*de Oratore*).

etiam apertiorem: in classical Latin, 'the comparative is often strengthened … by the insertion of **etiam**, *even*' (Gildersleeve & Lodge 190).

ille numquam nudus est contionatus: tuum hominis simplicis pectus vidimus: Cicero now resolves the puzzle built into the previous sentence by upbraiding Antony once more for his sartorial negligence at the Lupercalia. His emulation of his grandfather in being an upfront and free-spoken (*apertus*) speaker found infamous expression in him going full frontal with the crowd at the Lupercalia — not a feat grandad can rival, as Cicero notes with sardonic alliteration (*numquam nudus*).

tuum hominis simplicis pectus: Cicero here compresses two related constructions, the possessive adjective (*tuum pectus*) and the possessive genitive (*hominis simplicis pectus*). See Pinkster (2015: 1066): 'Since possessive adjectives to some extent function as genitives of corresponding personal pronouns, it is not surprising to find instances where a descriptive Noun Phrase in the genitive functions as apposition with a possessive adjective'. 'We saw your chest — the chest of a plain (sincere / simple-minded) human being'. Like *apertus*, *simplex* can have a range of meanings: in a positive sense it is a virtual synonym of *apertus* ('sincere'); Cicero in fact often uses the two terms together (see the passages cited above). But it can also have the pejorative sense of 'plain', 'naive', 'simple minded', 'unsophisticated'. The oscillation between a literal and a metaphorical sense also applies to *pectus*, which can mean both 'chest' and 'personality': so Antony revealed not just his body, but also what kind of person he is.

vidimus: first person plural perfect active indicative. Cicero identifies with the senatorial collective that witnessed Antony's strip-show.

respondebisne ad haec, aut omnino hiscere audebis?: *aut* extends the first part of the question by rephrasing it slightly: 'Will you reply to this, *or, put differently*, will you dare to open your mouth at all?'

ecquid reperies ex tam longa oratione mea cui te respondere posse confidas?: *ecquid* is an interrogative pronoun in the neuter accusative, the object of *reperies* (second person singular future indicative active) and the antecedent of the relative pronoun *cui*. The assonance (*ecquid* – *cui*) and alliteration (*reperies* – *respondere*) might have been part of the reason why Cicero changes the construction of *respondere* + *ad* in the previous sentence to *respondere* + dative (*cui*) here. *te* and *respondere* are the subject accusative and infinitive of an indirect statement governed by *confidas*: 'Will you find anything in this long speech of mine which you are confident that you can reply to?'

§ 112: The Senate Under Armour

As we are nearing the end of the speech, Cicero once again calls attention to the time and the location of the (imaginary) delivery of the speech — a specific moment on 19 September in the temple of Concordia — before opening up, via a strong rebuke of Antony's decision to bring along an armed body guard, to discuss the relation between statesmen and the wider civic community, with a special focus on the issue of 'personal safety'. As far as he is concerned, a politician who inspires hatred within his community has to fear for his life even if he tries to protect himself with the help of armed forces; the only effective source of security is the goodwill of the citizens. The passage therefore prepares the ground for the following paragraphs, where Cicero warns Antony that a tyrannical individual who rules through fear and the threat of violence must in turn fear for his life — since he ought to be killed. At the end of the paragraph Cicero accordingly shifts from a critique of Antony's past behaviour and remonstrance against his present actions to the possibility of impending retribution. The sketch of a scenario situated in the not-too-distant future coincides with a corresponding change in rhetorical register: invective flak morphs into cautionary counsel as not-so-veiled threat.

Sed praeterita omittamus: hunc unum diem, unum, inquam, hodiernum diem, hoc punctum temporis, quo loquor, defende, si potes: the imperative *defende* takes three all but synonymous accusative objects, arranged asyndetically and climactically and standing in antithesis to *praeterita*: (i) *hunc unum diem*; (ii) *unum ... hodiernum diem*; (iii) *hoc punctum temporis*. In the course of the tricolon Cicero homes in on the (it bears repeating: imaginary) moment of delivery with ever-greater precision.

praeterita: *praeteritus* is the perfect passive participle of *praetereo* — 'to pass by, go past', here used as a noun (in the neuter accusative plural): 'the matters that have occurred' = 'the past'.

omittamus: exhortative subjunctive: 'let us disregard past matters'.

inquam: first person singular present indicative active.

hoc punctum temporis, quo loquor: the antecedent of the relative pronoun *quo* (an ablative of time) is *punctum*: 'this moment of time in which I am speaking'.

defende, si potes: a simple condition in the present, though with an imperative *defende* (rather than an indicative) in the apodosis. Cicero's tone is challenging and derisive: the idea that Antony can actually defend himself for his current actions is dismissed as laughable even before his transgressions are spelt out.

cur armatorum corona senatus saeptus est, cur me tui satellites cum gladiis audiunt, cur valvae Concordiae non patent, cur homines omnium gentium maxime barbaros, Ituraeos, cum sagittis deducis in forum?: a sequence of four questions all introduced by *cur* in asyndetic sequence.

cur armatorum corona senatus saeptus est: the basic meaning of *corona* is 'wreath' or 'crown' but it was also used to refer to a throng of people surrounding a place. With reference to the civic sphere, this tended to be 'a circle of bystanders, spectators, or listeners', around a court of law or the senate; in military matters, it was 'a ring of soldiers' surrounding an enemy position. Here Cicero paints the picture of the Roman senate being encircled by a cordon of armed troops instructed to enforce Antony's whim and will. The sentence features a descending number of syllables: the instrumental ablative phrase *armatorum corona* (4 + 3) overpowers the subject and verb (assimilated by means of alliteration, homoioteleuton and sound-play) *senatus saeptus est* (3 + 2 + 1). The theme recurs at the opening of the pseudo-Ciceronian *Epistula ad Octauianum*, where the anonymous author in the context of a declamatory exercise postures as 'Cicero' and uses words and phrases employed by Cicero against Antony to inveigh against Caesar Octavianus: *cohortibus armatis* *circumsaeptus*. The first such enclosure of the senate by an armed force occurred in 88 BCE under Sulla (Valerius Maximus 3.8.5).

cur me tui satellites cum gladiis audiunt: a *satelles* (our English 'satellite' comes from it) is someone who (obsequiously) attends a higher ranking person, as bodyguard, escort, or partisan supporter; the word often has derogatory connotations (as here). Cicero likes a crowd, but not if it consists of Antony's henchmen with their swords (drawn?).

cur valvae Concordiae non patent: already in § 19, Cicero drew attention to the paradox of armed henchmen forming a divisive presence at a senate meeting in the temple of Concordia. Now towards the end of the speech he again gestures to the setting of the senate meeting at which we are to imagine he delivered *Philippic* 2, i.e. the temple of Concordia. As Clark (1999: 173–74) points out, 'This "speech" illustrates the potential richness of the temple of Concordia as an ideological location, but it also demonstrates that, had Cicero actually delivered it in Concordia's temple, as he purported to be doing in the circulated tract, he would in fact have conceded little to Concordia's presence in terms of the aggressiveness of his speech'. The fact that the temple doors are closed may owe itself to the need to protect the senators from Antony's supporters, but also signals that under Antony the conduct of civic business, which relies on open spaces and a sense of community, has been severely compromised through the threat of violence — and the absence of concord. The temple of Concordia was also the scene of his zenith speech, the fourth oration against Catiline (see below).

cur homines omnium gentium maxime barbaros, Ituraeos, cum sagittis deducis in forum?: *homines omnium gentium maxime barbaros* is the elaborate accusative object of *deducis*: 'of all foreign peoples the most savage human beings'. *omnium gentium* is a partitive genitive — indicating the whole of 'barbaria' (*gentes* here = foreign ethnicities) of which the *Ituraei* form the most savage part. *Ituraeos* stands in apposition to *homines … barbaros*. The Ituraeans lived in the Levantine region; some served as archers in the auxiliary forces of the Roman army. See Caesar, *Bellum Africum* 20.1, Virgil, *Georgics* 2.448, Lucan 7.230 and 514–15, further Isaac (2017: 144–46).

praesidi sui causa se facere dicit: Cicero imagines an explanatory interjection by Antony, held contemptuously in the third person (*sui – se – dicit*). The indirect statement governed by *dicit* features a subject accusative (*se*) and an infinitive (*facere*), but lacks a direct object (supply something like *hoc*). *causâ* (in the ablative) is as usual placed behind the genitive it governs: 'for the sake of his protection'.

non igitur miliens perire est melius quam in sua civitate sine armatorum praesidio non posse vivere?: the verb is the copula (*non*) *est* with (*miliens*) *melius* as predicate: 'is it not a thousand times better…' The subjects are the two infinitives *perire* and *non posse + vivere* coordinated by *quam* (following on the comparative *melius*) 'to perish than not to be able to live…'

sed nullum est istud, mihi crede, praesidium: caritate te et benevolentia civium saeptum oportet esse, non armis: Cicero now addresses Antony's justification from a different perspective — what Antony considers a safeguard, he claims, is not one. Instead of arms, Antony should endeavour to be enclosed for his safety by the affection and goodwill of the citizens. The subject of the impersonal verb *oportet* is the indirect statement *te* (subject accusative) *saeptum esse* (infinitive): (for safety) 'it is necessary that you are surrounded by…'. *caritate, benevolentia,* and *armis* are instrumental ablatives. Not coincidentally, Cicero uses the same verb (*saepire*) to express the idea of a protective wall, which he had used earlier on with reference to Antony's bodyguard in a threatening sense. A wall of love should replace a wall of arms. Cicero may be alluding contrastively to the *Fourth Catilinarian*, where he believes himself to be protected by the safest possible wall as long as the people remember his heroic service on behalf of the commonwealth (4.23: … *tutissimo me muro saeptum esse arbitror*). Put differently, Cicero says: 'a tyrant should die — and lives dangerously', irrespective of his armed guards. The idea that the best protection for a ruler is the devotion of his subjects becomes a topic in imperial panegyric. See Seneca, *de Clementia* 1.19.6 (*unum est inexpugnabile munimentum, amor civium* — with *civium* as subjective genitive), Pliny, *Panegyricus* 49.3 (building on Seneca), *Panegyrici Latini* 2.47.3–4, 3.24.5 (*Arma igitur et iuvenes cum gladiis atque pilis non custodiae corporis sunt, sed quidam imperatoriae maiestatis sollemnis ornatus. quid enim istis opus est, cum firmissimo sis muro civici amoris obsaeptus?* — 'Therefore the weapons and the young men with swords and pikes are not guardians of your body, but a kind of solemn adornment of your imperial majesty. What need is there for these, when you are surrounded by the firmest of walls, the citizens' love?'), Claudian 8.281–82, 24.221–22. See Nixon and Rodgers (1994: 427).

mihi crede: this colloquial 'metadirective imperative' ('believe me'), designed to reinforce the truth of the utterance (Spevak 2010: 210), does not affect the syntax of the surrounding sentence. It signals Cicero's shift in focus from past and present to the future, from invective to admonition, which continues in the following paragraph. The word order *mihi crede* (rather than *crede mihi*) is noteworthy. See Adams (2016: 204): 'Imperatives are often placed in the first position and unemphatic pronouns for their part do not as a rule come in first position. The order *mihi crede* is thus abnormal on two counts, and cannot but have given special emphasis to the personal pronoun. *Crede mihi* was more self-effacing than the reverse order, and it would only have been a person of marked self-esteem who would regularly have written *mihi crede*'. Cicero does so several times in short order: see also §113, §116, and §118.

§ 113: The *Res Publica* Has Watchers!

The previous paragraph ended on the dictum that only a life in harmony with the wider civic community guarantees personal safety. Cicero now explores what this general truth implies for the occasion at hand. A range of political agents (both individual and collective) and entities (*populus Romanus, gubernatores rei publicae, res publica, adulescentes nobilissimi*) are ready to take a stand against Antony if he persists in behaving like an enemy of the state. Cicero's tone — set up by another instance of *mihi crede* — remains aggressively didactic. But the paragraph ends on another gnomic pronouncement. Cicero differentiates between (desirable) *pax* and (intolerable) *servitus* and asserts that *libertas*, without which there cannot be any genuine *pax*, is a value to die for. His discourse here rises above the level of invective and turns into a personal manifesto about the principles of communal life. His guiding ideas, which will resonate throughout his peroration, are worth a more detailed look, in particular his notion of 'freedom' (*libertas*), which has a complex historical pedigree. Cicero combines at least four different ways of thinking with and about the term:[80]

(1) **Legal**: ancient Rome (just like ancient Greece and other cultures across the ancient Mediterranean) was a slave society, and the institution of slavery shaped every aspect of Greco-Roman life (including literature).[81]

---

80 The following draws on Wirszubski (1950), Brunt (1988a), Fantham (2005), Cowan (2008), Arena (2007b) and (2012), all with further bibliography. Some further aspects of *libertas* — such as its role in international relations, for instance, are less pertinent here.

81 See e.g. Bradley, K. R. (1994), Fitzgerald (2000), Mouritsen (2011), the papers in Bodel and Scheidel (2016), and Hunt (2018).

The most basic meaning of *libertas* thus concerns the legal distinction between free persons and slaves (with 'freed(wo)men', i.e. individuals who had once been enslaved but gained manumission, an intermediary category). As the *Digest* of Justinian puts it: 'all humans are either free or slaves' (1.5.3: *omnes homines aut liberi sunt aut servi*). This fundamental social divide ultimately informs all the other meanings of *libertas*. The foundational importance of the distinction between free / slave for the cultural imaginary of ancient Rome invited metaphorical exploitation, even when legal status was not literally at issue. Invoking *libertas* implied that those deprived of it were reduced to the lowest form of existence, that of slaves. (Modern definitions often work with the idea that slavery is tantamount to 'social death'.)

(2) **Political**: in the civic sphere, two distinct understandings of *libertas* — one associated with the ruling elite, the other with the people — shaped the practice of politics in republican Rome:

(i) for members of Rome's ruling elite *libertas* consisted primarily in the absence of a tyrant or, put differently, the preservation of oligarchic equality that ensured more or less equal opportunities to vie for offices and military commands in the pursuit of power and glory.

(ii) for the citizen body more generally, *libertas* manifested itself primarily in a set of rights and privileges that found expression in the notion of popular sovereignty (not least in passing legislation), the exercise of *suffragium* (voting), the magistracy of the tribune of the plebs (tasked originally and primarily with protecting the common citizen from abuse by magistrates), and the right to *provocatio* (i.e. the right of each citizen to appeal to the people against a magistrate who threatened to enforce capital or physical punishment).

With Caesar's rise to the dictatorship and his subsequent assassination, both of these traditions fused in interesting ways: they found emblematic articulation in both Caesar's self-promotion and that of his assassination.

To start with Caesar: his decision to go to war, he argued, was in part designed to protect *libertas*, in both the elite and the popular understanding of the term. He pulls off this conceptual caper at *Bellum*

Civile 1.22, which features himself in conversation with one of his senatorial adversaries, Lentulus Spinther:

> Cuius orationem Caesar interpellat: se non maleficii causa ex prouincia egressum, sed uti se a contumeliis inimicorum defenderet, ut tribunos plebis in ea re ex civitate expulsos in suam dignitatem restitueret, ut se et populum Romanum factione paucorum oppressum in libertatem uindicaret.

> [Caesar interrupts his speech, observing that he had not crossed the boundary of his province with any evil intent, but to defend himself from the insults of his enemies, to restore to their position the tribunes of the people who had been expelled from the civic community in the course of this affair, and to assert the freedom of himself and the Roman people who were oppressed by an oligarchic clique.]

Caesar contends that the senatorial grouping around Pompey formed an oligarchic clique that abused their power so as to deprive himself and the Roman people of their *libertas*. In his case, the lack of freedom consisted in the refusal of Pompey and his followers to recognize his achievements according to meritocratic criteria: Pompey, so Caesar insinuates in *Bellum Civile* 1.3, comported himself like a tyrant who would not tolerate a rival, thus violating the principles of oligarchic equality, equal opportunity, and the economy of merit that made up the 'optimate' understanding of freedom in politics. (Elsewhere, he prefers to make this point with reference to his *dignitas* — a notion indicating (earned) rank and standing within the ruling elite, which he here uses with reference to the constitutional status of the tribunes of the people.)[82] The 'popular' loss of liberty (and notional enslavement of the people) manifested itself above all in the flight of some of the tribunes of the plebs (one of them Antony) from Rome to Caesar's camp because they

---

82 Cf. Caesar, *Bellum Civile* 3.91 (before the decisive battle of Pharsalos): *Erat C. Crastinus evocatus in exercitu Caesaris, qui superiore anno apud eum primum pilum in legione X duxerat, vir singulari virtute. hic signo dato, 'sequimini me,' inquit, 'manipulares mei qui fuistis, et vestro imperatori quam constituistis operam date. unum hoc proelium superest; quo confecto et ille suam dignitatem et nos nostram libertatem recuperabimus.'* [There was in Caesar's army a reservist, G. Crastinus, *Mr. Morrow*, who *in the previous year* (get it?) had served under him as first centurion in the Tenth Legion, a man of remarkable courage. On the signal being given, he said: 'Follow me, who have been my comrades, and give your commander your usual loyal service. This one battle alone remains; when it is over he will recover his dignity and we our liberty.']

feared for their safety after interceding in senatorial proceedings on Caesar's behalf: this 'expulsion' of magistrates charged with upholding the rights of the common citizen served Caesar as a perfect pretext to pursue his personal agenda by violent means: he could claim to be protecting the rights, privileges, and sovereignty of the Roman people.[83] Caesar continued to style himself as a proponent of liberty even after gaining autocratic power. Following the Battle of Munda in 45 BCE, the senate honoured him with the title *Liberator* for having freed Rome from the evil of civil war.[84]

Caesar's assassins, of course, tried to pull off exactly the same conceptual move as the dictator: they w(h)etted their daggers to restore *libertas* both for themselves and the commonwealth at large, with freedom from tyranny benefitting both the ruling elite (*senatus*) and the people (*populus Romanus*). By choosing the label *liberatores* for the assassins, Cicero might even have been inspired by Caesar's — from his point of view perverse — cooption of the title *Liberator* and the ideology of *libertas* as ideological veneer for his tyrannical regime. It also enabled him to maintain that the assassins freed Rome from Caesar (and are therefore deserving of the highest praise) without, however, restoring *libertas* to the *res publica* since Caesar's underlings, in particular Antony, remain in charge.[85]

(3) **Philosophical**: after Caesar all but eliminated political *libertas* (as understood by Cicero), Cicero began to invest in a philosophical notion of freedom, which, in its purest form, does not require a political (or any other) context for its realization: it rests entirely in an internal disposition of virtuous self-sufficiency, embodied by the Stoic sage. Cicero elaborates the idea in his fifth *Paradoxon Stoicorum*, which maintains *Solum sapientem esse liberum, et omnem stultum servum* ('That only the wise man is free, and that every foolish man is a slave'). The fools include all those who are beholden to desires — whether for wealth, political office, or military commands. In his treatise *On Duties* (*de Officiis*), composed at the same time as the *Philippics*, Cicero builds on this Stoic notion of *libertas*, to develop an understanding of freedom

---

83   See further Raaflaub (2003).
84   See Cassius Dio 43.44.1 with Weinstock (1971: 142–43).
85   For this argument see Leber (2018).

tailor-made for the political struggles of the day. This sense of liberty continues to denote primarily an individual's 'freedom from (enslaving) passions', in particular the desire for glory (*Off*. 1.68):[86]

cavenda etiam est gloriae cupiditas, ut supra dixi; eripit enim libertatem, pro qua magnanimis viris omnis debet esse contentio. nec vero imperia expetenda ac potius aut non accipienda interdum aut deponenda non numquam.

[As I said before, we must also beware of desire for glory; for it robs us of liberty, and in defence of liberty a high-spirited man should stake everything. And one ought not to seek military commands; rather they ought sometimes to be declined, sometimes to be resigned.]

In this passage, Cicero turns the individual who desires *gloria* and *imperia* (read: a potential tyrant) into a slave of his passions, while at the same time elevating *libertas* (both philosophical and, importantly, as we shall see, political) into a priceless good for those 'high of spirit'. For in this treatise, Cicero imbricates philosophical reflection about the self and its disposition with politics broadly conceived as part of a larger effort to come to terms with the paradox that the same desire for glory and military commands that animated Rome's rise to imperial greatness also caused the downfall of the *libera res publica*. To combat the threat of tyranny (a regime that annihilates *libertas*) Cicero here hammers out a civic ethics in which each individual citizen is co-responsible for protecting the community and the commonwealth from enslavement. The contemporary thrust of his philosophical reflections resonates throughout the work, as in *Off*. 2.23–24 — a passage worth quoting in full not least since it also offers a philosophical take on the discussion of security in the previous paragraph:

Omnium autem rerum nec aptius est quicquam ad opes tuendas ac tenendas quam diligi nec alienius quam timeri. praeclare enim Ennius 'Quem metuunt oderunt; quem quisque odit, perisse expetit'. multorum autem odiis nullas opes posse obsistere, si antea fuit ignotum, nuper est cognitum. nec vero huius tyranni solum, quem armis oppressa pertulit civitas ac paret cum maxime mortuo interitus declarat, quantum odium hominum valeat ad pestem, sed reliquorum similes exitus tyrannorum, quorum haud fere quisquam talem interitum effugit. malus enim

---

86   See in more detail Arena (2007b).

est custos diuturnitatis metus contraque benivolentia fidelis vel ad perpetuitatem. (24) sed iis, qui vi oppressos imperio coercent, sit sane adhibenda saevitia, ut eris in famulos, si aliter teneri non possunt; qui vero in libera civitate ita se instruunt, ut metuantur, iis nihil potest esse dementius. quamvis enim sint demersae leges alicuius opibus, quamvis timefacta libertas, emergunt tamen haec aliquando aut iudiciis tacitis aut occultis de honore suffragiis. acriores autem morsus sunt intermissae libertatis quam retentae. quod igitur latissime patet neque ad incolumitatem solum, sed etiam ad opes et potentiam valet plurimum, id amplectamur, ut metus absit, caritas retineatur. ita facillime quae volemus et privatis in rebus et in re publica consequemur. etenim qui se metui volent, a quibus metuentur, eosdem metuant ipsi necesse est.

[But, of all motives, none is better adapted to secure influence and hold it fast than love; nothing is more foreign to that end than fear. For Ennius says admirably: 'Whom they fear they hate. And whom one hates, one hopes to see him dead.' And we recently discovered, if it was not known before, that no amount of power can withstand the hatred of the many. The death of this tyrant, whose yoke the state endured under the constraint of armed force and whom it still obeys more humbly than ever, though he is dead, illustrates the deadly effects of popular hatred; and the same lesson is taught by the similar fate of all other despots, of whom practically no one has ever escaped such a death. For fear is but a poor safeguard of lasting power; while affection, on the other hand, may be trusted to keep it safe for ever. But those who keep subjects in check by force would of course have to employ severity — masters, for example, toward their servants, when these cannot be held in control in any other way. But those who in a free state deliberately put themselves in a position to be feared are the maddest of the mad. For let the laws be never so much overborne by some one individual's power, let the spirit of freedom be never so intimidated, still sooner or later they assert themselves either through unvoiced public sentiment, or through secret ballots disposing of some high office of state. Freedom suppressed and again regained bites with keener fangs than freedom never endangered. Let us, then, embrace this policy, which appeals to every heart and is the strongest support not only of security but also of influence and power — namely, to banish fear and cleave to love. And thus we shall most easily secure success both in private and in public life. Furthermore, those who wish to be feared must inevitably be afraid of those whom they intimidate.]

To appreciate the pronounced political dimension of Cicero's philosophy, it is important to note that the philosophical understanding of freedom, i.e. being in rational control of one's emotions, does not inevitably lead to socio-political activism, an interest in justice, and a diehard dedication to keeping the commonwealth 'free'. The Stoic thinker Seneca the Younger (4 BCE–65 CE), for instance, writing during the reign of the emperor Nero, uses *libertas* in the philosophical sense to propound the paradox that a master beholden to his passions is enslaved, whereas his slaves, if they manage to master their emotions and live according to reason, are free. Given that this philosophical freedom is freedom in its supreme form, it is immaterial for Seneca if these philosophically free individuals are legally speaking slaves or live in conditions of political servitude (under a tyrannical regime).[87] By contrast, in *On Duties* Cicero repeatedly criticizes this kind of 'self-centred' philosophical conception of freedom as not good enough: for him, *self*-control in the form of freedom from noxious desires forms the basis for *political* engagement designed to ensure the *libertas* of the civic community and the *res publica* as well.

In the *Philippics*, Cicero, from the outset, looks back in admiration to the assassination of Caesar as a blow for liberty.[88] Initially, Antony gave hopeful signs that he would support the restoration of a free and peaceful citizenry and a senate unaffected by anxieties (*Phil.* 1.4, 31). But (according to Cicero) it soon emerged that the aimed for the same tyrannical power and position (*dominatus*) as Caesar, enslaving the people in a reign of fear. Against this threat, Cicero marshals the *Philippics* to establish a universal consensus among the assassins of Caesar (hailed as liberators — *liberatores*), the rest of the senate, and the people of Rome (as well as Caesar's adoptive son Caesar Octavianus) to ensure the (political) annihilation of the fledging tyrant Antony in the

---

87   See e.g. Seneca, *Letters to Lucilius* 47, where he explores the possibility that a slave is 'free in spirit' (*liber animo*), whereas those who are supposedly free are enslaved to various emotions and desires: *alius libidini servit, alius avaritiae, alius ambitioni, omnes spei, omnes timori.*

88   Caesar figures as *rex* and his reign as illegitimate *regnum* or *dominatio* throughout the corpus of *Philippics*. Conversely, from *Philippic* 1 onwards Cicero hails Brutus and Cassius for restoring *libertas* and rescuing *res publica* and *patria* from *regnum, dominatio,* and *servitus.* See e.g. *Phil.* 1.13: *fuerit ille L. Brutus qui et ipse dominatu regio rem publicam liberavit et ad similem virtutem et simile factum stirpem iam prope in quingentesimum annum propagavit* — 'Let us say it was Lucius Brutus, who freed the Commonwealth from regal despotism and now, almost five hundred years later, has inspired his descendants to a courage and a deed like to his own...'. See further Stevenson (2008: 106).

name of (universal) peace and freedom. The end of *Philippic* 2 (starting with § 113) is the first time this agenda comes fully into focus. *Libertas* will remain a rallying cry throughout the rest of the corpus, as Cicero tries to muster support for the violent reconstitution of the *libera res publica* through the killing of any would-be tyrant, irrespective of whether he addressed the senate or the people (though with certain differences in emphasis). As Cowan (2008: 151) notes, '*Libertas* in the *Philippics* was used broadly enough to accommodate widely differing understandings of the term (both "optimate" and *popularis* visions are accounted for) and could, therefore, serve as a platform for trying to generate consensus'. Our paragraph is an excellent illustration of the way in which Cicero tries to merge the elite and the popular sense of (political) *libertas*: he starts out by imagining the Roman People as the political agent who will confront Antony (*Eripiet et extorquebit tibi ista populus Romanus...*), but then gradually shifts to the senatorial collective (*utinam salvis nobis*), singles out generic individuals to whom the Roman people entrust the helm of the state (*habet populus Romanus ad quos gubernacula rei publicae deferat*), and ends up by hailing members of the traditional senatorial elite (*adulescentes nobilissimi*) who will take decisive political action on behalf of the commonwealth. (The choice of *adulescentes* is suitably vague and can conveniently comprise both the liberators who killed Caesar and Caesar's adoptive son Octavian — elsewhere referred to as *iuvenis*.)

It is important to note, however, that Cicero's claim that the Roman People were much invested in *libertas* as a political ideal was by and large wishful thinking: 'Cicero's assertion to the contrary notwithstanding [*Fam.* 10.12.4; *Phil.* 3.32], it is on the whole true that after the assassination of Caesar the Roman People showed little enthusiasm for the cause of republican freedom'.[89]

Eripiet et extorquebit tibi ista populus Romanus, utinam salvis nobis!: Cicero inverts natural word order, leading with the verbs (the futures *eripiet* and *extorquebit* — note the alliteration, enhanced by the intervening *et* — before adding the indirect object (*tibi*), the direct object (*ista*), and the subject (*populus Romanus*). The front-loading of the action is particularly pronounced because the verbs also push back the

---

89   Wirszubski (1950: 95).

demonstrative pronoun *ista*, which, in referring back to *armis*, provides the bridge to the previous sentence. The popular uprising, so Cicero's word order optimistically suggests, will be fell and swift.

utinam salvis nobis!: a nominal ablative absolute *salvis nobis* (nominal, since it consists of an adjective (*salvis*) and a personal pronoun (*nobis*), without a participle) that the particle *utinam* turns into a wish: 'I wish we [Cicero refers to himself and his senatorial peers] remain unharmed'. Translators tend to interpret the threat to the physical safety of the senators as coming from the popular uprising: 'may we be unscathed in the process!' (Lacey); 'I pray that we do not perish in the process' (Shackleton Bailey); and a feeling of unease on Cicero's part about the people taking matters into their own hands (however welcome their disarmament of Antony's henchmen might be) is in line with his elite prejudices elsewhere. But this reading produces an odd clash with the following sentence where Antony is clearly identified as the source of danger, and it might thus be better to understand *utinam salvis nobis* in the sense of 'may we (still) be unharmed [sc. by you and your henchmen] (when that moment comes)'.

sed quoquo modo nobiscum egeris, dum istis consiliis uteris, non potes, mihi crede, esse diuturnus: irrespective of the way in which Antony will have ended up dealing with Cicero and the senate (*nobiscum* — picking up *utinam salvis nobis*) at present (*egeris* is second person singular future-perfect active of *ago, egi, actum*), he will get his comeuppance from the people (*non potes, mihi crede, esse diuturnus*) if he continues his tyrannical agenda (*istis consiliis* is the ablative object of the deponent *uteris*, in the second person singular present indicative).

etenim ista tua minime avara coniunx, quam ego sine contumelia describo, nimium diu debet populo Romano tertiam pensionem: Cicero chooses to evoke Antony's violent death via a gratuitous insult to his wife Fulvia. The conceit here is to imagine her in significant debt to the Roman people, of which she has so far paid two of three instalments quite cheerfully (cf. the deeply ironic *minime avara*) through (causing) the slaughter of her first two husbands, i.e. Clodius and Curio. The third and final payment, however, i.e. the killing of Antony, is by now long overdue (cf. *nimium diu*; note the paronomasia *minime ~ nimium*). Antony, Clodius, and Curio form a disreputable set throughout the speech, with

Antony in line for the same fate as Fulvia's previous spouses. See esp. 2.11: *quis autem meum consulatum praeter te et P. Clodium qui vituperaret inventus est? cuius quidem tibi fatum, sicuti C. Curioni, manet, quoniam id domi tuae est quod fuit illorum utrique fatale* ('Who was ever heard abusing my consulship except yourself and Publius Clodius, whose fate awaits you, as it awaited Gaius Curio, since you have that in your house which proved fatal to them both?'). In the *Philippics*, Fulvia's hallmarks are greed (*avaritia*) and cruelty (*crudelitas*): see 1.33, 2.93, 2.95, 3.4, 3.10, 3.16–17, 4.4, 6.4, and 13.18, with Delia (1991).

habet populus Romanus ad quos gubernacula rei publicae deferat: Cicero again places the verb upfront ('The Roman People *do* have…'). He does not spell out the accusative object of *habet* (and antecedent of *ad quos*), inviting the reader to supply a word or phrase (most simply *eos* — or perhaps something conceptually more elaborate such as *principes civitatis*). The reference to politically motivated violence in the following sentence (*ulta est*) suggests that the liberators, and in particular Brutus and Cassius, are foremost in Cicero's mind. But when it comes to taking on the helm of the state, he will surely also have thought of himself.

ad quos ... deferat: the subjunctive is potential — in the event of a popular uprising that would disempower Antony, there would be other (= better) statesmen around to take the tiller.

gubernacula rei publicae: the literal meaning of *gubernaculum* is 'steering-oar of a ship', here used *pars pro toto* in what is known as the 'ship-of-state metaphor': see § 92 above.

qui ubicumque terrarum sunt, ibi omne est rei publicae praesidium vel potius ipsa res publica, quae se adhuc tantum modo ulta est, nondum reciperavit: *qui* is a connecting relative (= *et ii*), *ubicumque* a relative adverb (corresponding with *ibi*), here construed with the partitive genitive *terrarum*: 'And wherever in all the lands these men are, there is…' In the main clause, Cicero brings into play an issue that preoccupied him greatly throughout his career: what does the *res publica* ultimately consist in — and where is it located?

Depending on his genre of writing and (constantly changing) personal circumstances, he gave different answers to these questions. Initially, his geopolitical outlook on the world was emphatically Romanocentric. Unlike his military-minded senatorial peers, who vied with each other over provincial commands and considered the periphery the place where they could acquire wealth and reputation, Cicero preferred the civic setting of Rome to advance his career. During his consulship he even bargained away a potentially lucrative provincial command in return for support from his consular colleague in the suppression of Catiline's conspiracy. In 58–57 BCE, he had to adjust his views when he was forced into exile — an experience that ruptured the way in which his personal and political identity had so far interlocked with a physical presence in Rome. Instead, he became invested in a new form of megalomania, claiming that the Roman commonwealth joined him in exile, according to the principle *ubi ego, ibi res publica*. The notion that one individual 'embodied' the commonwealth made it possible to uproot the *res publica* from the urban topography of power — the physical setting for the institutions and procedures that comprised Roman republican politics. (Not coincidentally, this personification of the commonwealth is a figure of thought appealing to exiles: compare the claim of Charles de Gaulle (1890–1970) during WW II that the 'true France' was not the regime of Nazi-collaborators located in Vichy, but his exile government and the resistance.)

Still, Cicero was thoroughly miserable in exile and could not wait to return to Rome. When civil war broke out a few years later and Pompey planned to pull a similar stunt, taking the *res publica* into exile with him, Cicero strongly objected to Pompey's decision to cede Rome and Italy to Caesar. This policy of retreat, he argued in the first letter to Atticus after the crossing of the Rubicon, ignored the salient fact that the *res publica* was rooted in the religious topography of the city (*Att.* 7.11.3 = 134 SB):

> redeamus ad nostrum. per fortunas, quale tibi consilium Pompei uidetur? hoc quaero, quid urbem reliquerit; ego enim ἀπορῶ. tum nihil absurdius. urbem tu relinquas? ergo idem, si Galli uenirent. 'non est' inquit 'in parietibus res publica.' at in aris et focis. 'fecit Themistocles.' fluctum enim totius barbariae ferre urbs una non poterat. at idem Pericles non fecit anno fere post quinquagesimo, cum praeter moenia nihil teneret; nostri olim urbe reliqua capta arcem tamen retinuerunt.

> [To come back to our friend. What *do* you think, for heaven's sake, of Pompey's line — I mean, why has he abandoned Rome? *I* don't know what to make of it. At the time it looked the most senseless thing.

Abandon Rome? I suppose you would have done the same if the Gauls were coming? 'House walls' he might answer 'don't make the Republic.' But altars and hearthstones do. 'Themistocles did it.' Yes, because one city could not stand against the tide of the whole barbarian world. But Pericles did not half a century later, though he held nothing except the town walls. Our own forebears still held the citadel after the rest of Rome was in enemy hands.]

In other words, he had no idea of the military realities, then — hopeless as Demosthenes.

At the time of the *Philippics*, circumstances had changed yet again. The civic unrest in Rome in the wake of Caesar's assassination forced Brutus and his fellow conspirators to leave Rome and then also Italy. As Cicero notes at *Philippic* 1.6: *patriae liberatores urbe carebant ea cuius a cervicibus iugum servile deiecerant...* ('the liberators of their country were banished from the city whose neck they had released from slavery...'). With the centre in the violent grasp of Antony and his henchmen and the republican heroes operating on the imperial periphery, Cicero's *res publica* needs to put her travelling boots back on. See Hodgson (2017: 216) (with reference to Dawes 2008: 271): 'Whereas *Phil.* 1 provided concrete criticism and recommendations, this formula returns us to the realm of a wandering *res publica*, which "defies locality and a definite semantic meaning" and is defined more in "moral rather than constitutional" terms'.

quae se adhuc tantum modo ulta est, nondum reciperavit: a powerful personification of the *res publica*, who is the subject of the reflexive *ulta est* and *reciperavit* (*se* is to be construed with both verbs). More commonly, human agents avenge, liberate, or restore the commonwealth (also in passive construction with implied human agency: 'the commonwealth ought to be restored', 'with the commonwealth having been restored'). Here Cicero says that the commonwealth avenged itself, but has not yet regained its former strength. The relative clause raises the question whether the assassination of Caesar has been sufficient to restore the commonwealth to its pre-Caesarian form — or whether further drastic actions are required. The matter receives constant airing in his contemporary correspondence.

habet quidem certe res publica adulescentis nobilissimos paratos defensores: Cicero again starts with the verb, reinforced by the particle *quidem* and the adverb *certe*: 'Yes, indeed, the commonwealth does surely have...'. *paratos defensores* is the accusative object, with *adulescentis* (= *adulescentes*) *nobilissimos* in apposition: 'defenders ready to act, young men of the most illustrious ancestry'. (*nobilis* denotes a person with a consul in their lineage.) The first individuals who come to mind are Cassius and Brutus (both in their early forties — but Roman age labels are quite flexible: see above 132–33), but Cicero may also have been thinking of Caesar Octavianus (23 September 63 BCE–19 August 14 CE), who was 19 at the time.

quam volent illi cedant otio consulentes; tamen a re publica revocabuntur: *volent* and *revocabuntur* are in the future tense, *cedant* is in the present subjunctive: 'Those may withdraw as they will wish, with a mind to preserving peace'. (*consulentes* is the present active participle in the nominative plural, used intransitively and governing the dative *otio*.) Cicero refers to the decision of the conspirators to withdraw from Italy out of fear that their presence would result in renewed outbreak of civil warfare. He appreciates their desire to maintain peace, but at the same time evokes the scenario of a call to arms issued by the commonwealth: *tamen a re publica revocabuntur* again personifies the *res publica*, which here appears in the ablative of agency.

et nomen pacis dulce est et ipsa res [est] salutaris; sed inter pacem et servitutem plurimum interest: Cicero is all for peace: the word itself is sweet and the actual state (*res*) beneficial. But there is a world of difference (cf. the superlative *plurimum*) between peace and servitude. He already explored the thematic nexus of *libertas* / *servitus* and *pax* towards the end of *Philippic 1*, where he praises Antony for his initial commitment to concord and collaboration in the hours and days right after Caesar's assassination, which freed the senate and the rest of the citizenry from fear and manifested itself not least in his willingness to hand over his son as a 'hostage of peace' (*pacis obses*) to the conspirators holed up on the Capitol (31). And in the following paragraph he programmatically endorses *libertas* as foundation for *pax* (*Phil.* 1.32: *Tum denique liberati per viros fortissimos videbamur, quia, ut illi voluerant, libertatem pax consequebatur*). It remains a permanent theme throughout the rest of the corpus. See e.g. *Phil.* 8.12: *Sed quaeso, Calene, quid tu? servitutem pacem vocas?* ('But I ask you Calenus, what do you mean? do you call slavery peace?').

nomen pacis: *pacis* is an 'appositional genitive' with *nomen*, used instead of apposition to specify the contents of the noun on which it depends. English prefers apposition: 'The word "peace"'.

ipsa res: i.e. 'peace'.

plurimum interest: *plurimum* is the neuter accusative singular used adverbially, a so-called 'internal' or 'adverbial' accusative modifying the verb — here specifying the extent of the difference between *pax* and *servitus*: it could not be greater.

pax est tranquilla libertas, servitus [est] **postremum malorum omnium non modo bello sed morte etiam repellendum**: *postremum*, the superlative of *posterus* here construed with the partitive genitive *malorum omnium*, is a (substantival) adjective in the neuter singular functioning as complement to the subject of the sentence (Pinkster 2015: 768): 'servitude is the worst of all evils...'. It is further modified by the gerundive *repellendum* ('to be rejected...'). *bello* and *morte* are most poignantly understood as ablatives of price: 'not only at the price of war but even of death' (Shackleton Bailey).

In 48 BCE, after Pompey's defeat at Pharsalus and his death shortly thereafter, Cicero decided to cease fighting and return to Caesar-occupied Italy. As a result, he found himself forced to justify a conciliatory stance towards Caesar that grated with those who wanted nothing to do with Caesar and continued to fight and ended up either dead (like Cato) or in exile, banned by dictatorial edict from re-entering Italy. His uncompromising attitude towards Antony may be explained in part as an (over-)reaction to his earlier willingness to play ball with a tyrannical regime. Cicero seems to have told himself 'Never Again!'. The possibility of tolerable subservience that he chose for himself under Caesar has ceased to be an option. In the *Philippics*, the alternative is stark: either death for Antony and liberty for the commonwealth or Antony triumphant and slavery and/or death for Rome. Our passage here has many parallels in the later speeches.[90]

---

90   See e.g. *Phil.* 3.29, 5.9, or 10.19. There is also a parallel discussion at *de Officiis* 1.57. Though Cicero also concedes — realizing his own track record — that suicide to escape a tyrannical regime, however admirable and appropriate in the case of Cato the Younger, is not necessarily the best option for everyone.

§ 114: Caesar's Assassination: A Deed of Unprecedented Exemplarity

The paragraph falls into two halves. In the first (*Quod si se … impetum fecerunt*), Cicero looks back: he assesses the assassination of Caesar against similar events in Roman history, reaching the conclusion that the recent act of tyrannicide outshines all precedents. In the second (*quod cum ipsum factum … esse contemnendam*), he explores the future implications of what the liberators did: they set an example for others to imitate and will reap immortality through everlasting glory as a reward for their deed. Both topics — exemplarity and immortality through memory — warrant some comments. (A third 'big idea' Cicero here gestures to in passing is the notion of conscience: see below).

Exemplarity: in ancient Rome, historical precedents mattered — as did the desire to outperform ancestral benchmarks of excellence, i.e. doing something unprecedented, not least to leave a mark on the collective memory of the civic community (and perhaps become exemplary in turn). A good way to validate controversial deeds was to argue that — however novel — they were in conformity with ancestral norms, re-enacting, at least partially, exemplary deeds from the past. In this paragraph, Cicero tries to situate the murder of Caesar within Rome's *exempla*-discourse, citing various historical precedents for the use of violence as a legitimate means in domestic politics. He thereby gives the impression that expelling or killing a (would-be) tyrant is a norm and practice co-extensive with the Roman republic. That was not the case: politically-motivated murder (and its justification) were hotly contested issues in Roman political thought, but only from 133 BCE onwards, when the *pontifex maximus* Scipio Nasica, without the backing of the consuls, took the lead in bludgeoning Tiberius Gracchus and several hundred of his supporters to death on the charge that he aimed for tyranny. This was a watershed moment in Roman politics, which arguably ruptured the republican political system irredeemably: with the genie of extreme physical violence as a means of politics out of the bottle, instances of politically-motivated bloodshed and episodes of full-scale civil war continued to occur until Octavian's final victory over Antony at Actium in 31 BCE, which signaled the end of the *libera res publica*. 'Tyrannicide' never became consensual: 'It was, in fact, an illegal procedure advocated as a last-ditch solution by the late-Republican *optimates*, and as such, it was opposed and contested by large sections of Roman society' (Pina Polo 2006: 72). In the *Philippics* and *On Duties* (*de Officiis*), Cicero does his best to validate the practice both in historical and ethical terms. Desperate times call for desperate measures (or do they?), and Cicero acts as cheerleader to endow them with a veneer of historical and moral legitimacy (should we chime in?).

Moreover, when it comes to the issue of politically motivated violence, Cicero suggests that the ground has shifted. In the past, violent action was directed against either a king who ruled at a time when kingship was an acceptable form of government at Rome (the case of Tarquinius); or aristocrats who aspired to kingship during republican times, but were unable to realize their ambition before being stopped dead in their tracks (the cases of Sp. Cassius, Sp. Maelius, and M. Manlius, see on § 84). By contrast, Brutus, Cassius, and their co-conspirators killed someone who had managed to instal himself as king at a time when this form of rule was deemed to be utterly unacceptable. They thereby rose up against a novel, extreme form of tyranny. The lesson here is complex: their glory is greater than those who did away with earlier strongmen — yet Cicero also implies that they acted (too) late. Their blow for freedom shines the brighter since they rescued Rome from actual enslavement; but Caesar ought to have been eliminated before he could impose tyranny on Rome. In the wake of this unprecedented achievement, a return to what Cicero here portrays as the ancestral practice of killing would-be tyrants (like Antony) emerges as doubly sanctioned by the ambiguous exemplary value of Caesar's assassination, which is praiseworthy for its unprecedented benefits in terms of restoring freedom to the community, but implicitly blameworthy since drastic action ought to have been taken much earlier. Put differently, there is a call to arms built into the text.[91]

Immortality: Traditionally, aristocratic immortality in republican Rome consisted in ensuring posthumous presence within various modes and media of commemoration. The patrician-plebeian ruling elite that emerged in the late fourth and early third centuries developed specific ways of constituting and remembering the past (a prime source of identity and legitimacy in pre-modern societies), which chimed well with, indeed was an integral part of, the political system and its peculiar culture. Rooted in individual families but oriented towards the *res publica* at large, these commemorative practices focused on the preservation of the names of former office-holders and their deeds and took place in a variety of media and settings. *Imagines, tituli, stemmata, laudationes* and *pompae funebres* formed a complex system of storage and reactivation, permanent display and ephemeral enactments, perfectly aligned with the competitive instincts of, and need for cohesion within, an oligarchic ruling elite that placed equal emphasis on merit and past family achievement within a wider civic context and invested heavily in intense communication with the larger populace. Successful magistrates and generals further inscribed their names and achievements into the topography of the city by means of monuments and statues, the display of spoils and strategically dedicated temples; together, the houses of noble families and the public spaces of the city thus formed an impressive, if by and large uncoordinated 'landscape of memory'.[92]

But as we have seen (above 350–52) in the course of the last centuries of the republic, imaginative Romans explored the interface (or indeed the possibility of cross-over) between the human and the divine sphere,

---

91 The thrust of the argument here is not dissimilar to the rhetoric that animates the first speech against Catiline: in the light of historical precedents of private figures taking vigilante action against potential tyrants and revolutionaries, Cicero portrays his inactivity as consul as potentially embarrassing; OR (as John Henderson puts it) as executive head of state he threatens an extreme immediate emergency crackdown by doing an 'I'm at the end of my tether and ready to crack at any moment' shtick on the basis that a consul's declaration of a crisis is a felicitous speech-act.

92 See in particular the by now classic studies by Flaig (1995) (2003) and Flower (1996).

which opened up new modes of posthumous existence, with Caesar finally managing outright deification in the eyes of many. Cicero too flirts with various unconventional forms of life after death (in some of his works he asserts that the souls of the most outstanding statesmen are immortal) and, as we have seen, makes at least some concession to Caesar's new status to keep Octavian sweet — even though he rejects the notion that Caesar has become a god elsewhere in the strongest possible terms. (One of the ways in which he negotiated the divide between human and divine is the strategic use of the ambiguous attribute *divinus*: see below.) In our paragraph, he alludes to the idiom and imagery of apotheosis (perhaps not least so as not to fall too short of the new standards of elevation set by Caesar and his followers) before claiming everlasting fame for the liberators as the proper republican reward for their outstanding deed.

Extra information:
Tyrannicide and anti-tyrannical activism also have a distinguished Greek background, both in practice (Harmodius and Aristogeiton: see Azoulay 2017) and theory (in particular Plato, who in turn inspired his disciple Chion of Heraclea to put theory back into practice with the assassination of the tyrant Clearchus who ruled in his hometown). Cicero eloquently evokes the heroization that tyrant-slayers received in Greece at *pro Milone* 80. Milo, Cicero argues, deserves similar reverence for his slaying of the quasi-tyrant Clodius:

> Graeci homines deorum honores tribuunt eis viris qui tyrannos necaverunt — quae ego vidi Athenis, quae in aliis urbibus Graeciae! quas res divinas talibus institutas viris, quos cantus, quae carmina! prope ad immortalitatis et religionem et memoriam consecrantur — vos tanti conservatorem populi, tanti sceleris ultorem non modo honoribus nullis adficietis sed etiam ad supplicium rapi patiemini? confiteretur, confiteretur, inquam, si fecisset, et magno animo et libenter, se fecisse libertatis omnium causa quod esset non confitendum modo sed etiam vere praedicandum.

> [The Greeks accord honours of the gods to those men who have slain tyrants. What have I seen at Athens and in other cities of Greece! What religious adoration put in place for such men! What musical compositions, what songs! They are worshipped almost at the level of observance and commemoration distinctive of immortality. Will you not only not bestow any honours upon the preserver of such a great people and the avenger of such a great crime, but even suffer him to

be dragged away for capital punishment? Had he done the deed, he would confess — indeed confess proudly and gladly — that he had done for the sake of everyone's liberty a deed that he ought not merely to confess, but in truth proclaim far and wide.]

Quod si se ipsos illi nostri liberatores e conspectu nostro abstulerunt, at exemplum facti reliquerunt: *quod* as connecting particle — here introducing a simple conditional clause stating a fact (hence the indicative) — often has an adversative force: 'But if…'. The main clause begins with the particle *at*, which 'after negative or [as here] virtually negative conditional clauses' (OLD s.v. *at* 13b) means 'at least', 'at any rate', 'yet'. The *si*-clause contains stylistic touches, such as alliteration (*si se, ipsos illi*) and chiasmus (*nostri liberatores – conspectu nostro*), and a deluge of pronouns or pronominal adjectives (*se, ipsos, illi, nostri, nostro*), which only partly compensates for the fact that Cicero here expresses a truth he considers awkward and unfortunate: to preserve peace, the liberators had left the capital. But they did leave behind a 'benchmark of excellence ready for imitation' or, more succinctly, a 'precedent' (*exemplum*): the killing of the tyrant (*facti*: genitive singular of the perfect passive participle of *facio* dependent on *exemplum*), lit. 'the example of the deed' (= of that which has been done).

liberatores: Cicero's standard term for the conspirators throughout the *Philippics*, starting with 1.6. The label turns Caesar into a tyrant who had enslaved the Roman people. This view was by no means consensual — quite the contrary: 'In the immediate aftermath of his death, Caesar alternated between tyrant, martyred popular politician, and god, but a solution was not quickly found' (Flower 2006: 108).

illi quod nemo fecerat fecerunt: *fecerat* is pluperfect, *fecerunt* perfect: 'they did what no-one had (ever) done (before)'. The sentence neatly picks up on the phrase *exemplum facti*: *fecerat* and *fecerunt* form a polyptoton with *facti* (see also below: *impetum fecerunt, quod … ipsum factum, pulcherrimi facti*); and Cicero's assertion that the killing of Caesar was unprecedented reinforces *exemplum*. There were other attacks on (would-be) tyrants (as Cicero goes on to explain), but they all differed in important respects from what the liberators achieved.

Tarquinium Brutus bello est persecutus, qui tum rex fuit cum [regem] **esse Romae licebat**: the oldest and most famous instance of opposition to tyranny was the expulsion of the last of the legendary kings of Rome, Lucius Tarquinius Superbus, by Lucius Iunius Brutus, which initiated a period of warfare (*bellum*) between Rome and the supporters of Tarquinius, as he tried to regain his throne. (Cicero here conflates the act of expulsion with the subsequent warfare.) But the parallel is not precise: Tarquinius' reign belongs to a period back when (*tum ... cum*) kingship still happened to be an acceptable form of government at Rome, which it ceased to be afterwards.

Extra information, courtesy of John Henderson:
The idea that Brutus was repeating historical destiny by 'regicide' was lurking in his family self-image all along, and the important distinction that Tarquin wasn't assassinated in the 'regifuge', so the *libera res publica* wasn't born in civil bloodshed, was blurred right away, as in Horace's version of what he claims became a popular anecdote about the showdown between the liberators and the second triumvirate, *Satires* 1.7.33–35: '*per magnos, Brute, Deos te | oro, qui reges consueris tollere, cur non | hunc Regem iugulas? operum hoc, mihi crede, tuorum est*' ('By the great gods, I implore you, Brutus, since it is in your line to take off kings, why not slay this Rex? This, believe me, is the task of your family'). Didn't both Brutuses 'get rid of kings'!

Tarquinium Brutus bello: the inversion of accusative object and subject places the emphasis on the tyrant and yields an alliteration (*Brutus bello*).

cum [regem] **esse Romae licebat**: *licebat* is an impersonal verb ('it was permitted...'), taking the infinitive (*regem*) *esse* as subject. (*regem* needs to be supplied from the previous clause; for the accusative, see Gildersleeve & Lodge 420: 'The Infinitive, when it stands alone, involves an indefinite Accusative Subject, and the Predicate of that Subject is ... in the Accusative Case'. Hence: *regem esse* = to be king.)

Romae: locative ('in Rome').

Sp. Cassius, Sp. Maelius, M. Manlius propter suspicionem regni appetendi sunt necati: hi primum cum gladiis non in regnum appetentem, sed in regnantem impetum fecerunt: Cicero moves on to the classical trio of so-called *adfectatores regni* ('men aiming for kingship'), who all came to a sticky end: see above § 84. *hi* refers to the *liberatores*. Spurius Cassius (thrice consul, twice triumphator, suspected of royal ambition, hence killed — in 485 BCE), Spurius Maelius (a plebeian suspected of using his wealth to install himself as king — hence killed in 439 BCE by the Master of the Horse Gaius Servilius Ahala), and Marcus Manlius Capitolinus (consul in 392 BCE, rescued Rome from the Gauls in 390/387 BCE, helped by the geese — hence Capitolinus, killed in 384 BCE for harbouring royal ambition) were all still in the process of striving for kingship (cf. *regnum appetentem* — 'someone striving for kingship', which applies to all three). By contrast, the liberators attacked someone who was already ruling as king (*regnantem*).

The three *exempla* Cicero mentions form an 'authoritative and canonical' set of Roman citizen traitors from early republican times (Flower 2006: 45), who acquired new relevance in the wake of 133 BCE (the year Scipio Nasica killed Tiberius Gracchus and many of his supporters under suspicion of tyranny: see above). As Flower (2006: 46) explains:

> ... the final versions [of their stories] produced in the late Republic, which are the only ones now extant, had been substantially recast to reflect the political conflicts and the violence of contemporary Rome. While this observation affects much of the account of the early Republic, it applies in a very special way to these three incidents, which had also come to be associated with each other in an ahistorical manner. It was precisely the stories of the disgraced traitors that took on a completely new relevance with the death of the Gracchi and throughout the series of conflicts that marked the most prominent stages of the Republic's decay, from the introduction of the *senatus consultum ultimum* to justify the attack on Gaius Gracchus and his associates, to the civil carnage under Marius and Sulla, to the outlawing of Catiline and the summary execution of his supporters. Assassination and judicial murder became commonplace in a development that could only be made sense of with reference to ancestral precedents.

propter suspicionem regni appetendi: the genitive dependent on *suspicionem*, here the gerundive phrase *regni appetendi*, expresses the evil suspected (*OLD* s.v. 1b). The gerundive (a verbal adjective) is passive, so a literal translation would be 'because of the suspicion of kingship to-be-aspired-to' = of aspiring to kingship. (The equivalent gerund expression would be ... *regnum appetendi*, with *regnum* the accusative object of the verbal noun *appetendi*.)

sunt necati: = *necati sunt* (third person plural perfect indicative passive).

hi ... non in regnum appetentem, sed in regnantem impetum fecerunt: Cicero uses the idiom *impetum facere in* + accusative, which here consists of the two present active participles *appetentem* and *regnantem*. So the first *in* goes with *appetentem* and *not* with *regnum* (which is the accusative object of *appetentem*). As Mayor (1861: 155) notes: 'Genitives and adverbs are often interposed between the preposition and its case; occasionally the object governed by an adjective or [as here] participle comes between it and the preposition on which it depends'.

primum: the adverb ('for the first time') underscores that the liberators were setting a precedent.

cum gladiis: Cicero equips the assassins with proper swords (onward Roman soldiers…) rather than the daggers they will have used, perhaps in part to counter the label *sicarii* ('murderers that use daggers to stab innocent victims in the back') that some attached to the conspirators. In addition, as John Henderson points out to us, this phrase has been a pulse throughout the speech — since § 8, let alone 19, and goes straight to the 'point' that this scenario may look like it's a normal meeting of the senate but actually it's a war zone in a city that's a war zone, where the gunfree zone of metropolis and temple are tellingly violated.

quod cum ipsum factum per se praeclarum est atque divinum, tum expositum ad imitandum est, praesertim cum illi eam gloriam consecuti sint quae vix caelo capi posse videatur: *quod* is a connecting relative (= *et id*), modifying *ipsum factum*: 'and this very deed…'. *cum* does not introduce a subordinate clause, but correlates with *tum*: this adverbial *cum* introduces 'one of two co-existing or co-ordinate circumstances of actions', with *tum* indicating 'the more particular or noteworthy circumstance': *OLD* s.v. *cum²* 14: 'not only', 'as well as'. In the main clause (*quod ... est*) Cicero plods along heavily and emphatically with homoioteleuton in *-um*: *c-um*, *ips-um*, *fact-um*, *praeclar-um*, *divin-um*, *t-um*, *exposit-um*, *imitand-um*, before lifting (his prose) off into the sky from *praesertim cum* onwards. In this and the following sentence Cicero outlines two different kinds of reward that Caesar's assassins received for their deed: external recognition that manifests itself in quasi-deification; and internal satisfaction deriving from the awareness of having performed an act of outstanding heroism.

praeclarum ... atque divinum: The semantics of *divinus* range from the literal (in the sense of *ad deum, divinitatem pertinens / a deo originem ducens*) to the metaphorical. In the latter sense *divinus* loses its essential association with the divine and becomes synonymous with more mundane markers of distinction such as *praeclarus, eximius,* or *mirabilis*.[93] Suggestive ambiguities arise when the adjective is made to refer not to the gods, but to human beings, their capacities, or their deeds (as is the case here). In those instances it remains unclear whether the literal or the metaphorical meaning of the attribute is in force. The ambiguity appealed to Cicero, both here and elsewhere in his oeuvre: it enabled him to evoke the possibility of deification or association with the divine in the literal sense, without committing himself to a mode of religious elevation to which he strongly objected. See further Gildenhard (2011: 266–67).

expositum ad imitandum est: *factum* continues to be the subject, *expositum ... est* is the verb: the deed 'has been put on display for imitation / to be imitated'. The preposition *ad* (followed by a gerundive) expresses purpose.

illi: the *liberatores*.

quae vix caelo capi posse videatur: the antecedent of *quae* is *eam gloriam,* 'which seems scarcely able to be contained within the vault of heaven' (Lacey). Cicero underscores the hyperbole via alliteration (*caelo capi*) and qualifies it with his favourite hedge (*videatur*). Cf. *Att.* 14.6.2 = 360 SB (12 April 44), cited below. In his correspondence with Atticus, he is much more outspoken and calls the liberators 'heroes' (= semi-divine; see *Att.* 14.4.2 = 358 SB: *nostri autem ἥρωες quod per ipsos confici potuit gloriosissime et magnificentissime confecerunt* — 'Our heroes achieved all

---

93   See, respectively, *Thesaurus Linguae Latinae* 5.1.1619, 48ff. and 5.1.1624, 11ff.

that lay with themselves most gloriously and magnificently') or even 'gods' (14.11.1 = 365 SB, cited below). This (Greek) idiom would have been inappropriate in an oration. (Despite the fact that *Philippic 2* was not delivered, Cicero tends to abide by the protocols of the genre, partly to maintain the fiction of live performance.)

etsi enim satis in ipsa conscientia pulcherrimi facti fructus erat, tamen mortali immortalitatem non arbitror esse contemnendam: the subject of the *etsi* clause is *satis*, which governs — across a massive hyperbaton — the partitive genitive *fructûs*. The hyperbaton entails the thematically appropriate juxtaposition of *facti* and *fructus*, reinforced by alliteration. The verb of the main clause is *non arbitror* which introduces an indirect statement with *immortalitatem* as subject accusative and *esse contemnendam* as infinitive. *mortali* is a dative of agency with the gerundive. Its placement right next to *immortalitatem* produces yet another *figura etymologica* in this paragraph. *immortalitas* glosses *gloria* ('eternal fame') from the previous sentence.

in ipsa conscientia pulcherrimi facti: in his philosophical writings and orations, Cicero invested much in the notion of conscience (*conscientia*) — understood as an instance that assesses innocence and guilt in absolute, objective terms and rewards the former while punishing the latter. Here the liberators reap the benefit of knowing that they performed a 'most beautiful' deed — or so Cicero asserts, ignoring those for whom the murder might have looked suspect, erroneous, or even criminal.

Extra information:
Cicero's correspondence with Atticus from April and May 44 BCE bears eloquent witness to how divided the Romans were over Caesar's assassination. Some constituencies are portrayed as being overjoyed. See e.g. *Att.* 14.6.2 = 360 SB (12 April 44):

nihil enim tam σόλοικον quam tyrannoctonos in caelo esse, tyranni facta defendi. sed vides consules, vides reliquos magistratus, si isti magistratus, vides languorem bonorum. exsultant laetitia in municipiis. dici enim non potest quanto opere gaudeant, ut ad me concurrant, ut audire cupiant mea verba de re <publica>.

[It is the acme of incongruity that the tyrannicides should be lauded to the skies while the tyrant's actions are protected. But you see our Consuls and the rest of our magistrates, if these people are magistrates, and the apathy of the honest men. In the country towns they are jumping for joy. I cannot tell you how delighted they are, how they flock to me, how eager they are to hear what I have to say on the state of the country.]

In Rome, however, people were hard at work singing the praises of the dead dictator and condemning his murderers (*Att.* 14.11.1 = 365 SB; 21 April 44):

ἀκολασίαν istorum scribis. an censebas aliter? equidem etiam maiora exspecto. cum [equidem] contionem lego de 'tanto viro,' de 'clarissimo civi,' ferre non queo. etsi ista iam ad risum. sed memento, sic alitur consuetudo perditarum contionum, ut nostri illi non heroes sed di futuri quidem in gloria sempiterna sint sed non sine invidia, ne sine periculo quidem. verum illis magna consolatio conscientia maximi et clarissimi facti; nobis quae, qui interfecto rege liberi non sumus? sed haec fortuna viderit, quoniam ratio non gubernat.

[You write about the licence of these people. What did you expect? I look for still worse to come. When I read a public speech about 'so great a man,' 'so illustrious a Roman,' I can't stomach it. Of course this sort of thing has become a joke. But remember that is how the habit of pernicious speech-making grows, so that those heroes, or rather gods, of ours will no doubt be glorious to all eternity, but not without ill will or even danger. However they have a great consolation in the consciousness of a grand and glorious deed. What have *we*, who are not free though the king is slain? Well, we must leave all this to chance since reason has no say.]

In a letter from 22 April 44, he expresses his worries about the Caesarians in the company of Caesar Octavianus and counterbalances their threats by resorting to the same language of external renown and immortality in memory as well as internal bliss on account of the *conscientia* of their deed as here (*Att.* 14.12.2 = 366 SB):

ita multi circumstant, qui quidem nostri<s> mortem minitantur, negant haec ferri posse. quid censes cum Romam puer venerit, ubi nostri liberatores tuti esse non possunt? <qui> quidem semper erunt clari, conscientia vero facti sui etiam beati.

[There are too many around him (sc. Octavian). They threaten death to our friends and call the present state of things intolerable. What do you think they will say when the boy comes to Rome, where our liberators cannot go safe? They have won eternal glory, and happiness too in the consciousness of what they did.]

But the lives of the assassins continued to be in danger. By the beginning of May, he praises Dolabella for his intervention against Caesarian rioters and ps-Marius' monument to Caesar (above 349–50) (*Att.* 14.15.1 = 369 SB, 1 May 44):

> sustulisse mihi videtur simulationem desideri, adhuc quae serpebat in dies et inveterata verebar ne periculosa nostris tyrannoctonis esset.

> [He seems to me to have quashed that affectation of regret for Caesar which was spreading from day to day. I was afraid it might become a danger to our tyrannicides if it took root.]

Julius Caesar had made sure he was an indispensable part of the future — so many directly owed him so much.

§ 115: Looking for the Taste of (Genuine) Glory...

In his treatise *On Duties*, Cicero explains the reasons for the catastrophic self-laceration of republican Rome as follows (*Off.* 1.26):

> Maxime autem adducuntur plerique ut eos iustitiae capiat oblivio cum in imperiorum honorum gloriae cupiditatem inciderunt. Quod enim est apud Ennium: 'nulla sancta societas nec fides regni est', id latius patet. Nam quidquid eius modi est in quo non possint plures excellere, in eo fit plerumque tanta contentio ut difficillimum sit servare 'sanctam societatem'. Declaravit id modo temeritas C. Caesaris, qui omnia iura divina et humana pervertit propter eum quem sibi ipse opinionis errore finxerat principatum. Est autem in hoc genere molestum, quod in maximis animis splendidissimisque ingeniis plerumque existunt honoris imperii potentiae gloriae cupiditates.

> [Above all, however, most are brought to the point of becoming oblivious to the demands of justice when they lapse into desire for military commands, political offices, and glory. Ennius' words 'No inviolate community nor trust exists under kingship' have a wider application. Any aspect, in which it is impossible for many to be pre-eminent, tends to generate such competition that it becomes exceedingly difficult to preserve an 'inviolate community'. The rashness of Gaius Caesar has demonstrated this recently: he overthrew all divine and human laws on account of the single rule that he had imagined for himself out of an erroneous belief. What irritates in this scenario is the fact that often the desires for public office, military command, raw power, and glory exist in the greatest souls and the most outstanding talents.]

Cicero's argument here unfolds against the backdrop of Rome's political culture, which he evokes at both the beginning and the end of the passage: *imperia* (military commands) and *honores* (public offices) are the two principal means of attracting praise (*laus*) and acquiring renown (*gloria*), a core ambition of Rome's ruling elite. Yet, shockingly, he presents these desirables and their pursuit as fostering civil strife (cf. *tanta contentio*), the rise of a single ruler (*principatus*), and the perversion of anything that is right and just. In effect, Cicero here questions nothing less than the basic principles of Roman republican culture, defined as it was by competition among members of the elite for magistracies, military commands, and battlefield glory: in his view, this desire for political success and public recognition of excellence undermines the bonds that hold civic communities together once it becomes oblivious to the demands of justice. Proceeding from the general to the specific, he first introduces the spectre of kingship or tyranny by means of a quotation from Ennius, before invoking recent Roman history and the breakdown of the *libera res publica* through Caesar's bloody usurpation of power. In his passionate, yet utterly misguided pursuit of single rule he rashly overturned all divine and human laws; his despotism thereby emerges as irreconcilably at variance with, indeed destructive of, the basic qualities that unite and animate a commonwealth: *sancta societas* and *fides*.

According to Cicero, then, the ultimate root of the evils affecting Roman politics are the wrongheaded priorities, mistaken beliefs in what is desirable, and blatant ignorance of what truly matters (cf. *opinione erroris* ~ erroneous belief) that affect and poison the conduct of his senatorial peers, who dedicate themselves to the pursuit of misguided glory. The (rhetorical) distinction between *gloria* as conventionally, but — so Cicero argues — wrongly, conceived and 'true glory' (*vera gloria, vera laus*) enables him to invalidate the cultural certainties that his fellow citizens lived (and died) by. He gave the matter sustained discussion in several of his philosophical writings, including the *Tusculan Disputations*, the *de Officiis*, and, presumably, the lost *de Gloria*.[94] It figures prominently in the speech on behalf of Marcellus — a piece of

---

94   See *Tusc.* 3.2–6 with Gildenhard (2007: 167–87) and *Off.* 2.31–38 with Dyck (1996).

epideictic rhetoric that gives thanks to Caesar in person for pardoning
Marcellus, one of his most inveterate enemies, a [blatantly un-civic] act
which Cicero hails as 'truly' much more glorious than any of Caesar's
[*really* laudable] military victories. And it is a constant presence in
the *Philippics*, from the first oration onwards. Addressing Antony's
colleague in the consulship Dolabella towards the end of the speech,
he is willing to grant the consular duo, *nobiles homines* that they are and
motivated by great aspirations, that they do not aim (as some wrongly
suppose) 'for wealth obtained by violence and power unendurable
by the Roman people' (*opes violentas et populo Romano minime ferendam
potentiam*); rather, they genuinely desire the affection of their fellow-
citizens and glory (*caritatem civium et gloriam*) (1.29). He then proceeds
to (re-)define *gloria* as follows (1.29):[95]

> Est autem gloria laus recte factorum magnorumque in rem publicam
> meritorum, quae cum optimi cuiusque, tum etiam multitudinis
> testimonio comprobatur.

> [Glory, moreover, consists in the public acclaim derived from honorable
> deeds and great services benefiting the commonwealth, approved by the
> testimony of the best and also by that of the multitude.]

This definition of *gloria*, which places the emphasis squarely on civic
ethics rather than martial prowess in insisting that deeds only result
in renown (*gloria*) if they meet moral criteria (cf. *recte factorum*), benefit
the commonwealth, and find the approval of the elite and the people
at large, is strikingly unorthodox. Unfortunately, Antony, says Cicero,
only has a dim understanding of what true glory entails: he acquired
some when he abolished the office of dictator, but then squandered it all
in his ignorance (*Phil.* 1.33):

> Num te, cum haec pro salute rei publicae tanta gessisses, fortunae tuae,
> num amplitudinis, num claritatis, num gloriae paenitebat? unde igitur
> subito tanta ista mutatio? ... illud magis vereor, ne, ignorans verum iter
> gloriae, gloriosum putes plus te unum posse quam omnes et metui a
> civibus tuis quam diligi malis. quod si ita putas, totam ignoras viam
> gloriae. carum esse civem, bene de re publica mereri, laudari, coli,

---

95   See further Long (1995), Christian (2008: 157–60), Gildenhard (2011), Ch. 5:
     'Definition and the Politics of Truth', and Chang (2013: 110–34).

diligi gloriosum est; metui vero et in odio esse invidiosum, detestabile, imbecillum, caducum.

[Did you, after these great achievements for the welfare of the commonwealth, regret your fortune, your distinction, your renown, your glory? Why, then, did you experience such a sudden and significant change of heart? ... What I more fear is that, blind to the true path of glory, you may think it glorious to possess in your single self more power than all, and to be feared by your fellow-citizens. If you think so, you are totally ignorant of the true way to glory. To be a citizen dear to all, to deserve well of the commonwealth, to be praised, courted, loved, is glorious; but to be feared and an object of hatred is invidious, detestable, a proof of weakness and decay.]

In contrast, the assassins know what true glory consists in (*Phil.* 2.5, 33, 86, 114, 117) — as does Caesar Octavianus, unlike his adoptive father (*Phil.* 5.49). Cicero closes rank against Antony around the notion of two variants of glory — genuine renown (such as that enjoyed by the liberators) that thrives in a functioning commonwealth and its perverse counterfeit pursued by Caesar and now Antony, which is based on a confusion of power and glory.

In our paragraph, Cicero replays the ending of the first *Philippic*: he again begins by praising Antony for abolishing the office of dictator, only to dwell on his subsequent U-turn, caused by his pathological inability to grasp the true nature of glory.

Recordare igitur illum, M. Antoni, diem quo dictaturam sustulisti: *recordare* is the second person imperative singular of the deponent *recordor*, going with the vocative *M. Antoni*. The antecedent of the relative pronoun *quo* (an ablative of time) is *diem*: 'Recall that day on which...'. For Antony's motion that outlawed the act of proposing anyone to be appointed dictator see § 91 above.

pone ante oculos laetitiam senatus populique Romani, confer [eam] **cum hac nundinatione tua tuorumque**: Cicero delivers two further imperative blows (*pone, confer*) in asyndetic sequence, inviting him to visualize (*pone ante oculos*) the joy he managed to spark when he scrapped the dictatorship and compare it to his disgraceful pursuit of tyrannical self-enrichment shortly thereafter: he refers to Antony putting the *res publica* up for sale for personal gain (see § 92 above).

His close friends and relatives profited from the process as well (§ 93: *sunt ea quidem innumerabilia quae a tuis emebantur non insciente te*: 'the items bought by persons close to you, and not without your knowledge, are innumerable'). *laetitiam* is the accusative object of both imperatives. The comparison is either (*a*) compressed or (*b*) imprecise. (*a*) Cicero asks Antony to compare joy with an (unspecified) negative emotion such as grief (*dolor*) at the trafficking (*nundinatio*) in favours that he and those close to him engaged in after the Ides of March. (*b*) Cicero compares the emotional *re*action to a laudable deed (*laetitia*) with a contemptible *action* (*nundinatio*).

The governing word of *tuorum* is *nundinatione*: the *-que* after *tuorum* thus coordinates the possessive adjective *tua* and the possessive genitive *tuorum*. This is one of only six instances in which Cicero ends a sentence on the enclitic *-que* (Kraus 1992: 321).

In his philosophical dialogue *Tusculan Disputations*, Cicero classifies 'excessive' (*gestiens*) *laetitia* (together with *aegritudo, metus*, and *libido*) as a mental disturbance to be avoided (*Tusc.* 4.8, elaborated at 4.13). In his orations, he tends to be rather less po-faced about emotions, and 'joy' (*laetitia* — though not the excessive variety) becomes another criterion for dividing the world into 'the good' and 'the bad'. Cicero is here in part responding to Antony's assertion that he experienced heinous and homicidal glee (*laetitia*) at the deaths of Clodius (2.21: *at laetatus sum. quid ergo? in tanta laetitia cunctae civitatis me unum tristem esse oportebat?*) and Caesar (2.29: *tu autem, omnium stultissime, non intellegis, si, id quod me arguis, voluisse interfici Caesarem crimen sit, etiam laetatum esse morte Caesaris crimen esse?*). Instead, he endorses a salvific variant of reciprocal joyfulness on the part of both public benefactors and their beneficiaries, which he already outlined at the end of the first *Philippic*. See *Phil.* 1.30 (addressing Dolabella): *Quem potes recordari in vita illuxisse tibi diem laetiorem, quam cum, expiatio foro, dissipato concursu impiorum, principibus sceleris poena affectis, urbe incendio et caedis metu liberata, te domum recepisti?* ('What day can you recall in life that shone upon you more joyously than that in which, when the Forum had been purged, concourse of impious wretches scattered, the ringleaders of the crime punished, the city delivered from burning and the fear of massacre, you betook yourself home?') There were moments when Antony participated in this economy: when he surrendered his son as hostage to the conspirators, the senate and the people of Rome were overjoyed (*Phil.* 1.32: *quo senatus die laetior, quo populus Romanus?*). But he has since then lost his way, exulting over the destruction of normal senatorial proceedings (§ 109); and he remains unaffected by the joy of right-minded citizens over civic-minded actions.[96]

senatus populique Romani: *senatus populusque Romanus* (here in the genitive singular dependent on *laetitiam*) is how Rome's political community self-identified. The City Council of Rome (Comune di Roma) still uses SPQR as its official emblem today: you'll find it embossed on all manhole covers, for instance.

tum intelleges, quantum inter lucrum et laudem intersit: the interrogative adverb *quantum* (how much?) introduces an indirect question (hence the subjunctive *intersit*). There are various ways to reproduce the deftly alliterated phrase *lucrum et laudem* in English: gain and glory, profit and plaudits, riches and renown, cash and kudos, lucre and laudation, Mammon and merit... It's the same principle of verbal homophony / conceptual polarity as 'chalk and cheese'. As Lacey (1986: 241) notes, '*laudem* starts a series of echoes': see *verae laudis gustatum*, *laus, laudo* in the following sentences.

sed nimirum, ut quidam morbo aliquo et sensus stupore suavitatem cibi non sentiunt, sic libidinosi, avari, facinerosi verae laudis gustatum non habent: Cicero launches into an analogy (*ut ... sic*): just as people whose taste buds are affected by illness have lost the ability to savour food, so various kinds of scumbags are unable to appreciate true glory. The diagnosis of socio-pathologies is a standard move in Cicero's invective repertory. *quidam* (masculine nominative plural: 'some') is the subject of the well-crafted *ut*-clause: note the chiastic hendiadys *morbo aliquo et sensus stupore*, the persistent *s*-alliteration (*sensus, stupore, suavitatem, sentiunt*) and the *figura etymologica* (*sensus ... sentiunt*). *quidam* correlates with the three adjectives in asyndetic sequence used as nouns

---

96 *Laetitia* in this sense later became an element of imperial ideology: see Noreña (2011: 171–74): 'the "happiness" of the emperor and that of the empire's inhabitants, intimately connected through this constellation of concepts [sc. *felicitas, hilaritas, laetitia*], helped to maintain the notional community of interests between emperor and subject'.

in the *sic*-clause: *libidinosi* ('the libidinous'), *avari* ('the greedy'), and *facinerosi* ('the criminal').

morbo aliquo et sensus stupore: *morbo* and *stupore* are causal ablatives best understood as a hendiadys: 'because of numbness of perception caused by some disease'. The two nouns are modified, respectively, by a pronominal adjective (*aliquo*) and an adnominal genitive (*sensus*): the arrangement is chiastic.

sed si te laus adlicere ad recte faciendum non potest, ne metus quidem a foedissimis factis potest avocare?: the conditional sequence cast as a rhetorical question offers Antony two possible reasons for behaving in a civic-minded fashion: in the (negated) *si*-clause Cicero mentions the ideal scenario only to rule it out: it consists in the prospect of renown (*laus*) exercising sufficient positive pull towards acting in the right way (*adlicere ad*). Conversely, the apodosis outlines the minimalist alternative of acceptable behaviour, i.e. fear (of punishment) holding Antony back from the vilest deeds (*a … avocare* correlates with *adlicere ad…*), which, so the rhetorical question implies, Antony does not meet either. The superlative *foedissimis* is deliberate: Cicero does not even demand abstention from *foeda facta*, just those that are vile in the extreme. The *figura etymologica* is profoundly pessimistic: *ad recte faciendum* is mentioned as a counterfactual possibility, the *foedissima facta* are established facts.

Extra information:
Cicero's choice of *adlicere* to capture the attraction of *laus* to which Antony is not susceptible is curious since it is a verb he elsewhere associates with dubious sensual pleasure. See for instance *pro Murena* 74, where he mockingly impersonates Cato the Younger objecting to the practice of wooing voters through the provision of sensual pleasures:

> At enim agit mecum austere et Stoice Cato, negat verum esse adlici benivolentiam cibo, negat iudicium hominum in magistratibus mandandis corrumpi voluptatibus oportere. ergo, ad cenam petitionis causa si quis vocat, condemnetur? 'Quippe' inquit 'tu mihi summum imperium, tu summam auctoritatem, tu gubernacula rei publicae petas fovendis hominum sensibus et deleniendis animis et adhibendis voluptatibus? utrum lenocinium' inquit 'a grege delicatae iuventutis, an orbis terrarum imperium a populo Romano petebas?'

[Cato, however, deals sternly with me like a true Stoic. He says that it is wrong to promote good-will with food and warp men's judgement by means of pleasure in an election of magistrates. Are we then to condemn everyone who gives an invitation to dinner for this purpose? 'Am I,' he says, 'going to have you seek supreme power, supreme authority, the very government of the State by pandering to men's senses, bewitching their minds and plying them with pleasures? Were you asking,' he says, 'a gang of spoilt youths for a job as a pimp or the Roman people for world dominion?']

As Fantham (2013: 180) notes: 'the accumulation of strong sensual vocabulary like *adlicere* and *delenire,* associated with pleasure, reinforces the contrast between the solemn metaphor of *gubernacula* and the image of the pander appealing to susceptible young men'.

iudicia non metuis? si propter innocentiam [non metuis], **laudo; sin propter vim** [non metuis], **non intellegis, qui isto modo iudicia non timeat, ei quid timendum sit?**: Cicero imagines a gesture of dismissal on Antony's part in response to the threat of legal proceedings. In turn, he once more affirms his ethics of praise, contrasting personal integrity (*innocentia*), which entails *laus*, with the reliance on the illegitimate use of physical force (*vis*). He ends by stressing that Antony's trust in *vis* is misplaced: as history shows, strongman-politics results in violent resistance. *ei* is dative of authorship (with the gerundive *timendum sit*) and the antecedent of *qui*. Translate in the following order: *non intellegis quid ei timendum sit* (indirect question), *qui....* Dependence on *vis*, far from quelling fear, ought to generate it.

§ 116: Caesar You Are Not!

Cicero continues to insist that Antony ought to be very much afraid for his life if he continues his pernicious politics of fear. His bodyguard, meant to keep would-be assassins at bay, will not help him in the long run — or, indeed, much longer: even those close to him will sooner than later rise up against him. What renders this apparently counterintuitive claim plausible is the spectre of Caesar: those who did him in included some who had benefitted most from his benevolence. Built into the fate of Caesar is an *a-fortiori* caution: if even someone like him ran foul of people who ought to have been beholden to him, Antony is all the more likely to meet a nasty end, inferior to the dead dictator as he is in every conceivable respect. Cicero drives home the point that Antony is no Caesar by launching into an enumeration of the qualities of the dead dictator, carefully tempering praise with blame. As in the *de Officiis* (1.26, cited above 418), Cicero figures Caesar as an outstanding talent who ended up deploying his abundant gifts to the detriment and destruction of Rome's civic community — and so then got what he had coming.[97]

A key issue that Cicero struggles with in this paragraph is Caesar's preternatural ability to render others beholden to him — through personal charm, exceptional generosity, or services rendered that put others in social and financial debt to him. Roman political culture was much invested in reciprocal relations, captured in idiom and imagery of duties, services, gratitude, expectations of reciprocity, as well as binding obligations and loyalties (*beneficium, gratia, amicitia, fides, officia, obligare,* etc.). Social and financial debts blurred into each other. Those

---

97   For a survey of other contemporary assessments of Caesar see Griffin (2009: 3–5).

who loaned out money exercised a significant degree of influence over the borrower, who was duty bound to oblige his business associate in other respects as well — beyond the repayment of the debt.[98]

Caesar purported to perform within this traditional paradigm when he distributed favours and largesse to his friends, acquaintances, and the people more generally and exploited the opportunity to generate social and financial debt through interest free loans to the hilt.[99] But the most extreme form of 'obliging' someone is to exercise leniency towards a (conquered) enemy and spare his life. This scenario, which could only arise in situations of civil conflict, wrecked republican conventions: there is no way to ever properly pay back someone who has saved one's life — one is forever indebted to (and hence metaphorically beholden, perhaps even enslaved, and certainly resentful of) this person.[100]

How did aristocrats deal with Caesar's willingness to spare their lives when caught fighting against him? Some simply ignored it and returned to battle — until they were captured again. Caesar mocks such repeat captives badly in his *Bellum Civile*. Cato, a man of principle, resorted to a more drastic action: terminal withdrawal from the dictator. In Plutarch's *Life of Cato the Younger* Cato categorically rejects the notion of begging Caesar for mercy, either directly or through intermediaries — even though he does not force others to adopt the same uncompromising stance: 'If I were willing to be saved by grace of Caesar, I ought to go to him in person and see him alone; but I am unwilling to be under obligations to the tyrant for his illegal acts. And he acts illegally in saving, as if their master, those over whom he has no right at all to be the lord' (66).[101]

---

98 For senatorial wealth and Roman politics see generally Shatzman (1975), further Andreau (1999: 139–58) and Verboven (2002: 116–82).

99 See Suetonius, *Life of Julius Caesar*, 27.1 for details. Cicero, too, was a beneficiary as the recipient of a loan for 800,000 HS in 54 BCE.

100 At *pro Plancio* 72, Cicero notes that soldiers are reluctant to concede that their life has been saved in battle by a comrade, which may happen even to the brave and hence is not in itself humiliating: 'but they shrink from the overpowering burden of being under the same obligation to a stranger that they owe to a parent' (*sed onus beneficii reformidant, quod permagnum est alieno debere idem quod parenti*). See Konstan (2016: 46) for discussion.

101 See also Cicero, *ad Brutum* 24: Brutus wouldn't accept a *beneficium* or *misericordia* from Antony.

This prehistory to the Ides of March generated the awkward paradox that many of the assassins had their own lives previously spared by the very person whom they murdered. Cicero invested a lot of effort in formulating an ethics of murder, which legitimized the deed as justified — indeed required — tyrannicide, rather than the cold-blooded and ungrateful killing of a lenient benefactor. A large part of his case rests on the denial that a tyrant can engage in meaningful socio-political relationships, let alone an economy of reciprocal obligations. He stands outside any form of human community, indeed is a wild beast that is human in appearance only — a monster that ought to be killed as a matter of civic ethics. See *On Duties* (*de Officiis*) 3.32.

Quod si non metuis viros fortis egregiosque civis, quod a corpore tuo prohibentur armis, tui te, mihi crede, diutius non ferent: *quod* here has adversative force 'but if…' and the indicative *metuis* implies that the protasis of the conditional sequence introduced by *si* captures the facts: Antony *is* unafraid. The second *quod* is causal ('because…'). The subject of the main clause is *tui* (the masculine nominative plural of the possessive adjective *tuus*, here used as a noun): 'your men / supporters'; the verb (*ferent*) is in the future tense; *te* is the accusative object.

viros fortis egregiosque civis: the *-que* after *egregios* links *viros* and *civis*. The design of this majestic accusative object (placed emphatically at the end of the *quod-si*-clause) is chiastic (noun + adjective :: adjective + noun), here enhanced by grammar: the first phrase features a second declension noun and a third declension attribute, the second a second declension attribute and a third declension noun (*fortis* and *civis* are the alternative accusative plural forms of the third declension: = *fortes*, *cives*). The phrase constitutes a powerful hendiadys: Cicero is not referring to two distinct kinds of persons — 'brave men and outstanding citizens' — but persons who possess two qualities: 'men who are brave and outstanding citizens'.

quod a corpore tuo prohibentur armis: the subject of the *quod*-clause are the brave and pre-eminent citizens: 'because they are kept away from your body by means of weapons'. Cicero's adjustments to natural word order (which would have been *quod a corpore tuo armis prohibentur*) results in a dramatic postponement of the decisive *armis* (an ablative of means) and an iconic enactment of the meaning in the design: the verb *prohibentur* placed in-between *a corpore tuo* and *armis* does what it says it does, i.e. keeping the arms away from Antony's body. Essentially, Cicero is saying: 'without your bodyguard, Antony, you are a dead man!' This isn't exactly a promising premise for disarmament — and stands in latent contradiction to his earlier complaint that Antony is filling the city with armed henchmen.

tui te ... non ferent: Cicero operates with an implied antithesis between *viros fortis egregiosque civis* and *tui*, implying that Antony's supporters lack masculinity (*viros*), bravery (*fortis*), pre-eminence (*egregios*), and a sound understanding of what Roman citizenship entails (*civis*). And even though they potentially lack all of these qualities (for otherwise they would hardly support Antony in the first place), they will — so Cicero is predicting: note the future tense of *ferent* — soon cease to put up with him. On what grounds does Cicero make this — as it turned out, entirely baseless — prediction? Implied here is the belief that political criminals and tyrants by definition self-destruct — a Platonic tenet that Cicero cherished as a ray of hope (however misplaced) in his darkest hours, and which seemed to have become a reality (though much later than anticipated) with the assassination of Caesar.

mihi crede: for the phrase, see above 391.

diutius: the comparative of the adverb *diu* ('long', 'for a long time'): 'longer'.

quae est autem vita dies et noctes timere a suis?: the infinitive *timere* functions as a predicative noun with the copula *est*: 'What kind of life is it to fear harm from / be afraid of your close associates day and night?' Note that *timeo* can be construed either transitively (with the object of fear appearing in the accusative) or intransitively (as here), where the source of fear is expressed by the ablative + *ab*. Hence:

- *timere alicui*: to fear *for* someone
- *timere ab aliquo*: to fear harm from someone
- *timere aliquid ab aliquo*: to fear something from someone
- *timere aliquem*: to fear someone

Cicero does not pursue the explosive potential of his prediction that a revolt among Antony's underlings is imminent. Instead, by switching from second person (*tui*) to third person (*a suis*), he steps back and generalizes, posing a quasi-philosophical question about (acceptable) terms of existence. In the subsequent sentence he returns to the second person, evaluating Antony against the generic norm implied in the rhetorical question here. Cicero already posed a similar question in the *first Catilinarian* addressed to Catiline (1.16: *Nunc vero quae tua est ista vita?*). And his proto-philosophical enquiry also brings to mind Caesar's decision to refuse a bodyguard on the grounds that he did not wish to live in constant fear for his life. See Plutarch, *Life of Caesar* 57.7: 'When his friends thought it best that he should have a body-guard, and many of them volunteered for this service, he would not consent, saying that it was better to die once and for all than to be always expecting death'. A paradox ensues: the most un-tyrannical action on the part of the reigning tyrant was at least in part responsible for getting him killed. The implications of the tyrant de-tyrannizing himself and paying for it with his life are rather awkward for Cicero's argument here, so the issue never comes properly into focus.

dies et noctes: accusative of duration.

nisi vero aut maioribus habes beneficiis [tuos] **obligatos quam** [illa beneficia quibus] **ille quosdam habuit ex eis** [obligatos] **a quibus est interfectus, aut tu es ulla re cum eo comparandus**: both Cicero's syntax and his line of thinking are highly elliptical. In responding to the rhetorical question he just posed ('And what sort of a life is it to be afraid day and night of one's own?'), Cicero suppresses the (obvious) answer ('it's no life at all') and application to the case at hand ('but you are bound to lead it'). He then moots two all but impossible scenarios (one specific, one general, which leads off into a different line of argument, loosely coordinated by *aut ... aut*), in which Antony might not have to fear violence from those close to him: 'unless, indeed, you either have your own men bound (to you) through greater benefactions than (those by which) he [sc. Caesar] had some of those bound (to him) by whom he was killed — or are to be compared to him in any way'. (Cicero then goes on to assert that any comparison between Caesar and Antony is absurd — unlike the former, the latter entirely lacks any kind of redeeming quality).

maioribus ... beneficiis: Caesar dispensed favours and (material) handouts liberally (Cicero will provide details in a moment), but arguably the greatest benefaction he imposed on other members of Rome's ruling elite was to spare their lives when he captured them on the battlefield — or indeed after he had won the war (unlike Sulla, there were no proscriptions, or 'killing lists', under Caesar — one by one, he pardoned virtually all of his adversaries). This policy of mercy is another topic to surface in the course of this paragraph. The ensuing degree of obligation is almost impossible to match.

quosdam ... ex eis a quibus: 'some out of those by whom...' *ex eis* describes the whole of which the *quosdam* form a part. For this use of *ex* (instead of a partitive genitive), see Gildersleeve & Lodge 237. Cicero here refers to those of Caesar's assassins who were tied to him through services rendered or, indeed, friendship: 'the reference is both to Caesarians who joined the conspiracy, such as P. and C. Servilius Casca, L. Tillius Cimber, C. Trebonius, L. Minucius Basilus, Servius Sulpicius Galba, and to those who, though Pompeians from the first, had been pardoned by Caesar, such as M. Brutus and C. Cassius' (Denniston 1926: 171).

a quibus: an ablative of agency with the perfect passive verb *est interfectus*.

ulla re: an ablative of respect.

fuit in illo ingenium, ratio, memoria, litterae, cura, cogitatio, diligentia: Cicero enumerates a subset of Caesar's personal characteristics in an asyndetic list. He puts the emphasis on mental, moral, and intellectual qualities, where the difference to Antony is (according to Cicero) most pronounced. He was not the only one who singled out the special calibre of Caesar's power of mind. Here is Pliny the Elder, *Natural History* 7.91:

> Animi vigore praestantissimum arbitror genitum Caesarem dictatorem; nec virtutem constantiamque nunc commemoro, nec sublimitatem omnium capacem quae caelo continentur, sed proprium vigorem

celeritatemque quodam igne volucrem. scribere aut legere, simul dictare atque audire solitum accepimus, epistulas vero tantarum rerum quaternas pariter dictare librariis.

[The most outstanding instance of innate mental vigour I take to be the dictator Caesar; and I am not now thinking of manliness and resolution, nor of a loftiness embracing all the contents of the firmament of heaven, but of native vigour and quickness winged as it were with fire. We are told that he used to write or read and dictate or listen simultaneously, and *to dictate* [NB!] to his secretaries four letters at once on his important affairs.]

Cicero's own praise of Caesar is more muted, and the style arguably recalls the threadbare register of a funeral oration: so Dufallo (2007: 54). He notes that 'the economy of expression demonstrated by Cicero's praise of Caesar ... is in keeping with Cicero's own prescriptions for the Roman *laudatio*: delivered in the forum as a testimony to character, it has *brevitatem ... nudam atque inornatam* (a bare and unadorned brevity); composed specifically as a funeral speech, it is *ad orationis laudem minime accommodata* (least suited to a display of oratorical excellence) (Cic. *de Orat.* 2.341)' (141).

ingenium: most basically, *ingenium* refers to 'natural disposition' and then to 'inherent quality or character', or, with a greater emphasis on talent, 'natural abilities', especially of the mental / intellectual kind: it can specifically refer to being gifted with words, whether in rhetoric or poetry. In rhetorical theory, *ingenium* is a key technical term (innate talent complementing *ars*, or 'exercise', in constituting the perfect orator, the *summus orator*). But in the sense of 'talent' it refers to inherent potential rather than inherent moral excellence, and in some of his later philosophical writings Cicero laments that some of the greatest talents (*ingenia*) in Roman history, such as Caesar, became corrupted through the desire for power.

ratio: the ability to use reason. Caesar valued expert knowledge and rational order. Thus Suetonius (*Life of Julius Caesar* 42) reports that 'he conferred citizenship on all who practised medicine at Rome, and on all teachers of the liberal arts, to make them more desirous of living in the city and to induce others to resort to it'. As Garcea (2012: 5) points out:

'This makes clear to us how he wished to make use of competent and highly specialized people in public life'. His legal reforms are another good example of Caesar relying on rational criteria for the pragmatic vetting of traditional bodies of knowledge (Suetonius, *Life of Julius Caesar* 44.2):

> Nam de ornanda instruendaque urbe, item de tuendo ampliandoque imperio plura ac maiora in dies destinabat ... ius civile ad certum modum redigere atque ex immensa diffusaque legum copia optima quaeque et necessaria in paucissimos conferre libros.

> [In particular, for the adornment and convenience of the city, also for the protection and extension of the empire, he formed more projects and more extensive ones every day ... to reduce the civil code to fixed limits, and of the vast and prolix mass of statutes to include only the best and most essential in a limited number of volumes.]

'Caesar's aim, then, was to eliminate unnecessary and redundant legislation, resolve issues of incompatibility, bring order to the *uolumina* ...' Garcea (2012: 5). Most significantly, perhaps is his application of *ratio* to the measurement of time in his reform of the calendar (Macrobius, *Saturnalia* 1.14.2):

> sed postea C. Caesar omnem hanc inconstantiam temporum vagam adhuc et incertam in ordinem statae definitionis coegit, adnitente sibi M. Flauio scriba, qui scriptos dies singulos ita ad dictatorem retulit ut et ordo eorum inveniri facillime posset et invento certus status perseveraret.

> [But Gaius Caesar took all this chronological inconsistency, which he found still ill-sorted and fluid, and reduced it to a regular and well-defined order; in this he was assisted by the scribe Marcus Flavius, who presented a table of the individual days to Caesar in a form that allowed both their order to be determined and, once that was determined, their relative position to remain fixed.]

memoria: memory — the ability to retain and recall data — is one of the five components of oratory, together with *inventio*, *dispositio*, *elocutio*, and *actio*. See *Rhetorica ad Herennium* 3.28–40. Caesar seems to have been gifted with a prodigious memory, which he used for multi-tasking.

litterae: Caesar's literary output was considerable. See Suetonius, *Life of Julius Caesar* 56 for an overview:

He left *memoirs* too *of his deeds in the Gallic war and in the civil strife with Pompey*; for the author of the Alexandrian, African, and Spanish Wars is unknown; some think it was Oppius, other Hirtius, who also supplied the final book of the Gallic War, which Caesar left unwritten. … He left besides a work in two volumes *On Analogy*, the same number of *Speeches against Cato*, in addition to a poem, entitled *The Journey*. He wrote the first of these works while crossing the Alps and returning to his army from Hither Gaul, where he had held the assizes; the second about the time of the battle of Munda, and the last one in the course of a twenty-three days' journey from Rome to Farther Spain. Some letters of his to the senate are also preserved, and he seems to have been the first to redact such documents in the columnar form of a note-book, whereas previously consuls and generals only sent their reports written right across the sheet. There are also letters of his to Cicero, as well as to his intimates on private affairs, and in the latter, if he had anything rather confidential to say, he wrote it in cipher, that is, by so changing the order of the letters of the alphabet, that not a word could be made out. If anyone wishes to decipher these, and get at their meaning, he must substitute the fourth letter of the alphabet, namely D, for A, and so with the others. Certain writings of his early youth are also left, as Quintus Tubero says, such as the *Praises of Hercules*, a tragedy *Oedipus*, and a *Collection of Apophthegms*; but Augustus forbade the publication of all these minor works in a very brief and frank letter sent to Pompeius Macer, whom he had selected to set his libraries in order.

cura: here 'care', in particular due and detailed attention, as applied to literary pursuits or the wellbeing of others (within this list, the emphasis is most likely on the former rather than the latter).

cogitatio: 'thoughtfulness' — the ability to reflect and reach a considered view on a range of issues. Fantham (2009: 155–56) outlines the scope of the topics that came within his ken: 'his intellectual interests included a number of areas — religion, historiography, ethnography, and political theory and ideology (such as his invention of the weapon of clemency)'. He was also much interested in language, rhetoric, geography, and natural phenomena (including astronomy).

diligentia: a virtual synonym of *cura* — 'careful and painstaking attention', applied to such activities as literary compositions.

res bello gesserat, quamvis rei publicae calamitosas, at tamen magnas: Cicero could not possibly pass over Caesar's feats in war, though he mentions them in as qualified a fashion as possible: the matter-of-fact opening 'deeds in war he had performed...' is utterly devoid of any panegyric embellishment (Caesar might as well have been an insignificant foot-soldier marching along...). Before any kind of praise, Cicero condemns Caesar's military deeds wholesale, in the strongest possible terms, as an utter calamity for the commonwealth. He does not even differentiate between his conquest of Gaul and his victory in the civil war — both his external and internal conquests are equally implicated in his destructive rise to the top. Likewise, while Caesar was still alive, Cicero considered his triumph in the civil war a blessing in disguise: a republican victory would have resulted, he was convinced, in much more post-war persecution and bloodshed. Any such nuance is here by the way. In a concessive tag-on (*at tamen*), Cicero ends by damning Caesar with a faint bit of praise: *magnas* is a run-of-the-mill attribute at the end of the sentence, strategically separated from the noun it modifies (*res*): the massive hyperbaton ensures that the acclaim remains a belittling afterthought that trivializes Caesar's military achievements.

multos annos regnare meditatus, magno labore, magnis periculis quod cogitarat effecerat: *multos annos* is an accusative of duration ('for many years'). Cicero here projects the origins of Caesar's monarchical ambitions back into the distant past, but neither he nor modern scholars can possibly know at what point Caesar began to aim at kingship — though for biographers that tends to be a key question. Suetonius, in his *Life of Julius Caesar*, imagines the spectre of Alexander the Great as a key moment in Caesar's quest for greatness (7):[102]

> As quaestor it fell to his lot to serve in Further Spain. When he was there, while making the circuit of the assize-towns, to hold court under commission from the praetor, he came to Gades, and noticing a statue of Alexander the Great in the temple of Hercules, he heaved a sigh, and as if out of disgust with his own incapacity in having as yet done nothing noteworthy at a time of life when Alexander had already brought the world to his feet, he straightway asked for his discharge, to grasp the first opportunity for greater enterprises at Rome.

---

102 See further Henderson (2014: 103–06).

The consensus nowadays is that this was a fairly late development in his career and only really took off after his victory in the civil war, in reaction to events. Cicero goes for a more decisive (and hence more sensational and damning) backdating, but remains prudently vague: for him, Caesar was at any rate never a 'naturally born' tyrant who harboured tyrannical ambitions from the get-go. Quite the contrary: he always singled him out as a formidable talent; and in *Philippic* 5.49 identifies failure to achieve insight into 'true glory' at an early stage in his career as the reason why he ended up as an autocratic demagogue — a failure compounded by the lack of rightful recognition from other constituencies of Rome's civic community:

> Ea natura rerum est, patres conscripti, ut qui sensum verae gloriae ceperit quique se ab senatu, ab equitibus Romanis populoque Romano universo senserit civem carum haberi salutaremque rei publicae, nihil cum hac gloria comparandum putet. utinam C. Caesari, patri dico, contigisset adulescenti ut esset senatui atque optimo cuique carissimus! quod cum consequi neglexisset, omnem vim ingeni, quae summa fuit in illo, in populari levitate consumpsit.

> [It is natural, members of the senate, that one who has grasped the meaning of true glory, one who feels he is regarded by the senate, by the Roman knights, and by the entire Roman people as a loved citizen and beneficial to the commonwealth, should deem nothing comparable with this glory. Would it had been the fortune of Caius Caesar — the father I mean — when a young man to be very dear to the senate and every loyal citizen! Because he neglected to secure this, he wasted all the power of his intellect — and in him it was of the highest — in pandering to popular fickleness.]

It is of course important to realize that in *Philippic* 5, Cicero is trying to sell Caesar Octavianus to the senate, on the grounds that unlike his adoptive father he understands what true glory consists in — and that the senate should not commit the same mistake with him as it did with Caesar, i.e. be invidiously stingy in rewarding him with the public recognition he deserves. At the same time, it is noteworthy that Cicero here and elsewhere identifies external circumstances as responsible for transmogrifying Caesar and his *summum ingenium* into a tyrant-figure. Even here Cicero, while repudiating Caesar's desire to rule as king, expresses grudging admiration for the amount of effort and energy that Caesar invested in turning his misconceived dream into a reality. The 'strenuous' m-alliteration reinforced by anaphora (*multos – meditatus – magno – magnis*) provides a proper soundtrack for the point. For a similar formulation (though on a different time-scale) see § 85: *meditatum et cogitatum scelus* (Antony at the Lupercalia).

cogitarat: the syncopated third person singular pluperfect indicative active form (= *cogita | ve | rat*).

muneribus, monumentis, congiariis, epulis multitudinem imperitam delenierat: in this and the following sentence, Cicero outlines how Caesar managed to consolidate his reign: he ingratiated himself with the masses; and obliged friends and adversaries with material and immaterial benefactions. Plutarch, *Life of Caesar* 57.8, suggests that Caesar tried to generate goodwill among his fellow citizens as a substitute for a bodyguard: 'And in the effort to surround himself with men's good will as the fairest and at the same time the securest protection, he again courted the people with banquets and distributions of grain, and his soldiers with newly planted colonies'. Unlike Plutarch, Cicero portrays these efforts as insidious ploys to consolidate tyrannical power. Suetonius, *Life of Julius Caesar* 38 gives an idea of the scope of the lavish expenditure that Caesar invested in generating personal loyalties:

> To each and every foot-soldier of his veteran legions he gave twenty-four thousand sesterces by way of booty, over and above the two thousand apiece which he had paid them at the beginning of the civil strife. He also assigned them lands, but not side by side, to avoid dispossessing any of the former owners. To every man of the people, besides ten pecks of grain and the same number of pounds of oil, he distributed the three hundred sesterces which he had promised at first, and one hundred apiece to boot because of the delay. He also remitted a year's rent in Rome to tenants who paid two thousand sesterces or less, and in Italy up to five hundred sesterces. He added a banquet and a dole of meat, and after his Spanish victory two dinners; for deeming that the former of these had not been served with a liberality creditable to his generosity, he gave another five days later on a most lavish scale.

In terms of style, he continues with asyndetic enumeration and m-alliteration (*muneribus, monumentis, multitudinem*).

muneribus: throughout the republic, politicians tried to advance their careers through public benefactions, both ephemeral (e.g. through feasts, games, spectacles) and permanent (e.g. through buildings). A competition ensued, with aristocrats vying with each other to outdo earlier gestures of public munificence. The idea was to impress one's name upon the collective memory, and thereby get a step up in elections to public office. There was some allowance for using state-funds for this purpose, but the resources were limited: wealthy patrons drew upon their personal fortunes, others took out massive loans, and successful generals supplemented their allocated budget through imperial plunder (*manubiae*) to outshine their rivals.[103] Caesar started to get in on the action early. See Suetonius, *Life of Caesar* 10, on his activities as aedile in 65 BCE:

> When aedile, Caesar decorated not only the Comitium and the Forum with its adjacent basilicas, but the Capitol as well, building temporary colonnades for the display of a part of his material. He exhibited combats with wild beasts and stage-plays too, both with his colleague and independently. The result was that Caesar alone took all the credit even for what they spent in common, and his colleague Marcus Bibulus openly said that his was the fate of Pollux: 'For,' said he, 'just as the temple erected in the Forum to the twin brethren bears only the name of Castor, so the joint liberality of Caesar and myself is credited to Caesar alone.' Caesar gave a gladiatorial show besides, but with somewhat fewer pairs of combatants than he had purposed; for the huge band which he assembled from all quarters so terrified his opponents, that a bill was passed limiting the number of gladiators which anyone was to be allowed to keep in the city.

Suetonius explicitly states that Caesar did this to win the goodwill of the masses (and succeeded in doing so).

monumentis: before Caesar, the title of Mr. Public Grandeur went to Pompey and his theatre complex, which he began in 61 BCE to memorialize in stone his third triumph. It included a temple dedicated to Venus Victrix, which was dedicated in 55 BCE. In the following year, Caesar, flush with booty extracted from Gaul, began construction of a new forum, no doubt partly in emulation of Pompey's theatre complex. It was not completed in his lifetime, but that did not prevent him from initiating further building projects alongside, especially after securing

---

103 Shatzman (1975), Veyne (1990), Lomas (2003).

victory in the civil war, such as the temple of Venus Genetrix, dedicated in 46 BCE, as part of the unfinished forum complex, or the Basilica Iulia, also dedicated in 46 BCE but again finished under Augustus. (For a full list of the works planned by Caesar, see Suetonius, *Life of Julius Caesar* 44.)

congiariis: the term *congiarium* derives from *congius*, which denotes a measure of wine or oil, which a magistrate or similarly elevated individual distributes to his followers or the people at large. A *congiarium* was 'a "gift" intended to display the giver's generosity and to reward and encourage the recipient's loyalty, but not constituting formal payment for a specific service' (Kaster 1995: 311). See further Rostovtzeff (1900: 875, who notes that the character and the scope of *congiaria* changed significantly under Caesar: he handed out not just wine and oil, but also money as part of the triumphal celebrations in 46 BCE (see Suetonius, *Life of Julius Caesar* 38, cited above) — and monopolized the practice.

epulis: on the word, see Donahue (2004: 7–8):

> By far, the most popular term for a Roman feast is *epulum*. Originally a technical term for a religious meal ..., the term conveyed a religious aspect from an early date through its link with two of Rome's most ancient festivals, the *Ludi Romani* and *Ludi Plebeii*. Both ceremonies included among their festivities the *epulum Iovis*, a repast in honor of Jupiter, overseen by a special class of priests, the *septemviri epulones*. ... Over time, its religious connotation diminished and *epulum* came to mean a luxurious secular meal offered on various occasions to large numbers.

This is another area of ostentatious consumption in which Caesar distinguished himself — though he was not the only one.[104] See Suetonius, *Life of Julius Caesar* 38 (cited above). As Donahue (2004: 256) notes: 'No one was more adept at such public magnanimity, however, than Julius Caesar. Even though kingship could never be tolerated at Rome, for him the ability to act like a monarch remained very much a consideration. The beneficiaries were the plebs, who readily accepted largess from the kingly triumphator, becoming in the process instruments of his grand ambitions. There can be no doubt that the public meal played a pivotal role in this scheme, as it reached new heights during this period. To

---

104 See e.g. Plutarch, *Life of Crassus* 2.2 and 12.2, and *Comp. Crass. et Nic.* 1.4.

be sure, it was not an invention of Caesar's; he simply changed the standard by extending the scope and scale of liberality at Rome, but not the principle itself'.

multitudinem imperitam: *multitudo* — as opposed to *plebs* or *populus* — is a derogatory way of referring to the populace. *populus* is a politico-legal category that refers, in the case of *populus Romanus*, to all Roman citizens, whereas *plebs* is a social term (of course with political significance) that refers to the 'plebeian' component of the *populus Romanus* (in complement and contrast to the 'patrician' element; cf. the so-called 'secession of the *plebs*'). By contrast, *multitudo* simply captures quantity, without any indication of the social, legal, or political status of those who make up the multitude. It is similar in sense to our 'the masses', which also implies a range of prejudices and stereotypes, well summed up by Morstein-Marx (2004: 68):

> A bestialized urban mob, whose enslavement to its appetites and desperate circumstances make it incapable of reason, is one of the stock characters of the Roman political drama scripted by ancient writers. ... Cicero seems — at least in public — to take a less harsh view of the People's character as a political agent, though it is still often characterized by 'rashness' (*temeritas*) and 'fickleness' (*levitas*) ... It is consistent with these conceptions of the multitude that the audiences of public meetings were frequently derided by Cicero, once out of earshot, as composed of *imperiti*, 'ignoramuses,' an adjective that adheres to references to the plebs or *multitudo* virtually as a formula.

Philippic 2 is a written speech disseminated among his largely senatorial peers, so there was no need for Cicero to pay particular respect to popular feelings.

delenierat: *delenire* in the sense of 'to seduce', 'to bewitch' is attested from New Comedy onwards: see e.g. Plautus, *Amphitruo* 844 or *Stichus* 457.[105] Cicero also uses it, as part of an imagery of enticement and corruption.[106] Here the term feeds into the image of mass psychology

---

105 Paschall (1939: 50–52).
106 *pro Cluentio* 13, *pro Murena* 74 (cited above 424–25) where he mockingly impersonates Cato the Younger objecting to the practice of wooing voters through the provision of sensual pleasures, *de Oratore* 1.36, *de Finibus* 1.33: *blanditiis ... voluptatum deleniti atque corrupti.*

that Cicero is peddling: the common people are happy to be bribed ('bewitched') by the tyrant, made compliant to his whim and will through the provision of material pleasures. Their mental powers can be infiltrated and weakened to the point of enslavement — and they are willing to acquiesce as long as they can indulge in pleasures of the body.

suos praemiis, adversarios clementiae specie devinxerat: the *Thesaurus Linguae Latinae* 5.1.859, 51–54 differentiates between:

- *devincire* (= *astringere, alligare*) *legibus, necessitate (fati)*, where the binding happens through impersonal forces, public institutions, cosmic constraints
- *devincire beneficiis, amore*, where the focus is on personal relationships, with persons tied together through services rendered and/or powerful emotional attachments
- *devincire calamitate, scelere*, where the binding results in unholy alliances grounded in immorality and crime

Cicero uses the verb in the second sense, but manages to imply that Caesar's way of building up networks of obligations through ties that bind lacks legitimacy: he used material gifts (*praemia*) with his friends and immaterial favours (*clementia*) with his adversaries to corroborate his tyrannical power. See Santoro L'Hoir (2006: 146): 'Cicero implies a … subtle influence [of "behind-the-scenes" control], clustering *devincire* with *delenire*, as well as *specie, regnare*, and *servitium* in a vituperative passage insinuating that by binding the people to him emotionally with specious largesse, Caesar has abused his power'. Cicero speaks from personal experience — having benefitted from both forms of generosity: he was the beneficiary of a substantial interest-free loan from Caesar and one of the first republicans Caesar pardoned. (With as liberally giving a patron as Caesar, the boundary between *sui* and *adversarii* often became blurred as he tried to turn his adversaries into supporters through material enticements.) As Mouritsen (2017: 128) puts it: 'Caesar's pursuit of popular favour was noted by all ancient commentators, suggesting he may have been unusual in continuing this strategy well after the early career stages when most politicians abandoned it. But it was essentially a style, involving gestures, spectacle and generosity, as well as a public show of defiance towards the nobility. Whether it had much impact on the lives of the poor is a different matter'.

clementiae specie: 'through a semblance of mercy'. Elsewhere Cicero praises Caesar highly for his commitment to *clementia* in the civil war (which caught everyone by surprise — not least since it stood in stark contrast to the bloodthirsty rhetoric of the republican party). At the same time, he laboured under no delusion about the strategic value of Caesar's policy of mercy. In one of his letters he labels the *clementia* Caesar practised *insidiosa* ('cunning'; *Att.* 8.16.2 = 166 SB), in another letter he shares Curio's view that Caesar was not 'by nature' predisposed towards *clementia* and would start to behave savagely in case his policy of clemency ceased to produce the hoped-for results (*Att.* 10.4.8 = 195 SB: ... *ipsum autem non voluntate aut natura non esse crudelem, sed quod putaret popularem esse clementiam. quod si populi studium amisisset, crudelem fore* '... and as for Caesar himself, it was not by inclination or nature that he was not cruel but because he reckoned that clemency was the popular line. If he lost favour with the public he would be cruel'). He certainly never blinked an eye when the enemies were Gauls or Germans, whom he slaughtered in genocidal numbers. In the domestic sphere, his policy of mercy also carried unwelcome ideological connotations: while *clementia* was in principle 'a welcome and approved quality of character' (Konstan 2005: 344), in the course of the civil war between Caesar and Pompey and Caesar's dictatorship the quality, while laudable in itself, became associated with an unwelcome power-differential between the benefactor and the recipient, placing the latter into the debt of the former: there is no greater power than to execute a verdict over life and death — and the spared adversary will find himself caught in the inextricable bonds of an unrequitable benefaction. Such acts of mercy extended between aristocratic peers, while preferable to merciless slaughter, were at variance with the republican principle of oligarchic equality: from this point of view, '*clementia* ... denoted the arbitrary mercy, bound by no law, shown by a superior to an inferior who is entirely in his power. It is the quality proper to a *rex*. In the free Republic there was no place for *rex* or *regnum*. The only body which could properly show *clementia* was the Roman people itself in its historical role of pardoning the humbled' (Earl 1967: 60). By using the noun *species* Cicero acknowledges that *clementia* as such is a positive quality, but manages to imply that Caesar's variant is only a 'semblance' of the real thing — without going into details why exactly that is the case. But the context suggests that he objects to *clementia Caesaris* as a tool of consolidating (tyrannical) power through the generation of social debts that cannot be repaid.[107] More generally, in the works written after the Ides of March 44, Cicero argues that a tyrant by definition exists outside any meaningful social bonds, not least those generated by acts of *clementia* and the extension of *beneficia* by which (some of) Caesar's killers were bound to the dictator. This argument frees the assassins from the charge of murderous ingratitude.[108]

quid multa [(verba) dicam]?: the ellipsis of *dicam* with *quid multa?, quid plura?, ne multa, ne plura* etc. is common: see *OLD* s.v. *multus* 16b: 'why say more', 'to be brief', 'in a word'. The brachylogy often conveys emotional agitation in preparation for an upcoming punch line (as here).

attulerat iam liberae civitati partim metu, partim patientia consuetudinem serviendi: Cicero again opts for unorthodox word order (verb – indirect object – ablatives of cause – direct object), which ensures that the key phrase *consuetudinem serviendi* comes at the end of the sentence.

partim metu, partim patientia: note the alliteration; the causal ablatives specify the reasons that enabled Caesar to enslave a free commonwealth: fear and forbearance. *patientia* can be a positive value when referring to the 'ability or willingness to endure hardship'. In *Phil.* 10, for instance, Cicero identifies this kind of *patientia* as a particular virtue of Brutus (who wrote a treatise *De Patientia*). Here, however, it connotes undue passivity — or indeed submissiveness — towards a tyrant.

---

107 Contrast *pro Ligario* 6 (a speech delivered before Caesar) where he hails Caesar's *clementia* in the most effusive terms: *o clementiam admirabilem atque omnium laude, praedicatione, litteris monumentisque decorandam!* ('O admirable clemency, how worthy to be adorned by everyone's praise and promotion, by being put on record in literature and monuments!'). See further Dyck (1996: 225–26).

108 See further Angel (2008).

§ 117: Once Burnt Lesson Learnt!

Cicero continues his exercise in compare and contrast. Antony merits comparison with Caesar in one respect only: the desire to wield power at all cost (*dominandi cupiditas*), which makes him a tyrant. And if there is one good thing that the Roman people have learned from the evils inflicted by Caesar it is a more skeptical disposition towards self-styled leaders — and the willingness to do away with those that turn out to be tyrants. He reiterates his *a-fortiori* conviction: if Caesar was considered intolerable, Antony surely too.

Cum illo ego te dominandi cŭpiditate conferre possum, ceteris vero rebus nullo modo [cum illo] **comparandus es**: Cicero comes back to the comparability of Antony and Caesar — a question he had left hanging in the previous paragraph (116: … *aut tu es ulla re cum eo comparandus*). Now he specifies the one respect [*cupiditate* and *ceteris rebus* are ablatives of respect], in which the two strongmen can be compared: their desire to rule as tyrant. Cicero opens the sentence with three personal pronouns, referring to Caesar (*cum illo*), himself (*ego*), and Antony (*te*) respectively — a finely calibrated sequence with him in the nominative at centre position like the pillar of a scale appraising the other two. The adversative *vero* is designed to convey the impression that Cicero here asserts a commonly accepted truth, i.e. that in all other respects the two men are distinctly dissimilar. Antony shares Caesar's major vice, without possessing any of his positive qualities.

nullo modo comparandus es: the second person singular gerundive of necessity / obligation: 'you are not to be compared in any way' (sc. with Caesar). The strong negation *nullo modo* (an ablative of manner) has a colloquial flavour: Hofmann (1951: 81).

sed ex plurimis malis quae ab illo rei publicae sunt inusta hoc tamen boni est quod didicit iam populus Romanus quantum cuique crederet, quibus se committeret, a quibus caveret: the subject of the sentence is *hoc* (on which the partitive genitive *boni* depends: 'this of good'), the verb is *est*: 'out of the many evils, which ..., there is nevertheless this of good (namely the fact) that...'. Cicero envisages the commonwealth as a material entity (*res publica* literally means 'the public thing', 'the property that belongs to all citizens') or perhaps even body of sorts (perhaps in the tradition of the 'body politic') that Caesar has indelibly branded with a great number of evils. Nevertheless (note the concessive *tamen*), this bruising treatment has one positive outcome: however tough the learning experience was, it contained valuable lessons for the present.

quae ab illo rei publicae sunt inusta: *quae* is the nominative neuter plural of the relative pronoun referring back to *malis*. *inuro* means literally 'to imprint by burning on', 'to brand on' and is construed with the dative (here *rei publicae*). *ab illo* (sc. Caesar) is an ablative of agency with the perfect passive verb.

didicit iam populus Romanus: 'has now learned' (since it did not really know beforehand). The recent nature of the learning experience stands *prima facie* in latent conflict to the argument in earlier paragraphs that the killing of prospective tyrants was a long-standing practice in Rome, with a series of venerable *exempla* going all the way back to the expulsion of Tarquinius Superbus. As in § 114 Cicero imagines a broad consensus of ruling elite and people, as he moves from *populus Romanus* to *viri fortes* and ends on the generic *homines*, plastering over the awkward problem that reactions to the murder were far from uniform, ranging from unalloyed enthusiasm to outright hostility. For a recent discussion of how the conspirators misjudged public opinion see Rosillo-López (2017: 188–94).

quantum cuique crederet, quibus se committeret, a quibus caveret: Cicero articulates the contents of this experience in an asyndetic — and, via the verbs *crederet*, *committeret*, *caveret* alliterated — tricolon of indirect questions. He imagines the Roman people asking themselves: 'how much trust are we to put in anyone?' 'to whom should we entrust ourselves?' and 'whom should we guard against?' It is not easy to see how the three questions cohere. The first seems to call for a limit to the extent to which the people ought to entrust civic business to any one person in particular; the second and third pose the question which kind of individual is to be trusted with or, conversely, kept away from, public affairs.

haec non cogitas, neque intellegis satis esse viris fortibus didicisse quam sit re pulchrum, [quam sit] **beneficio gratum,** [quam sit] **fama gloriosum tyrannum occidere?:** *intellegis* governs an indirect statement with (the indeclinable) *satis* as subject accusative, *esse* as infinitive copula, and *didicisse* as predicative complement: '… that it is sufficient for brave men to have learned how…' *quam*, an adverb expressing degree, can be either interrogative or exclamatory (Pinkster 2015: 337, with reference to Bodelot 2010); here it is clearly the latter. It goes with all three adjectives (*pulchrum, gratum, gloriosum*), which all function as predicative complements to the subject of the clause, the infinitive phrase *tyrannum occidere*: 'how beautiful … it is to kill a tyrant!' (The copula *sit* is in the subjunctive because of indirect speech.) Each adjective comes with an ablative (*re … beneficio … fama*), perhaps best taken as ablatives of respect (the deed itself – the service rendered – the renown achieved), though Ramsey (2003: 335) suggests that *beneficio* and *fama* are best understood as causal ablatives.

Extra information:
In a letter of 4 August 44 BCE addressed to Antony, M. Brutus and Cassius also invoke the spectre of Caesar in an attempt to persuade Antony to desist from his Caesarian politics: *tu etiam atque etiam vide, quid suscipias, quid sustinere possis; neque, quam diu vixerit Caesar, sed quam non diu regnarit, fac cogites* ('On your part, consider well what you undertake and what you can sustain. Bear in mind, not only the length of Caesar's life, but the brevity of his reign'.) (Cicero, *ad Familiares* 11.3.4 = 336 SB).

an, cum illum homines non tulerint, te ferent?: the particle *an* here introduces a contemptuous direct question addressed to Antony that calls for a negative answer: 'given that people did not tolerate him (*illum*, placed up front for contrastive emphasis with *te*, refers to Caesar), will they tolerate *you*?'

ferent: future tense.

§ 118: Here I Stand.
I Can Do Naught Else

Cicero now works towards a rousing conclusion by shifting the focus from Antony back to himself: he combines a personal profession with the notion of self-sacrifice for the benefit of the wider community, intertwining liberty and death.

Certatim posthac, mihi crede, ad hoc opus curretur neque occasionis tarditas exspectabitur: Cicero proceeds to answer the rhetorical question he posed at the end of the previous paragraph, suggesting that Antony will soon face an attack of men vying with each other to kill him. The alliterated *certatim … curretur* (an impersonal passive in the future: 'there will be an emulous onrush to perform this task') underscores both the speed of the assault and the indiscriminate hatred among the populace, which Cicero further reinforces in the (somewhat tautological and compressed) follow-up clause, which literally means 'the lateness of an opportunity will not be waited for'. In other words: 'no-one will wait for an opportunity to present itself; they'll take action now'.

posthac: 'from now on'. Cicero seems to be hoping, rather optimistically, that the delivery (or the perusal) of his speech will stir everyone into taking violent action against Antony right away.

mihi crede: for the phrase see above 391.

ad hoc opus: the killing of Antony the tyrant.

respice, quaeso, aliquando rem publicam, M. Antoni: in sentences expressing commands, *aliquando* signifies 'now at last', 'while there is time', 'before it is too late': see *OLD* s.v. 5. Cicero urges Antony to make a U-turn in his attitude towards the commonwealth — for his own sake. Unless he (finally) starts heeding the welfare of the *res publica*, he will end up dead. So he is not begging on behalf of the commonwealth — rather, showing some consideration for the commonwealth is the only way for Antony to save his skin.

quaeso: in parenthesis, here added to lend the imperative *respice* even greater urgency: 'I implore you' — for your own sake just as much as that of everyone else.

quibus ortus sis, non quibuscum vivas, considera: Cicero exhorts Antony to comport himself in line with the illustrious representatives of his family tree rather than the rabble with whom he has ended up living, not least his wife Fulvia and his brother Lucius. Cicero inveighs against both throughout *Philippic* 2. The rhetoric of the rotten fruit of a glorious tree is a familiar weapon in the rhetorical arsenal of the *homo novus*, who uses the notion of generational decline to attack the established nobility and their conceit that they pass down ancestral excellence from generation to generation. The second person singular present imperative *considera* governs two indirect questions (hence the subjunctives *ortus sis* and *vivas*). *orior*, in the sense 'to be born *of*', 'to descend *from*', can be construed with the prepositions *ab* and *ex* or (as here) with the plain ablative (*quibus*).

quibuscum: = *cum quibus*.

mecum [age], **ut voles: redi cum re publica in gratiam**: the opening of the sentence is elliptical. It is possible to supply *redi in gratiam* with *mecum* from what follows ('reconcile yourself with me whenever you wish — but reconcile yourself *now* with the state') or a more general imperative like *age*: 'treat me as you like — but reconcile yourself with the state'). *redi* is the second person singular present imperative active of *redeo, redire*. *redire in gratiam* is idiomatic: 'to become reconciled (with)' (Cf. *reducere in gratiam* = to reconcile). *gratia* here signifies 'goodwill between two parties'.

sed de te tu videris; ego de me ipse profitebor: *videris* is second person singular future perfect active of *video*, indicating future anterior value but with a hortatory touch: 'but it will have been / is up to you to see to yourself'. This use of the so-called *futurum exactum* 'is idiomatic Latin to express that one leaves a debatable point to others to decide, and will continue with an idea about which one is certain oneself. In other words, it is a formula indicating something like "it is immaterial to me"' (Bremmer and Formisano 2012: 171; cf. Kühner-Stegmann II.1, 149). By contrast *profitebor* is in the simple future. The contrastive use of the second and first personal pronouns (*de te tu – ego de me*), further reinforced by the chiastic design and the addition of the reflexive *ipse*, could not be more pronounced. Right after dismissing Antony, Cicero indulges in a proto-Lutheran moment: he professes his civic creed.

defendi rem publicam adulescens, non deseram [rem publicam] **senex**: *defendi* is the first person singular perfect indicative active (note that the present passive infinitive looks identical); *deseram* is in the simple future. It is rather remarkable that Cicero labels himself an *adulescens* with reference to the year 63 BCE (the year of his consulship, when he quashed the conspiracy of Catiline): he was 43 years old at the time. But Roman age-labels were fluid: *adulescens* here captures Cicero's life before the onset of old age (*senectus*), when he becomes a *senex*. And Cicero wants to convey the image of an entire life spent in civic service.

contempsi Catilinae gladios, non pertimescam [gladios] **tuos**: Cicero claimed that he was a target for assassination for Catiline and his followers (see e.g. *Cat.* 1.11). Juvenal alludes to the sentence in *Satire* 10.114–26, a passage in which he also praises *Philippic* 2 as 'immortal' (*divina*):

> Eloquium ac famam Demosthenis aut Ciceronis
> incipit optare et totis quinquatribus optat 115
> quisquis adhuc uno parcam colit asse Minervam,
> quem sequitur custos angustae vernula capsae.
> eloquio sed uterque perit orator, utrumque
> largus et exundans leto dedit ingenii fons.
> ingenio manus est et cervix caesa, nec umquam 120
> sanguine causidici maduerunt rostra pusilli.

'o fortunatam natam me consule Romam':
Antoni gladios potuit contemnere si sic
omnia dixisset. ridenda poemata malo
quam te, conspicuae divina Philippica famae,   125
volveris a prima quae proxima.

[The eloquence and reputation of Demosthenes or Cicero is what boys keep on praying for throughout the spring holidays, every boy who goes to school accompanied by a house slave to guard his narrow satchel and who still worships thrifty Minerva with a single tiny coin. But it was because of their eloquence that both orators died. It was the abundant, overflowing gush of talent that sent both to their deaths. It was talent that had its hands and neck severed. The rostrum was never drenched in the blood of a feeble advocate. 'O Rome, you are fortunate, born in my consulate.' **He could have laughed at Antony's swords** if everything he said had been like this. I prefer his ridiculous verses to you, immortal *Philippic*, next to the first on the roll, with your distinguished reputation.]

quin etiam corpus libenter obtulerim, si repraesentari morte mea libertas civitatis potest, ut aliquando dolor populi Romani [id] **pariat quod iam diu parturit!**: Cicero now amplifies and corroborates (see *OLD* s.v. *quin* 3a: 'and moreover') his record of public service by pronouncing his willingness to sacrifice himself gladly (the subjunctive *obtulerim* is potential: 'I would gladly offer my body / life') if his death were to ensure the revival of freedom (or, literally: 'if the freedom of the community could be re-established through my death'). He concludes with a lyrically elusive consecutive *ut*-clause: 'so that finally the pain of the Roman people gives birth to (*parere*) what they have for so long carried in the womb / been in labour for (*parturire*)'. In this image, Cicero's self-sacrifice (*devotio*) will cause the Roman people such pain that they will finally manage to restore / give birth to *libertas* for good. (Since the assassination of Caesar, which did away with the tyrant but did not quite restore *libertas*, they were 'in labour' with it: Cicero's violent death would induce birth.) A good way to wind up any speech — but spot on for one where 'delivery' has been delayed for quite a while. But now (*iam diu*) begins the onslaught in earnest, with *Phil.* 3 coming up next, and then, for ever, within our box set of the dozen CDs of *Phil.* (with a few more to come, but not to reach us (?)).

pariat ... parturit: Cicero here strikes a notably feminine note in his otherwise pronounced masculine discourse. As Myers (2003: 337) observes: 'With this feminine metaphor of the womb and birth, Cicero ends the vitriolic *Second Philippic* against Mark Antony (Marcus Antonius) by calling for a return to the republic even at the expense of his own life. As both a productive and generative act, this climactic moment, in which the male body politic fuses with the politic of the female body, operates as the nexus of masculine and feminine, public and private, and oration and circulated pamphlet in the Roman society of the first century BCE. Moreover, of all the female allusions Cicero employs in the *Second Philippic*, it is the only one that focuses on the feminine as the potential for rebirth, rejuvenation, and renewal of what had been the Roman republic'. She offers three possible readings of this remarkable imagery (348): (i) Cicero fashions himself as a pregnant (fe)male: 'Tied to Cicero's invocation of his death, the phrase means that Cicero is the woman dying in childbirth to offer new life to the republic, because the Roman practice was to cut out the fetus if a woman died in labor' [this interpretation seems difficult to reconcile with the fact that the (labour-)pangs are experienced by the Roman people]; (ii) Cicero conceives of himself as a metaphorical midwife who, through his self-sacrifice, helps the *populus Romanus* give birth to a free commonwealth; (iii) as *paterfamilias* (and *pater patriae*) he is the one to legally recognize liberty as the offspring of the people (in Roman culture, 'the power and continuation of family name lies in the father's recognition of the child, not in the mother's delivery').

Extra information:
However we read this imagery, its presence here offers an opportune moment to recall that Roman oratory (whether delivered in a public space or distributed through backstage channels in pamphlet form) was a gendered practice. See Richlin (1997: 91): 'A full study of the issue [sc. the interrelation of gender and rhetoric in ancient Rome] would have to consider the nature of the forum as gendered space; the socialization of Roman citizen boys into manhood through the study of rhetoric; the rhetorical handbooks as guides to gender construction; the subject matter of the extant rhetorical exercises; the analogy between gender and geography in the Atticist-Asianist debate; the relation between Greeks, Romans, and others in the rhetorical schools; the contrast between Greek ideas of the meaning of rhetoric and Roman ideas; and the ways in which womanhood is constructed in Roman culture through exclusion from rhetoric'.

§ 119: Give Me Liberty
or Give Me Death!

Cicero clinches the account with his public service — and a twin focus on liberty and death. The final thought (or wish) of *Philippic* 2 is one of cosmic justice: that the fate of the individual reflects the nature of his actions within the public sphere. Those who invested much in the commonwealth ought to see their efforts rewarded; those who harmed the civic community ought to suffer accordingly. Much to Cicero's regret, reality proved recalcitrant to this principle: throughout much of his career, and certainly for the final two decades, he had to cope with the unpalatable scenario that those who acted on behalf of the *res publica* suffered (through exile and other forms of humiliation, as well as death), whereas perpetrators of the worst transgressions seemed to get off scot free: Piso and Gabinius, Clodius (until his death in 52), Caesar (until his death in 44). At best, the wheels of cosmic justice were working slowly.

Etenim si abhinc annos prope viginti hoc ipso in templo negavi posse mortem immaturam esse consulari, quanto verius nunc negabo [posse mortem immaturam esse] **seni!**: Cicero concluded the previous paragraph by recalling his attitude during the conspiracy of Catiline: *defendi rem publicam adulescens, non deseram senex; contempsi Catilinae gladios, non pertimescam tuos*. Now he uses a logical conditional sequence (with both verbs in the indicative) to explain this assertion in the form of an *a-fortiori* argument, with his past actions (detailed in the *si*-clause) as premise for the conclusions to be drawn about his attitude and actions now.

negavi introduces an indirect statement with *mortem immaturam* as subject accusative, *posse* as verb, *esse* as supplementary infinitive with *posse*, and the dative *consulari* dependent on *immaturam* ('… premature for someone of consular rank...'). In the apodosis, Cicero reiterates the finite verb (switching from perfect to future), but elides much of the indirect statement *negabo* governs: it is represented only by the dative *seni* (from *senex*), which has a syntactical position identical to *consulari*. The rest — *posse mortem immaturam esse* — has to be supplied from the protasis.

The sentence is designed to strengthen the notion of Cicero as a warrior on behalf of the commonwealth throughout his adult years: the two biographical markers used in the previous paragraph, *adulescens* and *senex*, recur in slight variation (*consulari – seni*); and his defiance of the 'swords of Catiline' receives chronological (*abhinc annos prope viginti*) and spatial (*hoc ipso in templo*) specification, as Cicero gestures back to the opening of the speech and also recalls a moment in his *Fourth Speech against Catiline*.

The temporal specification *annos prope viginti* at the opening of the concluding paragraph gestures back to the initial sentence of the speech (§ 1):

> Quonam meo fato, patres conscripti, fieri dicam, ut nemo his annis viginti rei publicae fuerit hostis, qui non bellum eodem tempore mihi quoque indixerit?

> [To what fate of mine, senators, should I attribute it that in these twenty years no man has been the enemy of the commonwealth without also declaring war on me at the same time?]

He then singles out Catiline and Clodius — but ignores Caesar, whom he considered a *hostis rei publicae* rather than a personal enemy. Put differently, he construes a historical arch from the hour of his greatest triumph, the suppression of the Catilinarian conspiracy in 63, the year when he held the consulship, to the present hour — his (last) stand against a prospective tyrant. Cicero begins the concluding paragraph of the speech by citing himself (*in Catilinam* 4.3):

> Quare, patres conscripti, consulite vobis, prospicite patriae, conservate vos, coniuges, liberos fortunasque vestras, populi Romani nomen salutemque defendite; mihi parcere ac de me cogitare desinite. nam primum debeo sperare omnis deos, qui huic urbi praesident, pro eo mihi, ac mereor, relaturos esse gratiam; deinde, si quid obtigerit, aequo animo paratoque moriar. *nam neque turpis mors forti viro potest accidere neque immatura consulari nec misera sapienti.*

[Take thought for yourselves, therefore, gentlemen; look to the preservation of your fatherland, save yourselves, your wives, your children and your fortunes, defend the name of the Roman people and their very existence; stop protecting me and cease your concern for me. Firstly, I am bound to hope that all the gods who watch over this city will recompense me as I deserve; and secondly, if anything happens to me, I shall die calm and resigned. A brave man's death cannot bring dishonour, a consul's cannot be before its time, a philosopher's cannot bring sorrow.]

abhinc annos prope viginti: *abhinc*, followed by the accusative of extent in time *annos prope viginti*, specifies the dating point: 'almost (*prope*) twenty years ago (*abhinc*)', i.e. 5 December 63 BCE, the day when he delivered the *Fourth Catilinarian*.

hoc ipso in templo: the temple of Concord.

mortem immaturam: for anyone who has reached the consulship, the apex of the *cursus honorum* and guaranteeing entry into the collective memory of the *res publica*, death can no longer be considered premature. For the topos (here inverted) see Nielson (1997: 198–202).

quanto verius: *quanto* is an ablative of the degree of difference, *verius* the comparative form of the adverb *vere*: 'how much more truthfully…'

mihi vero, patres conscripti, iam etiam optanda mors est, perfuncto rebus eis quas adeptus sum quasque gessi: the subject is *mors*, the gerundive *optanda … est* the verb. *mihi* is a dative of agency with the gerundive, deftly linked to *mors* by alliteration. *perfuncto* is a perfect passive participle in the dative, modifying *mihi*. The deponent *perfungi* (like *uti* and *frui*, the simplex *fungi*, *vesci*, and *potiri*) takes an ablative object — here *rebus eis*; the *res* in question are further detailed in the two relatives clauses (linked by the -*que* after the second *quas*) *quas adeptus sum* and *quas gessi*. This splitting of *res* in what amounts to a *husteron proteron* (*res quas adeptus sum* refers to the honours he attained, *res quas gessi* to the deeds for which he received those honours) renders a literal translation difficult: 'Death, senators, is now even something to be wished for by me, given all the things I have accomplished — the honours I attained, the deeds (*res gestae*) I performed'. Essentially, Cicero is now delivering his own funeral oration.

duo modo haec opto, unum ut moriens populum Romanum liberum relinquam — hoc mihi maius ab dis immortalibus dari nihil potest — alterum ut ita cuique eveniat ut de re publica quisque mereatur: Cicero concludes the speech with a twofold prayer: 'I pray for the following two things only (*modo*), first (*unum*), that ..., second (*alterum*), that...'. In between the two parts, Cicero includes a parenthetical gloss on the first (*hoc ... potest*): it signals that he subordinates his desire for (cosmic) justice on the level of the individual to his ardent wish that freedom be restored to the Roman people.

moriens: circumstantial present active participle in the nominative masculine singular modifying the subject of the *ut*-clause ('I'). Cicero is reaching the end: of the speech, of his life. And he looks beyond his own demise to the prospect of a revival of freedom for the Roman people, which he tries to help bring about in a spirit of self-sacrifice.

liberum: in predicative position: '... that I leave the Roman people free'.

hoc mihi maius ab dis immortalibus dari nihil potest: the subject of the parenthesis is *nihil*, which takes *maius* as predicative complement. *hoc*, which refers back to the Roman people being free (again) by the time Cicero dies, is an ablative of comparison with the comparative *maius*. Literally: 'nothing can be given to me by the immortal gods greater than this'. Cicero foregrounds *hoc mihi maius* by front position and alliteration.

ut ita cuique eveniat ut de re publica quisque mereatur: literally: 'that for each man (*cuique*) it turns out in such a way as each (*quisque*) behaves towards the commonwealth'. The first *ut* follows *opto* and is substantive (I pray that...), the second *ut* correlates with the preceding *ita*. Here construed with the dative of the person affected (*cuique*), *evenio* is value-neutral: the thing that happens can be good, bad, or neutral. Cicero prays that whatever happens to an individual reflects his (dis-) service to the commonwealth. It's what he has coming.

Extra information:
Cicero revisits the theme of just rewards in the last *Philippic*: at *Phil.* 14.19 he imagines the Roman people enquiring about each senator's views to judge him accordingly: *ita de quoque, ut quemque meritum arbitrantur, existiment* ('they hold each in the opinion they believe he merits').

Bibliography

1. On-line Resources

You can find the Latin text of Cicero's *Philippics* on-line at *The Latin Library*: http://www.thelatinlibrary.com/cicero/phil.shtml

The *Perseus Project* has the Latin text of the Oxford Classical Text of A. C. Clark (1918), hyperlinked to the *Lewis and Short Latin Dictionary*, and with the translation by C. D. Yonge (1903). See http://www.perseus.tufts.edu/hopper/collections, Greek and Roman Materials.

The website *LacusCurtius: Into the Roman World* (http://penelope.uchicago.edu/Thayer/E/Roman/home.html) features many Greek and Roman texts in translation (some with the original Greek and Latin) that are of relevance to the study of Cicero's *Philippics* (and are cited in the commentary), including:

- Caesar, *Commentarii*
- Cassius Dio, *Roman History*
- Cicero, *On Duties* (*de Officiis*)
- Suetonius, *The Lives of the Twelve Caesars*
- Varro, *On Farming* (*de Re Rustica*)

2. Secondary Literature

Adams, J. N. (1982), *The Latin Sexual Vocabulary*, Baltimore.

Adams, J. N. (1983), 'Words for "Prostitute" in Latin', *Rheinisches Museum* 126, 321–58.

Adams, J. N. (2016), *An Anthology of Informal Latin, 200 BC–AD 900: Fifty Texts with Translations and Linguistic Commentary*, Cambridge.

Adams, R. and Savran, D. (eds) (2002), *The Masculinity Studies Reader*, Malden, MA.

Adkins, L. and Adkins, R. A. (2014), *Handbook to Life in Ancient Rome*, Infobase Publishing.

Allcroft, A. H. (1901), *Cicero: Philippic II*, London.

Andreau, J. (1999), *Banking and Business in the Roman World*, trans. by Janet Boyd, Cambridge.

Angel, N. (2008), '*Clementia* and *Beneficium* in the *Second Philippic*', in T. Stevenson and M. Wilson (eds), *Cicero's Philippics: History, Rhetoric and Ideology* (= *Prudentia* 37 and 38), Auckland, 114–30.

Arena, V. (2007a), 'Roman Oratorical Invective', in W. Dominik and J. Hall (eds), *A Companion to Roman Rhetoric*, Malden, Oxford, Victoria, 149–60.

Arena, V. (2007b), 'Invocation to Liberty and Invective of *Dominatus* at the End of the Roman Republic', *Bulletin of the Institute of Classical Studies* 50, 49–73.

Arena, V. (2012), *Libertas and the Practice of Politics in the Late Roman Republic*, Cambridge and New York.

Atkins, E. M. (1990), '*Domina et regina virtutum*: Justice and *societas* in *De Officiis*', *Phronesis* 35, 258–89.

Azoulay, V. (2017), *The Tyrant-Slayers of Ancient Athens: A Tale of Two Statues*, Oxford.

Babcock, C. L. (1965), 'The Early Career of Fulvia', *American Journal of Philology* 81, 1–32.

Badian, E. (1996), 'Alexander the Great between two Thrones and Heaven', in A. M. Small (ed.), *Subject and Ruler: The Cult of the Ruling Power in Classical Antiquity*, Ann Arbor, 11–26.

Balsdon, J. P. V. D. (1969), *Life and Leisure in Ancient Rome*, New York.

Barr, W. (1981), 'Res = "a thing"? Persius 4,1', *Papers of the Liverpool Latin Seminar* 3, 422–23.

Barsby, J. (1999), *Terence, Eunuchus*, Cambridge.

Beard, M. (2014), *Laughter in Ancient Rome: On Joking, Tickling, and Cracking Up,* Berkeley etc.

Beard, M., North, J., and Price, S. (1998), *Religions of Rome,* vols 1–2, Cambridge.

Bechtold, C. (2011), *Gott und Gestirn als Präsenzformen des toten Kaisers: Apotheose und Katasterismos in der politischen Kommunikation der römischen Kaiserzeit und ihre Anknüpfungspunkte im Hellenismus,* Göttingen.

Bendlin, A. (2000), 'Looking Beyond the Civic Compromise: Religious Pluralism in Late Republican Rome', in E. Bispham and C. Smith (eds), *Religion in Archaic and Republican Rome and Italy: Evidence and Experience,* Edinburgh, 115–35 and 167–71.

Berthelet, Y. (2016), 'Violence, obstruction augurale et crise de la République romaine', in L. Gilhaus, S. Kirsch, I. Mossong, F. Reich, and S. Wirz (eds), *Elite und Krise in antiken Gesellschaften / Élites et crises dans les sociétés antiques,* Stuttgart, 83–95.

Bettini, M. (2000), 'The Origin of Latin *mustela*', *Glotta* 76, 1–19.

Bleicken, J. (1962), 'Der Begriff der Freiheit in der letzten Phase der römischen Republik', *Historische Zeitschrift* 195, 1–20.

Bodel, J. and Scheidel, W. (eds) (2016), *On Human Bondage: After Slavery and Social Death,* Malden, MA.

Bodelot, C. (2010), '*Quam*: Marqueur de degré interrogatif et/ou exclamatif', in M. Fruyt and O. Spevak (eds), *La quantification en latin,* Paris, 335–51.

Bradley, G. (2006), 'Colonization and Identity in Republican Italy', in G. Bradley and J.-P. Wilson (eds), *Greek and Roman Colonization, Origins, Ideologies and Interactions,* Swansea, 161–87.

Bradley, G. (2007), 'Romanization: The End of the People of Italy?', in G. Bradley, E. Isayev, and C. Riva (eds), *Ancient Italy, Regions without Boundaries,* Exeter, 295–322.

Bradley, G. (2014), 'The Nature of Roman Strategy in Mid-Republican Colonization and Road Building', in T. D. Stek and J. Pelgrom (eds), *Roman Republican Colonization: New Perspectives from Archaeology and Ancient History,* Rome, 61–72.

Bradley, K. R. (1994), *Slavery and Society at Rome,* Cambridge.

Bremmer, J. N. and Formisano, M. (2012), *Perpetua's Passions,* Oxford.

Brennan, T. C. (2012), 'Perceptions of Women's Power in the Late Republic: Terentia, Fulvia, and the Generation of 63 BCE', in S. L. James and S. Dillon (eds), *A Companion to Women in the Ancient World,* Chichester, 354–66.

Broughton, T. R. S. (1991), *Candidates Defeated in Roman Elections: Some Ancient Roman 'Also-Rans'* (= Transactions of the American Philosophical Society 81.4), Philadelphia.

Brunt, P. A. (1988a), '*Libertas* in the Republic', in *The Fall of the Roman Republic and Related Essays*, Oxford, 281–350.

Brunt, P. A. (1988b), '*Amicitia* in the Late Republic', in *The Fall of the Roman Republic and Related Essays*, Oxford, 351–81.

Burton, G. P. (2012), '*immunitas*', *Oxford Classical Dictionary*, 4th edn, Oxford.

Burton, P. J. (2011), *Friendship and Empire: Roman Diplomacy and Imperialism in the Middle Republic (353–146 BC)*, Cambridge and New York.

Butterfield, D. (ed.) (2015), *Varro Varius: The Polymath of the Roman World*, Cambridge.

Campanile, D. (2017), 'The Patrician, the General and the Emperor in Women's Clothes: Examples of Cross-Dressing in Late Republican and Early Imperial Rome', in D. Campanile, F. Carlà-Uhink, and M. Facella (eds), *TransAntiquity: Cross-Dressing and Transgender Dynamics in the Ancient World*, London and New York, 52–64.

Cantarella, E. (1992), *Bisexuality in the Ancient World*, New Haven.

Cantarella, E. (2003), 'Fathers and Sons in Rome', *Classical World* 96, 281–98.

Cerutti, S. (1994), 'Further Discussion on the Delivery and Publication of Cicero's *Second Philippic*', *Classical Bulletin* 70, 23–28.

Chaniotis, A. (2003), 'The Divinity of Hellenistic Rulers', in A. Erskine (ed.), *A Companion to the Hellenistic World*, Oxford, 431–45.

Chang, K. E. (2013), *The Community, the Individual and the Common Good: 'To Idion' and 'To Sympheron in the Greco-Roman World and Paul*, London etc.

Chassignet, M. (2001), '"La construction" des aspirants à la tyrannie: Sp. Cassius, Sp. Maelius et Manlius Capitolinus', in M. Coudry and T. Späth (eds), *L'invention des grands hommes de la Rome antique = Die Konstruktion der grossen Männer Altroms: actes du colloque du Collegium Beatus Rhenanus, Augst, 16–18 septembre 1999*, Paris, 83–96.

Christian, E. (2008), 'A Philosophy of Legitimacy in Cicero's *Philippics*', in T. Stevenson and M. Wilson (eds), *Cicero's Philippics: History, Rhetoric and Ideology* (= *Prudentia* 37 and 38), Auckland, 153–67.

Chrystal, P. (2015), *In Bed with the Romans*, Stroud.

Clark, A. J. (2007), *Divine Qualities: Cult and Community in Republican Rome*, Oxford.

Clarke, J. R. (1991), *The Houses of Roman Italy, 100 B.C.-A.D. 250: Ritual, Space, and Decoration*, Berkeley.

Clarke, J. R. (1998), *Looking at Lovemaking: Constructions of Sexuality in Roman Art 100 B.C.–A.D. 250*, Berkeley.

Classen, C. J. (1963), 'Gottmenschentum in der römischen Republik', *Gymnasium* 70, 312–38.

Cleland, L., Harlow, M., and Llewellyn-Jones, L. (eds) (2005), *The Clothed Body in the Ancient World*, Oxford.

Coffee, N. (2016), *Gift and Gain: How Money Transformed Ancient Rome*, Oxford.

Cokayne, K. (2003), *Experiencing Old Age in Ancient Rome*, New York.

Cole, S. (2014), *Cicero and the Rise of Deification at Rome*, Cambridge.

Connolly, J. (2007), 'Virile Tongues: Rhetoric and Masculinity', in W. Dominik and J. Hall (eds), *A Companion to Roman Rhetoric*, Malden, Oxford, Victoria, 83–97.

Corbeill, A. (1996), *Controlling Laughter: Political Humor in the Late Roman Republic*, Princeton.

Corbeill, A. (1997), 'Dining Deviants in Roman Political Invective', in J. P. Hallett and M. B. Skinner (eds), *Roman Sexualities*, Princeton, 99–128.

Corbeill, A. (2002), 'Ciceronian Invective', in M. J. May (ed.), *Brill's Companion to Cicero: Oratory and Rhetoric*, Leiden, 197–218.

Corbeill, A. (2007), 'Rhetorical Education and Social Reproduction in the Republic and Early Empire', in W. Dominik and J. Hall (eds), *A Companion to Roman Rhetoric*, Malden, Oxford, Victoria, 69–82.

Corbeill, A. (2008), '*O Singulare Prodigium*: Ciceronian Invective as a Religious Expiation', in T. Stevenson and M. Wilson (eds), *Cicero's Philippics: History, Rhetoric and Ideology* (= Prudentia 37 and 38), Auckland, 240–54.

Cornell, T. J. (2013), 'M. Porcius Cato', in T. J. Cornell (ed.), *The Fragments of the Roman Historians, Volume 3: Commentary*, 63–159.

Cornwell, H. (2017), *Pax and the Politics of Peace: Republic to Principate*, Oxford.

Cowan, E. (2008), '*Libertas* in the *Philippics*', in T. Stevenson and M. Wilson (eds), *Cicero's Philippics: History, Rhetoric, and Ideology* (= Prudentia 37 and 38), Auckland, 140–52.

Craig, C. P. (1993), *Form as Argument in Cicero's Speeches: A Study of Dilemma*, Atlanta.

Craig, C. P. (2004), 'Audience Expectations, Invective, and Proof', in J. G. F. Powell and J. Paterson (eds), *Cicero the Advocate*, Oxford, 187–204.

Crawford, J. W. (1984), *M. Tullius Cicero: The Lost and Unpublished Orations*, Göttingen.

Crawford, M. H. (1974), *Roman Republican Coinage*, Cambridge.

Dahlmann, H. (1935), 'M. Terentius Varro', *RE Suppl.* VI, 1172–277.

Dart, C. J. (2014), *The Social War, 91 to 88 BCE: A History of the Italian Insurgency Against the Roman Republic*, Farnham and Burlington.

Davidson, J. (1998), *Courtesans and Fishcakes: The Consuming Passions of Classical Athens*, London.

Davidson, J. (2001), 'Dover, Foucault and Greek Homosexuality: Penetration and the Truth of Sex', *Past & Present* 170, 3–51.

Davidson, J. (2007), *The Greeks and Greek Love: A Radical Reappraisal of Homosexuality in Ancient Greece*, London.

Davies, G. (2005), 'What Made the Roman Toga *virilis*?', in L. Cleland, M. Harlow, and L. Llewellyn-Jones (eds), *The Clothed Body in the Ancient World*, Oxford, 121–30.

Dawes, T. (2008), 'The Encomium of Brutus in *Philippic Ten*', in T. Stevenson and M. Wilson (eds), *Cicero's Philippics: History, Rhetoric, and Ideology* (= Prudentia 37 and 38), Auckland, 266–81.

Delia, D. (1991), 'Fulvia Reconsidered', in S. B. Pomeroy (ed.), *Women's History and Ancient History*, Chapel Hill and London, 197–217.

de Libero, L. (2009), '*Precibus ac lacrimis*: Tears in Roman Historiography', in T. Fögen (ed.), *Tears in the Graeco-Roman World*, Berlin and New York, 209–34.

Deniaux, E. (2003), 'Amatius et la naissance du culte de César au forum romain', in F. Lecocq (ed.), *Rome An 2000* [= Cahiers de la MRSH 33], Caen, 113–23.

Denniston, J. D. (1926), *M. Tulli Ciceronis in M. Antonium orationes Philippicae prima et secunda. Edited, with Introduction, Notes (mainly historical) and Appendices*, Oxford.

Devine, A. M. and Stephens, L. D. (2006), *Latin Word Order: Structured Meaning & Information*, Oxford.

Dionisotti, C. (2007), '*Ecce*', *Bulletin of the Institute of Classical Studies* 50, 75–91.

Dixon, J. (2014), 'Dressing the Adulteress', in M. Harlow and M.-L. Nosch (eds), *Greek and Roman Textiles and Dress: An Interdisciplinary Anthology*, Oxford and Philadelphia, 298–305.

Dolansky, F. (2008), '*Togam virilem sumere*: Coming of Age in the Roman World', in J. Edmondson and A. Keith (eds), *Roman Dress and the Fabrics of Roman Culture*, Toronto, Buffalo, London, 47–70.

Donahue, J. (2004), *The Roman Community at Table During the Principate*, Ann Arbor.

Drummond, A. (2013), 'M. Terentius Varro', in T. J. Cornell (ed.), *The Fragments of the Roman Historians, Volume I: Introduction*, Oxford, 412–23.

Dufallo, B. (2007), *The Ghosts of the Past: Latin Literature, the Dead, and Rome's Transition to a Principate*, Columbus.

Dugan, J. (2001), 'How to Make and Break a Cicero', *Classical Antiquity* 20, 35–77.

Dyck, A. R. (1996), *A Commentary on Cicero, De Officiis*, Ann Arbor.

Dyck, A. R. (2001), 'Dressed to Kill: Attire as Proof and Means of Characterization in Cicero's Speeches', *Arethusa* 34, 119–30.

Dyck, A. R. (2017), 'Textual Notes on Cicero's *Philippics'*, *Classical Quarterly* 67, 312–14.

Earl, D. (1967), *The Moral and Political Tradition of Rome*, London.

Edmondson, J. (2008), 'Public Dress and Social Control in Late Republican and Early Imperial Rome', in J. Edmondson and A. Keith (eds), *Roman Dress and the Fabrics of Roman Culture*, Toronto, Buffalo, London, 21–46.

Edwards, C. (1993), *The Politics of Immorality*, Cambridge.

Edwards, C. (1996), *Writing Rome: Textual Approaches to the City*, Cambridge.

Erskine, A. (1991), 'Hellenistic Monarchy and Roman Political Invective', *Classical Quarterly* 41, 106–20.

Evans, R. J. (2008), 'Phantoms in the *Philippics*: Catiline, Clodius and Antonian Parallels', in T. Stevenson and M. Wilson (eds), *Cicero's Philippics: History, Rhetoric and Ideology* (= Prudentia 37 and 38), Auckland, 62–81.

Fantham, E. (1972), *Comparative Studies in Republican Latin Imagery*, Toronto.

Fantham, E. (2005), 'Liberty and the People in Republican Rome', *Transactions of the American Philological Association* 135, 209–29.

Fantham, E. (2009), 'Caesar as an Intellectual', in M. Griffin (ed.), *A Companion to Julius Caesar*, Chichester, 141–56.

Fantham, E. (2011), '*Stuprum*: Public Attitudes and Penalties for Sexual Offences in Republican Rome', *Roman Readings: Roman Response to Greek Literature from Plautus to Statius and Quintilian*, Berlin and New York, 115–43.

Fantham, E. (2013), *Cicero's Pro L. Murena Oratio*, Oxford.

Farnsworth, W. (2011), *Farnsworth's Classical English Rhetoric*, Boston.

Feeney, D. C. (1998), *Literature and Religion at Rome: Culture, Contexts, and Beliefs*, Cambridge.

Feeney, D. C. (2007), *Caesar's Calendar: Ancient Time and the Beginnings of History*, Berkeley.

Fischer, R. A. (1999), *Fulvia und Octavia: Die beiden Ehefrauen des Marcus Antonius in den politischen Kämpfen der Umbruchszeit zwischen Republik und Principat*, Berlin.

Fitzgerald, W. (2000), *Slavery and the Roman Literary Imagination*, Cambridge.

Flaig, E. (1995), 'Die *Pompa Funebris*: Adlige Konkurrenz und annalistische Erinnerung in der Römischen Republik', in O. G. Oexle (ed.), *Memoria als Kultur*, Göttingen, 115–48.

Flaig, E. (2003), *Ritualisierte Politik: Zeichen, Gesten und Herrschaft im Alten Rom*, Göttingen.

Flower, H. I. (1996), *Ancestor Masks and Aristocratic Power in Roman Culture*, Oxford.

Flower, H. I. (2006), *The Art of Forgetting: Disgrace and Oblivion in Roman Political Culture*, Chapel Hill.

Forbis, E. (1996), *Municipal Virtues in the Roman Empire: The Evidence of Italian Honorary Inscriptions*, Stuttgart and Leipzig.

Fraenkel, E. (1957), *Horace*, Oxford.

Freudenburg, K. (1997), 'Review of Corbeill, *Controlling Laughter* (1996)', *Bryn Mawr Classical Review* 97.3.25.

Freyburger-Galland, M.-L. (2009), 'Political and Religious Propaganda between 44 and 27 B.C.', *Vergilius* 55, 17–30.

Frisch, H. (1946), *Cicero's Fight for the Republic: The Historical Background of Cicero's Philippics*, Copenhagen.

Garcea, A. (2012), *Caesar's De Analogia: Edition, Translation, and Commentary*, Oxford and New York.

Gargola, D. J. (1995), *Lands, Laws & Gods: Magistrates & Ceremony in the Regulation of Public Lands in Republican Rome*, Chapel Hill & London.

Gargola, D. J. (2017), *The Shape of the Roman Order: The Republic and Its Spaces*, Chapel Hill.

George, M. (2008), 'The "Dark Side" of the Toga', in J. Edmondson and A. Keith (eds), *Roman Dress and the Fabrics of Roman Culture*, Toronto, Buffalo, London, 94–112.

Gibbs, L. (2009), *Aesop's Fables in Latin: Ancient Wit and Wisdom from the Animal Kingdom*, Mundelein.

Gildenhard, I. (2007), *Paideia Romana: Cicero's Tusculan Disputations*, Cambridge.

Gildenhard, I. (2011), *Creative Eloquence: The Construction of Reality in Cicero's Speeches*, Oxford.

Gildenhard, I. (2018), 'A Republic in Letters: Epistolary Communities in Cicero's Correspondence, 49–44 BCE', in P. Ceccarelli, L. Doering, T. Fögen, and I. Gildenhard (eds), *Letters and Communities: Studies in the Socio-Political Dimensions of Ancient Epistolography*, Oxford, 205–38.

Gildersleeve, B. L. and Lodge, G. (1997), *Gildersleeve's Latin Grammar*, 3rd edn, London.

Gladhill, B. (2016), *Rethinking Roman Alliance: A Study in Poetics and Society*, Cambridge and New York.

Gotter, U. (1996), *Der Diktator ist tot! Politik zwischen den Iden des März und der Begründung des zweiten Triumvirats*, Stuttgart.

Gowers, E. (2012), *Horace, Satires Book 1*, Cambridge.

Griffin, M. T. (2009), 'Introduction', in M. T. Griffin (ed.), *A Companion to Julius Caesar*, Chichester, 1–8.

Griffin, M. T. and Atkins, E. M. (1991), *Cicero, On Duties*, Cambridge.

Grillo, L. (2015), *Cicero's De Provinciis Consularibus Oratio: Introduction and Commentary*, Oxford.

Gruen, E. S. (1974), *The Last Generation of the Roman Republic*, Berkeley.

Gunderson, E. (2000), *Staging Masculinity: The Rhetoric of Performance in the Roman World*, Ann Arbor.

Habicht, C. (1956/2017), *Divine Honors for Mortal Men in Greek Cities: The Early Cases* (Translated from the German by John Noël Dillon; first edition 1956; second edition 1970), Ann Arbor.

Habinek, T. (1998), *The Politics of Latin Literature: Writing, Identity, and Empire in Ancient Rome*, Princeton.

Hales, S. (2009), *The Roman House and Social Identity*, Cambridge.

Hales, S. (2013), 'Republican Houses', in J. DeRose Evans (ed.), *A Companion to the Archaeology of the Roman Republic*, Chichester, 50–66.

Hall, J. (2002), 'The *Philippics*', in J. M. May (ed.), *Brill's Companion to Cicero: Oratory and Rhetoric*, Leiden, Boston, Cologne, 273–304.

Hall, J. (2009), *Politeness and Politics in Cicero's Letters*, Oxford.

Hallett, J. (2015), 'The Representation of an Elite Roman Woman Warrior', in J. Fabre-Serris and A. Keith (eds), *Women & War in Antiquity*, Baltimore, 247–65.

Hallett, J. P. and Skinner, M. (eds) (1997), *Roman Sexualities*, Princeton.

Harlow, M. and Nosch, M.-L. (eds) (2014), *Greek and Roman Textiles and Dress: An Interdisciplinary Anthology*, Oxford and Philadelphia.

Harnett, J. (2017), *The Roman Street: Urban Life and Society in Pompeii, Herculaneum, and Rome*, Cambridge.

Haynes, I. (2013), *Blood of the Provinces: The Roman Auxilia and the Making of Provincial Society from Augustus to the Severans*, Oxford.

Hellegouarc'h, J. (1963), *Le vocabulaire latin des relations et des partis politiques sous la République*, Paris.

Hemelrijk, E. A. (1999), *Matrona Docta: Educated Women in the Roman Élite from Cornelia to Julia Domna*, London and New York.

Henderson, J. (2006), *Oxford Reds: Classic Commentaries on Latin Classics*, Bristol.

Henderson, J. (2007), '"… when who should walk into the room but…": Epistoliterarity in Cicero, *Ad Qfr*. 3.1', in R. Morello and A. D. Morrison (eds), *Ancient Letters*, Oxford, 37–85.

Henderson, J. (2010), 'Review of Tom Stevenson and Marcus Wilson (eds), *Cicero's Philippics: History, Rhetoric and Ideology* (= *Prudentia* 37–38), Auckland 2008', *BMCR* 2010.03.16.

Henderson, J. (2014), 'Was Suetonius' Julius a Caesar?', in T. Power and R. K. Gibson (eds), *Suetonius the Biographer: Studies in Roman Lives*, Oxford, 81–110.

Heskel, J. (1994), 'Cicero as Evidence for Attitudes to Dress in the Late Republic', in J. L. Sebesta and L. Bonfante (eds), *The World of Roman Costume*, Madison, 133–45.

Hodgson, L. (2017), *Res publica and the Roman Republic: 'Without Body or Form'*, Oxford and New York.

Hofmann, J. B. (1951), *Lateinische Umgangssprache*, 3rd edn, Heidelberg.

Hölkeskamp, K.-J. (2014), 'Under Roman Roofs: Family, House, and Household', in H. I. Flower (ed.), *The Cambridge Companion to the Roman Republic*, 2nd edn, Cambridge, 101–26.

Holleran, C. (2012), *Shopping in Ancient Rome: The Retail Trade in the Late Republic and the Principate*, Oxford.

Housman, A. E. (1896/1972), 'Cicero *Pro Milone* c. 33 §90', *Classical Review* 10, 1896, 192–93 [reprinted in: *The Classical Papers of A. E. Housman, collected and edited by J. Diggle & F. R. D. Goodyear, Volume I: 1882–1897*, Cambridge, 378–79].

Houston, G. W. (2014), *Inside Roman Libraries: Book Collections and their Management in Antiquity*, Chapel Hill.

Hubbard, T. (ed.) (2014), *A Companion to Greek and Roman Sexualities*, Malden, MA.

Hughes, J. J. (1992), 'A "Paraklausithyron" in Cicero's *Second Philippic*', in C. Deroux (ed.), *Studies in Latin Literature and Roman History VI*, Brussels, 215–27.

Hunt, P. (2018), *Ancient Greek and Roman Slavery*, Malden MA.

Hutchinson, G. O. (2005), 'Pope's Spider and Cicero's Writings', in T. Reinhardt, M. Lapidge, and J. N. Adams (eds), *Aspects of the Language of Latin Prose*, Oxford and New York, 179–94.

Huzar, E. G. (1978), *Mark Antony: A Biography*, Minneapolis.

Huzar, E. G. (1982), 'The Literary Efforts of Mark Antony', *Aufstieg und Niedergang der Römischen Welt* 2.30.1, 639–57.

Icks, M. and Shiraev, E. (eds) (2014a), *Character Assassination throughout the Ages*, New York.

Icks, M. and Shiraev, E. (2014b), 'Introduction', in M. Icks and E. Shiraev (eds), *Character Assassination throughout the Ages*, New York, 1–13.

Icks, M. and Shiraev, E. (2014c), 'Editorial Reflections: Modern Cases' & 'Epilogue', in M. Icks and E. Shiraev (eds), *Character Assassination throughout the Ages*, New York, 271–78.

Isaac, B. (2017), *Empire and Ideology in the Graeco-Roman World: Selected Papers*, Cambridge.

Jenkyns, R. (2013), *God, Space, and City in the Roman Imagination*, Oxford.

Jocelyn, H. D. (1967), *The Tragedies of Ennius*, Cambridge.

Johnson, W. R. (1969), 'Tact in the Drusus Ode: Horace, *Odes* 4.4', *Classical Antiquity* 2, 171–81.

Kamen, D. and Levin-Richardson, S. (2015), 'Lusty Ladies in the Roman Imaginary', in K. Ormand and R. Blondell (eds), *Ancient Sex: New Essays*, Columbus, 231–52.

Kaplow, L. (2012), 'Creating *popularis* History: Sp. Cassius, Sp. Maelius, and M. Manlius in the Political Discourse of the Late Republic', *Bulletin of the Institute of Classical Studies* 55.2, 101–09.

Kaster, R. A. (1995), *C. Suetonius Tranquillus: De Grammaticis et Rhetoribus*, Oxford.

Kaster, R. A. (1998), 'Becoming CICERO', in C. Foss and P. Knox (eds), *Style and Tradition: Studies in Honor of Wendell Clausen*, Stuttgart, 248–63.

Kaster, R. A. (2006), *Cicero: Speech on Behalf of Publius Sestius*, Oxford.

Kelly, D. (2008), 'Publishing the *Philippics*, 44–43 BC', in T. Stevenson & M. Wilson (eds), *Cicero's Philippics: History, Rhetoric and Ideology* (= *Prudentia* 37 and 38), Auckland, 22–38.

Kelly, R. B. (2014), *Mark Antony and Popular Culture: Masculinity and the Construction of an Icon*, London and New York.

Kennedy, G. A. (2002), 'Cicero's Oratorical and Rhetorical Legacy', in M. J. May (ed.), *Brill's Companion to Cicero: Oratory and Rhetoric*, Leiden, 481–502.

Ker, J. (2010), '"*Nundinae*": The Culture of the Roman Week', *Phoenix* 64, 360–85.

Kienpointner, M. (2014), 'Freiheit oder Tod. Zu einem Leitmotiv politischer Rhetorik innerhalb und außerhalb Europas', G. Ueding and G. Kalivoda (eds), *Wege moderner Rhetorikforschung*, Berlin, 595–615.

Kierdorf, W. (1980), *Laudatio Funebris: Interpretationen und Untersuchungen zur Entwicklung der römischen Leichenrede*, Meisenheim am Glan.

Kirchner, R. (2007), '*Elocutio*: Latin Prose Style', in W. Dominik and J. Hall (eds), *A Companion to Roman Rhetoric*, Oxford, 181–94.

Konstan, D. (1997), *Friendship in the Classical World*, Cambridge.

Konstan, D. (2005), 'Clemency as a Virtue', *Classical Philology* 100, 337–46.

Konstan, D. (2016), 'The Freedom to Feel Grateful: The View from Classical Antiquity', in D. Carr (ed.), *Perspectives on Gratitude: An Interdisciplinary Approach*, London, 41–53.

Koortbojian, M. (2013), *The Divinization of Caesar and Augustus*, Cambridge.

Koster, S. (1980), *Die Invektive in der griechischen und römischen Literatur*, Meisenheim am Glan.

Kraus, C. (1992), 'How (Not?) to End a Sentence: The Problem of -*Que*', *Harvard Studies in Classical Philology* 94, 321–29.

Kroon, C. (1995), *Discourse Particles in Latin: A Study of nam, enim, autem, vero and at*, Amsterdam.

Kühner, R. and Stegmann, C. (1966), *Ausführliche Grammatik der Lateinischen Sprache, Zweiter Teil: Satzlehre. Erster Band*, Hannover.

Kunkel, W. and Wittmann, R. (1995), *Staatsordnung und Staatspraxis der römischen Republik, zweiter Abschnitt: Die Magistratur*, Munich.

Lacy, W. K. (ed.) (1986), *Cicero: Second Philippic*, Warminster.

Langlands, R. (2006), *Sexual Morality in Ancient Rome*, Cambridge.

Larsen, J. (2008), 'Cicero, Antony and the *Senatus Consultum Ultimum* in the *Second Philippic*', in T. Stevenson and M. Wilson (eds), *Cicero's Philippics: History, Rhetoric and Ideology* (= Prudentia 37 and 38), Auckland, 168–80.

Latham, J. A. (2016), *Performance, Memory, and Processions in Ancient Rome: The Pompa Circensis from the Late Republic to Late Antiquity*, Cambridge.

Leber, N. (2018), 'Cicero's *Liberatores*: A Reassessment', *Classical Quarterly*, 1–18.

Lee, M. M. (2015), *Body, Dress, and Identity in Ancient Greece*, Cambridge.

Leigh, M. (1995), 'Wounding and Popular Rhetoric at Rome', *Bulletin of the Institute of Classical Studies* 40, 195–212.

Lévy, C. (1998), 'Rhétorique et philosophie: la monstruosité politique chez Cicéron', *Revue des Études Latines* 76, 139–57.

Lewis, R. G. (1991), 'Sulla's Autobiography: Scope and Economy', *Athenaeum* n.s. 69, 509–16.

Lewis, R. G. (1993), 'Imperial Autobiography: Augustus to Hadrian', *Aufstieg und Niedergang der Römischen Welt* 2.34.1, 629–706.

Linderski, J. (1986), 'The Augural Law', *Aufstieg und Niedergang der Römischen Welt* 2.16.3, 2146–312.

Linderski, J. (1995), *Roman Questions*, Stuttgart.

Linderski, J. and Kaminska-Linderski, A. (1974), 'The Quaestorship of Marcus Antonius', *Phoenix* 28, 213–23.

Lintott, A. (1999), *The Constitution of the Roman Republic*, Oxford.

Lomas, K. (2003), 'Public Building, Urban Renewal and Euergetism', in K. Lomas and T. Cornell (eds), *Bread and Circuses: Euergetism and Municipal Patronage in Roman Italy*, London, 28–45.

Long, A. A. (1995), 'Cicero's Politics in *De Officiis*', in A. Laks and M. Schofield (eds), *Justice and Generosity: Studies in Hellenistic Social and Political Philosophy*, Cambridge, 213–40.

Lurie, A. (1981/2000), *The Language of Clothes*, New York.

Ma, J. (1999/2002), *Antiochos III and the Cities of Western Asia Minor*, Oxford.

Ma, J. (2003), 'Kings', in A. Erskine (ed.), *The Blackwell Companion to the Hellenistic Age*, Oxford, 177–95.

Mahy, T. (2013), 'Antonius, Triumvir and Orator: Career, Style, and Effectiveness', in C. Steel and H. van der Blom (eds), *Community and Communication: Oratory and Politics in Republican Rome*, Oxford, 329–44.

Malitz, J. (1987), 'Die Kanzlei Caesars: Herrschaftsorganisation zwischen Republik und Prinzipat', *Historia* 36, 51–72.

Manuwald, G. (2003), 'Review of J. T. Ramsey (ed.), *Cicero: Philippic I and II*', *Bryn Mawr Classical Review* 2003.11.28.

Manuwald, G. (2007), *Cicero, Philippics 3–9. Edited with Introduction, Translation and Commentary. Vol. 1: Introduction, Text and Translation, References and Indexes; Vol. 2: Commentary*, Berlin and New York.

Manuwald, G. (2008), 'Cicero versus Antonius: On the Structure and Construction of the *Philippic* Collection', in T. Stevenson & M. Wilson (eds), *Cicero's Philippics: History, Rhetoric and Ideology* (= *Prudentia* 37 and 38), Auckland, 39–61.

Manuwald, G. (2011), 'The Function of Praise and Blame in Cicero's *Philippics*', in C. J. Smith and R. Covino (eds), *Praise and Blame in Roman Republican Rhetoric*, Swansea, 199–214.

Manwell, E. (2010), 'Gender and Masculinity', in M. B. Skinner (ed.), *A Companion to Catullus*, Malden and Oxford, 111–28.

Martelli, F. (2016), 'Mourning Tulli-*a*: The Shrine of Letters in *ad Atticum* 12', *Arethusa* 49, 415–37.

Martin, P.-M. (2013), 'La manipulation rhétorique de l'Histoire dans les *Philippiques* de Cicéron', in D. Côté and P. Fleury (eds), *Discours politique et Histoire dans l' Antiquité*, Franche-Comté, 109–42.

Matijević, K. (2006), 'Cicero, Antonius und die "*acta Caesaris*"', *Historia* 55, 426–50.

Matijević, K. (2018), 'Nochmals zur Verteilung der Provinzen nach Caesars Ermordung und zur Bedeutung Octavians für die Politik des Antonius im April / Mai 44 v. Chr.', *Hermes* 146, 219–34.

May, J. M. (1980), 'The Image of the Ship of State in Cicero's *Pro Sestio*', *Maia* 32, 259–64.

May, J. M. (1996), 'Cicero and the Beasts', *Syllecta Classica* 7, 143–53.

Mayer, R. G. (2005), 'The Impracticability of Latin "Kunstprosa"', in T. Reinhardt, M. Lapidge, and J. N. Adams (eds), *Aspects of the Language of Latin Prose*, Oxford, 195–210.

Mayor, J. E. B. (1861), *Cicero, Second Philippic*, London.

McDermott, W. C. (1972), 'Curio *Pater* and Cicero', *American Journal of Philology* 93, 381–411.

McDonnell, M. (2006), *Roman Manliness: Virtus and the Roman Republic*, Cambridge.

McGinn, T. A. (1998), *Prostitution, Sexuality, and the Law in Ancient Rome*, Oxford.

McGinn, T. A. (2004), *The Economy of Prostitution in the Roman World: A Study of Social History and the Brothel*, Ann Arbor.

McIntyre, G. (2016), *A Family of Gods: The Worship of the Imperial Family in the Latin West*, Ann Arbor.

Meyer, E. A. (2004), *Legitimacy and Law in the Roman World: Tabulae in Roman Belief and Practice*, Cambridge.

Mikalson, J. D. (1998), *Religion in Hellenistic Athens*, Berkeley, Los Angeles, London.

Morstein-Marx, R. (2004), *Mass Oratory and Political Power in the Late Roman Republic*, Cambridge.

Mouritsen, H. (2011), *The Freedman in the Roman World*, Cambridge.

Mouritsen, H. (2017), *Politics in the Roman Republic*, Cambridge.

Myers, N. (2003), 'Cicero's (S)Trumpet: Roman Women and the *Second Philippic*', *Rhetoric Review* 22, 337–52.

Naiden, F. S. (2006), *Ancient Supplication*, Oxford.

Nicols, J. (2014), *Civic Patronage in the Roman Empire*, Leiden and Boston.

Nielson, H. S. (1997), 'Interpreting Epithets in Roman Epitaphs', in B. Rawson and P. Weaver (eds), *The Roman Family in Italy: Status, Sentiment, Space*, Canberra and Oxford, 169–204.

Nisbet, R. G. M. (1960), 'Cicero, *Philippics* ii. 103', *Classical Review* New Series, 10.2, 103–04.

Nisbet, R. G. M. (1961), *Cicero: In L. Calpurnium Pisonem Oratio*, Oxford.

Nisbet, R. G. M. and Hubbard, M. (1970), *A Commentary on Horace: Odes Book 1*, Oxford.

Nixon, C. E. V. and Rodgers, B. S. (1994), *In Praise of Later Roman Emperors: The Panegyrici Latini*, Berkeley, Los Angeles, Oxford.

Noreña, C. F. (2011), *Imperial Ideals in the Roman West: Representation, Circulation, Power*, Cambridge.

North, J. A. (2008), 'Caesar at the Lupercalia', *Journal of Roman Studies* 98, 144–60.

Nussbaum, M. (2010), 'Foreword', in C. A. Williams, *Roman Homosexuality*, 2nd edn, Oxford, ix–xiv.

Oakley, S. P. (2013), 'Notes on the Text of Cicero's *Philippics*', *The Classical Quarterly* 63, 277–91.

Olson, K. (2002), '*Matrona* and Whore: The Clothing of Women in Roman Antiquity', *Fashion Theory* 6.4, 387–420.

Olson, K. (2008), *Dress and the Roman Woman: Self-Presentation and Society*, Abingdon and New York.

Ormand, K. (2018), *Controlling Desires: Sexuality in Ancient Greece and Rome*, 2nd edn, Austin.

Osgood, J. (2009), 'The Pen and the Sword: Writing and Conquest in Caesar's Gaul', *Classical Antiquity* 28, 328–58.

Osgood, J. (2018), *Rome and the Making of a World State, 150 BCE–20 CE*, Cambridge.

Ott, F.-T. (2013), *Die zweite Philippica als Flugschrift in der späten Republik*, Berlin.

Parkin, T. G. (2003), *Old Age in the Roman World: A Cultural and Social History*, Baltimore.

Paschall, D. M. (1939), 'The Vocabulary of Mental Aberration in Roman Comedy and Petronius', *Language* 15, 4–88.

Pasco-Pranger, M. (2006), *Founding the Year: Ovid's Fasti and the Poetics of the Roman Calendar*, Leiden.

Pelling, C. B. R. (1988), *Plutarch: Life of Antony*, Cambridge.

Pelling, C. B. R. (2011), *Plutarch Caesar: Translated with an Introduction and Commentary*, Oxford.

Pina Polo, F. (2006), 'The Tyrant Must Die: Preventive Tyrannicide in Roman Political Thought', in F. Marco Simón (ed.), *Repúblicas y ciudadanos: modelos de participación cívica en el mundo antiguo*, Barcelona, 71–102.

Pinkster, H. (2015), *Oxford Latin Syntax: Volume 1: The Simple Clause*, Oxford.

Pitcher, R. A. (2008), 'The *Second Philippic* as a Source for Aristocratic Value', in T. Stevenson and M. Wilson (eds), *Cicero's Philippics: History, Rhetoric and Ideology* (= *Prudentia* 37 and 38), Auckland, 131–39.

Powell, J. G. F. (2007), 'Invective and the Orator: Ciceronian Theory and Practice', in J. Booth (ed.), *Cicero on the Attack: Invective and Subversion in the Orations and Beyond*, Swansea, 1–23.

Price, S. R. F. (1984), *Rituals and Power: The Roman Imperial Cult in Asia Minor*, Cambridge.

Raaflaub, K. A. (2003), 'Caesar the liberator? Faction Politics, Civil War and Ideology', in F. Cairns and E. Fantham (eds), *Caesar Against Liberty? Perspectives on His Autocracy*, Cambridge, 35–67.

Raaflaub, K. A. (2004), 'Aristocracy and Freedom of Speech in the Greco-Roman World', in I. Sluiter and R. M. Rosen (eds), *Free Speech in Classical Antiquity*, Leiden, 41–61.

Ramage, E. S. (1991), 'Sulla's Propaganda', *Klio* 73, 93–121.

Ramsey, J. T. (1994), 'The Senate, Mark Antony, and Caesar's Legislative Legacy', *Classical Quarterly* 44, 130–45.

Ramsey, J. T. (2001), 'Did Mark Antony Contemplate an Alliance with His Political Enemies in July 44 B.C.E.?', *Classical Philology* 96, 253–68.

Ramsey, J. T. (2003), *Cicero: Philippics I–II*, Cambridge.

Ramsey, J. T. (2004), 'Did Julius Caesar Temporarily Banish Mark Antony from his Inner Circle?', *Classical Quarterly* 54, 161–73.

Ramsey, J. T. (2005), 'Mark Antony's Judiciary Reform and Its Revival under the Triumvirs', *Classical Philology* 96, 253–68.

Rasmussen, S. W. (2003), *Public Portents in Republican Rome*, Rome.

Rawson, E. (1985), *Intellectual Life in the Late Roman Republic*, London.

Rawson, E. (1987), '*Discrimina ordinum*: The *Lex Julia Theatralis*', *Papers of the British School at Rome* 55, 83–114.

Richlin, A. (1983/1992), *The Garden of Priapus: Sexuality and Aggression in Roman Humour*, 2nd edn, Oxford.

Richlin, A. (1991), 'Zeus and Metis: Foucault, Feminism, Classics', *Helios* 18.2, 160–80.

Richlin, A. (ed.) (1992), *Pornography and Representation in Greece and Rome*, New York and Oxford.

Richlin, A. (1993), 'Not Before Homosexuality: The Materiality of the *cinaedus* and Roman Law against Love between Men', *Journal of the History of Sexuality* 3, 523–73.

Richlin, A. (1997), 'Gender and Rhetoric: Producing Manhood in the Schools', in W. J. Dominik (ed.), *Roman Eloquence: Rhetoric in Society and Literature*, London, 90–110.

Roller, M. B. (1997), 'Color Blindness: Cicero's Death, Declamation, and the Production of History', *Classical Philology* 92, 109–30.

Roller, M. B. (2018), *Models from the Past in Roman Culture: A World of Exempla*, Cambridge.

Rosenberger, V. (1998), *Gezähmte Götter: Das Prodigienwesen der römischen Republic*, Stuttgart.

Rosenstein, N. (1995), 'Sorting out the Lot in Republican Rome', *American Journal of Philology* 116, 43–75.

Rosenstein, N. (2012), *Rome and the Mediterranean 290 to 146 BC: The Imperial Republic*, Edinburgh.

Rosillo-López, C. (2017), *Public Opinion and Politics in the Late Roman Republic*, Cambridge.

Rostovtzeff, M. (1900), 'Congiarum', *Real-Encyclopädie* 4.1, 875–80.

Ruebel, J. S. (1979), 'The Trial of Milo in 52 B.C.: A Chronological Study', *Transactions of the American Philological Association* 109, 231–49.

Ruffell, I. (2003), 'Beyond Satire: Horace, Popular Invective and the Segregation of Literature', *Journal of Roman Studies* 93, 35–65.

Rüpke, J. (2007), *Religion of the Romans* (trans. and ed. by Richard Gordon), Cambridge.

Russell, A. (2016), *The Politics of Public Space in Republican Rome*, Cambridge.

Saller, R. P. (1982), *Personal Patronage under the Early Empire*, Cambridge.

Saller, R. P. (1994), *Patriarchy, Property and Death in the Roman Family*, Cambridge.

Santangelo, F. (2005), 'The Religious Tradition of the Gracchi', *Archiv für Religionsgeschichte* 7, 198–214.

Santangelo, F. (2007), 'Pompey and Religion', *Hermes* 135, 228–33.

Santangelo, F. (2013), *Divination, Prediction and the End of the Roman Republic*, Cambridge.

Santoro L'Hoir, F. (1992), *The Rhetoric of Gender Terms: 'Man', 'Woman', and the Portrayal of Character in Latin Prose*, Leiden, New York, Cologne.

Santoro L'Hoir, F. (2006), *Tragedy, Rhetoric, and the Historiography of Tacitus' Annales*, Ann Arbor.

Schäublin, C. (1986), '*Ementita Auspicia*', *Wiener Studien* 20, 165–81.

Scheid, J. (1998/2003), *An Introduction to Roman Religion*, trans. by J. Lloyd, Cambridge.

Scheidegger-Lämmle, C. (2017), 'Last Words: Cicero's Late Works and the Poetics of a Literary Legacy', in A. Gavrielatos (ed.), *Self-Presentation and Identity in the Roman World*, Newcastle, 17–36.

Scott, K. (1933), 'The Political Propaganda of 44–30 B.C.', *Memoirs of the American Academy in Rome* 11, 7–49.

Seager, R. (2007), 'Ciceronian Invective: Themes and Variations', in J. Booth (ed.), *Cicero on the Attack: Invective and Subversion in the Orations and Beyond*, 25–46.

Sebesta, J. (2005), 'The *toga praetexta* of Roman Children and Praetextate Garments', in L. Cleland, M. Harlow, and L. Llewellyn-Jones (eds), *The Clothed Body in the Ancient World*, Oxford, 113–20.

Sedley, D. (1997), 'The Ethics of Brutus and Cassius', *Journal of Roman Studies* 87, 41–53.

Shackleton Bailey, D. R. (1967), *Cicero's Letters to Atticus, Volume VI: 44 B.C. 355–426 (Books XIV–XVI)*, Cambridge.

Shackleton Bailey, D. R. (1979), 'On Cicero's Speeches', *Harvard Studies in Classical Philology* 83, 238–85.

Shackleton Bailey, D. R. (1982), 'Notes on Cicero's *Philippics*', *Philologus* 126, 217–26.

Shackleton Bailey, D. R. (1986), *Cicero, Philippics, edited and translated*, Chapel Hill and London.

Shackleton Bailey, D. R. (1992), *Onomasticon to Cicero's Speeches*, 2nd edn, Stuttgart.

Shatzman, I. (1975), *Senatorial Wealth and Roman Politics*, Brussels.

Shiraev, E. (2014), 'Character Assassination: How Political Psychologists Can Assist Historians', in M. Icks and E. Shiraev (eds), *Character Assassination throughout the Ages*, New York, 15–33.

Skinner, M. B. (2005), *Sexuality in Greek and Roman Culture*, Malden and Oxford.

Slapek, D. and Luc, I. (eds) (2016), *Marcus Antonius: History and Tradition*, Lublin.

Smith, C. (2006), '*Adfectatio regni* in the Roman Republic', in S. Lewis (ed.), *Ancient Tyranny*, Edinburgh, 49–64.

Solodow, J. B. (1978), *The Latin Particle quidem*, Missoula.

Spevak, O. (2010), *Constituent Order in Classical Latin Prose*, Amsterdam and Philadelphia.

Staveley, E. S. (1972), *Greek and Roman Voting and Elections*, Ithaca.

Steel, C. (2005), *Reading Cicero: Genre and Performance in Late Republican Rome*, London.

Steel, C. (2006), *Roman Oratory*, Cambridge.

Steenblock, M. (2013), *Sexualmoral und politische Stabilität: Zum Vorstellungszusammenhang in der römischen Literatur von Lucilius bis Ovid*, Berlin and Boston.

Stevenson, T. (1996), 'Social and Psychological Interpretations of Graeco-Roman Religion: Some Thoughts on the Ideal Benefactor', *Antichthon* 30, 1–18.

Stevenson, T. (2008), 'Tyrants, Kings and Fathers in the *Philippics*', in T. Stevenson & M. Wilson (eds), *Cicero's Philippics: History, Rhetoric and Ideology* (= *Prudentia* 37 and 38), Auckland, 95–113.

Stevenson, T. (2009), 'Antony as "Tyrant" in Cicero's First *Philippic*', *Ramus* 38, 174–86.

Stevenson, T. and Wilson, M. (2008), 'Cicero's *Philippics*: History, Rhetoric and Ideology', in T. Stevenson and M. Wilson (eds), *Cicero's Philippics: History, Rhetoric and Ideology* (= *Prudentia* 37 and 38), Auckland, 1–21.

Stockton, D. (1971), *Cicero: A Political Biography*, Oxford.

Stone, A. M. (2008), 'Greek Ethics and Roman Statesmen: *De Officiis* and the *Philippics*', in T. Stevenson and M. Wilson (eds), *Cicero's Philippics: History, Rhetoric and Ideology* (= *Prudentia* 37 and 38), Auckland, 214–39.

Stroh, W. (1982), 'Die Nachahmung des Demosthenes in Ciceros Philippiken', in W. Ludwig (ed.), Éloquence et Rhétorique chez Cicéron (= Entretiens sur l'Antiquité Classique 28), Vandoeuvres-Geneva, 1–31 and 32–40 (discussion).

Strong, A. K. (2016), *Prostitutes and Matrons in the Roman World*, Cambridge.

Stroup, S. C. (2010), *Catullus, Cicero, and a Society of Patrons: The Generation of the Text*, Cambridge.

Sumi, G. S. (2005), *Ceremony and Power: Performing Politics in Rome Between Republic and Empire*, Ann Arbor.

Sussman, L. A. (1994), 'Antony as *Miles Gloriosus* in Cicero's *Second Philippic*', *Scholia* 3, 53–83.

Sussman, L. A. (1998), 'Antony the *Meretrix Audax*: Cicero's Novel Invective in *Philippic* 2.44–46', *Eranos* 96, 114–28.

Tahin, G. (2016), *Heuristic Strategies in the Speeches of Cicero*, Heidelberg.

Tatum, W. J. (1999), *The Patrician Tribune: Publius Clodius Pulcher*, Chapel Hill and London.

Taylor, L. R. (1966), *Roman Voting Assemblies: From the Hannibalic War to the Dictatorship of Caesar*, Ann Arbor.

Thomas, J.-F. (2007), *Déshonneur et Honte en Latin: Étude Sémantique*, Louvain, Paris, Dudley, MA.

Thorp, J. (1992), 'The Social Construction of Homosexuality', *Phoenix* 46, 54–61.

Toher, M. (2016), *Nicolaus of Damascus: The Life of Augustus and The Autobiography: Edited with Introduction, Translations and Historical Commentary*, Cambridge.

Trapp, M. (ed.) (2003), *Greek and Latin Letters: An Anthology with Translation*, Cambridge.

Treggiari, S. (1997), 'Home and Forum: Cicero between "Public" and "Private"', https://doi.org/10.2307/284406

Usher, S. (1965), '*Occultatio* in Cicero's Speeches', *American Journal of Philology* 86, 175–92.

Usher, S. (2010), 'Cicero's *First Philippic* and the Fall of the Republic', *Bulletin of the Institute of Classical Studies* 53, 129–36.

van den Berg, C. (2008), 'The *pulvinar* in Roman Culture', *Transactions of the American Philological Association* 138, 239–73.

van der Blom, H. (2010), *Cicero's Role Models: The Political Strategy of a Newcomer*, Oxford.

van der Blom, H. (2014), 'Character Attack and Invective Speech in the Roman Republic: Cicero as Target', in M. Icks and E. Shiraev (eds), *Character Assassination throughout the Ages*, New York, 37–57.

van der Blom, H. (2016), *Oratory and Political Career in the Late Roman Republic*, Cambridge.

Verboven, K. (2002), *The Economy of Friends: Economic Aspects of Amicitia and Patronage in the Late Republic*, Brussels.

Veyne, P. (1990), *Bread and Circuses: Historical Sociology and Political Pluralism* (abridged with introduction by Oswald Murray), London.

Vout, C. (1996), 'The Myth of the *Toga*: Understanding the History of Roman Dress', *Greece & Rome* 43, 204–20.

Vout, C. (2013), *Sex on Show: Seeing the Erotic in Greece and Rome*, Berkeley.

Wallace-Hadrill, A. (1994), *Houses and Society in Pompeii and Herculaneum*, Princeton.

Watkins, T. (1997), *L. Munatius Plancus: Serving and Surviving in the Roman Revolution*, Atlanta.

Weeks, J. (1991), *Against Nature: Essays on History, Sexuality and Identity*, London.

Weeks, J. (2001), *Making Sexual History*, Cambridge.

Weinstock, S. (1971), *Divus Julius*, Oxford.

Weische, A. (1966), *Studien zur politischen Sprache der römischen Republik*, Munster.

Welch, K. (1995), 'Antony, Fulvia, and the Ghost of Clodius in 47 B.C.', *Greece & Rome* 42, 182–201.

Welch, K. (2008), '*Nimium Felix*: Caesar's *Felicitas* and Cicero's *Philippics*', in T. Stevenson and M. Wilson (eds), *Cicero's Philippics: History, Rhetoric and Ideology* (= *Prudentia* 37 and 38), Auckland, 181–213.

White, P. (1993), *Promised Verse*, Chicago.

White, P. (2003), 'Tactics in Caesar's Correspondence with Cicero', in F. Cairns and E. Fantham (eds), *Caesar Against Liberty? Perspectives on his Autocracy*, Cambridge, 68–95.

Whitehead, S. M. and Barrett, F. J. (eds) (2001), *The Masculinities Reader*, Cambridge.

Wiestrand, E. (1978), *Caesar and Contemporary Roman Society*, Göteborg.

Williams, C. A. (1995), 'Greek Love at Rome', *Classical Quarterly* 45, 517–39.

Williams, C. A. (1999/2010), *Roman Homosexuality: Ideologies of Masculinity in Classical Antiquity*, 2nd edn, Oxford.

Williams, C. A. (2012), *Reading Roman Friendship*, Cambridge.

Wilson, M. (2008), 'Your Writings or Your Life: Cicero's *Philippics* and Declamation', in T. Stevenson and M. Wilson (eds), *Cicero's Philippics: History, Rhetoric and Ideology* (= *Prudentia* 37 and 38), Auckland, 305–34.

Wirszubski, C. (1950), *Libertas as a Political Idea at Rome during the Late Republic and Early Principate*, Cambridge.

Wirszubski, C. (1961), '*Audaces*: A Study in Political Phraseology', *Journal of Roman Studies* 51, 12–22.

Wood, S. (2010), '*Horti* in the City of Rome: Emulation and Transcendence in the Late Republic and Early Empire', in A. Moore, G. Taylor, E. Harris, P. Girdwood, and L. Shipley (eds), *TRAC 2009: Proceedings of the Nineteenth Annual Theoretical Roman Archaeology Conference, Michigan and Southampton 2009*, Oxford, 75–90.

Wooten, C. W. (1983), *Cicero's Philippics and their Demosthenic Model: The Rhetoric of Crisis*, Chapel Hill and London.

Worman, N. (2008), *Abusive Mouths in Classical Athens*, Cambridge.

Wright, A. (2001), 'The Death of Cicero: Forming a Tradition: The Contamination of History', *Historia* 50, 436–52.

Wyke, M. (1994), 'Woman in the Mirror: The Rhetoric of Adornment in the Roman World', in L. Archer, S. Fischler, and M. Wyke (eds), *Women in Ancient Societies*, Basingstoke and London, 134–51.

Yakobson, A. (1999), *Elections and Electioneering in Rome: A Study in the Political System of the Late Republic*, Stuttgart.

Yavetz, Z. (1983), *Julius Caesar and his Public Image*, London.

Younger, J. G. (2005), *Sex in the Ancient World from A to Z*, Abingdon and New York.

Zarecki, J. (2014), *Cicero's Ideal Statesman in Theory and Practice*, London.

This book need not end here…

At Open Book Publishers, we are changing the nature of the traditional academic book. The title you have just read will not be left on a library shelf, but will be accessed online by hundreds of readers each month across the globe. OBP publishes only the best academic work: each title passes through a rigorous peer-review process. We make all our books free to read online so that students, researchers and members of the public who can't afford a printed edition will have access to the same ideas.

This book and additional content is available at:
https://www.openbookpublishers.com/product/845

Customise

Personalise your copy of this book or design new books using OBP and third-party material. Take chapters or whole books from our published list and make a special edition, a new anthology or an illuminating coursepack. Each customised edition will be produced as a paperback and a downloadable PDF. Find out more at:

https://www.openbookpublishers.com/section/59/1

Donate

If you enjoyed this book, and believe that research like this should be available to all readers, regardless of their income, please become a member of OBP and support our work with a monthly pledge — it only takes a couple of clicks! We do not operate for profit so your donation will contribute directly to the creation of new Open Access publications like this one.

https://www.openbookpublishers.com/supportus

Like Open Book Publishers

Follow @OpenBookPublish

Read more at the Open Book Publishers BLOG

You may also be interested in…

Cicero, *On Pompey's Command (De Imperio)*, 27–49.
Latin Text, Study Aids with Vocabulary,
Commentary, and Translation
by Ingo Gildenhard, Louise Hodgson, et al.

http://www.openbookpublishers.com/product/284

Ovid, *Metamorphoses*, 3.511–733.
Latin Text with Introduction, Commentary, Glossary
of Terms, Vocabulary Aid and Study Questions
by Ingo Gildenhard and Andrew Zissos

http://www.openbookpublishers.com/product/293

Tacitus, *Annals*, 15.20–23, 33–45.
Latin Text, Study Aids with Vocabulary, and
Commentary
by Mathew Owen and Ingo Gildenhard

http://www.openbookpublishers.com/product/215

Virgil, *Aeneid*, 4.1–299.
Latin Text, Study Questions, Commentary and
Interpretative Essays
by Ingo Gildenhard

http://www.openbookpublishers.com/product/162